CONTENTS

AF194405

Bredene beach (p135)

Caramelized Liège
waffle (p35)

Grand-Place (p59), Brussels

BELGIUM & LUXEMBOURG
THE JOURNEY BEGINS HERE

If I had to describe Belgium and Luxembourg in one word, it would be 'crossroads'. Nestled in the heart of Europe, these two small countries sit between Germanic and Latin worlds, shaped by influences greater than them. My own family reflects this blend: a French grandmother, Flemish grandfather, Brussels-born mother, and Italian heritage from my father's side. Migration waves like these have long enriched both nations, making them among Europe's most diverse. Childhood here often mixes multiculturalism with deeply rooted traditions: carnavals, *kermesses,* and local folklore. Being at a crossroads also means openness: to trade, ideas, and artistic innovation. It's no surprise that Belgium and Luxembourg punch well above their weight economically and culturally. For visitors, the attraction lies not only in their layered histories and rich cultures but also in their fiercely unique identities, proving that crossroads are not mere passages but destinations in their own right.

Mélissa Monaco

@mellovestravels

Mélissa is a travel blogger and guidebook author. Brussels has been her home for 20 years. She wrote the Brussels chapter.

My favourite experience is walking the streets of **Brussels** (p44), being amazed as architecture and mood shift from one street to the next. It's a beautiful mess.

WHO GOES WHERE

Our writers and experts choose the places which, for them, define Belgium and Luxembourg.

My favourite experience is somehow surviving the chaotic swirling sea of humanity that is the **Ducasse de Mons** (p209), with hundreds of bodies heaving and straining to grab a hair from the tail of Doudou the dragon.

Mark Elliott

@markbekaz

Mark has contributed to over 70 guidebooks. He writes cultural and pro-conciliation articles for the CaspianPost *website and is the author of* Culture Shock! Belgium. *He wrote the Antwerp & Northeast Belgium, Wallonia and Luxembourg chapters.*

Ghent (p110) combines all the old-world pleasures you could want from a Belgian city – gables, canals, jewel-bright medieval art works – with contemporary panache. It's a music-loving place, with great record stores to browse and intimate little venues. Somewhere to get lost down a canal path, and somewhere to find yourself at the superb free music festival in July.

Helena Smith

@helenasmithpix

Helena loves to write about eco travel, community and the outdoors. She wrote the Ghent, Bruges & Northwest Belgium chapter.

Brussels

Majestic central square, brilliant art and characterful cafes (p44)

North Sea

Bruges

Postcard-perfect archetype of canal-side medieval beauty (p121)

Westerschelde

Vlissingen

Berge op Zoor

Knokke-Heist

Blankenberge

Terneuzen

Lillo

De Haan

Zeebrugge

Ostend

Bruges

Strait of Dover

Eeklo

Nieuwpoort

Veurne

Lokeren

Dunkirk

Ghent

Dendermonde

Willebro

Diksmuide

Torhout

Ypres

WWI Flanders Fields tragedies retold in the Lakenhalle (p146)

Roeselare

Deinze

FLANDERS

Aalst

Meise

Poperinge

Ypres

Leie

Oudenaarde

Ninove

Menen

Kortrijk

BRUSSELS

Mouscron

Roubaix

Schelde

Geraards-bergen

Halle

Armentières

Rônse

Waterfo

Lille

Tournai

Enghien

Nivelles

Leuze

Soignies

Lens

Mons

La Louvièr

Binche

Ghent

Perfect blend of medieval magic and contemporary life (p110)

Valenciennes

Sambre

Beaum

FRANCE

Amiens

Chimay

Cou

Mons

Descend from the belfry for the folkloric Doudou, the Ducasse (p206)

Hirson

Binche

The spookiest folkloric carnival anywhere, plus a museum celebrating it (p217)

Reims

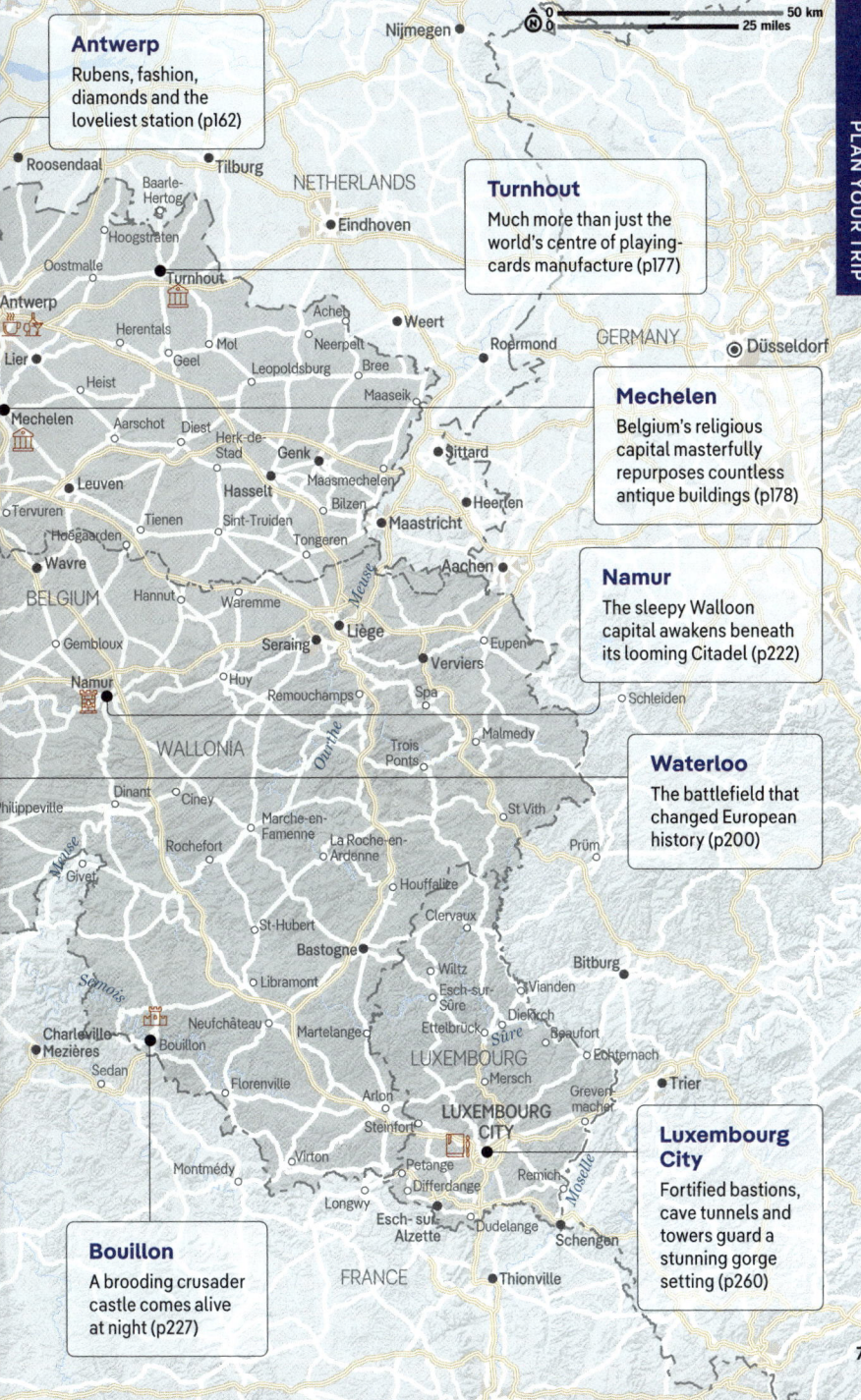

Antwerp
Rubens, fashion, diamonds and the loveliest station (p162)

Turnhout
Much more than just the world's centre of playing-cards manufacture (p177)

Mechelen
Belgium's religious capital masterfully repurposes countless antique buildings (p178)

Namur
The sleepy Walloon capital awakens beneath its looming Citadel (p222)

Waterloo
The battlefield that changed European history (p200)

Luxembourg City
Fortified bastions, cave tunnels and towers guard a stunning gorge setting (p260)

Bouillon
A brooding crusader castle comes alive at night (p227)

50 km
25 miles

NETHERLANDS

GERMANY

BELGIUM

WALLONIA

LUXEMBOURG

FRANCE

Nijmegen

Roosendaal
Tilburg
Baarle-Hertog
Hoogstraten
Eindhoven
Oostmalle
Turnhout
Achel
Weert
Antwerp
Herentals
Mol
Neerpelt
Roermond
Düsseldorf
Lier
Geel
Leopoldsburg
Bree
Heist
Maaseik
Mechelen
Aarschot
Diest
Herk-de-Stad
Genk
Sittard
Leuven
Hasselt
Maasmechelen
Bilzen
Heerlen
Tervuren
Tienen
Sint-Truiden
Tongeren
Maastricht
Hoegaarden
Wavre
Hannut
Waremme
Aachen
Gembloux
Liège
Eupen
Namur
Huy
Seraing
Verviers
Remouchamps
Spa
Schleiden
Malmedy
Dinant
Ciney
Trois-Ponts
Philippeville
Marche-en-Famenne
La Roche-en-Ardenne
St Vith
Rochefort
Prüm
Givet
Houffalize
Clervaux
St-Hubert
Bastogne
Bitburg
Libramont
Wiltz
Vianden
Esch-sur-Sûre
Dietkirch
Beaufort
Neufchâteau
Echternach
Charleville-Mézières
Bouillon
Martelange
Ettelbrück
Mersch
Grevenmacher
Trier
Sedan
Florenville
LUXEMBOURG
Arlon
Steinfort
LUXEMBOURG CITY
Montmédy
Virton
Petange
Differdange
Remich
Longwy
Esch-sur-Alzette
Dudelange
Schengen
Thionville

Meuse
Ourthe
Semois
Sûre
Moselle

7

MEDIEVAL MARVELS

As well as great churches and monasteries, medieval Flanders developed *begijnhoven,* religious refuges for single women who stopped short of becoming nuns. What's now Belgium was also one of the first places in Europe where the economic power accumulated through crafts (especially weaving) led townsfolk to assert their civic rights, helped by trade guilds. Despite many a fight with reticent nobility, this power shift was demonstrated architecturally through guildhalls, belfries and grand market squares.

Beautiful Belfries

No less than 33 Belgian belfries are UNESCO-listed, representing visually – in stone and brick – the development of secular municipal power in the early Middle Ages.

Market Squares

The heart of each medieval city is a grand central square, Grand-Place in French or Grote Markt in Dutch, typically ringed by beautifully gabled guild houses.

Idyllic Begijnhoven

The idea of a *begijnhof* dates from the 13th century but the very last resident *begijn* only died in 2013. There are 13 UNESCO-listed Flemish *begijnhoven.*

BEST MEDIEVAL EXPERIENCES

Swoon at the fabulous canals in ❶ **Bruges** (p121), climb the belfry, admire sumptuously detailed paintings by the Flemish Primitives, then stroll to the peaceful 800-year-old *begijnhof*.

Stroll around the ❷ **Grand-Place** (p59) in Brussels and wonder: how did such an incredibly ornate enclosed square survive so many wars?

Explore northeast Belgium comparing the many lovely *begijnhoven*. Do you prefer those in ❸ **Lier** (p176), ❸ **Turnhout** (p177) or ❸ **Diest** (p192)?

Learn about how the nobility had a rude awakening at the Battle of the Golden Spurs, at the ❹ **Kortrijk 1302** (p152) museum.

Stand on the little Grasbrug bridge in ❺ **Ghent** (p114) to admire the picture-perfect 'medieval' scene of waterfront gabled houses, gorgeous if largely rebuilt in 1913.

PHILIP REYNAERS / PHOTONEWS VIA GETTY IMAGES

Euro Space Center (p230)

INDUSTRIAL INNOVATOR

People in what's now Belgium and Luxembourg have been at the forefront of trade and new technologies for millennia. Both countries were major metallurgical centres and today they're hubs for international business and cooperation symbolised in part through the EU institutions based here.

Industrial Heritage

The Borinage around Mons, the hinterland of Liège and the Minett region of southern Luxembourg all have mining museums and heavy industry experiences open to visitors.

Always Cutting Edge

From transport infrastructure and space technology to the use of block chain in tracing genuine diamonds, this region is proud of its track record in innovation.

BEST TRADE & INDUSTRY EXPERIENCES

Learn all about the trade and processing of diamonds at DIVA (p167) in ❶ **Antwerp** or the ways in which 16th-century printing changed the world at Museum Plantin-Moretus (p171).

Appreciate human resilience by going down the ❷ **Blégny coal mine** (p251) near Liège, or the ❷ **MNM iron-ore mine** (p271) at Rumelange.

Be wowed by the rapid advances in science and technology at ❸ **Technopolis** (p182) near Mechelen.

Experience reduced-gravity training exercises that ESA astronauts undergo before heading into space at the ❹ **Euro Space Center** (p230).

Stay in the mind-bending ❺ **Ghostel** (p219) while trying to process the bleak dystopia that is post-industrial Charleroi.

THE GREAT OUTDOORS

Whether for sport, relaxation or as a spectator, cycling is a passion for many Belgians. But there's myriad ways to get outside here including kayaking and gentle river cruises, ziplines and activity parks, sporting events and long distance hikes. There's also many a cave to explore and the Belgian coast has some remarkably fine beaches.

On Your Bike

Cyclists get both the flat, well-tended canal-side routes of northern Flanders and the steep hills and high fenlands of the Ardennes.

Caving In

You don't need to be a speleologist to enjoy some of the numerous beautiful caves that form part of Belgium's newly declared Famenne-Ardenne UNESCO Global Geopark (p232).

Forest Walks

Head out on a musical hike on the Flanders–Wallonia border in Ronse's so-called Musical Forest, Muziekbos (p120), to enjoy the sounds of nature.

BEST OUTDOOR EXPERIENCES

Climb the classic ❶ **Muur van Geraardsbergen** (p120), the cobbled killer that's one of cycling's greatest sprint-tests. While in Geraardsbergen don't miss the cycle-sport museum.

Test your mountain-bike legs on the forest trails around ❷ **La Roche-en-Ardenne** (p233), or take a contrastingly gentle glide at FDHW near ❷ **Bokrijk** (p191) where you appear to be cycling right through a lake.

Take an idyllic walk through the beechwoods and mossy micro-canyons of Luxembourg's ❸ **Müllerthal/Mëllerdall** region (p275).

Delve deep underground at Rochefort's awe-inspiring ❹ **Grotte de Lorette** (p232), or for more stalactites and fewer steps, choose the **Grottes de Han** (p232) at Han-sur-Lesse.

Exhaust the family with countless activities at the extensive Adventure Valley complex at **Durbuy** (p233), Belgium's 'smallest city'.

PERENNIAL SURVIVOR

For centuries the region has seen battles between dukes and counts, between nobles and townsfolk and at the hand of many an outside enemy sweeping across the land. The result is a vast number of castles, forts and historic battlefields. Today a great deal of what once represented the worst of human aggression and the indulgence of overlords has been transformed into beautiful or moving sites for 21st-century visitors.

Castles & Forts

Impenetrable medieval castles like Bouillon's, grandiose châteaux like Chimay, Modave and Beloeil (above), and harsh fortresses like Namur and Luxembourg are all fascinating in their own way.

Battlefields

Some of Europe's defining battles have been fought on Belgian and Luxembourg soil with various attractions helping visitors to envisage what really happened.

World War Memorials

Silent memorials, vast white graveyards and many a moving museum commemorate the appalling tragedies of the world wars for soldiers and civilians alike.

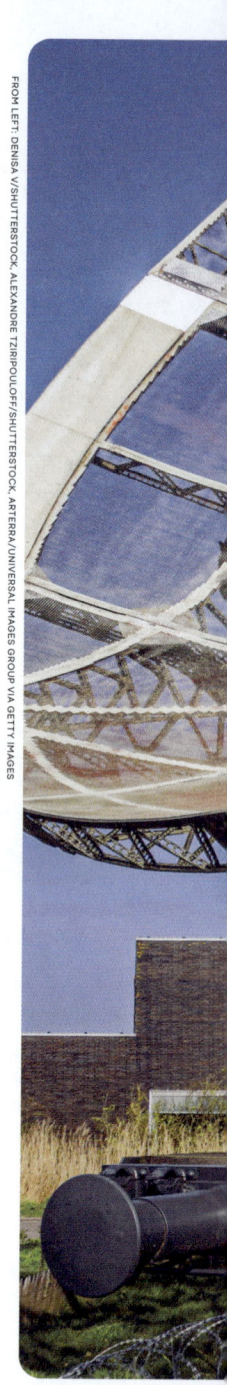

BEST WAR-RELATED EXPERIENCES

Find yourself right in the midst of the horrifically bloody Battle of Waterloo with a 3-D experience that's part of the highly interactive ❶ **Mémorial 1815** (p200) complex.

Be gripped by ❷ **Atlantikwall Raversyde** (p142), a remarkably extensive complex of WWI and WWII bunkers, gun emplacements and linking brick tunnels created by occupying German forces.

Hear personal stories from the terrible WWI trench warfare at the magnificently rebuilt ❸ **Lakenhalle** (p146) in Ypres (Ieper). Grave sites abound.

Visit specialist ❹ **war museums** (p235) in the Ardennes region, which was pummelled in Hitler's last ditch counter-attack at Christmas 1944.

Learn more of the moving histories of WWII occupation horrors and murderous deportations at ❺ **Kazerne Dossin** (p181) in Mechelen.

Westvleteren beers, Abdij Sint-Sixtus (p153)

BOOZY BRILLIANCE

Belgium is globally famous for its beers. The world's biggest brewer grew out of a family business based in Leuven, and the country has some truly fabulous drinking holes. Viniculture is a maturing novelty in Belgium but well established in Luxembourg, whose sparkling wines and pinot blancs are great discoveries.

Belgian Beer

Classics range from self-fermenting lambics to classic Trappist masterpieces created by monks in active monasteries. Enjoy them in hipster bars or timeless brown cafes.

Fizzy Fun

The beautiful undulating countryside east of St-Truiden is increasingly planted with vines, but for archetypal vineyard scenes do a tasting tour of Luxembourg's Moselle Valley.

BEST BEER & WINE EXPERIENCES

Seek the holy grail of Trappist beers, a glass of Westvletteren 12, at ❶ **In de Vrede** (p153), located beside Abdij Sint-Sixtus where it's brewed.

Take one of the most amusing brewery tours imaginable at ❷ **De Koninck** (p175) in Antwerp, then do a city cafe-crawl.

Go direct to the source with a tour of the historic ❸ **Cantillon Brewery** (p83) and *gueuze* museum.

Visit Belgium's last ❹ **'steam' brewery** (p213) at Pipaix.

Taste wines at the prestigious ❺ **Poll-Fabaire's** (p272) imposing winery building in Wormeldange, which offers still and *crémant* (sparkling) wine on the river-facing terrace.

CULTURE CLUSTER

Belgium's artistic pedigree is out of all proportion to its size. The van Eycks and Breughels, Rubens, van Dyck and surrealist superstar Magritte all lived and worked here. Cartoons are also a major art form. And then there's all those wildly idiosyncratic festivals and carnivals. Who said Belgium was boring?!

Crazy Carnivals

Certain Belgian towns seem to live for their carnivals, some of them deliciously weird. Foremost choices are at Binche (above), Stavelot and Malmédy.

Museum Marvels

So much culture and so many collectors mean that if you look hard enough you'll find museums celebrating virtually anything from 17th-century clocks to chips to ribbon-making.

Arrays of Art

On top of some truly world-beating galleries, Belgium also has a vibrant fashion scene (centred in Antwerp) and a penchant for large-scale street art.

BEST CULTURAL EXPERIENCES

Be blown away by the collection of Flemish Primitive artworks at the ❶ **Groeningemuseum** (p128) in Bruges.

Peruse the astonishing wealth of street art in ❷ **Berchem** (p175) and avoid Rubens overload at the majestic **KMSKA gallery** (p174) in Antwerp.

Jump on a bicycle in ❸ **Mons** (p210) and follow a route around the Borinage mining villages whose miseries turned Vincent van Gogh from wannabe priest to painter.

Immerse yourself in the surreal carnival world of the Gilles at ❹ **Binche** (p217).

Go on the trail of prolific Maigret author Georges Simenon in the ❺ **Outremeuse quarter** (p249) of Liège, a district that semi-comically declares independence every year.

15

WHAT'S NEW?

Belgium and Luxembourg may have a long and distinguished history with established museums and traditions, but that does not mean they are monolithic. Quite the contrary. Find out what's new – from new trends to new openings and new activities – across both countries.

More Street Art

Street art is brightening cities and villages alike as more locals embrace it. Explore new street art in Verviers, Namur, Lier, Leuven/Kessel-Lo, Louvain-la-Neuve, and Esch-sur-Alzette.

Coming Soon...

Many museums are being renovated or expanded. Look out for the opening of the Kanal Pompidou in Brussels or Antwerp's Maritime Museum and Design Museum Gent's (above) reopening.

More Immersion

Immersive experiences are popular now and expressed in various ways. You'll find accommodation, museum tours, activities and exhibitions all centring on immersive experiences.

BEST NEW EXPERIENCES

Admire Louvain-la-Neuve, Belgium's newest city (1972), with its brutalist architecture, and visit ❶ **Musée L** (p205).

Get close to wildlife at ❷ **Pairi Daiza** (p212) in a unique stay: a farmhouse near the petting zoo, a lodge by the wolves and rooms overlooking polar bears.

Mark the 100th anniversary of Art Deco at Brussels' ❸ **Musée Art et Histoire** (p65), where rooms are dedicated to Art Nouveau and Art Deco.

See Bruges' revamped ❹ **Museum Sint-Janshospitaal** (p129), showcasing Memling masterpieces in a glass shrine alongside contemporary art and medieval treasures.

Cross the city of ❺ **Liège** from north to south on a brand new tramway line (p245).

REGIONS & CITIES

Find the places that tick all your boxes.

Ghent, Bruges &
Northwest Belgium
p105

BRUSSELS
p44

Ghent, Bruges & Northwest Belgium

MEDIEVAL CITIES AND AN EVOCATIVE COASTLINE

Miles of sandy beach, poignant WWI memorials and flat expanses of hop fields are punctuated with fine medieval towns. Veurne and Oudenaarde are lovely, Ghent is magnificent, but Bruges grabs the limelight with its fairy-tale confection of pretty canals, soaring towers and step-gabled houses.

Brussels

MULTICULTURAL AND FESTIVE CAPITAL OF EUROPE

History meets bureaucracy meets bizarre in this multicultural jumble that's fabulous for art, museums, chocolate shops and unforgettable cafe-bars. The 1960s term Brusselisation was coined to describe places that wantonly wreck their own historical cityscapes, but much has survived nonetheless and Brussels' magnificent Grand-Place remains a global wonder.

Antwerp & Northeast Belgium

CENTURIES OF CREATIVITY, CONTINUED CUTTING EDGE

Antwerp is Belgium's second city, biggest port and fizzing hub of cultural cool. Medieval charmers like Mechelen and Lier fly under the radar, while further east, orchards and vineyards roll in emerald waves towards Gallo-Roman Tongeren and the 'gin' city of Hasselt.

Antwerp & Northeast Belgium
p156

Wallonia

BELGIUM'S FRANCOPHONE SOUTH

Expect more contours as you head south and switch linguistically from Dutch to French. Beyond a mishmash of post-industrial fascination, rolling farmlands and riverside fortress towns lies the sports-magnet that is the well-wooded Ardennes. Here you'll find caves, rivers to kayak, adventure parks and the nearest Belgium comes to mountains.

Wallonia
p195

Luxembourg

THE WORLD'S RICHEST COUNTRY

Don't think that Luxembourg is all banks and no trousers. The capital is a dramatic once-fortified canyon. Beyond are magical castles nestled in hilly green country with great walking trails, quaffable sparkling wines and totally free public transport that, despite the cheap petrol, might make you want to put your car away.

Luxembourg
p256

Canal tour, Bruges (p125)

ITINERARIES

The Main Marvels

Allow: 8 days   **Distance:** 260km

Belgium's fab four historic cities are all within a hour or so from one another by train. Each could entertain you for days at a time but with just a week you can still get a pretty good taster.

① BRUSSELS ⏱ 2 DAYS

As Belgium's capital, **Brussels** (p44) is a logical starting point. Its flamboyant Grand-Place is a phenomenal sight and the Manneken Pis is comical if underwhelming, while the streets around Saint-Géry and Sainte-Catherine are brimming with lively bar-cafés. Central Brussels has world-class galleries and amazing museums, and on the outskirts there are countless more, including the extraordinary Atomium.

② WATERLOO BATTLEFIELDS ⏱ 1 DAY

This is a battlefield that changed the whole course of European history, and the state-of-the art Mémorial 1815 experience is powerful enough to appeal even to those who thought Napoleon was a brandy trademark. There are several sub-sites, museums, walks and summer 'animations' making **Waterloo** (p200) a very satisfying day trip from Brussels.

③ BRUGES ⏱ 2 DAYS

Bruges (p121) has it all. Romantic canals lined by picture-perfect houses, a towering belfry, a mysterious secret in a medieval church, an idyllic *begijnhof* (pictured) and so many great museums. The one caveat is that everyone knows. Ideally visit out of season, stay overnight, and rework your itinerary if necessary to avoid being here at weekends when visitor numbers peak.

FROM LEFT: RAFAEL_WIEDENMEIER/GETTY IMAGES, KURT VANSTEELANT/SHUTTERSTOCK, GUS MARTINIE/GETTY IMAGES

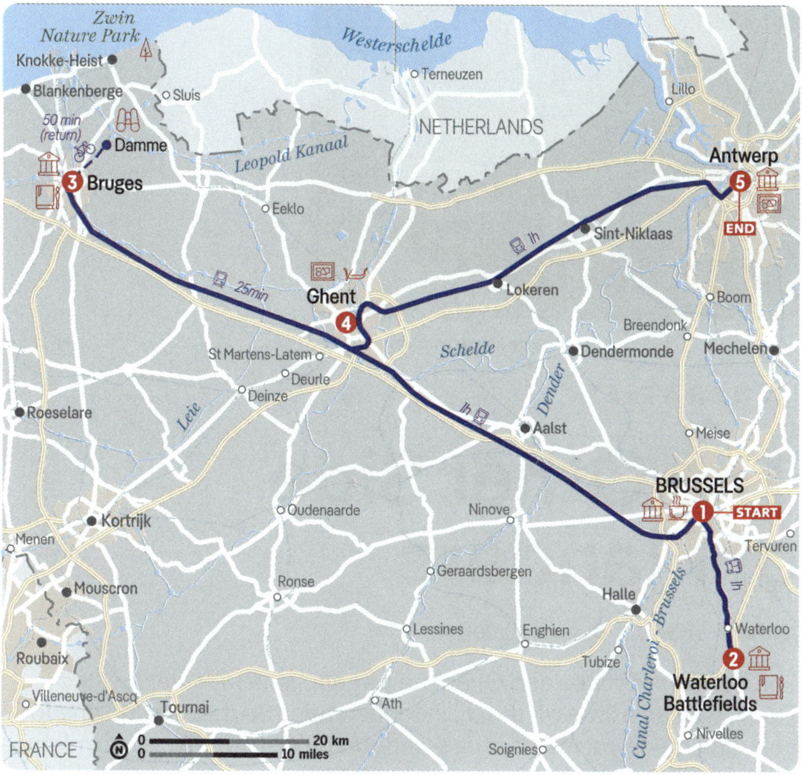

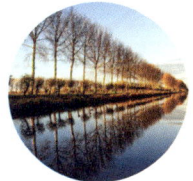

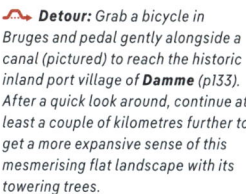

Detour: *Grab a bicycle in Bruges and pedal gently alongside a canal (pictured) to reach the historic inland port village of* ***Damme*** *(p133). After a quick look around, continue at least a couple of kilometres further to get a more expansive sense of this mesmerising flat landscape with its towering trees.*

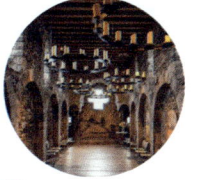

4

GHENT 1 DAY

With majestic canal views and spectacular medieval architecture, gorgeous **Ghent** (p110) feels like a slightly grittier, more lived-in version of Bruges. A day here will leave you wanting more but it's enough to climb the belfry, take a canal boat trip, explore Gravensteen castle (pictured), and adore the *Mystic Lamb*, a 20-panel altarpiece by Jan van Eyck in Sint-Baafskathedraal.

5

ANTWERP 2 DAYS

The old core of **Antwerp** (p162) has plenty of medieval majesty, including some fabulous museums and a Rubens connection at every turn. Antwerp is also a buzzing cradle of creativity, where immersive experiences give insights into the diamond industry, as well as chocolate making and beer brewing. There is also a cutting-edge fashion district and plenty of alternative lifestylers.

FROM LEFT: SL-PHOTOGRAPHY/SHUTTERSTOCK, OKSANA YERMOSHENKO/SHUTTERSTOCK, RENATA SEDMAKOVA/SHUTTERSTOCK

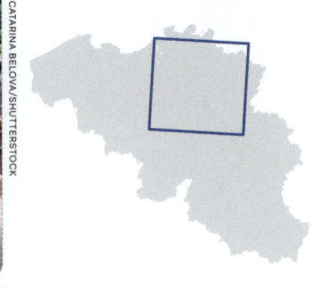

Historic city center, Antwerp (p162)

ITINERARIES

The Other Side of Flanders

Allow: 4–5 days   **Distance:** 220km

The dazzle of Bruges and Ghent helps keep several other historic Flemish cities a little off the main tourist radar. So if you're looking for beautiful medieval townscapes without the crowds, this route might suit as an alternative, or addition to, the Main Marvels itinerary.

1

ANTWERP ⏱1 DAY

On top of the couple of days you've done on the previous itinerary (p20), add an extra night in **Antwerp** (p162) and explore some of the great *bruin café* (p171). Next morning use the short-hop bicycle system to admire Art Nouveau architecture in Zurenborg and street art around Berchem. Drop off the bicycle beside Antwerpen-Berchem station and take the train to Lier.

2

LIER ⏱½ DAY

If you arrive at **Lier** (p176) by 11.30am, there's time to stroll into the centre and catch the noon 'performance' of Lier's signature Zimmertoren clock (pictured). Spend the rest of the afternoon enjoying the canal, *begijnhoven* and bar-cafés that give this underrated city such a sense of effortless class. There's a decent hostel here if you don't want to go back to Antwerp or continue on to Mechelen.

3

MECHELEN ⏱1½ DAYS

If it were located in a country with fewer superb medieval cities, **Mechelen** (p178) would be internationally famous. Attractions include a photogenic main square, several grand churches, a toy museum and an experiential centre that brings science to life. If possible, time your itinerary so that you overnight here at the weekend when accommodation prices typically fall.

FROM LEFT: ERIK AJV/SHUTTERSTOCK, CHEDKO/SHUTTERSTOCK, JORISVO/SHUTTERSTOCK

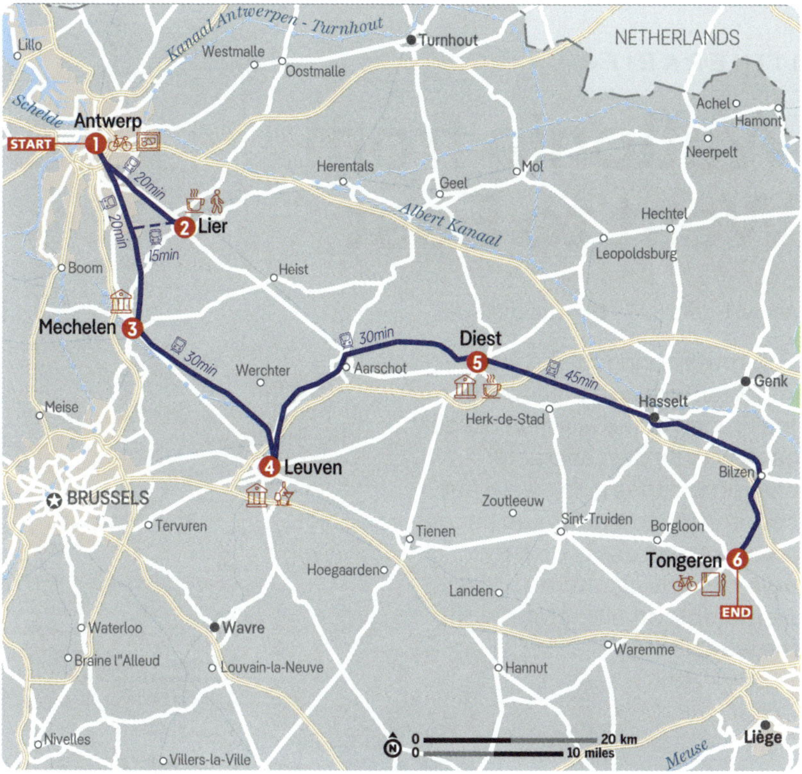

Kanaal Antwerpen - Turnhout
Lillo
Westmalle
Oostmalle
Turnhout
NETHERLANDS
Schelde
Antwerp
START
1
20min
20min
2
Lier
15min
Boom
Herentals
Geel
Mol
Achel
Hamont
Neerpelt
Albert Kanaal
Hechtel
Leopoldsburg
Heist
Mechelen
3
30min
Werchter
Aarschot
30min
Diest
5
45min
Herk-de-Stad
Hasselt
Genk
Meise
4
Leuven
BRUSSELS
Tervuren
Tienen
Zoutleeuw
Sint-Truiden
Borgloon
Bilzen
Tongeren
6
END
Hoegaarden
Landen
Waterloo
Wavre
Braine l'Alleud
Louvain-la-Neuve
Hannut
Waremme
Nivelles
Villers-la-Ville
0
20 km
0
10 miles
Meuse
Liège

4

LEUVEN ⏱ ½ DAY

You could happily spend days in **Leuven** (p183), a major university (pictured) and brewing centre where there's always lots going on. However, if you're on a tight deadline, a few hours give you just enough time to walk down from the station, climb the university belfry, admire the fabulous Stadhuis and inspect Oude Markt, sometimes nicknamed the 'world's longest bar'.

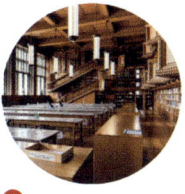

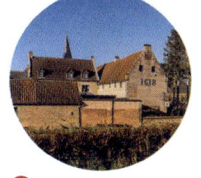

5

DIEST ⏱ 2½ HOURS

While it's not an essential destination, many railway routes in northeastern Belgium pass through the handsome city of **Diest** (p192). It's well worth jumping off the train for an hour or two to stroll through the older sections of town and into the UNESCO-listed *begijnhof* (pictured). It's one of Belgium's loveliest and a soothing place to unwind with a snack in a former chapel turned bar-café.

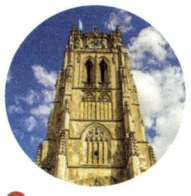

6

TONGEREN ⏱ 1 DAY

Come to **Tongeren** (p188) if you're interested in Gallo-Roman history and to discover another lovely old Flemish city with a small, historic core. Alternatively get off the train 15 minutes earlier in Hasselt (p189), visit the *jenever* (local gin) museum, then head for Bokrijk, spending most of the day amid re-assembled antique buildings before renting a bicycle to 'cycle through water'.

FROM LEFT: HENK VRIESELAAR/SHUTTERSTOCK, BERT BECKERS/SHUTTERSTOCK, BOERESCUL/GETTY IMAGES

ITINERARIES

Wallonia from West to East

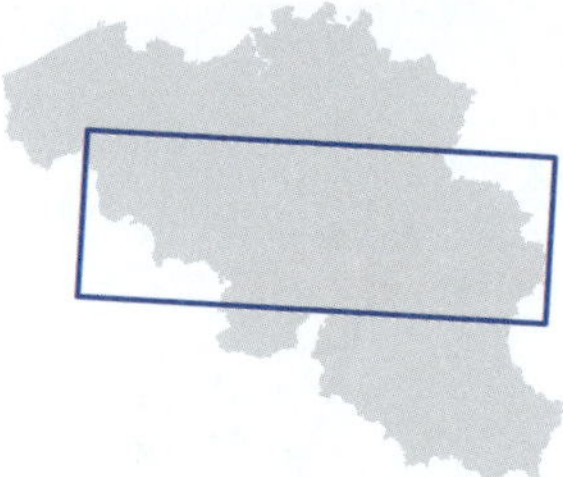

Allow: 8 days **Distance:** 248km

This route connects the more important cities in Wallonia from the French to the German border, each with its own character and landscapes going from flat countryside to the rugged Fagnes area. You can easily do it by train, but driving offers access to memorable smaller stops along the way.

1

TOURNAI 1 DAY

As Belgium's second-oldest city, **Tournai** (p213) oozes Flemish-style charm with its triangular Grand-Place, its slender Belfry tower and its gigantic Cathédrale Notre-Dame, framed by five spired towers (pictured). Take a walk along the Schelde River to the medieval Pont des Trous before heading to Mons for the night.

2

MONS 1 DAY

Perched atop its hill, **Mons** (p206) features a lovely and compact city centre that can be easily explored by following the 'L'Art habite la Ville' street art trail. Be sure to visit the Grand-Place, the Collégiale Sainte-Waudru, and the Mons War Museum dedicated to World War I.

Detour: *Visit Maison Van Gogh in* ***Cuesmes*** *(p210), where Vincent lived and discovered his true calling.*

3

CHARLEROI 1 DAY

Love it or hate it, the 'world's ugliest city' is perversely fascinating, and some budget airlines fly here. **Charleroi** (p218) has a surprisingly impressive choice of cultural options: art galleries, the out-of-town photo museum and the Bois de Cazier mine site (pictured), which offers an insight into the region's industrial history. Then drive on to spend the night in nearby Namur.

FROM LEFT: NINA ALIZADA/SHUTTERSTOCK, ANIBAL TREJO/SHUTTERSTOCK, USLATAR/SHUTTERSTOCK

④ NAMUR ⏱ 2 DAYS

Namur (pictured, p222), the once-sleepy Walloon capital, is reborn: new museums, a cable car, and projects complement its baroque centre and vast Citadelle – so impressive that Napoleon dubbed it 'Europe's Anthill'.

🌉 *Detour: On your way to Liège, make time to walk the streets and squares of **Huy** (p253) and its gigantic fort, looming over the Meuse river.*

⑤ LIÈGE ⏱ 2 DAYS

Liège (pictured, p245) takes a bit of effort to love, but it's rewarding to stroll around Hors Chateau, visit the Grand Curtius museum, cruise down to La Boverie on a river ferry and practise your French with ebullient, fun-loving locals. Timing your visit to be here on a Sunday adds to the fun.

🌉 *Detour: Driving to Eupen, stop in lovely little **Limbourg** (p243), underrated **Verviers** (p244) or the abbey-brewery gardens at **Val-Dieu** (p253).*

⑥ EUPEN ⏱ 1 DAY

Welcome to **Eupen** (p242), the capital of the German-speaking community. It's a little different here – even the buildings (pictured) have a distinct German flair. Close to the Fagnes moors and Belgium's highest 'summits', it's easy to reach Signal de Botrange (p241), the tallest of them all at 700m. Alternatively, hike from town through the forest to the Vesdre Dam.

ITINERARIES

The Two Luxembourgs

Allow: Around 9 days   **Distance:** 351 km

Belgian Luxembourg and the Grand Duchy all in one! This is a splendid drive to take in beautiful, forested landscapes, witness history visiting the many castles along the way, and explore the reminders that WWII left in this region. A car will be necessary.

❶ SPA ⏱ 1 DAY

The elegant original spa of **Spa** (p237) is a charmer, whether for dining well, 'taking the waters', or pampering yourself with massages and steam baths.

🚗 *Detour: On your way to Durbuy for the night, stop to explore the Grottes de Remouchamps (p232) and discover what it feels like to glide along Europe's longest underground river.*

❷ DURBUY ⏱ 1 DAY

Durbuy (p233) may be the world's smallest city, but it packs a serious punch with its fairy-tale centre, luxury restaurants and charming hotels. If you're active or travelling with children, don't miss Adventure Valley – an exciting outdoor recreation park.

🚗 *Detour: If you have time en route to La Roche-en-Ardenne, a visit to the Grottes de Hotton (p232) is well worth it.*

❸ LA ROCHE-EN-ARDENNE ⏱ 1 DAY

Rise early to take on the picturesque town of **La Roche-en-Ardenne** (p233), Wallonia's outdoor capital, with its ruined castle and museum dedicated to WWII.

🚗 *Detour: In the afternoon, drive to Redu (p230) and lose yourself in its many bookshops. Alternatively, spend the afternoon at the Euro Space Centre (p230) and discover if you have what it takes to become an astronaut.*

❹ BOUILLON ⏱ 1 DAY

Gorgeously set in a curl of the Semois River, the town of **Bouillon** (p227) – with its dominating castle (pictured) built by Godefroid, one of the most famous crusaders – deserves a full day's exploration, if only to see it illuminated at twilight. There's much to see here: the castle itself; the Archeoscope, where the Crusades come to life; the Ducal Museum; and much more.

❺ BASTOGNE ⏱ 1 DAY

For history buffs, **Bastogne** (p235) is unmissable – this was where Allied forces withstood Nazi Germany's counter-offensive in 1944: the Battle of the Bulge. The Bastogne War Museum vividly recounts those dreadful days, while the Mardasson Memorial (pictured) honours the fallen American soldiers.

🚗 *Detour: En route to Vianden, visit the Family of Man exhibition at Clervaux Castle (p277).*

❻ VIANDEN ⏱ 1 DAY

Hilly Luxembourg is a feast of castles, most impressively the ruins at rural Bourscheid or the brilliantly restored monster crowning **Vianden** (p277). Vianden town (pictured) has a steep, cobbled main street on which you can sleep in an atmospheric, heavy beamed inn.

🚗 *Detour: On the way to Echternach, go a little off road to Beaufort (p276). Yes, another fabulous castle!*

FROM LEFT: REMI FOLLET/SHUTTERSTOCK, SERGEY DZYUBA/SHUTTERSTOCK, CLEMENT LEONARD/GETTY IMAGES

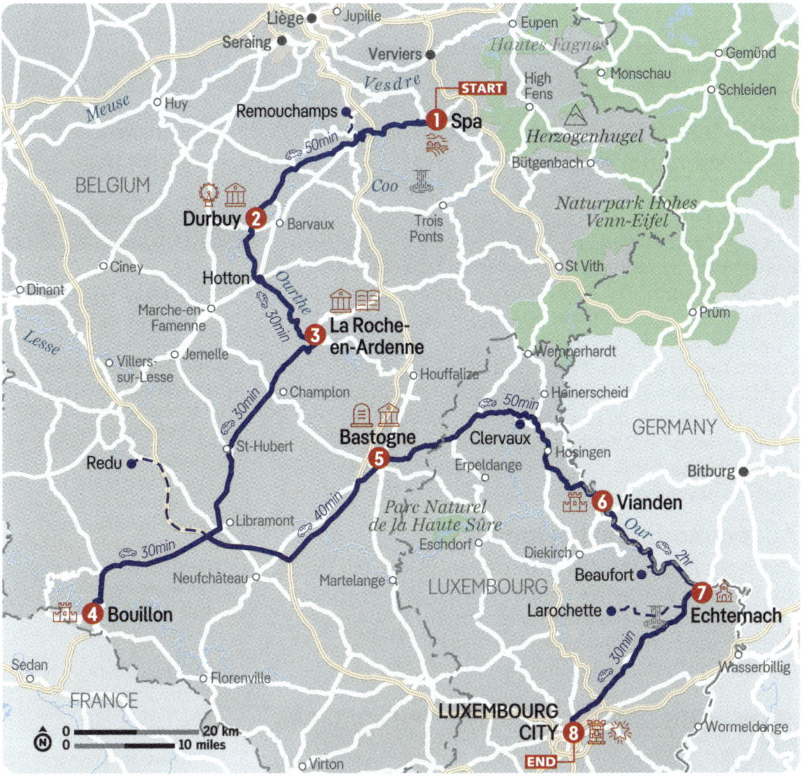

Durbuy (p233)

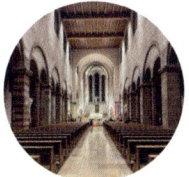

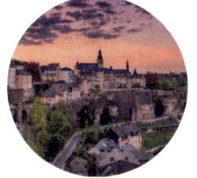

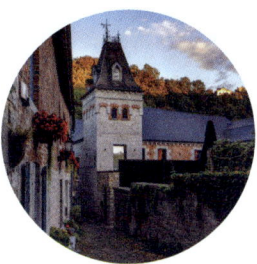

7

ECHTERNACH 1 DAY

Luxembourg's oldest city, **Echternach** (p273) is a true gem. Take some time to soak in the atmosphere of its main square and visit its St-Willibord's Cathedral (pictured) and Echternach Abbey.

Detour: *On your drive from Echternach to Luxembourg City, it's worth visiting* ***Larochette*** *(p276) and its castle.*

8

LUXEMBOURG CITY 2 DAYS

Luxembourg City (pictured, p260) is the capital of Europe's richest country, but while much is pricey, there are plenty of free attractions and public transport is gratis. Enjoy endlessly photogenic valley views and consider day trips to the post-industrial Minett region, local castle villages or Remich for some wine-tasting along the Moselle.

FROM LEFT: ILONA LABLAIKA/SHUTTERSTOCK, TEFIK RUSTEMOV/SHUTTERSTOCK, PABLO MEILAN CAMPAGNALE/GETTY IMAGES

WHEN **TO GO**

With a temperate climate, Belgium and Luxembourg are enjoyable all year long, although November and January–February are often gloomy.

Belgium is known for overcast skies and rainy, unpredictable weather while Luxembourg, with a slightly more continental climate, has a reputation for colder winters and sunny summers. Regardless, you will need to pack an umbrella or a raincoat, no matter the season.

Brussels and the Belgian art cities (Antwerp, Ghent and especially Bruges) are flooded with tourists between May and September and during weekends. Try to avoid these periods, and visit during the week if you can.

Things are a bit quieter in below-the-radar Luxembourg, although Luxembourg City may feel crowded at times because of its small size.

Accommodation Lowdown

There are no real low or high seasons, although prices drop slightly during the winter, especially in Bruges and the North Sea towns. In Brussels and Luxembourg City, both 'congress towns', rates may be a bit cheaper on the weekend but prices can jump in case of large events.

FROM LEFT: SARA WINTER/SHUTTERSTOCK, MANTONATURE/GETTY IMAGES

Hautes Fagnes (p241)

⭐ I LIVE HERE

HIKING IN THE HIGH FENS

Maxime Alexandre is a passionate outdoors lover and content creator @trekkingetvoyage

In wintertime, dawn is spectacular in the High Fens. I typically spend the night at **Malmedy Youth Hostel**, park my car at the **Signal de Botrange** and start walking on the trail until sunrise. It's simply fantastic. With luck, you get to see wildlife as well. When the crowds start coming in, I head for the nature centre or the restaurant at **Baraque Michel** for a meal.

THE GOOD LAND AND THE BAD

An extension of the Ardennes, Oesling, roughly covering a third of Luxembourg in the north, is called the 'bad land', while Gutland ('good land') makes up the rest of the country. Winters and summers are a bit colder there because of the higher altitude.

Weather through the Year: Brussels

JANUARY Avg. daytime max: **5°C** Days of rainfall: **12**	**FEBRUARY** Avg. daytime max: **6°C** Days of rainfall: **10**	**MARCH** Avg. daytime max: **9°C** Days of rainfall: **12**	**APRIL** Avg. daytime max: **13°C** Days of rainfall: **10**	**MAY** Avg. daytime max: **18°C** Days of rainfall: **10**	**JUNE** Avg. daytime max: **21°C** Days of rainfall: **10**

THE COAST EFFECT

The North Sea coast benefits from the most 'even-tempered' climate in Belgium. In winter, it's warmer than the rest of the country. In summer, it's cooler. And with the influence of the sea and the winds, it has its own microclimate. Check the regional weather forecast.

Major Festivals and People-Pleasers in Belgium & Luxembourg

Carnival In Belgium, the festival season kicks off with carnival. Binche (p217) and its UNESCO-listed celebration see its Gilles de Binche dressed in intricate costumes and masks, throwing oranges to repel evil spirits. 🌐 **February**

Wiltz Festival (p270) is the largest in Luxembourg, with the picturesque backdrop of Wiltz Castle. Originally focused on theatre, it also showcases concerts, dance shows and young public performances. ☀️ **First half of July**

Gentsefeesten (p111) During ten vibrant days, the city of Ghent is engulfed by music, arts and culture. The Gentsefeesten (Ghent Festivities) is one of the longest, and largest, festivals of its kind in Belgium. ☀️ **July**

Christmas markets Every large city has a Christmas market but the main one is Winter Wonders in Brussels. Don't miss the sound-and-light show on Grand-Place (p59). 🌐 **December**

Folklore and Traditions

Springprozession (p273) On Whit Sunday, Echternach hosts this UNESCO-listed event, commemorating the founding of the abbey by St Willibrord. This dancing procession is the last of its kind. ☀️ **May or June**

Ducasse (p209) In Mons, during the UNESCO-listed Ducasse de Mons, the Lumeçon reenacts Saint George's battle against the dragon. Join in the crowd to try and grab a hair of the dragon... if you dare! ☀️ **May or June**

Ommegang (p59) Brussels welcomes summer with the Ommegang, commemorating Emperor Charles V's visit in 1549, complete with Renaissance pageantry and flag-throwers. It's also on the UNESCO list! ☀️ **June**

Mittelalterfest (p277) Step back in time at Vianden Castle, with Luxembourg's largest medieval festival: Mittelalterfest. Aside from tourney, taste the food served during the Middle Ages or try some calligraphy. ☀️ **August**

GRAND DUCHY PLEASURES

Sharon Taylor is an expat living in Luxembourg for over two decades

I always enjoy early summer: the sun is often out, trees are green, terraces come alive and people are excited with the prospect of the warm months. City walks or forest hikes are a particular pleasure at this time of year, while at home, the outdoor furniture comes out and the BBQs fire up as we make the most of the weekends and the many bank holidays of May.

Late spider orchid

THE GAUME EFFECT

Being located far from the sea and sheltered by the Ardennes, the Gaume region (south of the Belgian Luxembourg around Virton) is the sunniest, warmest place in Belgium. The 'Little Provence' is warm enough to allow orchids to grow in the wild.

JULY	AUGUST	SEPTEMBER	OCTOBER	NOVEMBER	❄️ DECEMBER
Avg. daytime max: **23°C**	Avg. daytime max: **23°C**	Avg. daytime max: **19°C**	Avg. daytime max: **14°C**	Avg. daytime max: **8°C**	Avg. daytime max: **5°C**
Days of rainfall: **9**	Days of rainfall: **9**	Days of rainfall: **9**	Days of rainfall: **9**	Days of rainfall: **11**	Days of rainfall: **12**

FROM LEFT: ROBERTO FINIZIO/GETTY IMAGES, PHOTO 12/ALAMY

Maarten Devoldere of Warhaus

GET PREPARED FOR BELGIUM & LUXEMBOURG

Useful things to load in your bag, your ears and your brain.

Clothes

Season appropriate Belgium and Luxembourg have four well-defined seasons. Bring light clothes in summer and warm attire in winter, and even proper winter gear if you plan on hiking; the Ardennes and Luxembourg can get cold (–5/5°C). Spring and autumn are trickier with unpredictable weather and temperature changes. Dressing in layers is recommended.

Comfortable shoes and/or boots Those cobblestone streets can be a pain. Unless you have a night out planned during your trip, leave the fancy shoes at home. Hiking in the Ardennes or Luxembourg? Pack your walking boots.

Umbrella and waterproofs With 200 days of rain on average, you never know what

Manners

Be mindful of languages This is especially important in Belgium where Dutch is spoken in Flanders, French in Wallonia, German in Ostbelgien and Brussels is bilingual (French and Dutch). In Luxembourg, French and German are dominant, with Luxembourgish as the third official language. If you are unsure which language to use, English is widely spoken in both countries.

Punctuality Don't be late if you have an appointment – being on time is highly valued.

you're in for, so it's best to be prepared. A windbreaker jacket is also worth it if you plan to visit the Belgian coast.

The Sorrow of Belgium
(Hugo Claus; 1983)
Semi-autobiographical
tale about growing up in
Flanders around WWII.

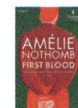

First Blood (Amélie
Nothomb; 2021) Award-
winning story about
fatherhood and legacy
by Belgium's most
prolific writer.

Speechless (Tom
Lannoye; 2018) After a
stroke silences his mother,
the author reflects on
her, his life and their
respective hardships.

**Your Heart of Ice Is
Hot as Vice** (Guy
Rewenig; 2016)
Four novellas by
Luxembourg's most
celebrated author.

Words

French
Salut (silent *t*) Hello
Bonjour *(Bon-joor)* Good morning
Bonsoir *(Bon-swar)* Good evening
Merci Thank you
S'il vous plaît *(Sil-voo-play)* Please (or 'Here you go')
Excusez-moi *(Ex-coo-say-mwa)* Excuse me
De rien *(Duh-reeyuh)* You're welcome
Au secours *(O-se-koor)* Help
Comment allez-vous? *(Ko-muh-alley-voo;* formal),
Comment vas-tu? *(Ko-muh-va-tu;* informal) How are you?

Dutch
Dag *(Dach)* Hello
Goeiedag *(Goo-ye-dach)* Good morning
Goedenavond *(Goo-den-ah-vond)* Good evening
Dank U *(Dank-oo* as in boot; formal), **Bedankt** *(Buh-dankt;* informal) Thank you

Alstublieft *(Ahl-stu-bleeft)* Please (or 'Here you go')
Sorry Excuse me
Graag gedaan *(Graag guh-daan)* You're welcome
Hulp (sounds like *help*) Help
Hoe gaat het? *(Hoo-gaat-hut)* How are you?

German
Hallo Hello
Guten Morgen *(Goo-ten Mor-gen)* Good morning
Guten Abend *(Goo-ten Ah-bend)* Good evening
Danke schön *(Dan-kuh-shun)* or **Danke** Thank you
Bitte *(Bi-tuh)* Please (or 'Here you go')
Entschuldigung *(Ent-shool-dee-gung)* Excuse me
Bitteschön *(Bee-tuh-shun)* You're welcome
Hilfe *(Heel-fuh)* Help
Wie geht es Ihnen? *(Vee-gayt-us-ee-nen;* formal), **Wie geht es dir?** *(Vee-gayt-us-ee-deer;* informal) How are you?

Rosetta (The Dardenne Brothers; 1999; pictured) A young unemployed girl in Wallonia is ready to do anything to find a job.

In Bruges (Martin McDonagh; 2008) After a job gone wrong, a hitman and his partner lay low.

Night Call (Michiel Blanchart; 2024) A student is thrust into a deadly spiral after being framed in an organised crime scheme.

High Tides (series; 2023–2025) A group of teens spend the summer in Belgium's most glamorous coastal town. Secrets and drama follow.

Capitani (series; 2019–2022) Detective Capitani investigates the death of a young woman in the small Luxembourg village of Manscheid.

Les 50 Plus Belles Chansons (Jacques Brel; 2008) The best songs by the best French-speaking singer of all time.

Brol (Angèle, 2018) The breakout album by Belgium's electro-pop princess, filled with massive hits, which paved the way to her performance in Coachella.

Karaoke Moon (Warhaus, 2024) Maarten Devoldere's one-man band is summoning the ghost of Leonard Cohen with his elegant and melancholy indie-pop-rock opus.

Miki (Graou, 2025) French electro-pop new sensation who grew up in Luxembourg. Her raw, cynicism-filled lyrics and sultry, hip-hop-like delivery make her an artist to follow.

Moules-frites/mossellen met frieten

THE FOOD SCENE

Belgians and Luxembourgers have a love for the finer things in life, and yes, that includes food.

Belgian and Luxembourgish cuisines are often described as a unique blend of French quality and German quantity, fashioned by the intersection of Latin and Germanic civilisations and various migration waves that shaped their modern societies. This fusion results in dishes rich in local elements heavily influenced by foreign cultures. Specialities vary across landscapes, environments and people, from north to south and east to west.

When you think of Belgian cuisine, classic specialities such as fries, mussels, waffles, chocolate and beer immediately jump to mind. However, Luxembourg's *Judd mat Gaardebounen* (smoked pork neck and fava beans) and *Gromperekichelcher* (potato pancake) are less well-known, and may draw a blank stare even from their close neighbours.

From humble dry sausages served with beer in brown cafes to world-class gastronomic restaurants, both Belgium and Luxembourg showcase their zest for life through their gastronomy. You can be sure that you won't leave either country feeling hungry.

A Gourmet's Paradise

The word 'gourmand' seems to have been coined to describe Belgian gastronomy. The traditional cuisine is essentially local, firmly rooted in the country's different regions. Grey shrimps and plaice from the North Sea, white asparagus from Flanders, chicory (au gratin), potatoes (whole, mashed, fried), meatballs, cured meats, game from the Ardennes and cheeses are among the classics of Belgian gastronomy. Plenty of

Best Belgian & Luxembourgish Dishes	MOULES FRITES/ MOSSELLEN MET FRIETEN	STOEMP	BOULETS SAUCE LAPIN	STOOFVLEES/ CARBONNADES FLAMANDES
	Mussels cooked in broth, with fries cooked in beef fat.	Mashed potatoes mixed with vegetables and served with sausage and bacon.	Liège veal-beef meatballs served in a syrup-based sauce.	Beef cheek stewed in a beer and carrot sauce.

cream and various sauces accompany these rich and satisfying dishes. And of course, there's the Belgian gold: *frites*. Cut from Bintje potatoes, twice-cooked in beef fat, to be enjoyed with one of the many sauces available at the fries kiosk, which you can find in almost every city and village. Belgian expertise also shines in sweets, with scrumptious waffles (from Liège, Brussels, and so on), *speculoos* (biscuits), *cuberdons* (raspberry jelly covered in a hard sugar shell) and, above all, chocolate, the making of which is elevated to the level of an art.

Luxembourg's Secret Delights

Luxembourg's gastronomy is unfortunately not well-known beyond its borders, but it's worth tasting. Although influenced by the recent waves of migration (especially Italian and Portuguese), its culinary essence remains rooted in rustic traditions. Staple ingredients include potatoes, river fish (such as trout) and pork (including sausages and charcuterie). Moselle wine is not only enjoyed as a beverage but also used in various dishes such as the *Rieslingpaschtéit,* a meat pie with Riesling wine jelly, or the *Hong am Rèisleck,* a chicken dish cooked in a creamy wine sauce. For dessert, the *Quetscheflued* (or *Quetschentaart),* a plum tart, is a must-try.

Filet américain

Time to Cheer

Belgium is the world's undisputed beer capital, with a countless array of different varieties to sample including those made by the country's five Trappist breweries, as well as by hipsters in their basements. *Jenever* is a kind of gin that comes straight or sometimes outrageously flavoured while wine has made a strong comeback in the past decade, producing excellent results, especially in both still and sparkling white wines.

Belgian Beer Weekend

FOOD & DRINK FESTIVALS

Antwerpen Proeft *(proeft.be; May)* Antwerp's established and promising chefs are showing off their skills in this multiday culinary event.

Festifood *(festifoodrtl.be; August)* In Mons, get a chance to sample food prepared by Michelin-starred chefs.

À l'Ostendaise *(ostendaise.be; June)* An annual food festival in Ostend where fresh seafood is the star of the show, of course!

StrEat Fest *(streatfest.be; May)* Chefs and artisans gather around Brussels to cook street food dishes. Concerts, DJ sets and workshops during the events.

Belgian Beer Weekend *(belgianbeerweekend.be; September)* Fifty breweries and more than 500 beers with Brussels' Grand-Place as a background.

WITLOOFGRATIN/ CHICON AU GRATIN	FILET AMERICAIN	JUUD MAT GAARDEBOUNENEN	F'RELL AM RÈISLECK
Gratinated ham-rolled chicory, topped with béchamel sauce and cheese.	Raw minced beef prepared with eggs, gherkins, mustard and Worcester sauce.	Luxembourg's national dish: smoked pork neck and fava beans.	Battered and fried trout served in a Riesling wine sauce.

In Luxembourg, the pride of the country is Moselle wine, which is just as good as its French and German neighbours, boasting a variety of grape types, with Riesling reigning supreme. The river slopes are lined with vineyards, making it a beautiful location to visit.

Chocolate Heaven

When people think of Belgium, chocolate often comes to mind – rightly so. Nowhere else (perhaps aside from Switzerland) has chocolate-making been elevated to such an art form.

Cocoa, native to Central and South America, reached Europe via Spanish ships. Antwerp, then part of the Spanish Empire, was an early adopter. At first, chocolate was a luxury drink. In 1831, Adolphe Meurisse began producing chocolate in Antwerp, and Antoine Jacques created the first Belgian chocolate bars. Both brands still exist today.

In 1857, Jean Neuhaus opened a pharmacy in Brussels' Galeries Saint-Hubert and began coating medicines in chocolate. His son had a brighter idea: filled chocolates, or pralines. Louise, his wife, followed up with the ballotin, the now-iconic box used to protect them.

With a direct supply of cocoa from the colonial plantations in the Belgian Congo, chocolate production boomed. A national law passed in 1894 set strict standards for chocolate: at least 35% cocoa and no vegetable fats — just pure cocoa butter. That law still stands.

Modern Belgian chocolatiers continue to innovate. Bean-to-bar makers like Pierre Marcolini control the entire production process, ensuring ethical sourcing and highlighting the character of single-origin cocoa. Brands like Belvas craft low-sugar and vegan creations.

Flavour-wise, anything goes: pralines are now infused with saffron, Earl Grey, yuzu, even Belgian beer or bacon (at Dominique Persoone's Chocolate Line).

Chocolate is more than a treat in Belgium – it's a passion. Locals eat an average of 6kg a year, placing them among the world's top 10 chocoholics. You'll undoubtedly understand why after just one bite.

OUR PICK OF CRAFT CHOCOLATIERS

Frédéric Blondeel (p96) Twice winner of best Brussels chocolate maker. His use of herbs and spices makes all the difference.

Jérôme Grimonpon (p87) Uccle's award-winning chocolatier. Fond of including tea in his ganache recipes.

Darcis (p244) Before trying the pralines of the 'goldsmith of chocolate-making', visit his chocolate museum and workshop in Verviers.

Chocolaterie Van Hoorebeke (p114) Elegant but indulgent traditional chocolate maker in central Ghent.

Sukerbuyc (p130) One of the tastiest chocolate shops in Bruges, delightfully old-fashioned with a modern twist.

Belgian pralines

Local Specialities

Frites Sauces

Andalouse Tomato-based with mustard and sweet chili.

Samouraï Spicy red-pepper sauce.

Américaine Spicy-sweet tomato sauce with onions, peppers and mustard.

Brasil Sweet and sour sauce with tomatoes and pineapple.

Sweet Pursuits

Waffles From Brussels (light and airy) or from Liège (thick and caramelised), these are the go-to sweet snacks.

Speculoos/speculaas Cookie made of brown sugar, ginger, cinnamon, nutmeg and cloves.

Lierse vlaaike A small cake made with candy syrup and four spices mix.

Gayette du Pays Noir A kind of chocolate truffle made to look like a lump of coal.

Pagnon borain A pie dusted with brown sugar and flavoured with coffee.

Bamkuch Luxembourg's 'tree cake', made by drizzling the dough onto a spinning spit.

Speculoos/speculaas

Try if You Dare

Paling in 't groen/anguille au vert Eel dressed in a green, herbal sauce.

Perzik met toninj/pêche au thon Half of a canned peach filled with a mix of tuna and mayo.

Caricoles Steamed periwinkle; a snail-like seafood cooked in its shell within a broth.

Konijn met pruimen/lapin aux pruneaux Rabbit stewed with prunes.

Kuddelfleck Fried beef tripes or stomach served with a tomato sauce.

MEALS OF A LIFETIME

Fiera (p163) An intriguing place to dine, Fiera is unforgettable if you come for their Handelbeurs by Night soirees.

Karel de Stoute (p114) Superbly presented dishes served in a smart Ghent's Patershol dining room.

Entropy (p62) Tantalising six-course, gourmet, plant-based dinner menu and surprising natural wines in the centre of Brussels.

Humus x Hortense (p71) Gastronomical vegan feast in a beautiful Brussels *maison de maître*.

L'Air du Temps (p205) Two Michelin stars for veggie-centric cuisine from the kitchen-garden of a stylish farmstead in rural Wallonia.

Dans le Noir? (p264) In Luxembourg City, taste fine food in pitch blackness, served by blind waiters: an extraordinary dining experience.

THE YEAR IN FOOD

SPRING

The first produce of the year appears: chicory and white asparagus. The latter is cooked, drizzled with melted butter, lemon, crushed hard-boiled eggs and parsley *(asperges à la flamande)*. In May, strawberries hit the shelves.

SUMMER

Make the most of the season's bounty: green-leaf veggies (spinach, lettuce), beans and peas, cabbages, cucumbers and tomatoes, plus raspberries, mulberries, blueberries and rhubarb. It's also the perfect timing for mussels.

AUTUMN

Harvest brings countless varieties of apples, pears and potatoes. People are going out in the woods looking for mushrooms and chestnuts. Hunting season means game meat (boar, doe, pheasant) will be on the menu.

WINTER

Time to enjoy the last root vegetables and pumpkins; it's also peak time to pluck the misunderstood Brussels sprouts. Sautéed with bacon and roasted potatoes, it's a great winter warmer.

Dulle Griet (p111), Ghent

NEVER JUST BEER

In the holy trinity of Belgian delights, beer – along with chocolate and *frites* – holds a special place. Deeply rooted in history and the land, it's a culture, a craft, a religion even (in a way). Belgian brewers have perfected the process to such height, and beer is so ingrained in the locals' way of life, that Belgium beer culture is listed as UNESCO Intangible Cultural Heritage.

WHAT IS BEER?

Beer is one of the world's oldest and most popular drinks, made by fermenting grains (usually barley) with water, hops (which add bitterness), and yeast (which converts sugar into alcohol). The result ranges from light and bitter to dark and strong, depending on ingredients and brewing techniques.

MONASTIC ROOTS

While beer dates back to Mesopotamia around 9000 BC, it was in medieval Europe – especially in monasteries – that Belgian brewing traditions took shape. With water often unsafe to drink, beer became a daily necessity, and brewing was a household task. Monks refined these methods, using their own grains, herbs, and spices (*gruit*) before hops were introduced. Today's Belgian *witbiers* still contain coriander and orange peel. Though Trappist beer gained renown only in the 19th century, monastic brewing had already laid the foundation of Belgium's brewing techniques.

FROM INDUSTRY TO INNOVATION

The Industrial Revolution brought mass production and pilsner-style lagers, but Belgian brewers resisted standardisation. Instead, they preserved complex, bottle-conditioned ales and wild-fermented styles like lambic. After WWII, many breweries disappeared – in Brussels the number

Westvleteren
The Holy Grail of Trappist beers can only be purchased at the Abdij Sint-Sixtus, or you can taste it at its nearby café **In de Vrede** (p153).

Barnabeer
Beer heaven (p226) in Namur with 46 different kinds on tap.

Dulle Griet
Ghent's medieval **tavern** (p111) serves more than 500 beers.

Cantillon
Brussels' long-standing, and renowned, **lambic-based beer brewers** (p83). Visit the brewery and have a taste.

Moeder Lambic
Brussels' most discerning beer bar; its **Place Fontainas** (p53) spot is more central.

Bierhuis Kulminator
Antwerp's **unique specialist** (p172) for tasting aged rarities.

shrank from 120 to just one by the 1990s (Cantillon; p83). But a craft beer revival has seen beer culture flourish again. Microbreweries now thrive, blending tradition with bold innovation and helping Belgian beer remain one of the world's most respected brewing traditions.

BEER CULTURE
Beer is serious business in Belgium. Each beer has its own branded glass, poured in a specific way to highlight its aroma, foam and flavour. Chalice-like glasses are used for Trappists, straight and narrow ones for Saisons or lambic-based beers, tulip-shaped for some blonde ales, and there are even more unusual options like hourglass-shaped (Kwak) or horn-shaped glasses. Not serving a beer in its appropriate glass is seen as disrespectful to the beer itself.

But Belgian beer culture goes beyond the brew. It's deeply tied to pub culture and its role in social life. From cosy *bruine kroegen* in Flemish villages to trendy beer bars in cities, *cafés* serve as key gathering places where conversation and connection matter more than drinking itself.

CLASSIC BELGIAN STYLE

Blondes, Dubbels, Tripels, Quadrupels
These refer to colour and strength – perfect for sampling Belgian artistry. Examples include Val-Dieu Blonde, Westmalle Dubbel, Tripel Karmeliet, Straffe Hendrik Quadrupel.

Witbier/Blanche
Pale and hazy wheat beer, spiced with coriander and citrus peel. Hoegaarden is the classic; Blanche de Namur offers more complexity.

Lambic-based beers
Spontaneously fermented beers from Brussels and the Pajottenland. *Gueuze* blends old and young lambic; *kriek* is flavoured with sour cherries. Funky, sour, fruity. Try Cantillon or 3 Fonteinen.

Saison
A spicy, dry farmhouse ale – a Walloon classic, originally brewed in winter to refresh farmworkers in summer (think Saison Dupont).

Flanders red/brown ales
A Flemish cousin to lambic, made with red malts. Sour, lightly acidic and fruity. Rodenbach and Bourgogne des Flandres are the standouts.

Trappist beers
Not a style of beer. Trappist beers are ales (often blondes, dubbels or tripels) brewed in monasteries by Trappist monks, or under monastic licence. The other requirement is that all profits must go to charity. Abbey beers have similar origins but aren't bound by the same strict rules. The five Belgian Trappist breweries are Chimay, Orval, Rochefort, Westmalle and Westvleteren.

Kriek lambic-based beer

Mullerthal Trail (p275)

THE **OUTDOORS**

Despite their small size, Belgium and Luxembourg have plenty to offer: from surfing and river kayaking to hiking in the Ardennes and, of course, cycling!

From the shores of the North Sea to the banks of the Moselle, small Belgium and Luxembourg pack a lot of punches. The 65km of Belgian coastline provide opportunities for all kinds of water sports, from sailing to windsurfing. Flanders and its flat terrain are the playground of cyclists, while mountain bikers will prefer the hilly, wooded trails of Wallonia. The south of Belgium and Luxembourg, with its lakes and rivers, is ideal for kayaking. In both countries, hiking trails abound.

Walking & Hiking

Even though they're heavily populated, both countries are rich in charming trails waiting to be explored. The Ardennes region of Belgium is an excellent choice for hikers, with its dense forests, rolling hills and meandering rivers. The famous GR 5, also known as 'Europe's trail', takes you through east Flanders and Liège before heading south to the Ardennes and Luxembourg, offering a long-distance hiking adventure amid breathtaking cultural and natural landscapes. Additionally, the High Fens, Belgium's largest nature reserve, boasts a unique moorland environment and is perfect for shorter day hikes.

The Mullerthal Trail explores the pretty riversides, woodlands, rock formations and intriguing 'microcanyons' in an area very optimistically dubbed Luxembourg's 'Little Switzerland'. Meanwhile, the challenging cross-border Escapardenne Eislek Trail will take you through Belgian Luxembourg and the Grand Duchy's most picturesque sceneries and villages.

Off-Beat Adventures

CRAZY BIKE RIDE
Biking through water? A clever cycle-path illusion makes it seem possible at **Bokrijk's Open-Air Museum** (p191).

BOATING
Take a guided 45-minute boat trip on **Ghent's inland waterways** (p114) to discover the history behind the downtown area.

BIRD-WATCHING
Grab a pair of binoculars and relax by watching bird species living full-time, or temporarily, at the **Zwin Nature Park** (p134).

Cycling

Cycling is Belgium's other national sport (with football) so it's no wonder that the country is criss-crossed with bike-friendly paths. Flanders is particularly well-equipped and suited for easy and safe bike escapes. For instance, you can discover Bruges on two wheels before heading to nearby Damme, following a tranquil canal. Another option is exploring WWI sites along one of the ten Flanders Fields Routes.

Brussels, Antwerp, Ghent and Namur each operate their own bike-sharing programs: Villo, Velo Antwerpen, Donkey Republic and Libiavello, respectively.

In contrast, Wallonia offers more challenging terrain, but for those who prefer leisurely rides, the RAVeL network is here. These former train and tram tracks were converted into a network of well-marked, car-free paths, suitable for biking and walking. Luxembourg, with its many hills, is also an excellent place for mountain bikers to explore.

There is a network of cycling nodes covering both regions and Brussels.

Water Sports

Famous for its strong winds, the Belgian coast is the perfect place for windsurfing and kitesurfing. However, sand yachting is a unique and exciting activity that is worth a try. De Panne is an excellent place to experience it. Did you know you could surf in the North Sea? There are clubs all along the coastline.

Over in Wallonia, the Lacs de l'Eau d'Heure are almost like an inland sea. For some, star of the water activities here is arguably a descent of the Lesse River by kayak from Houyet or Gendron to Anseremme, but it's arguably prettier to paddle the Semois River from Bouillon.

In Luxembourg, the Moselle River and the Upper-Sûre artificial lake are the perfect spots for water-sports enthusiasts, with kayaking, water-skiing and windsurfing on offer.

Sand yachting, De Panne (p144)

ACTION AREAS

Where to find Belgium & Luxembourg's best outdoor activities.

North Sea

Strait of Dover

Westerschelde

Schelde

Lete

Schelde

Dender

Sambre

Vlissingen
Bergen op Zoom
Terneuzen
Lillo
Knokke-Heist
Zeebrugge
Blankenberge
De Haan
Ostend
Nieuwpoort
Dunkirk
Veurne
Calais
Diksmuide
Torhout
Poperinge
Ypres
Menen
Mouscron
Armentières
Roubaix
Lille
St-Omer
Lens
Cambrai
Valenciennes
Maubeuge
Hirson
Couvin
Chimay
Philippeville
Beaumont
Binche
Charlero
La Louvière
Mons
Soignies
Nivelles
Waterloo
Halle
Tervuren
BRUSSELS
Enghien
Ath
Leuze
Tournai
Ronse
Geraardsbergen
Ninove
Oudenaarde
Aalst
Meise
Dendermonde
Mechelen
Willebroek
Aalst
FLANDERS
Ghent
Deinze
Eeklo
St-Niklaas
Lokeren
Antwerp
Bruges
Kortrijk
Roeselare

Water Sports

1. De Panne (p144)
2. Lacs de l'Eau d'Heure (p221)
3. Semois River (p229)
4. Dillingen to Echternach (p275)

Walking/Hiking

1. Muziekbos (p120)
2. Borgloon Art Trail (p187)
3. The Hautes Fagnes (p241)
4. Rochehaut (p229)
5. Luxembourg's Mullerthal Trail (p275)

Nature Parks

1. Zwin Nature Park (p134)
2. Remerschen's Biodiversum (p272)

FRANCE

Rotterdam
• Dordrecht
NETHERLANDS
Den
Bosch
Breda
Tilburg
Roosendaal
Baarle-
Hertog
Hoogstraten
Oostmalle
Turnhout
Eindhoven
Herentals
Achel
Weert
Mol
Neerpelt
Roermond
Lier
Geel
Leopoldsburg
Bree
Heist
Aarschot
Diest
Maaseik
Herk-de-
Stad
Genk
Sittard
Leuven
Hasselt
Maasmechelen
Bilzen
Heerlen
Tienen
Sint-Truiden
Tongeren
Maastricht
Hoegaarden
Wavre
Hannut
Waremme
Meuse
Aachen
BELGIUM
Gembloux
Liège
Eupen
Namur
Huy
Verviers
Seraing
Remouchamps
Spa
Schleiden
Ourthe
Trois
Ponts
Malmedy
GERMANY
WALLONIA
Dinant
Ciney
Marche-en-
Famenne
St Vith
Rochefort
La Roche-en-
Ardenne
Prüm
Meuse
Givet
Houffalize
Clervaux
St-Hubert
Bastogne
Wiltz
Bitburg
Libramont
Esch-sur-
Sûre
Vianden
Semois
Neufchâteau
Martelange
Ettelbrück
Diekirch
Beaufort
Echternach
Charleville-
Mézières
Bouillon
LUXEMBOURG
Mersch
Grevenmacher
Trier
Sedan
Florenville
Arlon
Sûre
Montmédy
Virton
Steinfort
LUXEMBOURG
CITY
Remich
Longwy
Petange
Differdange
Moselle
Esch-sur-
Alzette
Dudelange
Schengen
FRANCE
Thionville

Street Art Trails
1 The Crystal Ship (p140)
2 Brussels' Parcours BD (p61)
3 Mons (p208)
4 Antwerp's Berchem district (p175)

Cycling
1 Flemish Ardennes at Oudenaarde (p120)
2 Bruges to Damme (p133)
3 Ypres Salient (p150)
4 Bokrijk Open-Air Museum (p191)
5 Namur to Dinant (p224)
6 La Roche-en-Ardenne (p233)
7 Zuunbeekroute (p100)

0   50 km
0   25 miles

THE GUIDE

Ghent, Bruges &
Northwest Belgium
p105

Antwerp &
Northeast Belgium
p156

✪ BRUSSELS
p44

Wallonia
p195

Luxembourg
p256

✪ LUXEMBOURG
CITY

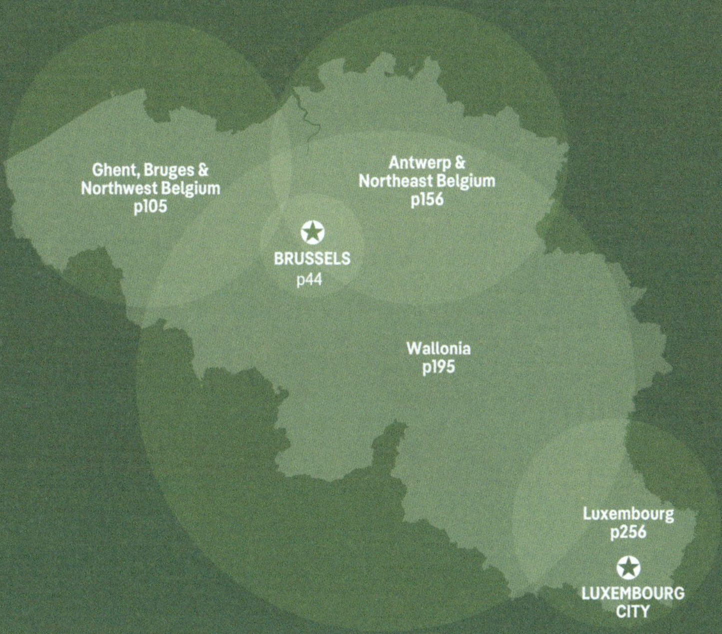

Chapters in this section are organised by hubs and their surrounding areas. We see the hub as your base in the destination, where you'll find unique experiences, local insights, insider tips and expert recommendations. It's also your gateway to the surrounding area, where you'll see what and how much you can do from there.

Luxembourg City (p260)
RUDY BALASKO/SHUTTERSTOCK

Researched by
Mélissa Monaco

Brussels

MULTICULTURAL AND FESTIVE CAPITAL OF EUROPE

Charming and far from boring, provincial yet global,
fundamentally open and epicurean, the Belgian
capital invites you to enjoy the finer things in life.

Brussels is, and has been for a long time: a haven, a respite. With over 180 nationalities (second only to Dubai), Brussels is a human-scaled global city. As the capital of a trilingual country and the decision-making centre for over 400 million Europeans, Brussels proudly embraces its identity as an open city, where almost everyone seems to come from somewhere else.

At first glance, Brussels can seem chaotic. Years of uncoordinated urban planning, with little regard to previous heritage, have left the city scattered with mismatched architecture. Grand squares, intricate guildhalls and Gothic churches stand alongside Art Nouveau, Art Deco and sleek glass buildings. This improbable mix has become an integral part of Brussels' landscape, adding to its distinctive character. And somehow, despite the clutter, Brussels grows on you. Maybe it's the slower pace compared to neighbours like Paris or Amsterdam? Or the easygoing, friendly locals?

It's a city of art, from Flemish masters in the Museum of Fine Arts to avant-garde galleries spread all around town. Many artists say the city gives them the freedom to create without judgment or pressure. Comics, known as the 9th art, have deep roots here: Hergé, creator of Tintin, was born in Brussels.

Foodies will feel right at home. From world-class Michelin-starred restaurants to humble but innovative cafes, the city offers a diverse range of gastronomic experiences. And then there are the ever-present temptations of chocolate, waffles, *frites* (chips or fries) and beers that you'll meet at every street corner.

But most of all, Brussels is all about conviviality and it knows how to party right. With its collection of 19 'villages' and different districts waiting to be discovered, you will never feel lost or overwhelmed. Brussels welcomes you, just as you are.

For clarity's sake, this guide refers to locations by their French names, the most widely spoken language among Brussels residents.

TANIA_WILD/SHUTTERSTOCK

THE MAIN AREAS

THE PENTAGON
Brussels' cultural, historic, vibrant heart. **p52**

EU QUARTER, CINQUANTENAIRE, SCHAERBEEK & ST-JOSSE
EU appreciation and great museums. **p63**

ST-GILLES, IXELLES & FOREST
Great food and Art Nouveau. **p70**

ALONG THE CANAL
Postindustrial heritage. **p78**

For places to stay in Brussels, see p102

TRABANTOS/SHUTTERSTOCK

Left: Serres Royales de Laeken (p92); Above: Sainte-Catherine Church (p60)

SOUTH & EAST BRUSSELS & FORÊT DE SOIGNES
The upper-class and green neighbourhoods. **p85**

NORTHWEST BRUSSELS
More than just the Atomium. **p92**

OUTSKIRTS OF BRUSSELS
Going beyond the capital. **p98**

FROM THE AIRPORT

Brussels Airport is about a 20-minute drive from the city. You can catch a train (just below the airport) to the city's main three stations, or take bus 12 (one floor below the Arrivals level) to the EU Quarter with connection to the Metro.

TAXI & RIDESHARES

For long-distance, late-night transport or if you have heavy luggage, taxi and rideshares are readily available. Be aware that not all taxis accept bank or credit cards. Most taxi companies offer packages to/from the airport. Don't forget to mention it when you order your taxi.

WALKING

With most of the main attractions within walking distance and the largest pedestrian area in Europe, you'll find it's quite easy to go from one sight to the next. Opt for comfortable footwear, as the cobbled streets might prove to be less than ideal for high heels.

PUBLIC TRANSPORT

The public transport network in Brussels consists of metros, trams, buses (operated by STIB/MIVB), and intra-urban trains (SNCB/NMBS). For late-night goers, Noctis buses (on Friday and Saturday nights) and Collecto, a shared taxi service, are available to ensure your safe return.

WEMMEL

HEYSEL

Mini-Europe   Atomium

Northwest Brussels
p92

GANSHOREN   JETTE   LAEKEN

BERCHEM-STE AGATHE   KOEKELBERG

Along the Canal
p78

The Pentagon
p52

MOLENBEEK

Galeries Royales
Saint-Hubert

Grand-Place

Manneken Pis

MAROLLES

Place du Jeu de
Balle Flea Market

Palais de
Justice

ANDERLECHT

St-Gilles, Ixelles & Forest
p70

ST GILLES

Canal de Charleroi

FOREST

UCCLE

DROGENBOS

THE GUIDE

BRUSSELS

46

Find Your Way

The heart of Brussels is rather compact, with the oldest section of the city retaining the winding charm of its medieval streets. While the central area, known as the Pentagon, is easily covered by foot, public transport is recommended for visiting other neighbourhoods and attractions, including the famous Atomium.

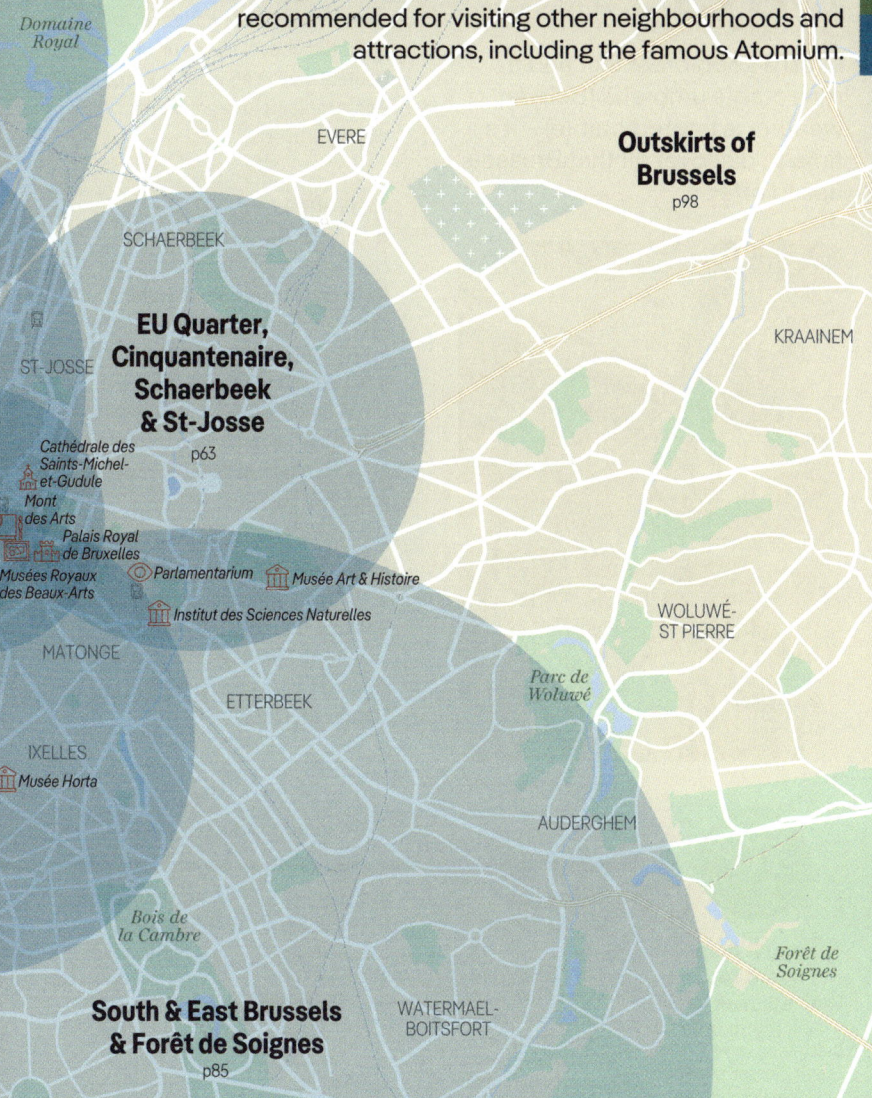

Domaine Royal

EVERE

Outskirts of Brussels
p98

SCHAERBEEK

KRAAINEM

EU Quarter, Cinquantenaire, Schaerbeek & St-Josse
p63

ST-JOSSE

Cathédrale des Saints-Michel-et-Gudule

Mont des Arts

Palais Royal de Bruxelles

Musées Royaux des Beaux-Arts

Parlamentarium

Musée Art & Histoire

Institut des Sciences Naturelles

WOLUWÉ-ST PIERRE

MATONGE

ETTERBEEK

Parc de Woluwé

IXELLES

Musée Horta

AUDERGHEM

Bois de la Cambre

Forêt de Soignes

South & East Brussels & Forêt de Soignes
p85

WATERMAEL-BOITSFORT

Forêt de Soignes

N

0   2 km
0   1 mile

Plan Your Days

Grab a good breakfast and a retractable umbrella (Belgian weather is unpredictable) – it's time to discover all that Brussels has to offer.

ALAN JOHN AINSWORTH/HERITAGE IMAGES/GETTY IMAGES

Musée Horta (p74)

Day 1

Morning
● Kick-start your day with a visit to the **Marolles Flea Market** (p61) and then explore antique shops and independent stores on Rue Haute. Take the elevator to **Place Poelaert** (p61) for a panoramic view of Brussels.

Afternoon
● Lunch in Brussels' historical centre and don't miss the allure of **Galeries Royales Saint-Hubert** shopping arcade (p53). Marvel at the breathtaking **Grand-Place** (p59), and if time permits, visit the **Hôtel de Ville** (p59) and **Brussels City Museum** (p59). Don't forget to greet **Manneken Pis** (p53) and his wardrobe.

Evening
● Relax with an aperitif at **58 Rooftop & Eatery** (p53) before heading to **Fin de Siècle** (p61) for dinner. Finish with a cocktail at **Life Is Beautiful** (p53).

You'll Also Want to...

Explore Brussels' green side, with its many parks and even a forest. Enjoy lesser-known neighbourhoods and go see a football game.

EXPLORE SCHAERBEEK
Make your inner child happy exploring the interactive **Train World museum** (p65), relax at **Parc Josaphat** (p68) and find beer heaven at **Le Barboteur** (p69), a place for hops enthusiasts.

GET LOST IN THE FOREST
Get some fresh air and closer to nature by spending time among the trees of the **Forêt de Soignes** (p89), Brussels' southern green girdle.

GET TO KNOW THE INDUSTRIAL BRUSSELS
Visit Molenbeek's **La Fonderie museum** (p84) of labour and industry and learn about the fascinating story of Brussels' working class. And why not book a guided tour as well?

Day 2

Morning
● Get your culture fix with a visit to one of the **Musées Royaux des Beaux-Arts** (p57). Don't miss the breathtaking view from **Mont des Arts** (p56) while heading back towards the centre.

Afternoon
● Enjoy a laid-back lunch at **Mer du Nord** (p59) and explore the stores and hidden delights of the **Ste-Catherine neighbourhood** (p60). Take a bike ride to admire the postindustrial architecture of **Tour & Taxis** (p80), and make a pit stop at **La Source microbrewery** (p84) for refreshments.

Evening
● Go back to Tour & Taxis' **Gare Maritime food court** (p81) for a meal, or take public transport to **Friture René** (p82) for traditional Belgian fare.

Day 3

Morning
● Make your way to the EU Quarter for a visit of the **Parlamentarium** (p66) and the **Hemicycle of the European Parliament** (p67). Alternatively, go to the **Institut des Sciences Naturelles** (p67) for some dinosaur viewing.

Afternoon
● Go grab a cone of *frites* at **Maison Antoine** (p65), then walk or take bus 54 to get to the start of the **Art Nouveau walking tour** (p75). If you have time, do visit **Musée Horta** (p74), dedicated to the master of Art Nouveau.

Evening
● Have a refreshing beer and enjoy the fun atmosphere at **Brasserie de l'Union** (p76) before treating yourself to a delightful meal at **iOda** (p76).

DISCOVER CONTEMPORARY ART
Witness Belgians' taste in contemporary art at **Centrale for Contemporary Art** (p53), **Fondation Boghossian/Villa Empain** (p87) or **Atelier 34zéro Muzeum** (p96).

TRY THE BEERS
Cantillon Brewery (p83), renowned for its lambic-based beers, offers brewery tours followed by a tasting. Other breweries with a taproom: **Brasserie de l'Ermitage** (p83) and **Brasserie de la Senne** (p84).

FEEL LIKE YOU'RE IN A MOVIE-SET
The **Floréal and Logis garden cities** (p90) and **Coin du Balai** (p90) feel straight out of a vintage movie, with their quaint houses, leafy streets, and timeless atmosphere.

CATCH A FOOTBALL GAME
Attend a game of top-league team Union Saint-Gilloise and discover why their fans are known as Belgium's friendliest **supporters** (p74). *Allez, l'Union!*

HELP ME PICK:

Craft Breweries

After losing all but one of its breweries, Brussels experienced a sort of brewery renaissance over the past 15 years, with sprouting craft breweries spearheaded by Brasserie de la Senne. A dozen of them are open to the public through their taprooms. But which one will tickle your taste buds?

Where to Try If You Like...

Traditional beers

Cantillon (p83) This legendary brewery makes traditional lambic-based beers (a spontaneous fermentation brew that can only be found in the Senne Valley), such as *gueuze, kriek*... low in alcohol, non-fizzy and a bit sour.

Brasserie de la Senne (p84) Its Zinnebir, a Belgian pale ale, has established itself as classic. It puts a modern twist on traditional Belgian beers, and its taproom behind Tour & Taxis is one of the more laid-back.

Bold flavours

Brasserie de l'Ermitage (p83) It all started in a friend's basement, and now l'Ermitage has its taproom close to Cantillon and its own bar in St-Gilles. Its focus: hoppy/sour beers and experimentation of mixed fermentation with grapes.

La Source (p84) If you like your IPAs pungent, and your sours... soury, this is the place for you! Its taproom is located inside a beautiful former warehouse.

Brasserie La Jungle Located along the canal, this brewery specialises in 'wild' beers, often macerated with fruits (peach, plum, cherry) in mixed fermentation.

Your beer with a side of fancy

Brussels Beer Project The 'naughty kid' of the Brussels brewery scene doesn't shy away from experimenting (Thai soup beer, anyone?). But it also shines with its minimalist bar on Rue Antoine Dansaert and the largest beer garden in Brussels (on the canal's banks).

Brasserie Surréaliste The Brasserie's taproom gets the 'Wow-effect' right. Part winter garden, part abbey, its stylish bar is the perfect setting for its

bold IPAs (especially the single hop series). Excellent food is also served.

German-style beers

Brasserie de la Mule In Schaerbeek's old tram stables (at the time where trams were drawn by horses), it brews German-style beers (think *helles, effenweise*...). Its enclosed terrace is a winner when the sun is out.

Outsiders

CoHop Located in a former army barracks, CoHop gathers four microbreweries, uniting their forces and visions. A great way to try different styles at the same place.

L'Annexe This Saint-Gilles brewery is also a fermentery. Known for its range of 'saison' beers (a rustic, dry kind of farmhouse ale), it also produces lemonade and tonics with fermented fruits.

HOW TO

When to go Aim to visit the taprooms during the weekends, as they are more likely to be open than during the week.

Book ahead Some breweries have tours (Cantillon, BBP, Brasserie de la Senne, Surréaliste). However, all of them must be booked in advance.

Before you taste Eat beforehand or order snacks – sausages and cheese are classic pairings with Belgian beer, which can be quite strong.

Budget A 33cl beer costs €4.50–6.50. Not all breweries offer flights, but if available, expect to pay €10–20 for four to six glasses (12cl each).

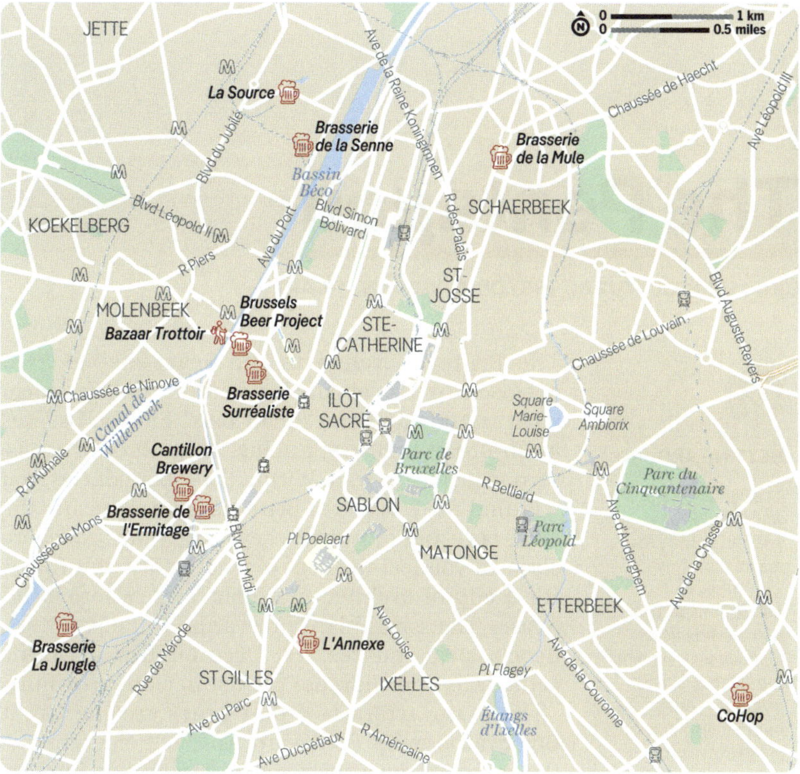

JETTE

La Source

Brasserie
de la Senne

Brasserie
de la Mule

Ave de la Reine Koninginnelaan

Chaussée de Haecht

Bld du Jubilé

Bassin
Béco

Blvd Simon
Bolivard

Blvd Léopold II

R des Palais

SCHAERBEEK

KOEKELBERG

R Piers

ST-
JOSSE

Ave du Port

MOLENBEEK

Brussels
Beer Project

Bazaar Trottoir

STE-
CATHERINE

Chaussée de Louvain

Blvd Auguste Reyers

Chaussée de Ninove

Brasserie
Surréaliste

ILÔT
SACRÉ

Square
Marie-
Louise

Square
Ambiorix

Canal de
Willebroek

Cantillon
Brewery

Parc de
Bruxelles

R Belliard

Parc du
Cinquantenaire

R d'Aumale

R de Mons

Brasserie de
l'Ermitage

SABLON

Pl Poelaert

MATONGE

Parc
Léopold

Ave d'Auderghem

Ave de la Chasse

ETTERBEEK

Brasserie
La Jungle

L'Annexe

Ave Louise

Pl Flagey

Ave de la Couronne

Rue de Mérode

ST GILLES

Blvd du Midi

IXELLES

Étangs
d'Ixelles

CoHop

Ave du Parc

Ave Ducpétiaux

R Américaine

0   1 km
0   0.5 miles

To Tour or Not to Tour

If you'd like to create your own 'Brussels Beers Tour', it's actually quite simple, as most of the breweries are located along the Canal or nearby. This makes for an interesting, if lengthy (and slightly boozy), walk from Anderlecht to Laeken, starting from the BBP Beer Garden or Cantillon, all the way to La Source, passing through less-visited parts of town. If walking sounds like too much, why not rent a bike for the afternoon – or even just part of the way? Villo!, the city's bike-share service, has over 360 stations where you can pick up and drop off bikes. Alternatively, Pro Velo, a well-known cycling advocacy group, also offers rentals and cycling resources.

Strangely enough, even though Brussels hosts numerous pub crawls and beer tours hopping from one bar to another, organised brewery tours are quite rare! **Bazaar Trottoir** (*bazaartrottoir.be*) specialises in alternative and 'forgotten neighbourhoods' tours. It has four different tours, each in a different part of the city, visiting different breweries along the way. The only downside? It's only possible to book for groups of at least 10. If you're travelling solo or in a smaller group, your best bet is to download a map of the breweries and explore at your own pace. Cheers to that!

Gueuze **beer, Cantillon brewery**

The Pentagon

BRUSSELS' CULTURAL, HISTORIC, VIBRANT HEART

GETTING AROUND

The Pentagon is easily walkable. Unless you feel tired by the end of the day, you won't need to use public transport. For a single-ride ticket, contactless payment is available. Simply swipe your bank card, smartphone or smartwatch on the grey validator at the entrance of metro stations or on buses and trams. Metro lines 1 and 5 run across the Pentagon from west to east, while underground tram lines 4 and 10 run from north to south, with De Brouckère station serving as the intersection of all three lines.

☑ TOP TIP

If you'd like to take postcard-worthy pictures of the Grand-Place, get up very early, as it will likely be deserted. After, go have breakfast at your hotel or in a nearby cafe.

The Pentagon refers to the heart-shaped area enclosed by the expansive boulevards that form what is known as the 'Small Belt.' This belt serves as an urban highway, tracing the path of Brussels' second defensive wall. Within these boundaries, you will find the essence of Brussels, encompassing the city's core and most of its key attractions. Nowhere else can you feel the beat of what is Brussels today. It's a city of architectural contrasts, where guild houses, Haussmannian boulevards, brutalist towers, neoclassical squares, Art Deco buildings, Gothic cathedrals and churches coexist in close proximity.

The main arteries of that heart are the Great Boulevards, with Boulevard Anspach emerging as the centre of the largest pedestrian area in Europe. It pulsates with the energy of the city, serving as a vibrant hub for pedestrians to explore and immerse themselves in the soul of Brussels.

A Gothic Masterpiece

MAP P54

Be wowed at Cathédrale Saints-Michel-et-Gudule

Perched atop one of Brussels' hills, the unmistakable twin Brabantine Gothic towers of the **cathedral** (*cathedralisbruxellensis. be*) soar through the sky. Built as the church of St-Michel-au-Mont, it was later replaced by a Romanesque collegiate in 1047, housing the relics of St Gudula (Brussels' other patron saint) brought from the church of St-Géry. Renamed 'St Michael and St Gudula,' the cathedral underwent multiple expansions, predominantly in Gothic style, and attained cathedral status in 1962. Notable features include a magnificent baroque pulpit sculpted from wood and exquisite 16th-century stained-glass windows in the side chapels, based on designs by Bernard van Orley. In addition to the church, you can also visit the Treasury and the Crypt (*€3/€4, respectively*). But the real kick is to climb the cathedral towers with a guide (*€10*) – 10am on the second Saturday of each month from March to October – for a bird's-eye view over the town. Don't forget to sign up two weeks ahead.

Cathédrale Saints-Michel-et-Gudule

The Largest Wardrobe for the Littlest Guy

MAP P54

Check out Manneken Pis and its many outfits

Meet the 'Most Disappointing Tourist Attraction in the World' (and Brussels' mascot): **Manneken Pis**. This little peeing boy has been relieving himself in the fountain below since 1619 when it was sculpted by Jérôme Duquesnoy the Elder. While its size may be underwhelming, his wardrobe is not. 'Little Julien' (Manneken Pis' given name) owns over 1100 costumes from around the world, gifted on various occasions, such as festivities or dignitary visits. Just up the street, the **Garde Robe Manneken Pis** (*mannekenpis.brussels; adult/under 18 €5/free*) proudly displays 150 rotating outfits.

The Continent's First Mall

MAP P54

Shop for chocolate and more

Built in 1847, the **Galeries Royales Saint-Hubert**, just 80m away from Grand-Place, is an elegant glass-covered shopping arcade – and was the first of its kind on the continent. With a delightful array of boutiques, chocolatiers, cafes and theatres, intricate architecture and high-end shops, it exudes a timeless charm that attracts both locals and tourists.

continues on p59

BEST ART-RELATED VENUES

ARGOS: Immerse yourself in the sights and sounds of Belgium's artistic audiovisual centre, the largest in the country.

Art & Bulles: Arts and crafts workshop to learn watercolour painting, unleash your creativity with acrylics, or create/paint with clay.

Centrale for Contemporary Art: Brussels' contemporary art centre highlights primarily local talent with rotating shows of emerging and experimental artists.

Vanhaerents Art Collection: One of the most prestigious private art collections in the world, with names such as Jeff Koons and Ai Weiwei.

Cloud Seven: Co-working space/art gallery, this beautiful *maison de maître* exhibits Frédéric de Goldschmidt's collection and guest artists.

 DRINKING IN THE PENTAGON: OUR PICKS ———— MAP P54

Life Is Beautiful: Sip gourmet craft cocktails, carefully prepared by Harouna and his team in an unpretentious atmosphere. *6pm-midnight Wed & Thu, to 1am Fri & Sat*

L'Archiduc: Ring the doorbell and step into the 1930s in this noteworthy cocktail bar/jazz lounge. Order its signature pisco sour and enjoy! *4pm-5am*

Moeder Lambic Fontainas: For discerning beer connoisseurs, an ever-changing list of craft beers. *4pm-midnight Mon-Thu, noon-1am Fri & Sat, noon-11pm Sun*

58 Rooftop & Eatery: Splendid city views from the 9th floor of the city's administrative building – no purchase required to just check the view. *hours vary*

THE PENTAGON

Cloud Seven (300m);
ARGOS 400m)

R du Grand- Hospice

R de Flandre

R de Laeken

Pl du
Béguinage

R de Flandre

R L'Epage

Marché aux
Poissons

STE-
CATHERINE

R des Augustii

R Antoine Dansaert

Pl du
Nouveau
Marché aux
Grains

Pl Ste-
Catherine

R de l'Evêque

R Ste-Catherine

R de la Vierge Noire

R Rempart des Moines

R du Marché aux Poulets

R des Fabriques

R des Chartreux

R Auguste Orts

ST-GÉRY

Blvd Anspach R Grétry

R Pletinckx

R Van Artevelde

Pl St-Géry

Pl de la
Bourse

R des Pierres

R des 6 Jetons

R des Riches
Claires

R de la Grande Ile

Blvd Anspach

R du Midi

R du Lombard

R d'Anderlecht

R du Marché au Charbon

Manneken
Pis

Pl
Fontainas

See Mont des Arts &
Museums Map p58

⭐ **HIGHLIGHTS**
1 Galeries Royales Saint-Hubert
2 Grand-Place
3 Manneken Pis

🔴 **SIGHTS**
4 Anspach Fountain

5 Bourse & Belgian Beer World
6 Brussels City Museum
7 Cathédrale Saints-Michel-et-Gudule
8 Centrale for Contemporary Art
9 Centre Belge de la Bande Dessinée

10 Hôtel de Ville
11 Pigeon Soldat Memorial
12 Rue de la Cigogne
13 Vanhaerents Art Collection
14 Vismet-Marché aux Poissons

⚫ **SLEEPING**
15 Art de Séjour B&B

16 Craves
17 Hôtel Amigo
18 Juliana Hotel
19 La Senne
20 LATROUPE Grand-Place
21 Made in Catherine

🟢 **EATING**
22 Chouke

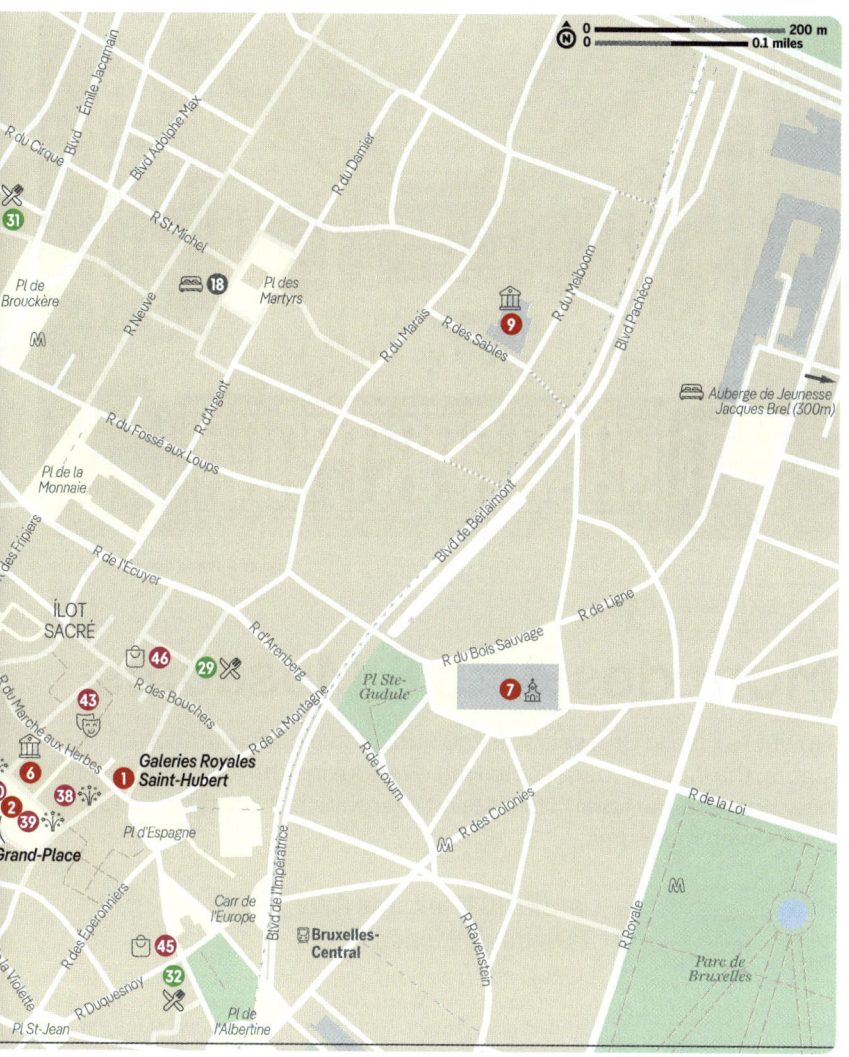

Auberge de Jeunesse
Jacques Brel (300m)

ÍLOT
SACRÉ

Galeries Royales
Saint-Hubert

Grand-Place

Bruxelles-
Central

Parc de
Bruxelles

KRISTOF VADINO

Musées Royaux des Beaux-Arts

TOP EXPERIENCE

Mont des Arts & Museums

Nowhere else in Brussels will you find such a concentration of sights: the Coudenberg (Cold Hill) overlooking the lower town is not only home to the lovely Mont des Arts gardens but contains no less than seven museums.

DON'T MISS

Musées Royaux des Beaux-Arts

Musée Magritte

MIM

Musée BELvue

Palais du Coudenberg

The garden and view from Mont des Arts

KBR Museum

Place du Musée

Jardin du Mont des Arts & Place du Musée

Linking the lower and upper town, the terraced garden and staircase of **Mont des Arts** have existed since 1910. Landscape architect René Pechère redesigned it for the 1958 World Fair. At the top, turn around for a beautiful view over the city – especially stunning at dusk. While you're there, pop by the nearby **Place du Musée**. This hidden square is the site of the palace of Charles of Lorraine (then governor of the Austrian Lowlands for Empress Maria Theresa), and a jewel of classical architecture.

Practicalities

● mim.be, fine-arts-museum.be, coudenberg.brussels, belvue.be, kbr.be/en/museum ● Prices vary ● Museums close Mondays

KBR Museum

Reopened in 2025, the **KBR Museum** inside the National Library hosts a precious collection of 15th-century manuscripts, from the golden age of Burgundian power. To provide historical context, the exhibition includes paintings, weapons, wall projections of drawings, and interactive screens where you can create your own illuminations or try your hand as a medieval copyist.

Musée des Instruments de Musique (MIM)

Strap on a pair of headphones, then step onto the automated floor panels in front of precious instruments (including world instruments and inventions by Adolphe Sax) to hear them being played. It's a sure hit with children. The **museum** is housed in the stunning Art Nouveau Old England Building, a former department store built in 1899 by Paul Saintenoy. At the time of research, the rooftop cafe remains closed for renovation.

Musées Royaux des Beaux-Arts

This **prestigious complex** includes the Musée Old Masters (ancient art), the Musée Fin-de-Siècle (1868–1914, closed for renovation since early 2025), and the purpose-built Musée Magritte. The Musée Old Masters showcases 15th-century Flemish Primitives, including Rogier Van der Weyden's *Pietà* with its hallucinatory sky, Hans Memling's refined portraits, and the richly textured *Madonna with Saints* by the anonymous Master of the Legend of St Lucy. Highlights continue with Bruegel the Elder (*The Fall of Icarus*), Rubens (*Four Studies of a Head*), and Van Dyck (*Portrait of an Elderly Lady*). The gallery concludes with *Marat Assassiné*, painted in exile in Brussels by Jacques-Louis David, Napoleon's favourite painter.

Musée Magritte

With new scenography, the **Magritte Museum** holds the world's largest collection of surrealist pioneer's paintings and drawings. Going from the top floor to the bottom, you can watch his style develop from colourful Braque-style Cubism in 1920 through a Dalí-esque phase and a late-1940s period of Kandinsky-like brushwork to his trademark bowler hats of the 1960s.

Musée BELvue & Palais du Coudenberg

Housed in an elegant 18th-century mansion once home to royals, **Musée BELvue** traces Belgium's history from the 1830 Revolution to today's federal state: a must for understanding the country. The museum is also the entrance to the underground ruins of the **Palais du Coudenberg**, all that remains of the former Palace of the Dukes of Brabant, once among Europe's grandest, destroyed by fire in 1731.

SAVE ON MUSEUMS

If you're planning to explore a few museums in Brussels, the Brussels Card might be a good deal – it gives you access to 48 museums, starting at €39 for 24 hours. For museum lovers, the Museum Pass (*€54.95*) lets you visit 263 museums all over Belgium for a full year.

TOP TIPS

● The Old Masters and Magritte museums are free on the first Wednesday of the month, starting at 1pm. Musée BELvue is free on the first Sunday of the month.

● The Palais du Coudenberg is partially accessible to non-electric wheelchairs. Please contact them at least three days before your visit.

● Feeling peckish? **albert** (p61), the National Library's restaurant on the top floor, offers splendid views of Brussels on one side and a lovely terrace full of greenery on the other.

MONT DES ARTS & MUSEUMS

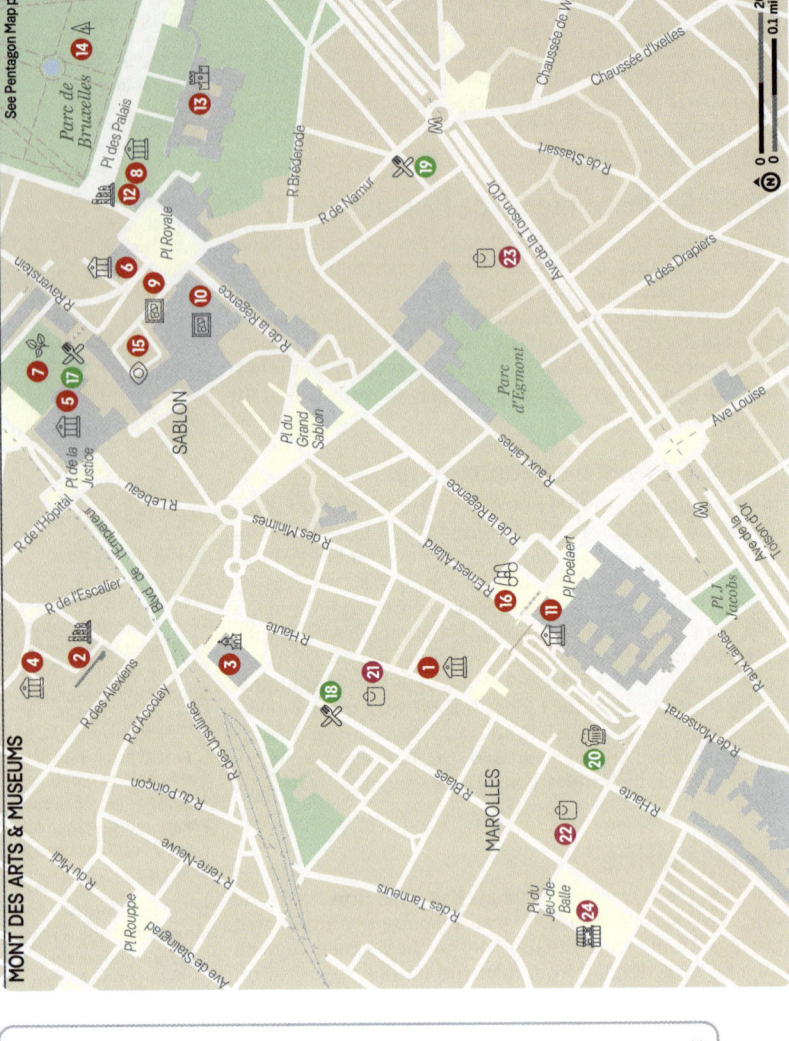

● **SIGHTS**
1 Bruegel House
2 Courtine and Tour de Villers
3 Église Notre-Dame de la Chapelle
4 GardeRobe MannekenPis
5 KBR Museum
6 MIM
7 Mont des Arts
8 Musée BELvue
9 Musée Magritte
10 Musées Royaux
   des Beaux-Arts
11 Palais de Justice
12 Palais du
   Coudenberg
13 Palais Royal de Bruxelles
14 Parc de Bruxelles
15 Place du Musée
16 Place Poelaert Viewpoint

● **EATING**
17 albert
18 La Bonne Chère
19 Umā

● **DRINKING & NIGHTLIFE**
20 Le Petit Lion

● **SHOPPING**
21 Belge une fois
22 Foxhole Vintage Marolles
23 Mayfair BXL & Filigranes
24 Place du Jeu de Balle Flea Market

continued from p53

Do not miss **Tropismes**, Brussels' prettiest bookshop, and have a waffle or *speculoos* biscuit at **Maison Dandoy** or at **Mokafé**. Additionally, the Galeries offer residential apartments on the upper floors. Fancy living like a resident? We recommend Hotel des Galeries or the Vaudeville B&B.

Explore Brussels' Crown Jewel   MAP P54 & P58

The awe of Grand-Place

It's impossible not to gawk at the gilded guildhalls of the **Grand-Place** (Grote Markt in Dutch). They are a testament to the power and resilience of the guilds and notable figures who rebuilt the Grand-Place after the devastating bombing of Brussels by the army of the King of France, Louis XIV, in 1695. The walls of the Gothic city hall remained standing as the sole testimony of the square's medieval past. Its tall and slender tower supports a golden statue of St Michel, one of Brussels' two patron saints. Since 2023, the **Hôtel de Ville** (*bruxelles.be/hotel-de-ville; adult €15*) has been open for daily visits. Across from the city hall, the neogothic Maison du Roi now houses the **Brussels City Museum**. Admission includes entry to the **GardeRobe Manneken Pis** (*brussels citymuseum.brussels; adult/under 18 €10/free;* p53). On the eastern side of the square, the House of the Dukes of Brabant is in fact several houses built under the same facade, making it look like a palace decorated with busts of the several dukes and duchesses of Brabant.

Admire the Royal & National Grounds   MAP P58

Palais Royal and Parc de Bruxelles

Further up Place Royale, the view opens onto Place des Palais, where major events like the National Day parade take place. On the right stands the **Palais Royal de Bruxelles**, and on the left, the Parc Royal. Beyond the park, the Palais de la Nation houses the Belgian Parliament. Built on the ruins of the Duke of Brabant's palace, the Royal Palace is not the king's residence but his workplace. King Philip lives in Laeken and, like any Belgian, commutes. If the flag is flying, he's in the country. From 23 July to 28 August, the palace is open to visitors, for free.

The **Parc de Bruxelles**, once a hunting ground, offers a peaceful escape from the city's buzz. It's filled with statues,

EVENTS ON THE GRAND-PLACE

Flower Carpet: Every even year, in mid-August, the square is adorned with begonias, dahlias, and other plants, creating a stunning floral tapestry.

Ommegang: This UNESCO World Heritage pageant, held late June to early July, commemorates Emperor Charles V and Prince Philip II's Joyous Entry.

Belgian Beer Weekend: In early September, the Grand-Place welcomes 50 breweries and their 500 beers.

Le Grand Rendez-Vous de la Fédération Wallonie-Bruxelles: Celebrate Belgium's French-speaking community with a star-clad, free concert in late September.

Christmas Tree & Show: The city's largest Christmas tree, a whimsical sound-and-light show, and traditional manger.

EATING IN THE PENTAGON: BUDGET PICKS   MAP P54

Mer du Nord/ Noordzee: Enjoy your shrimp croquettes at this outdoor venue by a fishmonger's window. *11am-6.30pm Tue-Sun* €

Chouke: Have the best *frites* in the city centre at this no-frills chip shop. Don't miss the homemade burgers. *noon-11pm Mon-Sun* €

Tonton Garby: Cheese-loving brothers serve custom sandwiches worth the wait, mixing vegs, fruits, sauces... Friendly, chatty service. *11am-5pm Mon-Sat* €

Super Fourchette: Vinyl shop meets café-cantine with homemade, seasonal dishes and a chill vibe. *noon-2pm & 6.30-9.30pm Mon-Fri* €

THE GUIDE

BRUSSELS THE PENTAGON

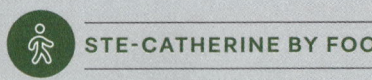

STE-CATHERINE BY FOOT

Welcome to Ste-Catherine, one of the oldest Brussels neighbourhoods and former site of the city's inland port.

START	END	LENGTH
Place Sainte-Catherine	La Bellone	1km; 45 mins

Start your walk at ❶ **Place Sainte-Catherine.** Until 1854, the square and church area were part of Brussels' port. The city authorities closed it and filled in the basins connected to the Willebroek Canal, which leads to Antwerp. This transformation coincided with the covering of the Senne River and the construction of the Haussmann-inspired Central Boulevards. The current church, designed by Joseph Poelaert, replaced the original one – only the baroque bell tower remains.

From here, head to ❷ **Vismet-Marché aux Poissons**, the public space named after the fish market established after the basins were filled in. Though dismantled in the 1950s, the surrounding streets still bear names linked to old merchandise quays. Two artificial basins and several historic fish restaurants recall the area's maritime past. At the end of the second basin, admire the ❸ **Anspach Fountain** with a bas-relief representing an allegory of the Senne River, resting in a tunnel. On the left, notice the Maison du Cheval-Marin, a former inn dating back to the 17th century.

Further along, the ❹ **Pigeon Soldat Memorial** pays homage to homing pigeons and their owners during WWI. Next, head to ❺ **Rue de la Cigogne** for Brussels' prettiest street. Rue de Flandre offers an array of good restaurants and independent stores. If open, check out ❻ **La Bellone**.

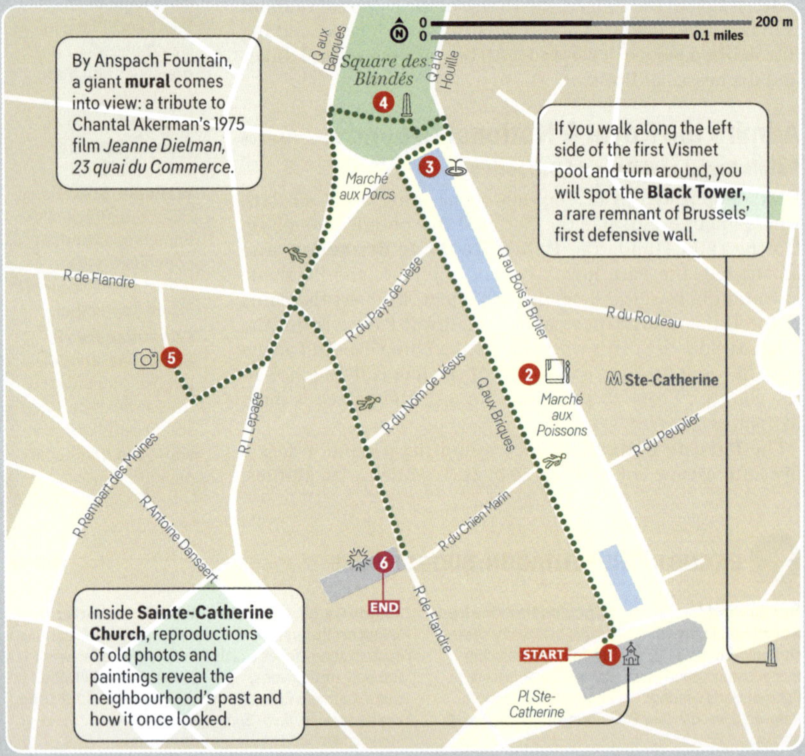

By Anspach Fountain, a giant **mural** comes into view: a tribute to Chantal Akerman's 1975 film *Jeanne Dielman, 23 quai du Commerce.*

If you walk along the left side of the first Vismet pool and turn around, you will spot the **Black Tower**, a rare remnant of Brussels' first defensive wall.

Inside **Sainte-Catherine Church**, reproductions of old photos and paintings reveal the neighbourhood's past and how it once looked.

0   200 m
0   0.1 miles

Q aux Barques
Square des Blindés
Q de la Houille
Marché aux Porcs
R de Flandre
R du Pays de Liège
Q du Bois à Brûler
R du Rouleau
Ⓜ Ste-Catherine
R du Nom de Jésus
Q aux Briques
❷
Marché aux Poissons
R du Peuplier
R L Lepage
R Rempart des Moines
R Antoine Dansaert
R du Chien Marin
R de Flandre
❻ END
START ❶
Pl Ste-Catherine

ponds, a bandstand, and outdoor bars. Among its quirks is a stone marking the spot where Russian Czar Peter the Great, after a night of excess, famously vomited his wine.

Browse & Bargain at the Marolles Flea Market

MAP P58

The spirit of Brussels

Brussels inhabitants will tell you that there's only one place where you can find the 'true' Brussels spirit alive and well: in the **Marolles** (Marollen in Dutch). This predominantly working-class and multicultural neighbourhood has always had a rebellious streak and a joke on its lips. The best way to experiment it is by visiting its flea market on **Place du Jeu de Balle**. Every morning, starting at 9am, vendors fill up the whole square to sell everything you can imagine, and what you did not think you needed: secondhand clothes, furniture, old cameras, books, paintings... You can try your hand at bargaining, especially if you buy several items from the same vendor, or simply enjoy the mood and have a cup of coffee in one of the many cafes surrounding the square. Afterwards, make your way to Rue Haute – and stop for a drink at the legendary **Le Petit Lion** for a true 'old Brussels' experience if you haven't had one yet – and the glass elevator to **Place Poelaert** and the **Palais de Justice** for a fantastic view.

Bruegel, Street Art & Comic Strips

MAP P54 & P58

Art is on the walls

In 1562, Pieter Bruegel the Elder settled in the Marolles, painting his masterpieces from Rue Haute 132 (**Bruegel House**). To commemorate the 450th anniversary of his death in 2019, 11 vibrant murals were created, offering a contemporary take on his daily life and biblical scenes, all infused with wonder and humour. Begin your journey on Rue de Rollebeek with *The Fall of the Rebel Angels* and **Église Notre-Dame de la Chapelle**, Bruegel's final resting place.

But art in Brussels extends beyond the Flemish masters. Belgium has a rich comic-strip culture, home to both the expressive Marcinelle school and Hergé's *ligne claire* style. While the **Centre Belge de la Bande Dessinée** (Comics Art Museum; *cbbd.be; adult/senior/youth under 12: €14/€11/€6*) celebrates this '9th Art', explore further by following the **Parcours BD** *(parcoursbd.brussels)* to find over 70 comic-strip murals scattered across the city *(parcoursstreetart.brussels)*.

BEST HIDDEN SURPRISES IN THE PENTAGON

Rue de la Cigogne: Small, hidden, medieval street: enjoy this pocket of serenity, especially in early May when wisterias bloom.

La Bellone: Push the door of this art centre dedicated to creation and stage artists, and go through the passageway to a splendid courtyard and 17th-century facade covered by a glass roof.

Grand Hospice Pacheco: Gardens of former hospice and retirement home transformed into a trendy open-air cafe.

Courtine and Tour de Villers: Discover a large and beautiful remnant of the 13th-century first city wall.

Théâtre Royal de Toone: At the end of an impasse, find this legendary puppet theatre and its charming pub.

 EATING IN THE PENTAGON: BEST FOR LUNCH/DINNER ———— MAP P54 & P58

Fin de Siècle: This laid-back brasserie draws crowds for its hearty dishes, buzzing vibe, and raw decor with Art Nouveau touches. *noon to midnight* €€

Nightshop: In a former garage, enjoy global, improvised cuisine and natural wines by former Londoner Jocasta Allwood. *5pm–11pm Thu, from noon Fri & Sat* €€

albert: On top of the Royal Library, albert serves farm-to-fork, seasonal dishes and pastries with a striking view of downtown Brussels. *10am–5pm* €€

Manneken Pis Café: Touristy location, but it makes the best carbonades (stewed beef in a beer sauce) in town. *hours vary, closed Mon* €€

TOP SHOPS IN THE PENTAGON

Manneke:
Not-your-average souvenir shop; locally made items and full of Belgian quirkiness.

Belge une fois:
Postcards, T-shirts, deco, food and trinkets: this family-run shop has everything Belgian.

Atelier Sainte-Catherine: This independent chocolatier crafts luscious chocolate bars and ice creams but also carries pralines from the acclaimed Frederic Blondeel.

Foxhole Vintage:
Vintage galore at two locations, in Saint-Géry and the Marolles. We prefer the second address with a larger assortment.

Mayfair BXL & Filigranes: A high-flying concept store and bookshop, where staging matters as much as what's on sale.

MIRKO KUZMANOVIC/SHUTTERSTOCK

Belgian Beer World, Palais de la Bourse

From Finance Temple to Beer Heaven   MAP P54

Hoppy pour-suits

The long-empty Bourse de Bruxelles (stock exchange) has finally found a purpose: hosting the **Belgian Beer World** (*belgianbeerworld.be; adult/16-25 €19/€16*). From the importance of beer to the Belgian culture, the brewing process, and of course, a tasting at the rooftop bar, you'll uncover all the secrets of beer-making. Even without visiting for beer, you can go inside the building and admire it. Its lavish interior (Auguste Rodin worked on some sculptures) is worth seeing.

The Rainbow Village   MAP P54

Come one, come all

Centred around the Plattesteen and rue du Charbon, the Rainbow Village grew organically as gay men claimed visibility and safe spaces. Today, it's a lively LGBTIQ+ hot spot, with bars (cruising or not), drag shows, cabarets, and queer-friendly shops. At its heart is the **Rainbow House**, a community centre with support and social activities for all. Amid ancient houses and cobbled streets, the Rainbow Village keeps the party alive from evening until late.

EATING IN THE PENTAGON: OUR PICKS FOR A SPLURGE   MAP P54 & P58

La Bonne Chère: Chef Alexandru Sapco crafts creative seasonal menus in a cosy Marolles house. Moldovan wines too. *7-8.30pm Tue-Sat, noon-1.30pm Thu-Fri* €€€

Entropy Restaurant: Tantalising six-course, gourmet, plant-based dinner menu. Organic wine list. *7.30-11pm Wed-Sat, noon-2.30pm Fri* €€€

Kline: In a raw, minimalist space, Kline serves seasonal, locally sourced but globally inspired small plates (think crisp asparagus with miso). *6-9.20pm Thu-Sat* €€

Umã: Nikkei-style dishes by Aurélie Kluyskens with bold contrasts and delicate flavours. The fish, leek and yuzu shine. *noon–2pm & 7–10pm Mon-Fri* €€€

EU Quarter, Cinquantenaire, Schaerbeek & St-Josse

EU APPRECIATION AND GREAT MUSEUMS

Some neighbourhoods stand out for their significance and charm, but the EU Quarter buzzes with its own unique energy. In larger-than-life buildings, politics that shape the lives of 447 million European citizens are discussed, decided and implemented. The 'EU Bubble' might seem somewhat removed from the rest of the population, but these people-in-suits, hailing from the 27 corners of the EU, are now as much part of Brussels as the Manneken Pis.

The imposing double triumphal arch of the Cinquantenaire was built to commemorate Belgium's 50th anniversary in 1880. It hosts captivating museums, a beautiful park and elegant cafes in nearby Etterbeek.

Schaerbeek is a vibrant and multicultural up-and-coming district and offers a blend of architectural styles, from Art Nouveau masterpieces to eclectic townhouses, but also parks, bars and theatres, and for railways enthusiasts, a train museum.

Finally, St-Josse, the smallest – and poorest – Brussels municipality holds some treasure of its own, including an Art Deco swimming pool and secret parks.

GETTING AROUND

Access most EU-related sites by taking metro line 1 or 5. Step off at Schuman. For Cinquantenaire, alight at Mérode and take the train, or take bus 71 or 95 and stop at Luxembourg for the European Parliament. The easiest way to reach Train World is either by train or tram 92 until Gare de Schaerbeek. For the Botanical Garden, take metro line 2 or 6.

The Seeds of Art Nouveau

Horta's statement

Victor Horta, the famous Art Nouveau architect, was 32 when his friend Eugène Autrique asked him to design his house in Schaerbeek. Completed in 1893, it was Horta's first private mansion. While still rooted in eclecticism, the seeds of what were to become the codes of Art Nouveau can be found here: the use of iron and glass, industrial materials and curves as ornamental elements make it a milestone. The **Maison Autrique** *(autrique. be; adult/senior & youth €9/6)* has been lovingly restored and is now a museum, preserving Horta's legacy.

☑ **TOP TIP**

If you are planning to visit the EU Quarter, and especially the Berlaymont area, make sure that the timetable for the European Council meetings, which bring together the heads of government of the 27 member states, does not coincide with your visit, as access to the quarter is partly cordoned off for security purposes.

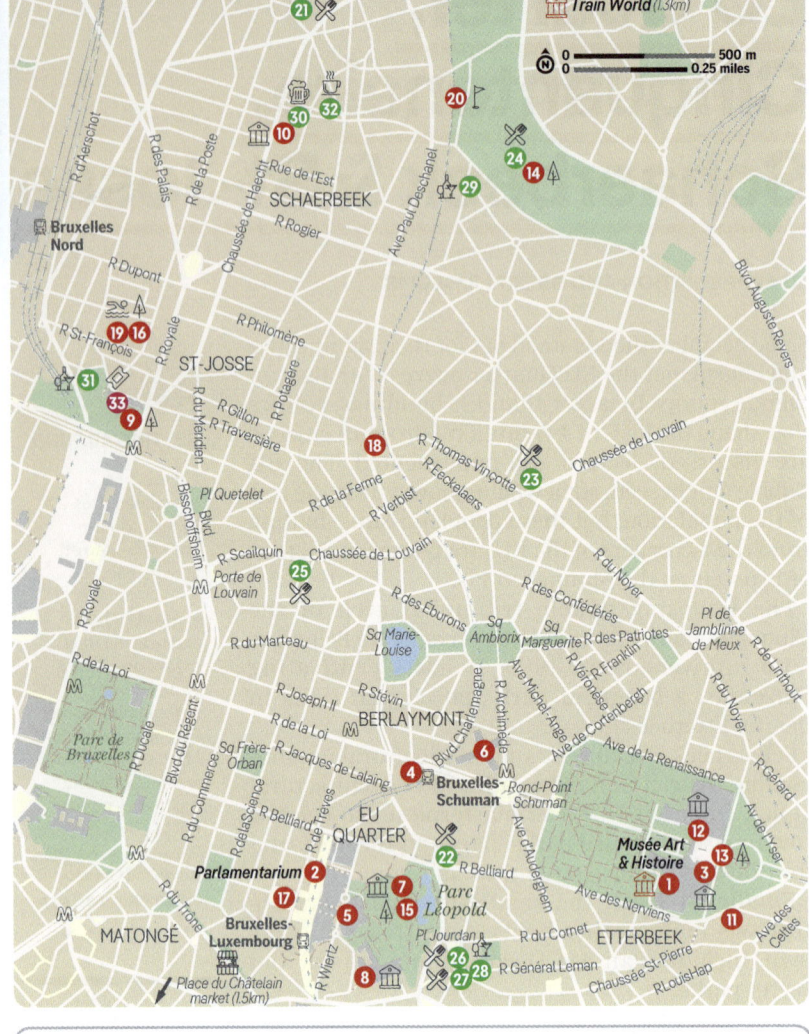

EU QUARTER, CINQUANTENAIRE, SCHAERBEEK & ST-JOSSE

Faubourg Saint-Antoine (900m);
Train World (1.3km)

0 — 500 m
0 — 0.25 miles

SCHAERBEEK

Bruxelles Nord

ST-JOSSE

BERLAYMONT

Bruxelles-Schuman

Rond-Point Schuman

EU QUARTER

Parc de Bruxelles

Parlamentarium

Parc Léopold

MATONGÉ

Bruxelles-Luxembourg

Place du Châtelain market (1.5km)

Musée Art & Histoire

ETTERBEEK

⭐ **HIGHLIGHTS**
1 Musée Art & Histoire
2 Parlamentarium

🔴 **SIGHTS**
3 Autoworld
4 Council of the European Union
5 European Parliament
6 European Commission building
7 House of European History

8 Institut des Sciences Naturelles
9 Jardin Botanique
10 Maison Autrique
11 Maison Cauchie
12 Musée Royal de l'Armée et d'Histoire Militaire
13 Parc du Cinquantenaire
14 Parc Josaphat
15 Parc Léopold
16 Parc Saint-François

17 Place du Luxembourg
18 Square Armand Steurs

🔴 **ACTIVITIES**
19 Bains de Saint-Josse
20 Mini-golf Josaphat

🟢 **EATING**
21 Achille
22 Grand Central
23 Groseille
24 La Laiterie
25 La Piola Pizza

26 Maison Antoine
27 Stirwen

🟢 **DRINKING & NIGHTLIFE**
28 Beers Bank
29 Fox Den
30 Le Barboteur
31 Tope
32 Winok

🔴 **ENTERTAINMENT**
33 Le Botanique

A Belgian Choo-Choo story

A world of trains

When the first railway linking Brussels to Mechelen was inaugurated in 1835, Belgium was the second country, after the UK, to welcome the train. It was only natural that a museum should be dedicated to it. Located in Schaerbeek's historic stations, **Train World** (*trainworld.be/fr; adult/teen/child €15/11/6*) features a permanent and temporary exhibition. Discover the history of the train; its effect on keeping Belgium synchronised; admire vintage steam engines, locomotives and royal carriages; explore interactive exhibits; listen to the captivating stories of the railway workers; and catch a glimpse of the future of train travel.

Where Brussels Shows Off

Park and museums

Parc du Cinquantenaire was built in 1880 to commemorate Belgium's 50 years of independence. It is renowned for its majestic triumphal arch monument and arcades. Standing tall in the centre of the park, the triple arch is an iconic symbol of the city. Surrounding the monument, there are no fewer than three museums for visitors to explore. The **Musée Art & Histoire** (*artandhistory.museum; adult/under 18 €10/free*) showcases an impressive collection of art and artefacts ranging from Egyptian sarcophagi to Art Nouveau ornaments. Surprisingly enough, the museum is quite overlooked, which means that you won't get swamped by visitors while looking at the South American sculpture that inspired Hergé for Tintin's *The Broken Ear*, or a magnificent Roman-Syrian mosaic. There is even an authentic moai from Rapa Nui/Easter Island, a gift from the Chilean government.

Choose carefully which section you want to see; the museum is so vast it can take a whole day to explore its treasures. The **Autoworld** museum (*autoworld.be; adult/4-18 €16/13*) could not be more different and presents a journey through the history of automobiles, with its remarkable assortment of vintage cars and temporary exhibitions. Finally, the **Musée Royal de l'Armée et d'Histoire Militaire** (*klm-mra.be; adult/student/child under 6 €12/9/free*) provides a comprehensive insight into Belgium's military heritage. Surprisingly, it also holds a collection of czarist Russia militaria. The best perk? The ticket also includes access to the top of the Cinquantenaire triumphal arches. Enjoy the view!

CITY OF DONKEYS

Schaerbeek's nickname dates back to the Middle Ages when it was a rural village rich with fields, orchards, and windmills. Its farmers secured the right from the Duke of Brabant to transport flour and produce on donkeys' backs to the market in Brussels. Among the goods they brought were the famous sour cherries, which brewers still use to make *kriek*, a lambic-based local beer.

Thanks to the donkeys, everyone in Brussels recognised where these farmers were coming from, and thus, Schaerbeek earned its unique nickname. To honour this tradition, the city takes care of two 'official' donkeys, Camille and Gribouille, who can often be seen grazing at Parc Josaphat or during the Cherry Festival, on the last Sunday of June.

 EATING & DRINKING IN ETTERBEEK: OUR PICKS

Maison Antoine: Some say that these are the best *frites* in town, but you be the judge. *11am-1am* €

Stirwen: Updated French-Belgian classics with modern flair and killer sauces. Precise and elegant cuisine. *7-9.30pm Tue-Sat, & noon-2.30pm Wed-Fri* €€€

Beers Bank: This friendly pub invites you to rob its vaults filled with 150 different kinds of beer. *3.30pm-1am Mon-Thu, to 2.30am Fri, 3pm-2.30am Sat, noon-midnight Sun*

Grand Central: Vast, industrial-chic bar with all-day dining and an EU Bubble favourite. *noon-midnight Mon-Wed, to 1am Thu-Fri, 11am-1.30am Sat, 11.30am-11.30pm Sun*

MONTICELLO/SHUTTERSTOCK

European Parliament building

TOP EXPERIENCE

The EU Quarter

Most of the EU bodies are located in Brussels, marking the urban landscape with their presence and transforming what was once a small capital into a cosmopolitan city. If you want to understand how these institutions work, affecting the lives of over 440 million Europeans, a visit is well worth your time. Some non-EU-related sights also deserve your attention.

DON'T MISS

Parlamentarium

European Parliament Hemicycle

House of European History

Institut des Sciences Naturelles

The Berlaymont

European Council

Parc Léopold

Place du Luxembourg after work

Parlamentarium

If there is only one place associated with the EU that you can visit, this should be it. The **Parlamentarium** explores the history of the European Parliament and how it works. Among the highlights: the 360-degree panorama of the Parliament, the interactive map of the EU member states, and first-hand accounts from Europeans and their experiences with legislative changes brought by the Parliament.

Practicalities

● european-union.europa.eu/contact-eu/visit-european-union-institution_en; historia.europa.eu and naturalsciences.be ● Free for EU-related sights. Natural Science Institute: adult/concession/child €13/10/5/free ● Check websites for opening hours.

The European Institutions

The **European Parliament** is the EU organ closest to the citizens since its members are directly elected, and guess what, you can visit it for free! An audio guide (in 24 languages) will be handed to you (or download the 'EP Visit' app on your smartphone). For a more in-depth approach, why not book a Hemicycle talks tour with a speaker? If you're eager to witness the Parliament in action, plan your visit during the week when the MEPs are in session. Limited spots are available to watch the debates, so make sure to register in advance.

The star-shaped **European Commission building** aka The Berlaymont has become the icon of the EU in Brussels. Built in 1967 on the site of the former convent of the Ladies of Berlaymont, it houses the offices of the President of the Commission and the college of Commissioners. If you take a good look at it, you'll notice that only the central part of the 'star' is connected to the ground, while its four branches seem to hover in the air, like tree branches. The Commission accepts group tours by reservation at least 10 weeks in advance. However, the exhibition centre **Experience Europe** is accessible to all.

At the **Council of the European Union**, guests are welcome to explore the visitor centre and common areas, with an opportunity to admire 'the egg' structure enclosed within the building.

House of European History

In a beautiful **Art Deco building** overlooking **Parc Léopold**, learn everything about the history of Europe and where it's headed. What is Europe? Is there such a thing as a shared European heritage? The interactive exhibition offers a fascinating journey through the continent's long and rich history while envisioning its future. The House also features dedicated spaces for young adults, a special route for children, and a temporary exhibition.

Institut des Sciences Naturelles

Part museum, part scientific research institute, the **Institut des Sciences Naturelles** hosts an impressive collection of 28 iguanodons found in a Belgian coal mine. The gallery displaying these dinosaurs is the largest of its kind in Europe. Do not miss the Evolution Gallery, Man Gallery or the Mineral Room. The Living Planet exhibit (inside the Evolution Gallery) and BiodiverCITY (about urban fauna and flora in Brussels) will keep you amazed at how resilient our natural world is. The museum also hosts temporary exhibitions.

PLACE DU LUXEMBOURG

The 'EU Bubble' is a work-hard, play-hard crowd. After a long day at the office, public servants and interns gather at **Place du Luxembourg** (aka Place Lux or Plux) to unwind and socialise. This square, located just in front of the Parliament, is filled with bars and provides the perfect opportunity to experience the life of an EU public servant and network.

TOP TIPS

● Avoid visiting the Institut des Sciences Naturelles on Wednesday afternoons, weekends or holidays, unless you don't mind large groups of children.

● The largest accessible toilet in the museum is on the 1st floor, near the dinosaur gallery.

● Remember to bring your ID card or passport, as it will be required for entry to the EU institutions.

● Audio guides and information are provided in 24 EU languages. Booking in advance is highly recommended.

● Don't miss the Place du Luxembourg after-work event every Thursday from April to October. It is the largest after-work gathering in Brussels, and the entire square is closed to traffic.

TOP PICKS IN SCHAERBEEK

Emmanuelle Hubert, a food and travel blogger *(augoutdemma.be)*, lived in Schaerbeek for several years.

Before living there, I knew little about Schaerbeek. For a long time, it was a neighbourhood overlooked by the rest of Brussels. So imagine my surprise when I discovered its cherry tree–lined streets and its stunning Art Deco and Art Nouveau architecture.
 On weekends, people gather in **Parc Josaphat** – and it's one of the friendliest places in Brussels. I saw Schaerbeek change over the years: today, the 'upper part' attracts far more trendy young people, and the **Chasseurs Ardennais market** is nearly as popular as **Châtelain's**. Still, it remains more culturally mixed – to me, that's one of its biggest strengths.

Brussels' Prettiest Facade?

Cauchie's masterpiece

Built in 1905, the stunning **Maison Cauchie** *(cauchie.be; adult/child €9.50/free)* was the home of married couple Paul Cauchie (1875–1952), an architect and painter, and Caroline Voet, also a painter. Its sgraffito facade, adorned with graceful female figures, is one of the most beautiful in Brussels. It looks like a Klimt painting transformed into architecture. The goal is much less romantic, as it was thought out as an advertisement for Cauchie's skills. A petition saved the house from demolition in 1971, and since 1975, it has been a protected monument. It's open 10am to 1pm and 2pm to 5pm on Saturdays.

Parc Josaphat, the People's Park

A Sunday afternoon family outing

Parc Josaphat is Schaerbeek's green lung and a main gathering spot for its residents. Amid the trees, winding paths and ponds of this English-style park, you can enjoy a leisurely stroll and admire statues of writers and artists, and children will have fun at the playground. Need a break from playing? Head to the **Buvette Sint-Sebastiaan** to grab a bite to eat, or something to drink. Belonging to the St Sebastian guild of archers (which still offers archery sessions on Wednesdays), this refreshment bar is a bit of a victim of its popularity: you'll have to be patient, but you'll understand why so many people love it.

 Next, continue your afternoon at the park's **mini-golf course** before stopping for a snack at **La Laiterie**. This contemporary cafe was built on the grounds of an old castle, which was transformed into a milk bar and reopened in 2018.

St-Josse's Little Treasures

Small is beautiful

Pint-sized St-Josse squeezes a lot of people and buildings into a tiny urban space. But that doesn't mean there's nothing to see. Start at the **Jardin Botanique**: its entrance lies just at the edge of the municipality. Especially delightful in spring, the gardens stretch out at the foot of beautiful greenhouses converted into concert halls: **Le Botanique** is one of Brussels' top venues, notably for the Nuits Botanique festival each May.

EATING IN SCHAERBEEK & ST-JOSSE: OUR PICKS

La Piola Pizza: Neapolitan pizzas so good they were elected the best in the country in 2025. *noon-2.30pm & 6.30-11pm Tue-Thu, 6.30-11pm Sat* €

Faubourg Saint-Antoine: French-Belgian dishes with Peruvian twist. Filled with Tintin memorabilia. *noon-2.30pm & 6.30-9.30pm Wed-Fri, 6.30-9.30pm Sat* €€

Groseille: Delighting Schaerbeek with locally produced, veggie-forward, Asian-inspired small plates, natural wines, cocktails. *6.30-10pm Tue-Sat, noon-2pm Fri* €€

Achille: Wine bar and sunny terrace facing showy Place Colignon. With a rotating roster of resident chefs, expect something new each time. *6pm-late, Mon-Fri* €€

Maison Cauchie

Feeling the heat or just need a swim? Head to the **Bains de Saint-Josse** *(sjtn.brussels/fr/sports-loisirs/sports/piscine-communale; adult/under 13 €3/€2.50)*. This swimming pool is an Art Deco gem. Restored in 2019 to its 1930s glory, the rows of changing rooms on two levels make it look like an aquatic theatre.

Another charming garden is hidden nearby at Rue de la Poste 53: **Parc Saint-François**, with its cherry trees. At the time of writing, it was nearing the end of renovation. Don't hesitate to check if it has reopened – this pocket park was codesigned with local residents and holds a few surprises.

Square Armand Steurs, surrounded by stately Art Deco apartment buildings and turn-of-the-century *maisons bruxelloises*, is especially lovely when the Japanese cherry trees are in bloom.

LITTLE ANATOLIA

In 1964, Belgium faced a shortage of workers to support its growth and sought foreign labour. Similar to the approach taken with Italy after WWII, Belgium signed agreements with Morocco and Türkiye. Tens of thousands of labourers arrived in the country. In Brussels, the Turkish community primarily settled in the northern municipalities of St-Josse and Schaerbeek. Many came from Anatolia, especially from towns like Emirdağ, and built a close-knit community. Over time, they opened bakeries, cafes, grocery stores, and mosques – notably the Fatih Mosque with its decorative minaret. The neighbourhood around Chaussée de Haecht won its nickname of 'Little Anatolia'. If you're itching for *pide*, *dürüm*, apple tea or anything typical from Türkiye, there's no better place to go.

DRINKING IN SCHAERBEEK & ST-JOSSE: OUR PICKS

Tope: The Hoxton Hotel's rooftop has wonderful views over Brussels and the Botanical Garden, plus spicy Mexican snacks. *4pm-midnight Sun-Wed, to 1am Thu-Sat*

Le Barboteur: Enjoy fine craft beers on tap or take one home from the 'beer library'. *4pm-late, Mon-Sat*

Fox Den: Original take on a cocktail bar, where each creation represents a country (cognac-based for France, pisco for Peru…). *6pm-late Thu & Fri, from 4pm Sat & Sun*

Winok: Sip on a single-origin espresso at this coffee roaster's cosy cafe or have a cocktail and small bites. *8am-11pm Mon-Fri, from 9.30am Sat & Sun*

St-Gilles, Ixelles & Forest

GREAT FOOD AND ART NOUVEAU

GETTING AROUND

Reach Flagey and the Ixelles ponds by taking bus 71. For the Châtelain neighbourhood, step into tram 8 or 93 and step off at Bailli. St-Gilles is best accessed through tramlines 4 and 10 with stops at Porte de Hal, Parvis de Saint-Gilles and Horta.

Nestled to the south/southeast of the Belgian capital, St-Gilles and Ixelles offer a captivating blend of culture, shopping and foodie hot spots. St-Gilles is renowned for its bohemian atmosphere, artistic affinities and Art Nouveau facades. The heart of the neighbourhood is Parvis de St-Gilles, where locals and visitors gather for the market or in the many cafes and bars.

Adjacent to St-Gilles, Ixelles is a vibrant kaleidoscope with the lively Congolese neighbourhood of Matonge, elegant treelined avenues, upscale and independent boutiques, renowned art galleries, and the most exciting dining spots in Brussels. Place Flagey serves as the unofficial centre of Ixelles, with its beautiful Art Deco buildings and the Ixelles Ponds.

Lastly, don't overlook Forest, with its leafy parks and charming residential streets. This up-and-coming commune holds hidden highlights, like the magnificent Abbaye de Forest, the tranquil Duden Park, Forest Park and the WIELS Contemporary Art Centre.

Wild Ponds

Looking for the 'ixelligator'

Next to the sprawling Place Flagey, the **Étangs d'Ixelles** (Ixelles Ponds) make for a gorgeous walk. These two large ponds are lined on both sides with mansions and villas in a variety of architectural styles, including Art Nouveau, Art Deco and eclecticism. It's the chicest address in Ixelles. Fun fact: in 2007, a pond keeper claimed to have seen someone release a large reptile into one of the ponds. The mayor had to send in the civil protection team to check, but the 'ixelligator' was never found.

☑ TOP TIP

Ixelles and Saint-Gilles are famous for their markets. In Ixelles, the **Place Flagey market** is on Saturday and Sunday morning, the **Place du Châtelain market** on Wednesday afternoon, and the **Parvis de St-Gilles market** takes place on Wednesday, Thursday and on weekends.

Musée Meunier

The Artist of the Industrial Revolution

Constantin Meunier's house and workshop

Part of the Musées Royaux des Beaux-Arts, the **Musée Meunier** is an intriguing place dedicated to one of the most prolific and significant artists of the 19th century: Constantin Meunier (1831–1905). He was born and raised in Brussels, and the museum is housed in the artist's former home and studio, where he also died. A competent painter, Meunier's career truly flourished after visiting factories and coal-mining sites. Struck by the industrial landscapes and the workers' hardships, he began depicting miners, men and women descending into or returning from the pits, steelworkers at their forges, and landscapes filled with chimney smoke. His sculptures, meanwhile, portrayed labourers in a magnified, almost heroic manner. The ultimate tribute came when the profile of one of his coal miners was reproduced on the Belgian franc until it was replaced by the euro. The museum traces the evolution of Meunier's work, with a particular focus on his last 30 years, when social and industrial themes came to dominate.

BEST SHOPPING IN BAILLI-CHÂTELAIN NEIGHBOURHOOD

LILU: Brussels designer Emmanuelle Adam crafts colourful, one-of-a-kind leather bags, handmade in her workshop-showroom.

Rose: Homeware riches, from pineapple lamps to leather birthday cards and unicorn-scented room-fragrance sprays.

Hopono: One of Brussels' biggest concept stores: 600m² of ecofriendly fashion, homeware, travel gear, toys, and gifts.

Makesenz: Sophie Trenteseaux offers a playful twist on skincare: Belgian, organic, preservative-free products.

Retro Paradise: Social economy organisation *Les Petits Riens* sets aside its best vintage clothing pieces so you can shop, feel beautiful and do good.

EATING & DRINKING IN IXELLES: OUR PICKS

Soif de Faim: Canteen-like restaurant for comforting lunches and gastronomic dinners. *10.30am-3.30pm Mon-Fri, 7.30–9.30pm Fri* €€

Humus x Hortense: Enjoy a Michelin-starred vegan feast and fine cocktails in a beautiful *maison de maître*. *6-11.30pm Wed-Sat, noon-2.30pm Fri & Sat* €€€

L'Amère à Boire: Searching for that elusive craft beer? This laid-back bar has got you covered. Their terrace is particularly lively in the evening. *4pm-2am*

Buddy Buddy: Nut/coffee roastery doubling as a vegan cafe. Try the bold coffee drinks (peanut, coffee and cocoa). *8.30am-7pm Mon-Fri, from 9am Sat & Sun*

GOODING/ALAMY

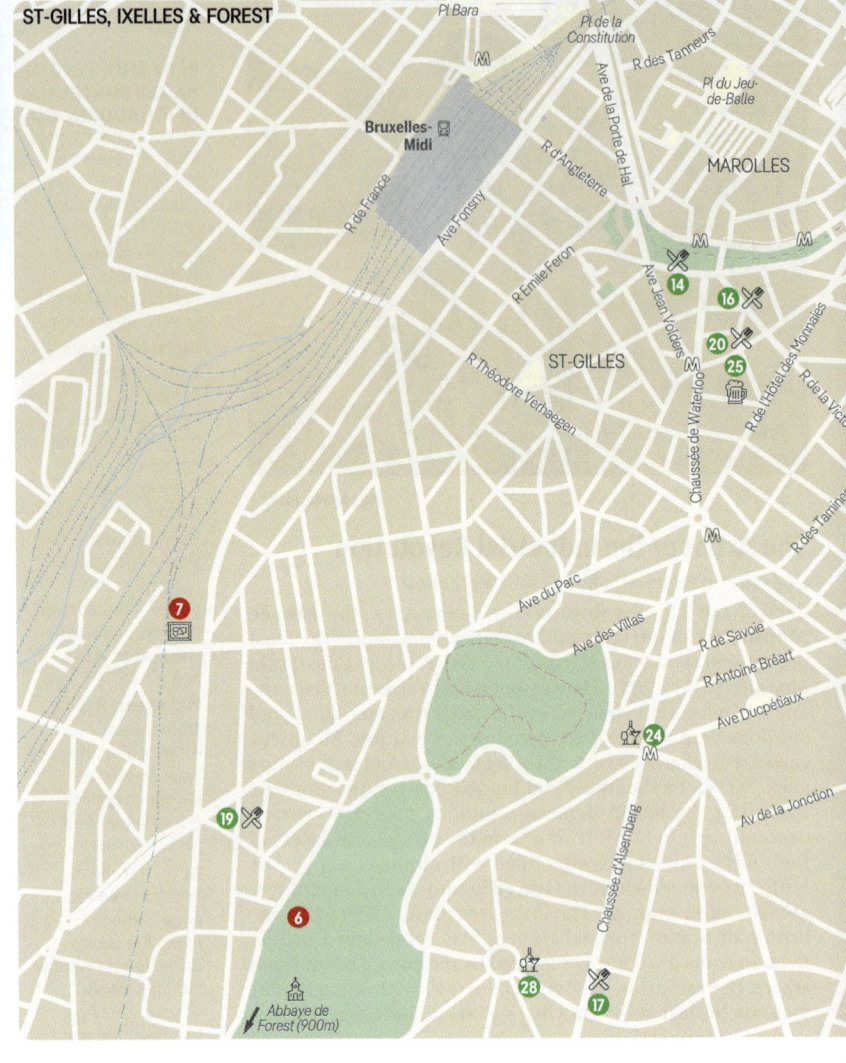

ST-GILLES, IXELLES & FOREST

Pl Bara
Pl de la Constitution
R des Tanneurs
Pl du Jeu-de-Balle
MAROLLES
Bruxelles-Midi
R d'Angleterre
Ave de la Porte de Hal
R de France
Ave Fonsny
R Émile Feron
Ave Jean Volders
14
16
20
25
Chaussée de Waterloo
R de l'Hôtel des Monnaies
R de la Victoire
R Théodore Verhaegen
ST-GILLES
R des Tamines
Ave du Parc
Ave des Villas
R de Savoie
R Antoine Bréart
Ave Ducpétiaux
7
24
Chaussée d'Alsemberg
Av de la Jonction
19
6
28
17
Abbaye de Forest (900m)

HIGHLIGHTS
1 Flagey
2 Musée Horta
3 Place du Châtelain market

SIGHTS
4 Maison Africaine

5 Musée Meunier
6 Stade Joseph Marien
7 WIELS Contemporary Art Centre

SLEEPING
8 Jam Hotel
9 L-Avenue

10 Le Berger
11 Maison Flagey
12 The Hotel
13 The Scott

EATING
14 Holy Smoke
15 Humus x Hortense

16 iOda
17 L'Altitude
18 Le Laakam
19 MangiaSempre
20 Parvis de St-Gilles market
21 Place Flagey market

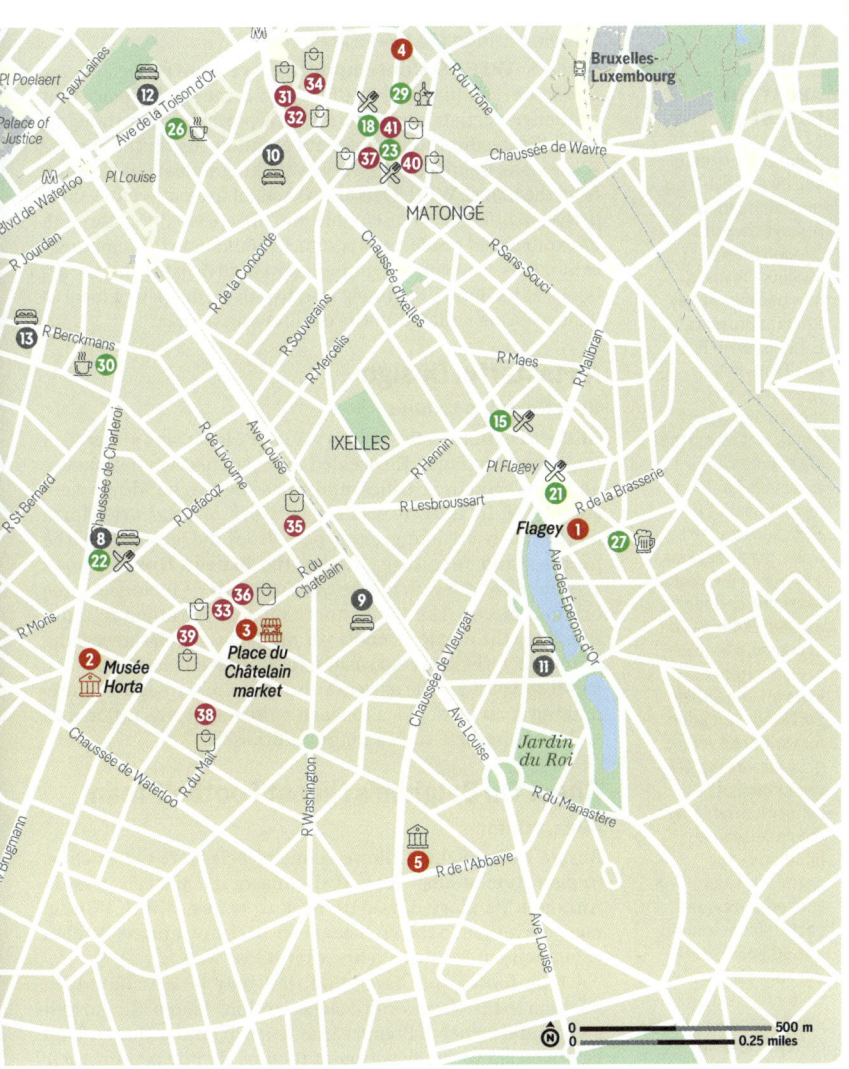

MATONGÉ

IXELLES

Flagey

Musée
Horta

Place du
Châtelain
market

Jardin
du Roi

0   500 m
0   0.25 miles

22 Soif de Faim	26 Buddy Buddy	32 Chez Nous Sawa	36 Makesenz
23 Soleil d'Afrique	27 L'Amère à Boire	see 32 Galerie Matongé	37 RCOOP
see 23 Thieyp	28 Lombric	and Galerie de la	38 Retro Paradise
	29 New Calebasse	Porte de Namur	39 Rose
● DRINKING &	30 Stella	33 Hopono	40 Wisu Kama
NIGHTLIFE		34 Jinny's	Art Shop
24 Bar du Matin	● SHOPPING	35 LILU	41 Zando ya Matonge
25 Brasserie de l'Union	31 Afrik'Wax		

ABBAYE DE FOREST

If you enjoy beer, you might have tried the blonde triple Abbaye de Forest. Though brewed in Hainaut province, its **namesake abbey** exists in Brussels. Established in 1105 as a Benedictine women's priory, the abbey played a significant role in the life of Forest until it was closed by French revolutionaries in 1796. Surrounded by walls, the abbey was a village in the village, with land, a windmill, a bakery, stables and, of course, a brewery.

Aside from worship, the abbey provided education for well-bred young girls. Unfortunately, the turmoil of history has left only the neoclassical buildings – the portal, crescent-shaped priory, and castle – constructed just 30 years before the abbey's demise. Under renovation, it will become the cultural pole ABŸ.

A Brewery Turned Art Centre
Building bridges between art forms

Forest's **WIELS Contemporary Art Centre** (*wiels.org; adult/concession/under 18 €12/5/free*) is the kind of place that challenges artists and visitors with powerful and thought-provoking exhibitions. Since its creation inside the former Wielemans Ceuppens Brewery (a striking industrial building from the 1930s), WIELS has always sought to create connections between different art disciplines and inspire creativity through its exhibits and residency program. In addition to the temporary exhibitions, the centre organises events and debates. Browse art books at its library or simply visit to enjoy a drink or a meal at its lovely cafe situated in the old brewing room.

A Masterful Design
Visit Horta's own house

At the turn of the 20th century, Victor Horta was already an important architect. He decided to design his own townhouse and workshop in St-Gilles, and when the two buildings were completed in 1901, it was a true work of total art. Horta meticulously created every aspect, from the letterbox to the mosaics and furniture – today the **Musée Horta** (*horta museum.be; adult/student/child €14/6/3.5*) includes some original pieces. The living area's interior is bathed in light, thanks to the windows and a stunning glass roof, showcasing the characteristic Art Nouveau style with its emphasis on glass, metal and curves. The museum also serves as a research centre, making it an ideal place to learn more about this influential style that has left such a mark on Brussels.

Cheer On Belgium's Nicest Football Team
Allez, l'Union

Royale Union Saint-Gilloise is one of Belgium's oldest clubs (registration number 10) and also one of the most successful. Although its glory days date back to before WWII, l'Union made its return to the Pro League in 2021, finishing as Belgian champions in 2025, 90 years after it last won.

A true footballing fairy tale that may be attributed, in addition to the players and coaches, to Tony Bloom, the current owner (and owner of Premier League's Brighton & Hove Albion FC) but also to the devotion of its fans. Renowned for their friendliness and good humour, the Unionists welcome anyone

EATING & DRINKING IN FOREST: OUR PICKS

L'Altitude: Audiophile bar with lunches/dinners, wines and DJ sets. *4.30-11pm Mon & Tue, 8.30am-11.30pm Wed-Fri, 10.30am-11.30pm Sat, 10.30am-4pm Sun €€*

Lombric: Natural wine bar, vegan-friendly cuisine. Several resident chefs in elegant rustic-chic space. *5.30pm-12.30am Thu-Sat, to 11pm Sun, to 11.30pm Mon €€*

MangiaSempre: Fall for Giulia's homemade pasta (eat in/takeaway), her bottega and award-winning meatballs. *10am-7pm Tue & Wed & Fri, to 10pm Thu, to 6pm Sat €€*

Bar du Matin: Forest's sunniest terrace (or welcoming counter if rainy) with friendly vibes and snacks from morning until night. *8am-1am Mon-Fri, 9am-1am Sat & Sun*

IN ART NOUVEAU'S FOOTSTEPS

Walk to discover the best of Art Nouveau, a style that left a lasting mark on Brussels' urban landscape.

START	END	LENGTH
Maison Hannon	Musée Horta	3.9 km; 2hrs if no visits

Take tramline 4 or 10 to Albert or Berkendael. Walk to Rue de la Jonction 1 to admire ❶ **Maison Hannon** – the only Art Nouveau building by Jules Brunfaut. Nearby, at Ave Brugmann 55, the twin owls of ❷ **Les Hiboux** have watched over the street since 1899. Its architect, Édouard Pelseneer, was the son of a cabinetmaker who worked with Victor Horta.

Cross to No 80 for your first Horta design: the ❸ **house and workshop of sculptor Fernand Dubois**. A few steps away, at Rue Darwin 15–17, is the ❹ **house and workshop of painter Louise De Hem** by Ernest Blerot. Continue to ❺ **Hôtel Max Hallet** (Ave Louise 346), a more sober Horta

work. At No 224 stands ❻ **Hôtel Solvay**, one of his masterpieces, built for the industrialist Armand Solvay. Take a moment to admire the bow windows and porches, or visit if you have the time.

At Rue Paul-Émile Janson 6, find Horta's first true Art Nouveau mansion: ❼ **Hôtel Tassel** (1894), the 'Manifesto of Art Nouveau', with details designed down to the door handles. On Rue Defacqz, find several houses built by Paul Hankar: the extravagant ❽ **Hôtel Ciamberlani** at No 48 and the ❾ **architect's own house, Maison Hankar**, at No 71. End your tour at ❿ **the Horta House and Museum**.

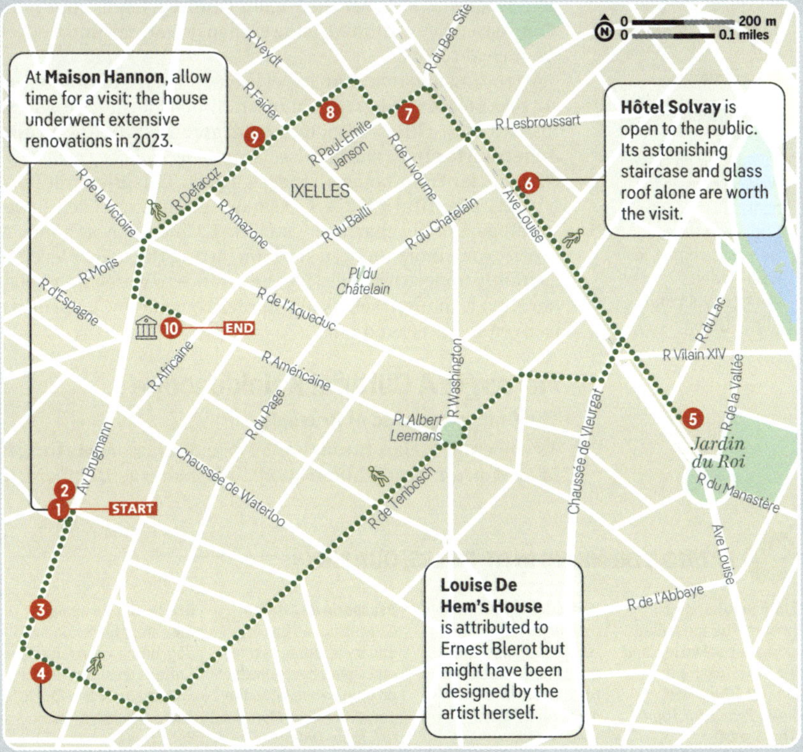

At **Maison Hannon**, allow time for a visit; the house underwent extensive renovations in 2023.

Hôtel Solvay is open to the public. Its astonishing staircase and glass roof alone are worth the visit.

Louise De Hem's House is attributed to Ernest Blerot but might have been designed by the artist herself.

IXELLES

START

END

Jardin du Roi

CHEER LIKE A UNIONIST

If you indeed go watch a Union game, get ready to sing. The supporters have a whole repertoire but this one is the most famous and must be sung to the tune of 'I Will Follow Him'. Here's something for you to practise, with a little translation:

Bruxelles ma ville, je t'aime,
Je porte ton emblème, tes couleurs, dans mon cœur,
Et quand vient le week-end, au parc Duden,
Je chante pour ton club:
Allez l'Union

'Brussels, my city, I love you,
I wear your emblem, your colours, in my heart,
And when the weekend comes, in Parc Duden,
I sing for your club:
Allez l'Union'

who wishes to support their club. Family-friendly and non-aggressive, they continue to sing even in defeat, earning respect from rival teams.

Attending a match is an experience in itself. Adding to the surreal Belgian twist, the Union stadium is located in Forest instead of St-Gilles. Although renovated in 2018, the **Stade Joseph Marien** *(rusg.brussels; online tickets from €15)* remains far from being a modern arena. This 1919 stadium, with its beautiful 1922 Art Deco facade, has changed little. It's all part of the charm of watching L'Union play at home. A project for a more modern stadium, fitting the team's level, is currently underway; time is of the essence to watch them play here, even though tickets are harder to come by, as priority is given to registered fans.

Matonge: A Cultural Kaleidoscope

The Congolese side of Brussels

As you enter Ixelles through the Porte de Namur, **Matonge**, named after a neighbourhood in Kinshasa, Democratic

EATING & DRINKING IN ST-GILLES: OUR PICKS

Holy Smoke: Here, brisket, ribs and pulled pork are cooked low and slow in a Texan smoke pit. *7-11.30pm Wed, noon-2pm & 7-11.30pm Thu-Sat €€*

iOda: Bold, pretty and flavourful vegetable dishes prepared with the same care usually reserved for the finest meat cuts. *7-9pm Wed-Sat €€*

Brasserie de l'Union: Old-fashioned bar, legendary lasagna, vast terrace, good beers. Perfect pit stop before/after the game. *8am-1am Mon-Wed, to 1.30am Thu-Sun*

Stella: Bassel named the cafe after his beloved dog, both Syrian refugees. Coffees, pastries, brunch. *7.30am-2pm Mon-Thu, to 3pm Fri, 8.30am-4pm Sat & Sun*

Union supporters, Stade Joseph Marien

Republic of the Congo, comes to life. The influx of a significant Congolese population began in the late 1950s when the Congo (along with Rwanda and Burundi) was still a **Belgian colony** (p98). The **Maison Africaine**, also known as Maisaf, served as a gathering place for students and scholarship recipients. With the country's independence in 1960, the migration to Belgium increased, leading Congolese expatriates to establish themselves in Matonge. Many opened shops in the neighbouring commercial galleries, transforming Matonge into a beacon of African culture in Europe. Over time, other African communities, including Rwandans, Guineans, as well as Indo-Pakistani and Latin American residents, also found a home here.

Take a leisurely stroll to the busy yet slightly neglected **Galerie Matongé** and **Galerie de la Porte de Namur**. Both areas are abuzz with hairdressers, occasional clothing stores and convenience shops. The main commercial artery, Chaussée de Wavre, has plenty of exotic fruit and vegetable stands, wax-print shops and cosy little restaurants.

WHERE TO SHOP IN MATONGE

Zando ya Matonge: If you're thinking of cooking a homemade African dish, you'll find all your ingredients here.

Jinny's: Everything you need for African hair care, from chemicals to wigs, as well as specific cosmetics.

Chez Nous Sawa: From wax fabrics to jewellery and bags, one for African design lovers.

Afrik'Wax: As the name suggests, this shop is all about wax: Dutch wax, grand wax... You name it!

RCOOP: Cooperative of beauty professionals, including hairdressers, beauticians and dressmakers, many specialising in ethnic care and styles.

Wisu Kama Art Shop: Compact gallery showcasing African culture through paintings, sculptures, books, CDs. Also hosts workshops.

 EATING & DRINKING IN MATONGE: OUR PICKS

Thieyp: Senegalese home-cooked meals. Two options for mains and a short list of fresh, homemade juice (baobab, *bissap...*). *noon-2.30pm & 6-10pm Mon-Sat* €

Soleil d'Afrique: A full immersion into African cuisine with specialities from the Congo, Senegal and Cameroon. Try the grilled goat, if you dare. *5-11.30pm* €€

Le Laakam: Cameroonian restaurant with traditional dishes *(ndole, poulet DG...),* as well as Congolese favourites *(moambe, saka-saka...).* *11am-11pm Wed-Fri & Sun-Mon* €€

New Calebasse: Lively pub where you can sample some *bissap* (ginger and hibiscus juice), have some grilled goat and... party like it's Kinshasa. *noon-late*

Along the Canal

POSTINDUSTRIAL HERITAGE

GETTING AROUND

Anderlecht's main metro station is Saint-Guidon on line 5, a five-minute walk from La Maison d'Erasme. For Molenbeek's highlights, take metro lines 1 or 5 to Comte de Flandre, or hop on bus 59 or tram 51 to Porte de Flandre. The Canal Park and Tour & Taxis are easiest via metro lines 2 or 6 to Yser, or by various buses stopping at Suzanne Daniel.

☑ TOP TIP

On the left bank of the canal is Brussels' busiest cycle path, and it's quite narrow. Make sure you stay well off the lane (close to the railing) if walking, or why not join the cyclists and rent a bike to explore the area?

When industries disappeared from the canal area, Brussels turned its back on it. The municipalities, which were home to a large working-class, often impoverished community, many of whom were immigrants, were forgotten along with it. Molenbeek, once a countryside hamlet, was turned into a factory town by the construction of the canal. It welcomed people who were seeking work, first from Belgium, then Italian and Spanish leftists fleeing fascism and the Franco regime, and then Moroccan workers who were invited to Belgium. This history makes Molenbeek a fascinating tapestry of cultures and architecture.

Similarly, Anderlecht (famous for its football club) is also affected by neglect and socioeconomic disparities. With a rich history, diverse population and a mix of residential and former industrial areas, it faces its own set of struggles. However, significant efforts are being made to invest in the canal's potential, which will likely shape the future of Brussels.

Stories of Migration

Newcomers' triumphs and heartaches

Ever since Molenbeek became a boomtown in the second part of the 19th century, it has attracted several waves of migration from near and far. The **MigratieMuseumMigration** (*mmm. brussels; adult/under 12 €8/free*) tells the story of Brussels as a city shaped by migration, highlighting the various types of migrants and their journeys to Brussels and Molenbeek. Fifty display cases, each filled with photos, objects, and official documents, are lined up neatly and waiting for visitors to pick up an earpiece. These feature voices of migrants from a variety of backgrounds, each with their own motivations and experiences (ranging from European Union civil servants and guest workers to refugees from the Petit Château reception centre across the canal). Fifty deeply moving human stories.

0   500 m
0   0.25 miles

GANSHOREN

Ave Charles-Quint

KOKELBERG

Blvd Léopold II

R de l'Intendant

R Picard

22

17

Canal de Willebroek

Q de Willebroek

Blvd du Jubilé

Blvd du Port

🏛 **Tour & Taxis**
3

9

4

R Piers
R de Ribaucourt
R du Courtois
R de l'Avenir

6 🏛

15 🍴

Blvd d'Anvers

Chaussée de Gand

16

Chaussée de Gand

12 🍴

R de Laeken

MOLENBEEK

5 🏛

20 ☕
R Antoine Dansaert

8 🛏

Blvd Barthélémy

BRUXELLES

Chaussée de Ninove

7

Canal de Charleroi

R d'Anderlecht / R Van Artevelde

14

Cantillon Brewery

R Otlet
Blvd du Midi
Blvd Maurice Lemonnier

1 🍺
18 **11** 🛏
10

Pl de la Constitution

23 🏛

Bruxelles-Midi 🚆

R des Fabriques
R Haute

ANDERLECHT

☕ **19**

Chaussée de Mons

R de l'Instruction

Pl Bara

MAROLLES

R des Tanneurs

Ave de la Porte de Hal

21 ☕ **2** 🗡 **13** 🏛

Pl de la Résistance

Ave Fonsny

La Maison d'Erasme

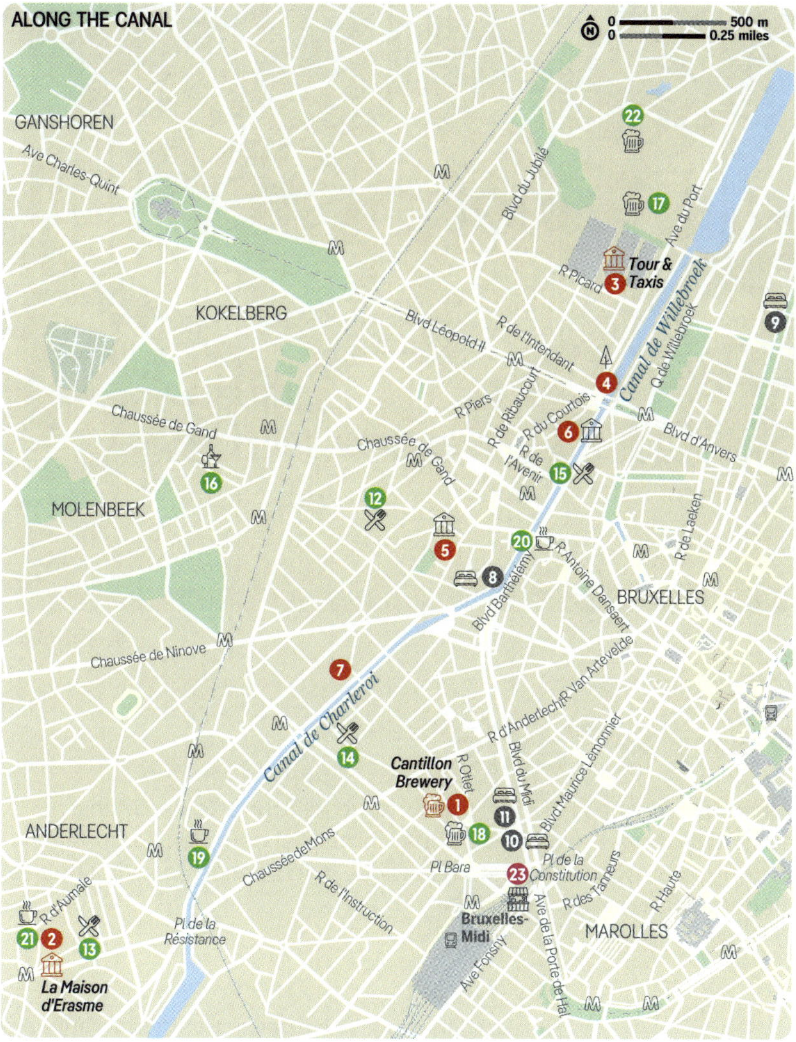

🟠 **HIGHLIGHTS**
1 Cantillon Brewery
2 La Maison d'Erasme
3 Tour & Taxis

🔴 **SIGHTS**
4 Bassin Béco
5 La Fonderie
6 MigratieMuseum Migration

7 Recyclart

⚫ **SLEEPING**
8 Meininger Bruxelles City Center
9 The Standard
10 Urban Yard
11 Yooma Urban Lodge

🟢 **EATING**
see 8 Belmundo
12 Cassonade
13 Friture René
14 La Paix
15 Phare du Kanaal

🟢 **DRINKING & NIGHTLIFE**
16 Bar Leo

17 Brasserie de la Senne
18 Brasserie de l'Ermitage
19 Coop Café
20 Koul
21 La Fourmilière
22 La Source

🔴 **SHOPPING**
23 Marché du Midi

KRISTOF BELLENS/SHUTTERSTOCK

Gare Maritime

TOP EXPERIENCE

Tour & Taxis

Witness the rebirth of a neighbourhood at Tour & Taxis. Sitting along the canal, it was once a busy industrial complex, featuring warehouses, post and customs offices, and serving as a vital hub for maritime and railway activities.

DON'T MISS

Royal Depot

Gare Maritime and its food court

World of Mind

Parc Tour & Taxis

Royal Depot

Of course, when you're building a multifunctional facility for import and export, you need a warehouse. A lot of goods were coming and going through Tour & Taxis and if they were needed to be held (for clearing customs, for instance), this is where they would end up. This stunning, four-floors-high building inundated by light, thanks to its glass roof, opened in 1910. Instead of merchandise, you can now find

Practicalities

● tour-taxis.com (hours vary according to the businesses)
● wom.brussels; 10am-6pm Tue-Sun, €15

restaurants and office spaces, and even a spa – curiously, it is a favourite spot for wedding pictures. Look for the glass-covered rail tracks in the middle of it, a reminder of the construction's past use.

Gare Maritime

The **Gare Maritime** is the showpiece of the whole T&T complex and one of Brussels' most beautiful buildings: three massive, connected halls made of bricks, iron, glass and a lot of wood since its long renovation. It's also a beautiful example of Art Nouveau applied to an industrial use, with its elegant curving arches and vinelike details, the work of architect Frédéric Bruneel.

As the name suggests, the 'maritime station' was Brussels harbour's freight station and the largest in Europe. It's a bit hard to imagine that trains would come through the massive doors via the quays just outside, to be loaded or offloaded. The site is so large it could fit 2km of rail tracks! Today, you're more likely to meet office workers who have the chance to spend the day 'in the city where it never rains', shoppers or diners who'd have a hard time choosing what to eat in its **food court**. Gare Maritime is also the site of many events such as **StrEAT Fest** (p33).

World of Mind

The old sheds are hosts to many different things, including a paddle club and a virtual karting experience, but if we had to pick our favourite, it would be **World of Mind**. Its 1500 sq metres are dedicated to mystifying the mind and your sense of perception with optical illusions, eye tricks and mirrors. It's perfect to visit with family or friends, and you'll want to have your smartphone fully charged and ready!

Parc Tour & Taxis

Formally known as 'Parc de la ligne 28', **Parc Tour & Taxis** is one of Brussels' newest parks. It was developed on the site of an old railroad, and you can still see remnants of its former use. The park is still a work in progress, with young trees and a micro-forest that needs time to grow, but it has a spacious grassy area for children to play. Students from the nearby circus school also train here.

Just beyond the large bridge that spans the park, you'll find **Parckfarm**, a social and urban farm that provides a space and the knowledge for those interested in growing vegetables. Run by local volunteers, the cafeteria welcomes visitors with homemade drinks and snacks, adding a refreshing touch to this already green space.

NEW BEGINNINGS

Once a thriving harbour zone, the **Quartier Maritime** in Molenbeek declined after the port moved and poor urban planning isolated it. Today, projects like Tour & Taxis and the future Kanal Pompidou contemporary art museum aim to breathe new life into the area and reconnect it with the rest of the city – though not without concerns about rapid gentrification and the displacement of longstanding communities.

TOP TIPS

● There is a convenient, and free, shuttle bus from Gare du Nord to Tour & Taxis. It runs approximately every 10 minutes.

● In addition to World of Mind, the Sheds offer a variety of entertainment options, including a BattleKart circuit, a paintball arena, and the Bubble Planet Experience.

● For a beautiful view of Tour & Taxis, cross the park and walk up to the Pont du Jubilée (there's a small trail on the right side of the bridge and stairs for easy access). From this vantage point, Brussels appears completely different.

Chill-Out Spot for a Great Mind

Where Erasmus lived

No wonder the EU student-exchange programme is named after Desiderius Erasmus from Rotterdam: the great scholar, called by his contemporaries the 'Prince of Humanists', travelled extensively across Europe. Between 1516 and 1521, he lived in the Leuven-Brussels area as counsellor to the young emperor Charles V. In rural Anderlecht, he found peace to revise the New Testament while staying with Canon Pieter Wijchman. The house, **La Maison d'Erasme** *(erasmushouse. museum; adult €5)*, now in central Anderlecht, dates from 1450 and is one of Brussels' oldest. It's beautifully decorated with period pieces, paintings, engravings and editions of Erasmus' works. The garden – part medicinal, part philosophical – is a delight.

Begin the Béguine

Belgium's smallest béguinage

Anderlecht, contrary to Brussels, managed to preserve its own *béguinage* (*begijnhof* in Dutch). *Béguines* were women who lived a religious life together without taking perpetual vows, allowing them the freedom to leave when desired. The movement was particularly prominent in Belgium, with some *béguinages* featuring hundreds of members. In time, it became a true influential power until the French Revolution swept over. Anderlecht's *béguinage (erasmushouse.museum/ decouvrir/beguinage; free)* is the smallest in Belgium, featuring two buildings surrounding an enclosed garden. After undergoing restoration work, the *béguinage* is open to visitors on the first Sunday of the month. At the time of writing, a new museum exhibition is set to be installed.

Scents & Colours from Around the World

One of Europe's largest markets

The huge **Marché du Midi** (South Market) is part of everyday life in Brussels, taking place every Sunday morning. For many Brussels families, the market is the place to go for a good bargain – the prices are simply unbeatable. Fruit, meat, clothes, fish, plants, bicycles, books – it's a dizzying array of smells and colours. The cosmopolitan mix that is Brussels is on full display at the stalls and in the aisles of the market.

 EATING & DRINKING IN ANDERLECHT: OUR PICKS

Friture René: Anderlecht's pride: great *frites*, even better meats and delicious mussels best eaten in season. *noon-2pm & 6-9.30pm Wed-Sun* €€

La Paix: Michelin-starred experience in a *belle époque* house. Refined Belgian-French cuisine with Japanese touches. *7–8pm Tue-Fri, noon–1pm Thu-Fri* €€€

La Fourmilière: Bohemian and welcoming cultural cafe in a pretty Art Deco building. Stop by for events, drinks or a bite. *noon-late Mon-Fri, from 10am Sat & Sun*

Coop Café: Perched on a converted flour mill, its wooden terrace with an expansive view over the canal alone is worth the visit. *9am-5pm Mon-Fri*

La Maison d'Erasme

It's *Gueuze*, not Gose!

Deep dive into beer heritage

Anderlecht is home to the last remaining lambic and *gueuze* brewery in Brussels: **Cantillon** *(cantillon.be)*. Lambic is a spontaneous-fermentation beer; rather than adding yeast, the lambic-to-be is exposed to the open air and fermented by the unique bacteria and yeasts found only in the Senne River valley, imparting its distinctively sour taste. *Gueuze,* on the other hand, is crafted by blending young and old lambics. Cantillon is not just a brewery; it is also an interesting museum, the **Musée Bruxellois de la Gueuze**, that is well worth a visit for beer enthusiasts. The Van Rooy-Cantillon family maintains exceptionally high standards for its beers and has gained celebrity status among zythologists. Just a few metres away, you'll discover **Brasserie de l'Ermitage** *(ermitagenanobrasserie.be)*, a nanobrewery that ranks among the best in town.

BEST NEIGHBOURHOOD BEERS TO TRY

Gueuze by Cantillon: The classic Brussels beer, low in alcohol, slightly fizzy with a refreshing, balanced sourness.

Kriek by Cantillon: A blend of lambics combined with morello cherries. Fruity with a hint of almond.

La Lanterne by L'Ermitage: An aromatic and hoppy pale ale, the first to come out of L'Ermitage's vats.

Le Zinnebir by Brasserie de la Senne: The firstborn from Brussels' first craft brewery: a golden pale ale, lightly bitter and citrusy.

Delta by Brussels Beer Project: The one that started it all for BBP. A fruity, tropical saison IPA.

 EATING IN MOLENBEEK: OUR PICKS FOR A GOOD CAUSE

Phare du Kanaal: Lively cafe serving organic food and drinks, with a sunny terrace along the canal. *8.30am-8pm Tue-Wed & Fri, to 11pm Thu, 10am-6pm Sat & Sun* €

Belmundo: Serves good-value meals from garden-grown, rescued local produce, while training jobseekers. *noon-2.30pm Mon-Fri & 6-9.30pm Thu-Fri* €

Recyclart: Trains vulnerable people in its workshops and warm industrial canteen: vegan, halal, classics and global flavours. *noon-3pm Tue-Wed, to 10pm Thu-Fri* €

Cassonade: Buying a meal here means providing one for someone in need, and the food is delicious (don't miss Friday, couscous day). *8am-2.30pm Mon-Fri* €

MY MOLENBEEK

Edgar Kosma is a writer, actor and comedian who lives on the Molenbeek-Anderlecht border. *@edgarkosma*

When it rains, I love walking my dog under the freshly renovated **Grande Halle** along the Quai de l'Industrie. And when the weather is good, you can stretch out on wooden loungers next to the playground; it's a great chill-out spot. If you're lucky, you might catch a concert or cultural event there.

In the heart of Molenbeek, at 4 rue Mommaert, go enjoy the energy of the **Maison des Cultures**. It's a beautiful venue for cultural events. I especially recommend the 'Good Vibes' evenings, which highlight talents in stand-up, rap and theatre, and actively involve local youth in the programming.

Brussels' Little Manchester

Molenbeek, a city of industries

The 1832 opening of the **Brussels–Charleroi Canal** turned Molenbeek from a rural village into a buzzing industrial hub of factories and workers' housing, earning it the nickname 'Little Manchester,' after the English city known for its booming industry.

For those interested in Brussels' industrial past, a visit to **La Fonderie** *(lafonderie.be, adult/concession €8/5)* is highly recommended. This former derelict bronze factory now houses the **Museum of Labour & Industry** and a study centre. La Compagnie des Bronzes, known for its quality, created statues for Queen Victoria and animal sculptures for the New York Zoo. La Fonderie also has guided tours of Molenbeek and other Brussels neighbourhoods; related to industry. The museum's cafe, open on the garden and casting hall, is blissfully quiet.

A Call to Sea

Walk and sail

The canal banks are evolving, starting with the left side from Sainctelette to Tour & Taxis. The transformed **Bassin Béco** features an attractive promenade with a sport field, large sandpit, and extensive skateboarding/BMX area. Enjoy walking along the water, watching barges, and admiring the Corto Maltese mural across the bank, while dreaming of faraway seas.

Bassin Béco also serves as the **Waterbus** starting point, operating from May to October. The mini-cruise to Vilvoorde *(waterbus.eu, adult/3-12 €3.50/1.75 one-way)* includes stops at the Dockx mall and Cruise terminal, taking about two hours round-trip. It will give you an unprecedented look at Brussels' industrial side.

DRINKING IN THE CANAL AREA: OUR PICKS

La Source: This micro-brewery is known for its intensely hopped beers and beautiful setting in a former warehouse. *4-11pm Wed-Fri, from 2pm Sat, 2-9pm Sun*

Brasserie de la Senne: Brussels' craft-beer pioneers use all organic ingredients. Get a taste at its laid-back taproom. *4-11pm Wed-Fri, from noon Sat, noon-9.30pm Sun*

Koul: Killer coffees and caffeine-based specialities and even better flatbreads in a minimalistic, cool space. *9am-6pm Mon-Fri, 9.30am-6.30pm Sat & Sun*

Bar Leo: Alternative vibes in this bar in the former Delhaize supermarkets HQ under temporary occupation. Concerts, comedy shows, bingo drag. *4-11pm Thu-Sat*

South & East Brussels & Forêt de Soignes

THE UPPER-CLASS AND GREEN NEIGHBOURHOODS

The communes of the second ring, located to the east and south of Brussels, far from the centre and its frenzy, have always been the favoured haunts of the upper classes. Quiet Woluwe-Saint-Lambert and Woluwe-Saint-Pierre, residential Auderghem, bohemian Watermael-Boitsfort and upmarket Uccle all share the fact that they are privileged, airy and blessed with beautiful parks. Brussels is said to be made up of 19 villages. This is even truer here. But that veneer of discretion does not mean that there's nothing to do or see – far from it, especially in Uccle, which is more dynamic than it seems.

For residents of the southern municipalities, the great Forêt de Soignes is just a stone's throw away. This verdant lung of the capital is Brussels' best place to relax and breathe. In the quiet of the forest, walking among towering beech trees, city life seems blissfully far away.

☑ **TOP TIP**

The two main gates of the Forêt de Soignes in Brussels are easily accessible by public transport. They are located near the **Hippodrome de Boitsfort** (p89; tram 8) and the **Rouge-Cloître park** (p87; bus 44, 'Auderghem-Forêt' stop).

Where East Meets West

An artistic conversation

At first sight, the **Villa Empain** is another Art Deco showstopper. Built in the early 1930s for Baron Louis Empain, a notable entrepreneur and philanthropist, by Swiss-Belgian

GETTING AROUND

Uccle's main transport link is tram 10, which runs from Brussels city centre to Stalle on the southern border (stop at Churchill for the Musée & Jardins van Buuren). Tram 92 also serves the Fort-Jaco neighbourhood. The train is another quick option, with Uccle-Stalle, Uccle-Calvoet and Uccle-St-Job as the main stops. Woluwe-Saint-Lambert is served by metro line 1, with Gribaumont, Tomberg and Roodebeek as its main stations, while tram 8 crosses Woluwe-Saint-Pierre all the way to Auderghem and Watermael-Boitsfort. Alternatively, for Auderghem, take metro line 5 to Beaulieu. Watermael and Boitsfort also have their own train stations.

SOUTH & EAST BRUSSELS & FORÊT DE SOIGNES

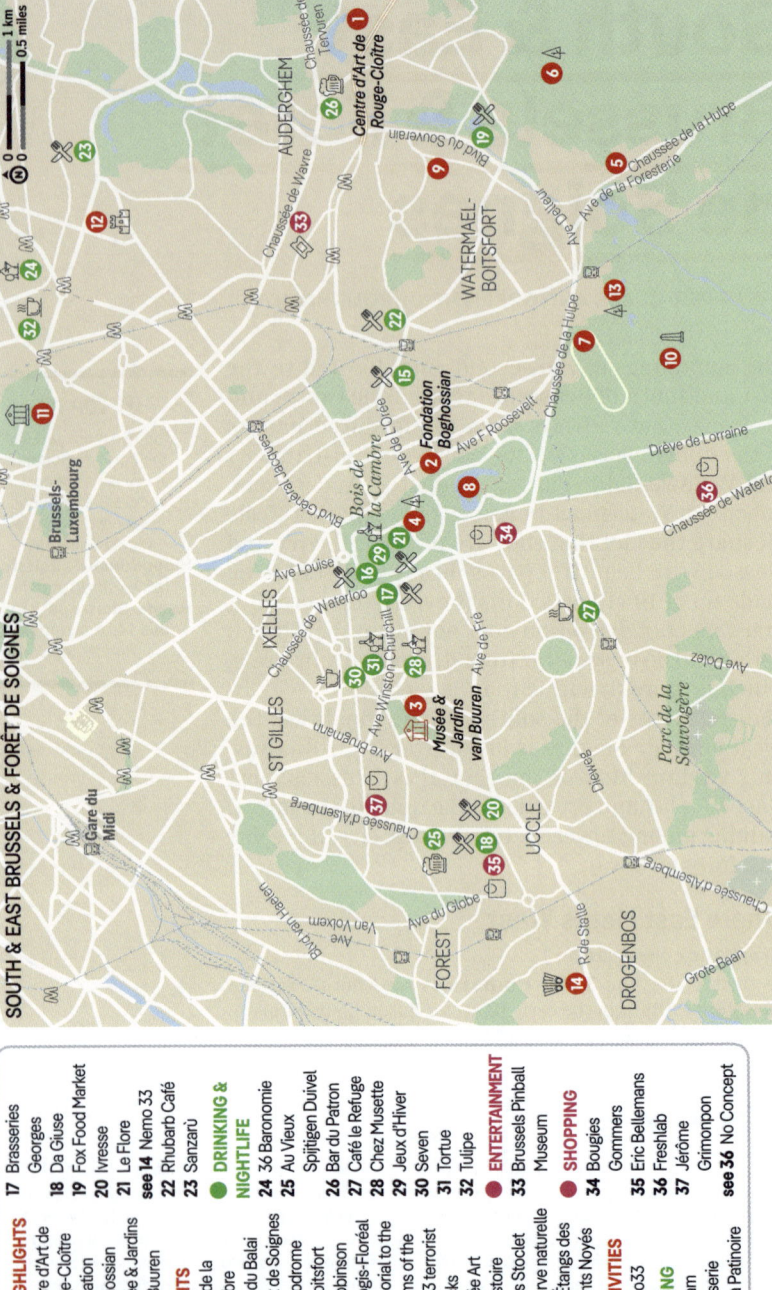

★ HIGHLIGHTS
Centre d'Art de Rouge-Cloître
1 Centre d'Art de Rouge-Cloître
2 Fondation Boghossian
3 Musée & Jardins van Buuren

SIGHTS
4 Bois de la Cambre
5 Coin du Balai
6 Forêt de Soignes
7 Hippodrome de Boitsfort
8 Île Robinson
9 Le Logis-Floréal
10 Memorial to the Victims of the 22/03 terrorist attacks
11 Musée Art & Histoire
12 Palais Stoclet
13 Réserve naturelle des Étangs des Enfants Noyés

ACTIVITIES
14 Nemo33

EATING
15 Babam
16 Brasserie de la Patinoire

17 Brasseries Georges
18 Da Giuse
19 Fox Food Market
20 Ivresse
21 Le Flore
see 14 Nemo 33
22 Rhubarb Café
23 Sanzarù

DRINKING & NIGHTLIFE
24 36 Baronomie
25 Au Vieux Spijtigen Duivel
26 Bar du Patron
27 Café le Refuge
28 Chez Musette
29 Jeux d'Hiver
30 Seven
31 Tortue
32 Tulipe

ENTERTAINMENT
33 Brussels Pinball Museum

SHOPPING
34 Bougies Gommers
35 Eric Bellemans
36 Freshlab
37 Jérôme Grimonpon
see 36 No Concept

architect Michel Polak, it was purchased in 2006 by the **Fondation Boghossian** *(villaempain.com; adult/concession €12/8)* and turned into a cultural institution and place of artistic dialogue between East and West. The wonderfully restored house is the backdrop for temporary exhibitions and events. Make time to have a drink at the gorgeous villa cafe. Gatsby would feel at home here!

Art in Nature

A peaceful retreat

The **Centre d'Art de Rouge-Cloître** *(rouge-cloitre.be; adult/concession €5/3)* combines the charms of a partially ruined monastery and the tranquillity of the nearby Forêt de Soignes. It was once one of the most prestigious abbeys of the Spanish Lowlands, but the final blow to a long story of glory and decline came when the French revolutionary troops invaded Brussels and suppressed all religious order. The Rouge-Cloître never recovered. Today the art centre occupies the remaining buildings, hosting year-round exhibitions with a focus on the relationship between art and writing. It's a wonderful opportunity to combine artistic discovery with a walk in the forest. There's also a children's playground on-site and a cafe along the priory's pond (a real showstopper).

Art Deco from Roof to Garden

A dream home turned art museum

It was the heyday of Art Deco when Dutch banker David van Buuren's house was finally completed in 1928. Married couple David and Alice were famous philanthropists and art collectors. They wanted their house to be a showcase for their collections and called on French, Belgian and Dutch decorators to embellish their home. The **Musée & Jardins van Buuren** *(museumvanbuuren.be; adult/concession €18/12)* is brimming with original Art Deco pieces – carpets, furniture, stained glass and vases – and every room is an opportunity to admire paintings or sculptures by famous artists, such as Constant Permeke or James Ensor. The gardens, supervised by Alice, are particularly beautiful, with their labyrinth, rose garden and the 'Garden of the Heart', which Alice had ordered built after her husband's death.

FANCY SHOPPING IN UCCLE

Jérôme Grimonpon: Award-winning chocolatier. One of his signatures? Including tea in his ganache recipes.

Freshlab: Pharmacy-like cosmetics store full of exclusive perfumes, skincare and hair products, as well as home scents.

Eric Bellemans: Eric is a jeweller who works with clients to design custom pieces based on their ideas. He also repurposes items into new jewellery.

Bougies Gommers: Making candles since 1863, from church to novelty types, with unrivalled expertise. The workshop looks like a magician's den!

No Concept: Two addresses in Uccle, but we prefer the one in Fort-Jaco with the largest assortment of ready-to-wear, shoes, accessories and decorative items.

EATING & DRINKING IN UCCLE: OUR PICKS

Da Giuse: Family-run Italian trattoria with freshly made pasta, sauces, desserts and panini. *10am-6pm Tue & Wed, from 8am Thu, 8am-9pm Fri & Sat* €

Ivresse: It's a grocery shop and a wine shop but, above all, a restaurant with inventive, local and season-based cuisine. *7.30-11pm, Wed-Sat* €€

Brasseries Georges: Belgian cuisine with an emphasis on seafood. Winners of the 2023 best shrimp croquettes award. *noon-10.30pm, to 11pm Fri-Sat* €€

Au Vieux Spijtigen Duivel: Charles V and Victor Hugo were patrons of this former inn in Uccle. It has hardly changed. *11.30am-1am Mon-Sat, to midnight Sun*

BOIS DE LA CAMBRE: PAST & PRESENT

Bois de la Cambre is more than just a spot for strolls, picnics and children's playgrounds. The day before the Battle of Waterloo, British soldiers, finding a large grassy area, improvised a game of cricket. It's since been baptised *La pelouse des Anglais* (Englishmen's green). Spot the commemorative plaque and tree near the former ice rink.

Fast-forward to today, and the park goes full throttle each spring for the **24 Heures Vélos**: a raucous, Boy and Girl Scouts bike relay, where teams pedal like mad from Saturday noon to Sunday noon. Expect costumes, fantasy bikes, concerts, animations, cheering crowds, and plenty of pedal-powered mayhem, a tradition rolling towards its 40th birthday in 2026 and the largest Scouts gathering in Belgium.

Brussels' Playground

A great and green escape

Bois de la Cambre is an extensive green space and a favourite escape from Brussels' urban chaos. Originally an extension of the Forêt de Soignes, it takes its name from the Abbaye de la Cambre, a former Cistercian abbey which, in true Belgian surrealist fashion, lies outside the wood (though not far away). Designed by German landscape architect Edouard Keilig (1827–95), it was conceived as the 'grand finale' of the newly built Avenue Louise, a prestigious thoroughfare named after one of Leopold II's daughters. Opened in 1866, La Cambre is a classic example of English-style landscaping, with pockets of the original forest somewhat preserved.

Within the park, you'll find **Île Robinson**, an island in the middle of a lake with a restaurant where you can enjoy a meal or a drink. Simply wait for the barge to whisk you there. Prefer to stay on solid ground? Visit **Le Flore** *(leflore.brussels)* for tapas-style aperitifs or a delightful Sunday brunch. For a refined dining experience, try la **Brasserie de la Patinoire**

 ## DRINKING IN UCCLE: OUR PICKS

Seven: One of Uccle's places-to-be, from breakfast to aperitif. Scrumptious pastries, healthy food and killer coffee. *8am-5pm Mon-Fri, from 9am Sat & Sun*

Chez Musette: A cute bistro decorated with antiques, serving locally sourced food, wines and craft beers. *noon-11.30pm, to 8pm Sun*

Tortue: Yann and Étienne share their love of natural wines (neatly arranged on wooden shelves), beers, cocktails and charcuterie: no fuss, just great taste. *5-10pm*

Café le Refuge: Friendly neighbourhood cafe with comfort food, chalet-style decor and great drinks, morning to evening. *8am-midnight Mon-Fri, from 9am Sat & Sun*

Île Robinson, Bois de la Cambre

(*brasseriedelapatinoire.be*), known for its seafood and fish dishes. It's open noon to 10.30pm Sunday to Monday and noon to 11pm Tuesday to Saturday. And if you're in the mood to dance, head to the nearby **Jeux d'Hiver** (*jeuxdhiver.be*), but be ready to get dressed to the nines.

Ominously Named Lakes & a Ghost Station

A walk in the forest

Head to the **Hippodrome de Boitsfort**, the former horse-racing track, to enter the **Forêt de Soignes**. Follow the track to the Réserve naturelle des **Étangs des Enfants Noyés**, three beautiful lakes with an ominous name. It originated from a watermill owned by Mr Verdroncken, known as the 'mill of the Verdroncken children'. Poor translation (*verdroncken* meaning 'drowned') resulted in the name 'drowned children'. The preserve is ecologically and archaeologically significant, with artefacts from the 3rd and 2nd millennia BCE found here and displayed at the Musée Art & Histoire (p65).

PUTTING ON THE RITZ

When you step off the tram at the Legrand stop, where Avenue Louise meets the Bois de la Cambre in northern Uccle, you'll find a square featuring a bronze statue of a horse rider. If you look a bit further back, you'll discover a gated cul-de-sac lined with stately houses, all meticulously well-kept.

Welcome to **Square des Milliardaires** (Billionaires' Square), one of the most exclusive addresses in Brussels. Officially named Square du Bois, this street is almost privatised and under constant surveillance to ensure the privacy of its well-to-do residents. This area has been home to French industrialists who fled wealth taxes, as well as local entrepreneurs, politicians, and high-ranking diplomats.

 EATING OUTSIDE OF UCCLE: OUR PICKS

Rhubarb Café: Perfect laid-back spot on Place Keym for a sweet or savoury break. Vegans, meat-eaters and families all welcome. *9am-6pm Mon-Fri, to 3pm Sat* €

Babam: Chef Thibaut cooks seasonal dishes in his modern inn-style space of Watermael. Warm, family-inspired vibe. *noon-2pm Wed-Fri, 7-11pm Mon-Fri* €€

Fox Food Market: In the former Royale Belge building (a brutalist stunner), this food court has all-day global eats. Big sunny terrace. *hours vary* €€

Sanzarù: Tastes and scents from Japan and Peru in colourful and classy decor in Woluwe-St-Pierre. *noon-2pm Tue-Fri, 7-10pm Tue-Thu, 7-10.30pm Fri & Sat* €€€

THE FORBIDDEN UNESCO HERITAGE SITE

Along the prestigious Avenue de Tervueren stands the impressive **Palais Stoclet**, a true architectural gem. Built between 1905 and 1911 for wealthy banker Adolphe Stoclet, it was designed by Austrian architect Josef Hoffmann, who had total creative freedom, regardless of expense. The result is a pinnacle of *Gesamtkunstwerk* – a total work of art – where every element, down to the cushions, was custom-designed. Inside, Gustav Klimt created stunning mosaics. A landmark of the Vienna Secession, it's considered Hoffmann's masterpiece and was listed as a UNESCO World Heritage Site in 2009. Unfortunately, it remains closed to the public, due to family restrictions. For now.

Continue through the marshy **Vallon du Vuylbeek** before a long and serene walk in the forest, surrounded by beeches and oaks. Along the way, you'll find the only remaining structure of the forest railroad services: an old shed serving now as storage for the foresters.

On the way back towards the ponds, take a little detour to the left to see the **Memorial to the Victims of the 22/03 terrorist attacks**. Designed by the renowned landscape architect Bas Smets, the memorial is composed of 32 beeches (the number of victims) placed in a circle, as if holding hands, surrounding a circular bench made of 32 stones. Return to the main path and you're back at the Hippodrome.

Birds, Flowers & a Broom
Watermael-Boitsfort's working-class heritage

Today **Watermael-Boitsfort** is essentially a 'bourgeois-bohemian' commune – but it wasn't always that way.

The neighbourhood is home to one of the largest and most beautiful garden cities in Brussels: **Le Logis-Floréal**. Constructed mainly between 1921 and 1930, these two social housing projects emerged from worker cooperatives. The area consists of numerous individual houses with gardens, resembling cottages, arranged around communal squares or picturesque streets lined with cherry and apple trees. Le Logis has green-painted doors and bird-themed street names, while Floréal's houses are yellow with flower-inspired street names. The area has often been used as a movie set.

Le **Coin du Balai** (the 'Broom's corner') has a distinct charm. Tucked away from the rest of Boitsfort on a lush hill, this neighbourhood was built initially to accommodate Marolles residents who were displaced when the Palace of Justice was constructed. Nowadays, the small tightly knit working-class houses have undergone significant changes. The area has become increasingly attractive to affluent newcomers and expats, due to its direct access to the Forêt de Soignes, transforming the village-like atmosphere that once captivated fauvist painter Rik Wouters. His memory still lingers in the streets.

Pinball Wizard World
Vintage arcade games

The arcade game defined pop culture for those who were young from the 1960s to the 1990s. The pinball cabinet, a wooden box with a decorative headboard perched on four metallic legs, is quite aesthetically pleasing. It's no wonder that Ludo, an avid pinball-machine collector, decided to open his **Brussels Pinball Museum** (*brusselspinballmuseum. com*) in Auderghem. And guess what? The machines aren't just for display – they are meant to be played! Ludo's collection, from the 1970s to the 2000s, is spread across three levels. Classic machines like 'Indiana Jones,' 'FunHouse,' and 'Back to the Future' are sure to evoke nostalgia in adults, while giving them the opportunity to introduce their children to

KARTOUCHKEN/SHUTTERSTOCK

Cottage in Le Logis

these timeless games. The 1st floor also includes a few retro arcade games like 'Pac-Man' and 'Street Fighter' for added fun. Visitors pay by the hour, although some machines on the ground floor are still coin-operated for those who don't want to stay long. It's open 11.30am to 11pm Thursday, 11.30am to 11.30pm Friday, noon to 11.30pm Saturday, and noon to 11pm Sunday.

Take the Plunge!

Divers' paradise

Missing the feeling of diving? Head to **Nemo33** *(nemo33. be)*. Its barrel-shaped, springwater pool is one of the world's deepest at 33m. Only tropical fish are missing to create the full illusion! Enjoy diving, try aqua-yoga, or just watch the divers from the **Thai restaurant**. Choose between the jungle-style terrace or dining inside with a view of the underwater action. It's a unique experience with good-value food, especially at lunchtime. The pool is open from 8am to 10.30pm Monday to Friday and from 10am until 10.30pm during the weekend. Prices vary according to the kind of activities you'd like to join.

 DRINKING OUTSIDE OF UCCLE: OUR PICKS

Tulipe: In a corner house near Mérode, this coffee bar charms with exposed brick, jazz tunes, coffee and pastries. *8am-6pm Mon-Fri, 9.30am-6pm Sat & Sun*

36 Baronomie: Swanky-looking bar with a mostly European selection of wines by the glass near Montgomery. Boards and plates to share if hungry. *5pm-12.30am Tue-Sat*

Bar du Patron: Auderghem's closest thing to a pub where regulars gather to relax, drink, sing and dance the night away. *5pm-late, Mon-Sat*

Northwest Brussels

MORE THAN JUST THE ATOMIUM

GETTING AROUND

For the Atomium and Mini-Europe, hop on metro line 6 to Heysel. To visit the Serres Royales de Laeken, take tram 7 or 35 to De Wand, or bus 59 to Serres Royales. Tramline 9 offers a particularly scenic ride to the Koekelberg Basilica. To reach Jette, the train to Gare de Jette is the simplest option. To explore the Cité Moderne in Berchem-Sainte-Agathe, take tram 82 (Schweitzer) or 9 (Goffin), while tram 55 to Tilleul brings you to Evere.

☑ **TOP TIP**

If you're planning on visiting the Serres Royales de Laeken, keep an eye on its website, as the opening is announced only a couple of weeks before (when gardeners estimate that the flowers will be at their most beautiful). Count on being there between late April and early May.

Brussels' northwest is mainly residential and may seem somewhat sleepy and secluded, but it does harbour some worthwhile sights, among them the distinctive Atomium and Heysel. There are more architectural marvels to behold, such as the huge Basilique du Sacré-Cœur de Koekelberg (an Art Deco masterpiece) or the Berchem-Ste-Agathe's modernist 'Cité Moderne'. Jette, a family-oriented village-like district, has the expansive Parc Roi Baudouin, connected to a sprawling marsh shared with neighbouring Ganshoren. Evere is known for housing the secretive NATO headquarters but also the serene Brussels graveyard (where many historical figures are buried) and the Musée de l'alimentation (Foods Museum) located in an old windmill. Laeken, the royal district, is home to the King of the Belgians' palace, and during spring, the Serres Royales de Laeken open their doors to the public. Lastly, the Church of Our Lady of Laeken is the final resting place of Belgium's past monarchs.

A Botanical Crystal Palace

Gorgeous greenhouses

The **Serres Royales de Laeken** (*koninklijke-serres-royales. be*), part of the royal grounds, open only once a year (from mid-April to mid-May). These palaces of iron and glass showcase a stunning variety of plants and flowers (especially fuchsias). Designed by Alphonse Balat at the request of King Leopold II, construction of these remarkable greenhouses began in 1873 and spanned over two decades. The showpiece of this crystal city is the **Winter Garden**, a magnificent dome able to accommodate towering palm trees. While visiting, you'll also see **Queen Elizabeth's cottage**, which she used as a workshop, and from the park, you'll get a beautiful view of the **Japanese Tower**. This pagoda-style tower and the

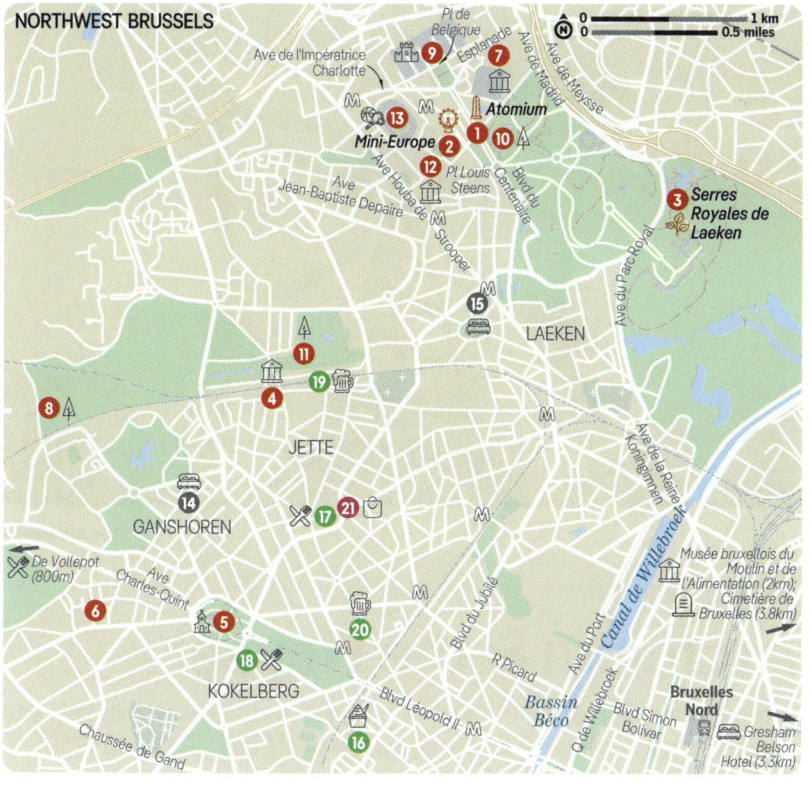

NORTHWEST BRUSSELS

HIGHLIGHTS
1 Atomium
2 Mini-Europe
3 Serres Royales de Laeken

SIGHTS
4 Atelier 34zéro Muzeum

5 Basilique Nationale du Sacré-Cœur de Koekelberg
6 Cité Moderne
7 Design Museum Brussels
8 Marais de Jette-Ganshoren
9 Palais des Expositions

10 Parc d'Osseghem
11 Parc Roi Baudouin
12 Planétarium
13 Stade Roi Baudouin

SLEEPING
14 B&B Basilique
15 Onyx Hotel Expo

EATING
see 1 Atomium Restaurant

16 Frederic Blondeel
17 French Kiss
18 New Luc

DRINKING & NIGHTLIFE
19 Excelsior Stam Cafe
20 Tipsy Tribe

SHOPPING
21 Jaune

accompanying **Chinese pavilion** were originally exhibited at the 1900 Paris World Fair. Leopold II was so taken by them he commissioned architect Alexandre Marcel to build him something similar at the edge of the royal grounds. While the Japanese Tower remains the original building from Paris (incorporating elements from Japan itself), the Chinese pavilion was custom-made, with specially ordered and crafted components from Shanghai.

The Atomium

TOP EXPERIENCE

Atomium & the Heysel

In the 1930s, the Heysel Plateau became an expansive exhibition site for Belgium's centenary. It hosted two World Fairs (1935 and 1958) that significantly affected Brussels' history and cityscape, leaving behind landmarks such as the Palais des Expositions, the national stadium and the peculiar Atomium.

DON'T MISS

Palais des Expositions

The Atomium

Mini-Europe

Design Museum Brussels

Stade Roi Baudouin

Planétarium

Parc d'Osseghem

Palais des Expositions

The first significant building on the Heysel Plateau is the gigantic **Palais des Expositions** (Exhibition Palace, also known as the Centenary Palace). Built to host part of the 1935 World Fair, this Art Deco palace, designed by architect Joseph Van Neck, remains the centrepiece of a series of 12 exhibition halls. It hosts Brussels' largest events, such as the Auto Fair, Batibouw (Construction, Renovation, and Interior Design Fair) and the Made in Asia convention.

PRACTICALITIES

- atomium.be, 10am-6pm, adult/concession : €17/8.50
- minieurope.com, 9.30am-7pm, adult/concession : €23.50/16.80

The Atomium

Funnily enough, the **Atomium** shares a similar story with the Eiffel Tower: it's a construction made of metal, built on purpose for a World Fair (this time in 1958), and it was meant to be dismantled after the event. However, it's still standing, and rightly so, as this monument is so quirky that it embodies the Belgian spirit. It consists of nine metal spheres connected by tubes, representing an iron crystal magnified 165 billion times. The Atomium, imagined by architects André and Jean Polak and engineer André Waterkeyn, was meant to symbolise faith in the advancement of sciences for all humankind in a postwar atmosphere of optimism. It remains one of the stars of Brussels' show. The visit starts with the panoramic view from the top sphere. Not only will you find information about what you see, but also panels presenting the view as it was in 1958. Then, go back down to the lower spheres and learn more about the construction of this iconic building and the 1958 World Fair that had such an effect on Brussels, and its current appearance. This is followed by temporary exhibitions, often based on digital art.

Mini-Europe

This one is for the kids and the kids at heart. **Mini-Europe**, a miniature park, is one of the most visited attractions in Brussels, with no less than 350 monuments chosen from among the 27 EU member states (and the UK) for their architectural value and recreated to the most minute details. The replicas are so well done that, if you take a close-up picture of a monument, it could pass as the real one. However, the park isn't just about walking through miniatures: there are interactive parts where you can trigger an eruption of Vesuvius, the chimes of Stockholm Town Hall, or bring down the Berlin Wall. The **Spirit of Europe** exhibition, supported by the EU, explains briefly how the Union is working and serves as an interesting finale to the visit.

Stade Roi Baudouin

The national football team's home was known as the Heysel Stadium until 1993. Following an extensive renovation, the decision was made to change its name to **Stade Roi Baudouin**, partly to distance itself from the fateful night of 29 May 1985. Before the kick-off of the European Cup final between Juventus and Liverpool, Liverpool supporters breached the (mostly) Juventus fans' section, pressing them against a wall. In the panic, people were crushed, and some trampled to death. Thirty-nine were killed, mostly Italian and Juventus supporters, with over 600 people injured. This tragic event became known as the Heysel Stadium Disaster.

THE DOOMED EUROSTADIUM

The Heysel's fate reflects Belgium's complexity. It was deemed too outdated for hosting one of the Euro 2020 matches, so plans were made to build a new stadium in Grimbergen, on Brussels' outskirts but situated in Flanders. It sparked disputes between the city, developer and Flemish authorities. UEFA withdrew Brussels' match organisation in 2017, acknowledging the project's delays. The project was withdrawn in shame and abandoned.

TOP TIPS

● In the top sphere, you will find the **Atomium Restaurant** (p96) (reservation highly recommended).

● Pay a visit to the **Design Museum Brussels**: great collection of interior design since the 1950s, and the price is included in the Atomium ticket.

● Need a breath of fresh air? Go relax at **Parc d'Osseghem** and its English-style gardens.

● Save much-needed euros by buying a combined Atomium-Mini-Europe ticket *(adults/teens/children €34/26.60/21.90)*.

● If you visit the Brussels **Planétarium**, present your Atomium ticket to get €1 off.

The Koekelberg Basilica is so vast that it houses two museums. The largest is the **Musée d'Art Religieux Moderne**, which safeguards the church's most valuable artworks alongside numerous pieces acquired over the years. It aims to show that religion and faith can be expressed through contemporary art and need not remain classical or static.

The second is the **Musée des Sœurs Noires** (Black Sisters' Museum). This religious order was particularly prominent in Belgium but could not escape secularisation. The convent relocated outside Brussels and donated its most treasured possessions – fine furniture, paintings, porcelain, lace, and more – to the Basilica, where they are now on display.

The Monster of Faith

Art Deco, art and religion

The **Basilique Nationale du Sacré-Cœur de Koekelberg** (Koekelberg Basilica; *basilicakoekelberg.be*) stands as 'the other monster' of the Brussels landscape with the Palace of Justice (p61). The sixth largest church in the world took 65 years to be completed (1905–70) and is a prime example of neo-Byzantian-inspired Art Deco. Sitting at the end of a triumphal boulevard crossing Parc Elisabeth, its huge green copper cupola can be spotted from very far away. Its cavernous interior shelters a Head of Christ sculpted by Constant Permeke, 31 engravings by Joan Miró and works by James Ensor. Don't hesitate to go up to the cupola's platform for an amazing view. The church is open 9am to 5pm from May to September, and from 10am to 4pm from October to April.

Wodek's Wonderland

Art meets food, meets vodka

The quirky **Atelier 34zéro Muzeum** (*atelier340muzeum.be; adult/child €10/2*) located near Jette station is the brainchild of artist Wodek, who initiated the project about 40 years ago. It has since grown, incorporating no fewer than 10 buildings and a garden. His primary objective is to promote contemporary art, and his preferences often lean towards the provocative and the humorous.

In addition to its permanent collection, the museum (open 11am to 7pm) organises temporary exhibitions, workshops and cooking classes. Visitors can also enjoy the garden and cafe, which serves homemade food, including Polish specialities and even vodka straight from Wodek's village.

Marshes & the City

Biodiversity and tranquility unite

One of the great unsung green spaces in Brussels is the **Marais de Jette-Ganshoren** (*gardens.brussels/fr/espaces -verts/marais-de-ganshoren*). Stuck between two railways, this reserve is the last remnant of the Molenbeek River valley marsh and a little treasure of biodiversity: rare plants, birds (mallards, herons, falcons), amphibians and even grass snakes are present here. The ever-flowing water adds an

EATING IN THE NORTHEAST: OUR PICKS

Frederic Blondeel: Workshop of an award-winning chocolatier. Enjoy pralines or homemade ice cream. *9.30am-6.30pm Mon-Sat, noon-6pm Sun* €

French Kiss: Classic surf-and-turf dishes, such as Chateaubriand, oysters, and mussels served in inviting brick-walled venue. *noon-2pm, 6.30-10pm Tue-Sun* €€

New Luc: Old-timey restaurant serving Belgian classics and meat. Don't miss its cassoulet. *noon-2.30pm Tue-Fri &Sun, 6.30-10pm Tue-Sat* €€

Atomium Restaurant: Just for the experience of dining at the Atomium's top sphere: honest Belgian cuisine. *10am-5pm & 6pm-midnight Mon-Sat, 10am-5pm Sun* €€

atmospheric and poetic touch to this sanctuary. However, it's important to note that some trails may be temporarily inaccessible, depending on rainfall and water levels. The opening hours vary.

Fit for A King

Family park

At the end of the marshes, just across Ave des Expositions, the contrast with the landscaped grounds of **Parc Roi Baudouin** is striking. Named after the uncle of King Philip, the park is dotted with lawns, orchards, woods, ponds and play areas, all well-suited for a family-oriented municipality like Jette. You could easily spend an afternoon exploring the various sections of the park. Among its interesting features are the remains of a Gallic-Roman villa uncovered in the late 1960s. Although the structure is quite degraded, you can still see the outlines of the walls marked by blue stones. It is quite busy with locals when the sun is out. **Guinguette Fabiola**, an open-air cafe, welcomes you with cold drinks and fresh food from the end of April to the end of September.

Faraway Evere

Of gravestones and food

Residential Evere feels far removed from the hustle and bustle of central Brussels. Perhaps that's why the **Cimetière de Bruxelles** – open 8.30am to 4pm – was established here. More park than cemetery (it's the city's largest), it was designed as a haven for the dead. Stately monuments line its alleys (the British Waterloo Memorial is particularly striking) and many famous Bruxellois are buried here, including mayor Jules Anspach and painter Jacques-Louis David.

Tucked away in an older part of Evere, the **Musée Bruxellois du Moulin et de l'Alimentation** (*moulindevere. be; adult/concession/child €4/2/0*) centres on an old windmill, illustrating the history of flour-making and hosting exhibitions on our relationship with food. Surrounded by a charming park, it's a firm favourite with children. The museum is open 10am to 12.30pm and 1.30pm to 5pm Tuesday to Saturday, and 1.30pm to 5pm on Sunday.

CITÉ MODERNE

Architecture enthusiasts venture a bit out of the way to visit la **Cité Moderne**, blocks of social housing built in the modernist style. Inspired by the British garden-cities, architect Victor Bourgeois and landscape architect Louis Van der Swaelmen designed a neighbourhood of over 200 houses, in 15 different styles, with private gardens, common areas and shops. Completed in 1925, it was among the first social housings to use concrete as a building material. The city, with its white facades, clean lines, and Cubist shapes was way ahead of its time, and is regarded as one of the finest garden cities, along with the **Logis-Floréal** (p90). Unfortunately, some of the houses are in dire need of a renovation.

DRINKING IN THE NORTHWEST: OUR PICKS

Tipsy Tribe: A 'brewstillery' in a beautiful Koekelberg house. Try the Chaotique beer and chocolate liqueur. *11am-4pm Mon, noon-7.30pm Thu-Sat*	**Excelsior Stam Cafe:** A true blue *stamcafé* (pub) in Jette, with wooden furniture, enamel plates on the wall and a long list of beers. *4pm-late*	**De Vollepot:** Berchem's cute bar-café is a charmer, with its squeaky wooden floor, beautiful antique counter and large terrace. *7am-midnight Mon-Fri, from 10am Sat & Sun*	**Jaune:** Family-friendly bookshop in Jette hides a lovely cafe out back. Enjoy a sweet break with a book! *10.30am-6.30pm Mon-Sat, 10am-1pm Sun*

Outskirts of Brussels

GOING BEYOND THE CAPITAL

GETTING AROUND

During your time in Brussels, you'll use the STIB/MIVB for public transport. If you don't have a car or bike, you can rely on De Lijn, Flanders' public-transport company, to reach the destinations mentioned below (except the AfricaMuseum, which is linked by STIB's tram 44).

Note that the Flemish municipalities surrounding Brussels can be reached by bus/train with a STIB Brupass XL ticket *(stib-mivb.be/buy/ metro-tram-bus -and-train-travel -in-the-brussels -capital-region-with -brupass).*

Often overshadowed by the capital, the outskirts are clearly worthy of exploration. Now a mainly French-speaking city, Brussels is surrounded by Flemish territory, serving as a reminder of its Dutch-speaking past before French took over as the language of power. The periphery is attracting urban dwellers seeking respite from the city's hustle and bustle, gradually changing the demographic, and linguistic, landscape.

History and nature buffs will feel lucky in this area teeming with castles (the medieval Kasteel van Beersel and the historic Kastel van Gaasbeek), green spaces (the Hallerbos with its famous bluebells, the Meise Botanical Gardens) and museums like the AfricaMuseum, which add to the region's cultural wealth.

Biking enthusiasts will find joy in exploring the countryside of Pajottenland, evoking scenes from Flemish Old Masters paintings. And don't miss a visit to a lambic brewery, a must-do in this captivating region.

Belgium's True Colonial Narrative
Slowly deconstructing colonial history

Your visit to the **AfricaMuseum** *(africamuseum.be; adult/ concession/under 18 €13/10/free)* begins before you even arrive. Tram 44 from Montgomery takes you along the scenic Avenue de Tervueren, originally built to link the Parc du Cinquantenaire with the Royal Museum for Central Africa.

The institution was established in 1898 on the impulsion of King Leopold II to glorify the colonisation of the Congo (now the Democratic Republic of the Congo). The museum we see today opened in 1910. From 1885 to 1908, the Congo Free State had been a private possession of the king. It was characterised by brutal exploitation, forced labour, malnutrition and human rights abuses, killing millions in

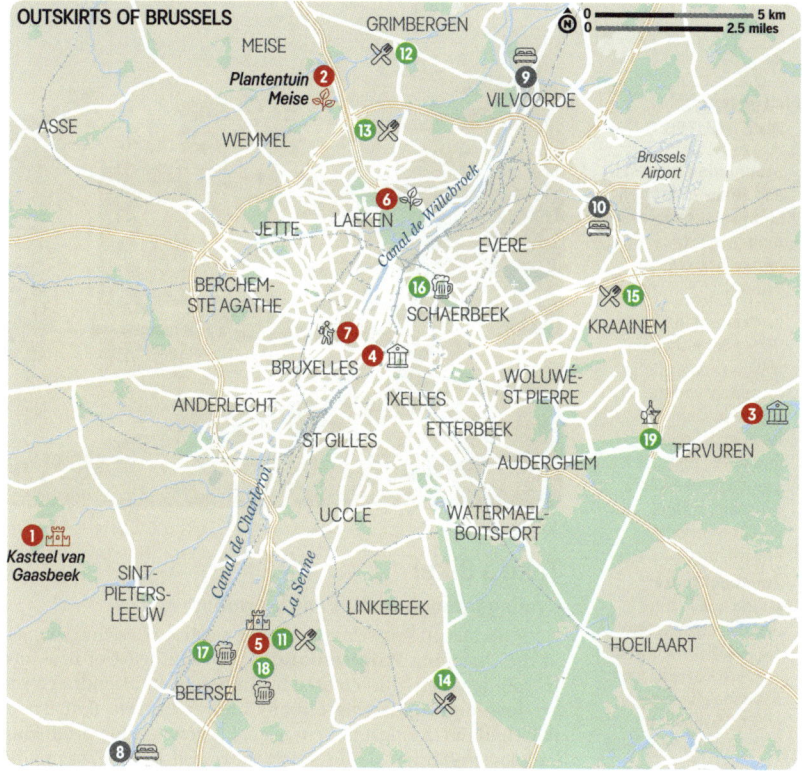

HIGHLIGHTS
1 Kasteel van Gaasbeek
2 Plantentuin Meise

SIGHTS
3 AfricaMuseum
4 Hôtel de Ville
5 Kasteel van Beersel

6 Serres Royales de Laeken

ACTIVITIES
7 Bazaar Trottoir

SLEEPING
8 Hotel Hallensis
9 Lodge Vilvoorde

10 Van der Valk Hotel Brussels Airport

EATING
11 3 Fonteinen Restaurant
12 Het Fenikshof
13 In de Patattezak
14 Marlu

15 Maxime Collin

DRINKING & NIGHTLIFE
16 Brasserie de la Mule
17 Brouwerij 3 Fonteinen
18 Oud Beersel
19 Soko Rooftop

the process. This led to such international outcry it forced Leopold to reluctantly relinquish the Congo to Belgium as a colony (until the Congo gained independence in 1960). Read more on p302.

The museum harbours an impressive collection covering ethnography, archaeology, geology, mineralogy, zoology, music from the Congo but also from Rwanda, Burundi (which became Belgian protectorates after WWI) and neighbouring countries; some of the exhibits are of questionable provenance. After an extensive renovation and a lot of soul-searching, it reopened in 2018 with a much-needed new museography, challenging the colonisation myth and exploring its effect in Africa and in Europe.

☑ **TOP TIP**

If you want to visit the famous Hallerbos while the bluebells are in bloom (April to May), there is a free shuttle service from Halle station on weekends.

Stéphanie Zawadski
and Jean-Sébastien
Liébin share some of
their favourite cycling
routes in/around
Brussels.

La Promenade Verte:
Sixty kilometres of
walking and cycling
routes around the
Brussels-Capital
Region, divided
into seven parts. A
great way to explore
Brussels' natural
and peri-urban
environment.

Zuunbeekroute:
A long ride in the
Flemish countryside
close to Brussels and
easily accessible from
the canal. It's a great
way to discover the
beautiful Pajottenland
while learning about
the cycling nodes
system.

Royalroute: You'll
pass through the
magnificent Tervuren
Park and Forêt de
Soignes, visit Kasteel
van Huldenberg
and discover the
unexpected grape
fields on the outskirts
of Brussels.

Take a Bike!
Cycling through castles and breweries

Hop on a bike in Brussels and in a few pedal strokes, find yourself
in the charming **Pajottenland**, to the southeast of Brussels.
Its rolling green hills, crossed by the Senne and Dendre rivers,
are fertile grounds where many breweries have flourished.
Pajottenland, alongside Brussels, is renowned for producing
lambic-based beers (p36). Explore the region, following a cycling
nodes itinerary that you can customise based on length and
points of interest. Depending on your itinerary, you'll come
across several castles – in **Beersel**, **Gaasbeek** and **Sint-Pieters-
Leeuw** – and famed breweries such as **Oud Beersel** and **3
Fonteinen** (in Beersel) and **Lindemans** (in Sint-Pieters-Leeuw).

The **Kasteel van Gaasbeek** (*kasteelvangaasbeek.be; adult/
concession/under 18 €12/8/free*) has a long, tumultuous and rich
history. First built in 1240 to protect Brabant and Brussels, it was,
oh the irony, destroyed by Brussels city troops seeking revenge
for the assassination of the popular councillor Everard t'Serclaes
(whose statue can be seen on the left side of the Brussels city
hall; p59). The castle, renovated in the late 19th century, is now
a museum with remarkable gardens. It's open 10am to 6pm.

DRINKING IN THE OUTSKIRTS: OUR PICKS

Brouwerij 3 Fonteinen:
One of the top lambic
beer breweries with
a fantastic taproom.
*2-8.30pm Fri-Sat,
1-7.30pm Sun*

Het Fenikshof: The
Grimbergen Abbey is a
brewery site, also with a
restaurant and hop yard.
noon-9pm

Soko Rooftop:
Stunning rooftop with a
360-degree view over
the Forêt de Soignes in
Kraainem. *5pm-1am Mon-
Sat, 11am-3pm Sun*

Oud Beersel: Another
top lambic brewery that
does not shy away from
experimenting (rhubarb or
walnut-infused lambics).
*2-10pm Thu-Fri, 10am-
10pm Sat, 11am-6pm Sun*

Château de Bouchout

The **Kasteel van Beersel** *(visitbeersel.be/Kasteel-Beersel; adult/concession/under 18 €5/2/free)*, on the other hand, is a fairy-tale-like moated castle straight out of the 15th century. It's open 10am to 6pm, Tuesday to Sunday.

Plants Paradise

Gardens, greenhouses and more

A short journey north of Brussels, the **Plantentuin Meise** *(plantentuinmeise.be; adult/concession/child €15/7/6)* is a plant lover's wonderland. Actually, it's one of the largest botanical gardens in Europe, spanning 94 hectares of greenhouses, gardens and parks. You can easily spend a whole day here. It's open 10am to 6pm.

Among the stars of the garden are the delicate **Ballat Greenhouse** (named after the architect who built the Serres Royales de Laeken; p92), the **Plants Palace**, an enormous greenhouse featuring specimens from all around the world representing different climates; and the historical gardens, where various facets of European garden design await discovery before visiting the exhibition inside the **Château de Bouchout**.

For young visitors, the 1km-long barefoot path is a treat, engaging them in guessing what they're walking on.

HALLERBOS, THE BLUE FOREST

Every year from mid-April to mid-May, social-media feeds are flooded with photos of a sun-dappled forest floor blanketed in soft blue-violet hues: the wild hyacinths (bluebells) of **Hallerbos** are in bloom. Thousands of visitors make the trip to witness nature's short-lived spectacle – so many, in fact, that trails had to be fenced off to stop overenthusi-astic selfie-seekers from trampling the flowers. Yes, the Hallerbos owes its oh-so-modern fame to social media. A blessing or a curse? You be the judge, but know that the wood is worth visiting in any season!

 EATING IN THE OUTSKIRTS: OUR PICKS

3 Fonteinen Restaurant: Not to be confused with the brewery. Belgian classics and lambic-based beers in Beersel. *noon-2pm & 6-9.30pm Fri-Mon €€*

In de Patattezak: In Grimbergen, discover 'Belgian spaghetti', freshly made, in a brown cafe decor. *noon-2pm Mon-Fri, 5-10pm Sun-Thu, 5pm-midnight Fri & Sat €€*

Marlu: Marlu's reputation extends beyond Sint-Genesius-Rhode with its seasonal, plant-focused cuisine and memorable, intimate meals. *noon-2pm & 7-9pm €€*

Maxime Collin: Gas-tronomic restaurant in Kraainem, where French cuisine meets global influ-ences in a subtle balance. *7.30-10pm Tue-Sat, noon-2pm Thu-Fri €€€*

Places We Love to Stay

€ Budget   €€ Midrange   €€€ Top End

The Pentagon   MAP p54

Auberge de Jeunesse Jacques Brel € HI-affiliated, no-frills hostel with a great bar, lovely courtyard, and free organic breakfast – simple, but with everything you need for a solid stay.

LATROUPE Grand Place € Near the Bourse, this hotel/hostel has dorms for budget travellers and private rooms for those needing privacy, plus a lively bar and communal space.

Made in Catherine €€ With just a few rooms, this cosy stay provides a warm welcome and free drink. Expect exposed beams, vibrant touches, comfy beds and local goodies.

Art de Séjour B&B €€ This charming B&B near the Rainbow Village has just two rooms, a two-night minimum stay, and generous breakfasts prepared by welcoming host Mario.

Craves €€ Superbly located, Craves oozes sexiness with its boudoir-like and velvet-clad rooms. Succulent Levantine food at its restaurant: Le Conteur.

La Senne €€ Charlotte hosts guests in her inviting corner-house and serves breakfast in her cosy downstairs cafe. Just a handful of rooms, each with its own colour scheme.

Hôtel Amigo €€€ Let impeccably polite staff usher you into Brussels' top address. Behind a Flemish facade lie stylish rooms with Art Deco flair, surreal touches and decorative Belgian icons.

Juliana Hotel €€€ This luxurious mansion-like hotel blends neoclassical charm and contemporary art with exquisite decor throughout, and a Murano glass mosaic pool as the showpiece.

European Quarter   MAP p64

B & B Place Jourdan €€ Stylish little B&B with some '50s-type furnishings, colourful touches and a breakfast buffet, which includes freshly baked bread and croissants.

Aloft Brussels Schuman €€ A short walk from Parc du Cinquantenaire, this relaxed hotel has bright loft-style rooms, walk-in showers and cocktails at the lively Wxyz bar.

Hôtel de Maître de Vaughan €€ Charming historic guesthouse, once King Leopold II's love nest for his mistress, Blanche Delacroix, the Baroness de Vaughan.

Stanhope Hotel €€€ Despite a corporate makeover, the Stanhope's public spaces retain their English manor charm. Breakfast beneath the magnolia trees in the courtyard remains a delight.

St-Gilles, Ixelles & Forest   MAP p72

Le Berger €€ Once a discreet lovers' hotel, Le Berger keeps its 1930s sultry charm after renovation. Guests also enjoy access to Le Jardin Secret's shared pool.

The Scott €€ Close to Avenue Louise, The Scott immerses guests in Gatsby's era with roaring '20s decor, retro cocktails, and elegant rooms draped in rich colours.

Jam Hotel €€ Jam embraces raw concrete and bold colours, with industrial-chic rooms, a rooftop plunge pool, and bar with cosy vibes and standout gin and tonics.

L-Avenue €€ This boutique palace has bright suites with kitchenettes, a copper-toned bar, sunny terrace, attentive staff, concierge service and a generous breakfast. Ideal for longer stays.

Maison Flagey €€€ Art Nouveau flair at this characterful B&B near Flagey. Be wowed by the entrance staircase and rooms lovingly decorated with period furniture.

The Hotel €€€ Modestly named, The Hotel has sleek rooms, stunning views, and a 25th-floor spa open in 2025 – one of the city's highest wellness escapes.

Along the Canal   MAP p79

Meininger Bruxelles City Center € Set in a restored brewery by the canal, this stylish hostel has spacious rooms (dorms and private), a beautiful bar, kitchen, laundry and bike rentals.

The Standard €€ Open in 2025, this hotel channels a playful '60s-'70s vibe throughout, from lobby to rooms. Don't miss Lila29, Belgium's highest rooftop bar-restaurant. Particularly caring staff.

Urban Yard €€ Close to Gare du Midi, Urban Yard blends industrial style with botanical touches. Zen vibes, family rooms, cute garden and a good breakfast (at an additional cost).

Yooma Urban Lodge €€ Comfy Yooma celebrates Franco-Belgian comics with themed rooms (for two to six guests) a game room, cinema, spa, comics library, board games and a terrace. A family favourite.

South & East of Brussels   MAP p86

Auberge des 3 Fontaines € By Forêt de Soignes, this hostel provides practical dorms, private rooms, a bar, a kitchen, and easy access to public transport. Perfect for nature lovers.

La Maison Chantecler €€ Françoise and Alain pamper their guests in their 1906 Anglo-Norman Uccle villa. Four charming rooms, a

cottage and an outdoor pool set in a lush garden.

Aspria Royal La Rasante €€ La Rasante's on-site hotel in Woluwé, built in a converted farm, gives guests full access to the upscale wellness club's spa, pool, gym and grounds.

Mix Brussels €€ Set in a 1970s landmark building, Mix impresses with bold design, vast luxe rooms, pools, spa, gym and one of Brussels' best breakfasts.

Northwest Brussels   MAP p93

Onyx Hotel Expo € Simple, efficient hotel conveniently located near the Atomium and ING Arena. Soundproofing could be better, but the staff's friendliness makes up for it.

Gresham Belson Hotel € Conveniently located between the airport (with free shuttle on request) and the city centre, this no-frills hotel could use a refresh but does the job.

B&B Basilique €€ Hostess Dominique welcomes you in her fully equipped guest studio by the Koekelberg Basilica. Belgian hospitality and a lovely terrace.

Outskirts of Brussels   MAP p99

Van der Valk Hotel Brussels Airport €€ This full-service hotel by the airport has it all (large rooms, restaurant, shuttle...), but its single, gadget-filled 'Superbox' rooms with common lounge really stand out.

Lodge Vilvoorde €€ The former prison-turned-hotel might well keep you as a willing prisoner. The original brick architecture has been cleverly preserved, and each room is unique.

Hotel Hallensis €€ Ready to bike the countryside? This fun, sleek small hotel in Halle rents them out. There is also a regional products shop on the ground floor.

Mix Brussels

GHENT, BRUGES & NORTHWEST BELGIUM

For places to stay
in Ghent, Bruges
& Northwest
Belgium, see
p154

INNA SHPORT/SHUTTERSTOCK

Above: Medieval architecture, Ghent (p110); Right: Nieuwpoort beach (p143)

Researched by
Helena Smith

Ghent, Bruges & Northwest Belgium

MEDIEVAL CITIES AND AN EVOCATIVE COASTLINE

Gorgeous cities with gabled buildings lining their canals offer rich artworks and fabulous food, while coastal dunes harbour the troubled story of two world wars.

The provinces of East Flanders (Oost-Vlaanderen) and West Flanders (West-Vlaanderen) make up Northwest Belgium, though they comprise only around half of the total Flemish region that covers the whole of northern Belgium.

The top highlights here are a series of enticing cities featuring fabulous medieval marketplaces, cobbled streets, belfries and *begijnhoven*. But it's beautiful Bruges and somewhat grittier Ghent – each with atmospheric age-old waterways – that steal the show. Bruges is home to the breathtaking Belfort and a cache of spectacular architecture, while Ghent boasts Art Nouveau buildings alongside the gables plus a big student population. Both cities helped foster a flowering of medieval art, particularly the jewel-bright work of the Flemish Primitives,

that remains as absorbing as the Italian Renaissance.

Buffer your explorations with the dunes and beaches of the Belgian coast, whose excellent tram service links a series of blustery coastal settlements, from high-end Knokke to pretty De Haan to lively Ostend. A key location during both world wars, the coast and surrounding area feature some wonderful museums that bring recent history painfully to light. The thought-provoking WWI sites and cemeteries of the Ypres Salient, and Ypres' Flanders Field Museum are also fascinating.

Explorations by train or bike of the landscapes of the 'Flemish Ardennes' around Geraardsbergen complete a gently compelling picture. It doesn't take long to understand why folks keep falling for Flanders.

THE MAIN AREAS

GHENT
Medieval and modern at once. **p110**

BRUGES
Picture-perfect postcard town. **p121**

OSTEND
Queen of the Belgian coast. **p138**

YPRES
Drenched in WWI history. **p146**

North Sea

0 ____ 20 km
0 ____ 10 miles

Bruges, p121

With its dreamy historic city centre and breathtaking canals around every corner, Bruges draws huge numbers of visitors.

Ostend, p138

This 12th-century fishing village has outgrown its humble origins and become an economic, cultural and artistic force to be reckoned with on the Belgian coast.

Vlissingen

Knokke-Heist

Zeebrugge

Blankenberge

De Haan   N34   Lissewege

Ostend
(Oostende)

Bredene   N9

Oostburg

Sluis   N49

Damme

Bruges (Brugge)

Eeklo

A18   E40

Nieuwpoort

St-Idesbald   Koksijde

De Panne

Veurne

Diksmuide

N8   Lo

IJzer

Oostvleteren

Dunkerque

N33

Torhout

N35   E403

E40   A10

Deinze

N35

Lys

Roeselare

Langemark

Poperinge

Ypres
(Ieper)

Cassel

Dranouter

HAZEBROUCK

FRANCE

Armentières

LILLERS

N19

Menen
(Menin)

Comines
(Komen)

Kortrijk

E17

Mouscron
(Moeskroen)

Tourcoing

Roubaix

Lille

Schelde

Ypres, p146

A key site during WWI, Ypres has become a beacon of peace and hope – and a stark reminder of the horrors of the past.

Find Your Way

Major sights are concentrated in heritage-rich Ghent and Bruges, historic Ypres and seaside resort Ostend. Public transport services within and between the cities are reliable and frequent. Otherwise, opt for a rental car or bike.

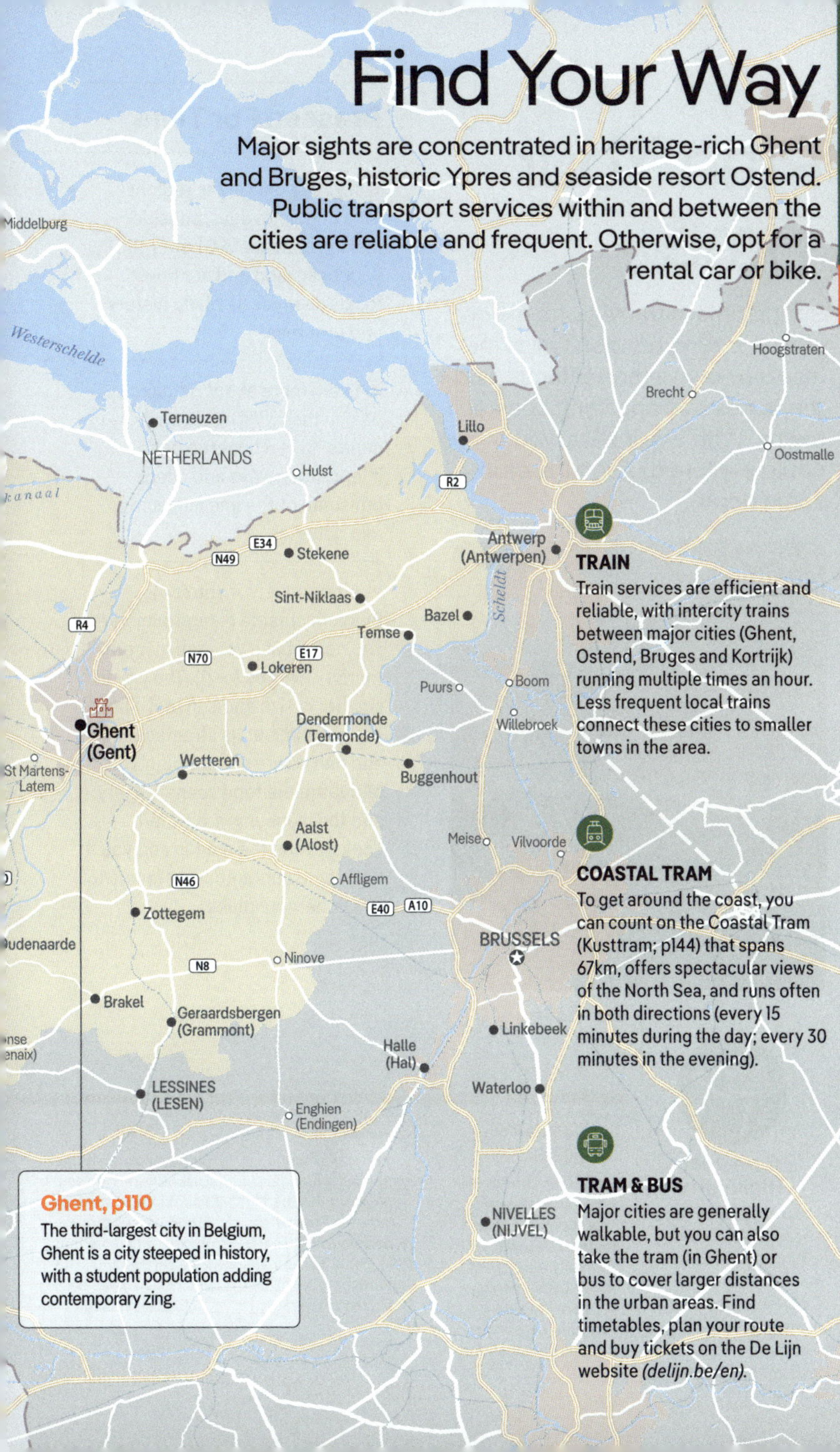

TRAIN

Train services are efficient and reliable, with intercity trains between major cities (Ghent, Ostend, Bruges and Kortrijk) running multiple times an hour. Less frequent local trains connect these cities to smaller towns in the area.

COASTAL TRAM

To get around the coast, you can count on the Coastal Tram (Kusttram; p144) that spans 67km, offers spectacular views of the North Sea, and runs often in both directions (every 15 minutes during the day; every 30 minutes in the evening).

TRAM & BUS

Major cities are generally walkable, but you can also take the tram (in Ghent) or bus to cover larger distances in the urban areas. Find timetables, plan your route and buy tickets on the De Lijn website (delijn.be/en).

Ghent, p110

The third-largest city in Belgium, Ghent is a city steeped in history, with a student population adding contemporary zing.

Plan Your Time

Spend time in the region's major cities for sure, but don't miss the lesser-known inland villages, and the dunes and engaging coastal towns. With two weeks, you could explore this small area in some depth.

STUDIO-ANNIKA/GETTY IMAGES

Damme village (p133)

Pressed For Time

● If you're only in the regions for a couple of days, consider making handsome **Ghent** (p110) your base, and find out how locals seamlessly blend history and progress.

● Learn more about Belgium's past in the city's historic city centre, take a boat trip on the inland waterways and check out some of the fine museums and galleries.

● Alternatively, if you're in Belgium outside of high summer, you could base yourself in more touristy **Bruges** (p121). The city is smaller in size and can feel a little set in aspic, but its streetscapes and canals are outstandingly beautiful, the food scene is tasty and the museums are superb. Look beyond the gables and you'll find some contemporary facets to this venerable place.

Seasonal Highlights

Like the rest of the country, northwest Belgium has moderate weather year-round – the perfect climate for a wide range of religious and sporting events, festivals and gatherings.

JANUARY/ FEBRUARY

With a focus on Flemish film and television productions, **Film Festival Ostend** (p142) is a truly local event. As well as screenings, there are acting masterclasses and a short film competition.

APRIL

Every year in spring, cycle-loving Flanders is all about this road race: the **Tour of Flanders** (p119). The steep cobbled Muur at Geraardsbergen (p120) is an icon of the race.

MAY

On Ascension Day, the UNESCO-recognised **Procession of the Holy Blood** passes through Bruges, with more than 1700 participants. The procession dates back to at least 1303.

The Best in Three Days

● Take your pick between the fine old cities of **Bruges** (p121) and **Ghent** (p110) and wander historic streets, enjoy the restaurants or explore some of Europe's finest museums and galleries.

● Then hop on a train to the nearby coast, with its spacious sandy beaches and tufty dunes. In **Ostend** (p138), known as the Queen of the Coast, explore the promenade and the unique local art museums.

● Board the **Coastal Tram** (p144) and spend an hour or two people-watching in decadent **Knokke-Heist** (p134), home to an arts centre and a couple of acclaimed restaurants, or head just west of Ostend to the excellent beachside **Atlantikwall Raversyde** museum (p142), which brings the conflicts of both world wars to vivid life.

A Week-Long Stay

● With a week or more, you can explore some smaller places around the major destinations, and uncover the rural character that makes Flanders tick. Near Ghent, the settlements of **Oudenaarde** (p120) and **Geraardsbergen** (p120) offer low-key slow charm, while **Damme** village (p133) just north of Bruges rewards a bike or boat trip up the canal.

● The **Coastal Tram** (p144) opens up almost 70km of absorbing holiday towns such as **De Panne** (p144) and **De Haan** (p135).

● Another option is to brave the winds and explore the coast – and indeed the rest of this region – by bike. The city of **Ypres** (p146) and the surrounding **Salient** (p150) offer a lasting reminder of WWI, when this quiet rural area was immersed in the horrors of war.

JULY
The fabulously raucous **De Gente Feesten** transforms the heart of Ghent into a youthful party, with excellent free music and street theatre, dance workshops, packed streets and alfresco drinking.

AUGUST
MA Festival Bruges, a week-long festival of medieval music, takes place in Bruges in the first week of August. The festival's remit is to intertwine innovation with early music.

OCTOBER
Among the most prestigious film festivals in Europe, **Ghent Film Festival** – first held in 1974 – hands out prizes for Best Film, Best Soundtrack, Best International Short and Best Belgian Student Short.

DECEMBER
Around holiday season, Ghent's city centre transforms into winter wonderland during the **Gentse Winterfeesten** (p111). Visitors will find an ice rink, a Ferris wheel, and 150 stalls selling food, drink and crafts.

Ghent

MEDIEVAL MASTERPIECES | CANAL-SIDE STROLLS | VIBRANT CULTURE

GETTING AROUND

Ghent's city centre is relatively large, but the different districts are well connected by public transport, including smoothly gliding modern trams. Download the De Lijn app *(delijn.be/en)* to find routes, buy tickets and consult up-to-date information.

The seat of the Counts of Flanders, medieval Ghent was a great cloth town that grew to become medieval Europe's largest city after Paris and Constantinople. In the early 19th century, Ghent was the first town in Flanders to harness the Industrial Revolution. Many historical buildings were converted into flax- and cotton-processing mills and the city became known as the 'Manchester of the Continent'.

Despite being one of Belgium's most historic cities, Ghent remains small enough to feel cosy but big enough to be a vibrant, relevant centre for trade and culture. There's a wealth of medieval and classical architecture here, contrasted by post-industrial areas undergoing urban renewal that give the city a gritty-but-good industrial feel.

In the centre, tourists remain surprisingly thin on the ground, but Ghent's large student and youth population means there's always people about, enjoying the city's fabulous canal-side architecture, abundance of quirky bars and restaurants, and some of Belgium's best museums.

Medieval Monuments

Head into Ghent's past

Ghent's UNESCO-listed 14th-century **Belfort** *(historische huizen.stad.gent/en/belfry; adult/child €11/2.20)* or belfry stands 91m high and is topped by a huge and magnificent dragon weathervane: he's become something of a city mascot. You'll meet two previous dragon incarnations on the 350-stair climb to the top (there are elevators to help some of the way). Enter through the **Lakenhalle**, Ghent's cloth hall that was left half-built in 1445 and only completed in 1903. Hear the carillon at 11.30am Fridays and 11am on summer Sundays.

Flanders' quintessential 12th-century stone castle, the **Gravensteen** *(historischehuizen.stad.gent/en/castle-counts;*

✅ TOP TIP

CityCard Gent *(48-/72-hour €42/48)* gives free entrance to all of Ghent's top museums and monuments and allows unlimited travel on trams and city buses, plus a boat trip and a day's free bike hire. It's excellent value. Buy one at participating museums, major bus offices or the **tourist office**.

Belfort

adult/child €13/2.70) comes complete with fairy-tale moat, turrets and arrow slits. It's all the more remarkable considering that during the 19th century the site was converted into a cotton mill. Meticulously restored since, the interior sports the odd suit of armour, a guillotine and torture devices. The lack of furnishings is compensated for with a handheld 45-minute movie guide, which sets a tongue-in-cheek historical costumed drama in the rooms, prison pit and battlements. There's a great castle viewpoint on St-Widostraat.

On the Water

Canals, bridges and boat trips

Ships have been docking on either side of the River Leie since the 11th century. The area on the east bank is known as **Graslei**; **Korenlei** is on the west. There are always people here milling about, wining, dining, or sitting on the stepped riverbank admiring the stunning architecture.

continues on p114

GOOD TIMES IN GHENT

Dating back to 1843, the **Ghent Festivities** *(gentsefeesten.be/en)* take over the inner city for 10 days in July, with free events including live music and workshops.

The main draw is 13 music squares, each with its own style and personality, which have grown organically over the years. Local favourites include Polé Polé (a sultry Latin pop feast on the historic Graslei), Emile Braunplein (a colourful Mardi Gras celebration in the shadow of Ghent's three iconic medieval towers) and Vlasmarkt (the place where merry-makers watch the sun come up after an eventful night).

Any movie fans in town in September should head to the long-standing **Ghent Film Festival**, while December's **Gentse Winterfeesten** (Ghent Winter Festivities) encompass over 150 wooden huts, pine trees and an ice rink.

A good bet for a late night out.

 GHENT'S BEST TRADITIONAL PUBS AND CAFES: OUR PICKS

Dulle Griet: Heavy beams, a heraldic ceiling, barrel tables, lacy lampshades and more than 500 beers. *noon-1am Tue-Sat, to 7pm Sun, 4.30pm-1am Mon*

Het Waterhuis aan de Bierkant: This photogenic classic beer-pub has an interior draped in dried hops, plus three exclusive house beers. *11am-1am*

De Brouwzaele: Local gents unwind with newspapers, and grannies lunch on shrimp croquettes in this classic bar-café set in a former brewery house. *11am-2am*

Het Spijker: Built in the late 12th century, this heavy-beamed stone bar-café is the oldest building on Graslei. *10am-5am*

GHENT

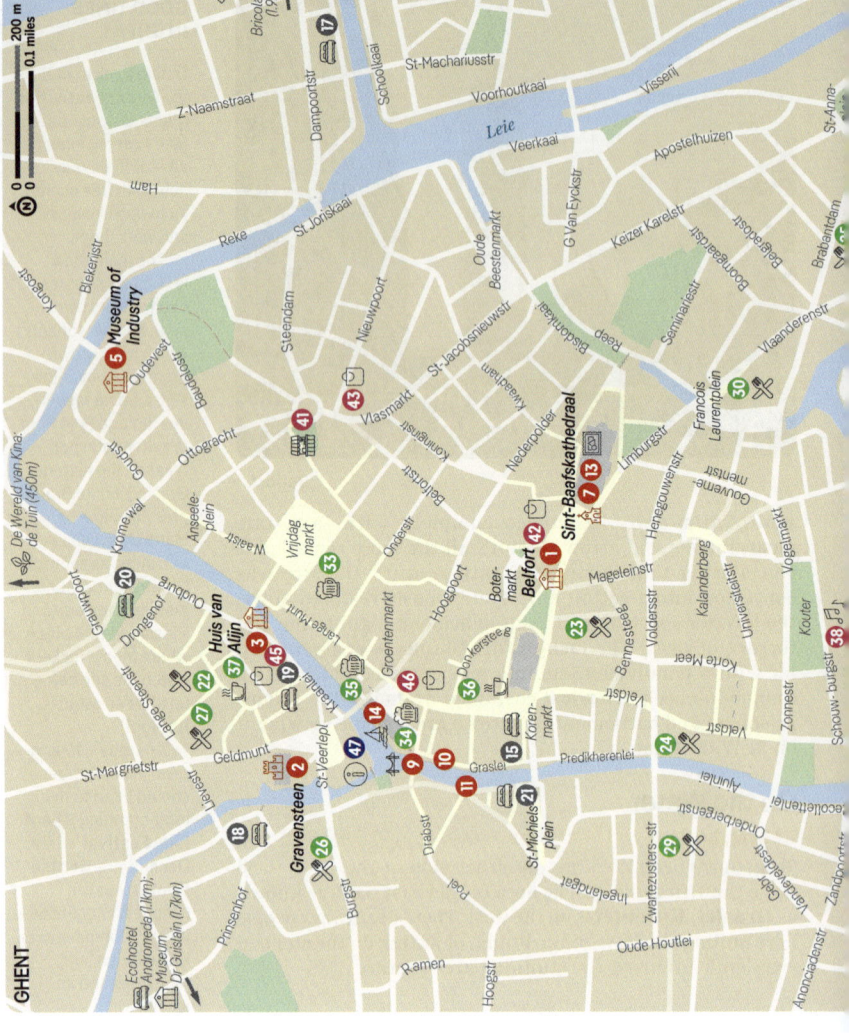

HIGHLIGHTS
1 Belfort
2 Gravensteen
3 Huis van Alijn
4 MSK
5 Museum of Industry
6 S.M.A.K.
7 Sint-Baafskathedraal

SIGHTS
8 De Wereld van
  Kina: het Huis
9 Grasbrug
10 Graslei
11 Korenlei
12 STAM
13 The Adoration
  of the Mystic Lamb

ACTIVITIES
14 Rederij De Gentenaer

SLEEPING
15 1898 The Post
16 ApartGent
  Apartments
17 Big Sleep
18 De Draecke
19 Hotel Harmony
20 Simon Says
21 Uppelink

EATING
22 Karel de Stoute
23 knol&kool
24 Le Botaniste
25 Madam Bakster

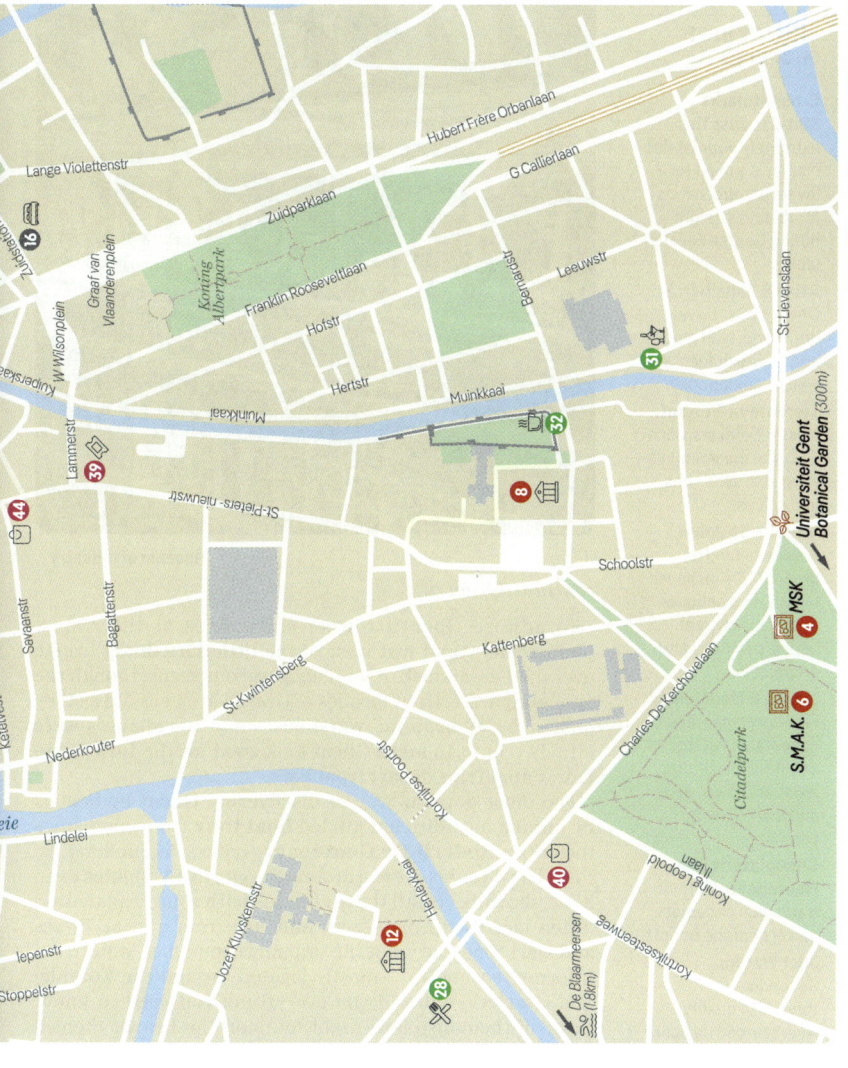

Universiteit Gent
Botanical Garden (300m)

MSK

S.M.A.K.

De Blaarmeersen (1.8km)

26 OAK
27 Roots
28 Soul Kitchen
29 't Oud Clooster
30 Vrijmoed
● **DRINKING &**
NIGHTLIFE
31 De Brouwzaele
32 De Geus
   van Gent
33 Dulle Griet
34 Het Spijker
35 Het Waterhuis
   aan de Bierkant
36 Mokabon
37 Rococo
● **ENTERTAINMENT**
38 Handelsbeurs
   Concert Hall
39 VIERNULVIER
● **SHOPPING**
40 Atlas & Zanzibar
41 Brocantmarkt
   Sint-Jacobs
42 Chocolaterie
   Van Hoorebeke
43 Gallerie St-John
44 Just Waldo
45 Louise & Madeleine
46 Tierenteyn-Verlent
● **INFORMATION**
47 Ghent Tourist Office

GHENT'S BEST SHOPPING

Brocantmarkt Sint-Jacobs: This extremely popular flea market is a must for lovers of retro. It runs for 10 days straight during Gentse Feesten (July).

Atlas & Zanzibar: Ghent's best travel bookshop, with globes and nature guides, as well as guidebooks.

Tierenteyn-Verlent: Mustard-makers since 1790: the museum-like shop also sells jams and spices.

Gallerie St-John: Hidden behind a grand 1748 almshouse facade, this antique shop sells ancient books, paintings and art objects.

Louise & Madeleine: Find contemporary collectables at this beautiful tiled store: jewellery, linen-ware and locally made ceramics.

Chocolaterie Van Hoorebeke: Elegant traditional chocolate maker near the Belfort.

Just Waldo: Secondhand threads of quality: well-sourced designer goods made with classy materials.

Museum of Industry

continued from p111

To admire Ghent's towers and gables at their most photogenic, stand just west of the little **Grasbrug** bridge over the Leie at dusk. It's a truly gorgeous scene, though the appealing waterfront facades of Graslei aren't as old as they look – these 'medieval' warehouses and townhouses were largely rebuilt to make Ghent look good for the 1913 World Fair. Canal trips depart from here.

The most popular way of discovering Ghent by boat is by joining a traditional guided **boat tour** from companies including **Rederij De Gentenaer** *(rederijdegentenaer.be; €10)*. These tours take you around the city in 45 minutes to an hour, showing you all the highlights with some explanation (often laced with dry Ghent humour) from a local. Prices and start times vary, but the shipping companies' waterfront information booths – mostly located around the Korenlei and Graslei – will tell you everything you need to know. Some of them also host night tours on the Leie or themed experiences, so it's always worth asking around.

 EATING IN GHENT: UPSCALE RESTAURANTS

OAK: In a 17th-century building with modern style, dishes reflect the chef's Italian-Brazilian heritage and love for local fish and global flavours. *noon-1.30pm, 7-10pm Tue-Fri* €€€

Karel de Stoute: Superbly presented dishes served in a smart Patershol dining room. *from noon & from 7pm Tue-Fri* €€€

Roots: Upmarket bistro vibe where North Sea fish dominates the menu. Locally sourced organic is key, and the natural wines delight. *noon-3.30pm & 7-10pm Mon-Fri, lunch only Wed* €€€

Vrijmoed: An elegant townhouse restaurant: Gallic-inspired cooking meets fermentation and inspired technical cooking. *noon-1.30pm, 7-9.30pm daily* €€€

Marvellous Museums

Explore local life, industry and psychiatry

Set in a restored 1363 children's hospice complex, delightful **Huis van Alijn** *(Museum of Daily Life; huisvanalijn.be; adult/children €9/2.50)* examines everyday life from the 1890s to the present, with a fabulous emphasis on the 1960s to the '80s. Most of the exhibits are refreshingly self-explanatory, including quaint recreated shop interiors, photos of wedding fashions and a disarmingly moving collage of family home videos. There's always something new happening. The annexed bar-café is a great spot to socialise and sample the local beers.

Shoehorned into a 17th-century former nunnery-hospital complex, **STAM** *(stamgent.be; adult/child €11/2.50)* is a fabulous, architecturally striking, ultra-modern museum that does a very thorough job of explaining Ghent's evolution from prehistoric times to the present. A giant satellite image vividly illustrates the vast extent of the docks; you could spend hours clicking between interactive map views of Ghent in different eras. City treaties and treasures are interspersed with choose-your-own film clips and a chance to peer into the future. Begin your city visit here.

In a five-floor 19th-century mill-factory building, thought-provoking **Museum of Industry** *(Industriemuseum; industriemuseum.be; adult/child €9/2.50)* celebrates Ghent's history of textile production and examines the damaging social effects of 250 years of industrialisation. An extensive collection of heavy mechanical weaving equipment comes deafeningly alive on Tuesday or Thursday mornings around 10am; earplugs are provided. Note: there are great city skyline views from the top floor.

Hidden away in an 1857 neogothic psychiatric hospital on the north side of town, enthralling mental-health **Museum Dr Guislain** *(museumdrguislain.be; adult/child €10/3)* takes visitors on a trilingual, multicultural journey through the history of psychiatry, from gruesome Neolithic trepanning to contemporary brain scans via cage beds, straightjackets, shackles and phrenology. Dr D'Arsonval's extraordinary 1909 radiographic apparatus looks like a Dr Frankenstein creation.

Guilt-free sweet things.

LIVE MUSIC SPOTS

Liz Aku, Ghent resident, singer and music teacher tells us about her favorite live music venues in the city. *@lizakumusic*

Bar Bricolage: An urban oasis in Ghent's Old Docks, with sandy boardwalk paths, cultural programming, live DJs and a relaxed campfire atmosphere.

VIERNULVIER: Known for concerts and parties, particularly in the Concert Hall and the new Club Wintercircus, which has an immersive sound system.

Handelsbeurs Concert Hall: Beautifully restored venue offering an intimate setting for jazz, world, soul music and acoustic performances.

Gentse Feesten: One of Europe's largest cultural festivals, transforming the entire city into a 10-day celebration filled with free live music on every corner, from folk to punk to techno. Crowded but definitely an amazing experience for all ages.

EATING IN GHENT: BEST VEGAN RESTAURANTS & CAKES

Madam Bakster: Sugar-free vegan pastries and desserts – be sure to try the lemon avocado cake. *10am-2pm Wed-Sun* €

knol&kool: With a glass-domed interior and an adjoining funky vegan refill store, this stylish but informal cafe serves fresh and inspiring plant-based dishes. *hours vary* €€

Le Botaniste: Prettily styled like an old-time pharmacy, this vegan buffet hits the spot, and the sweets are great too. *11.30am-9.30pm daily* €€

Soul Kitchen: Fresh, organic and plant-based food prepared with locally sourced ingredients. *noon-2pm & 6-9pm Wed-Sat, noon-4pm Sun* €

The Mystic Lamb

The towering interior of Sint-Baafskathedraal (*sintbaafskathedraal.be; adults/children €16/8*) features some fine stained glass, an unusual combination of brick vaulting with stone tracery and a big original Rubens opposite the stairway that leads down into the partly muralled crypts. However, most visitors come to see just one magnificent work – the Van Eyck brothers' 1432 Flemish Primitive masterpiece, *The Adoration of the Mystic Lamb*.

JAN VAN EYCK/WIKIMEDIA/PUBLIC DOMAIN

The Adoration of the Mystic Lamb, Hubert & Jan Van Eyck

TOP TIP

Consider taking the augmented reality tour. This reveals the *Mystic Lamb's* dramatic story and its impossibly fine detail, such as the chapel window reflected in painted jewels. Viewings of the artwork itself, located in the upper church, are headset-free.

PRACTICALITIES

● intbaafskathedraal.be/en/history/the-ghent-altarpiece
● adult/augmented reality tour €12.50/16
● Mon-Sat 10am-5pm, Sun 1-5pm

Earliest Oil Painting?

A lavish representation of medieval religious thinking, this is one of the earliest-known oil paintings. Completed in 1432, it was painted as an altarpiece by Flemish Primitive artist brothers Hubert and Jan Van Eyck, and has 20 luminous panels, which are in the process of a remarkable restoration.

The work represents an allegorical glorification of Christ's death: on the upper tier sits God the Father flanked by the Virgin and John the Baptist. On the outer panels are the nude Adam and Eve. The lower tier centres on the lamb, symbolising the sacrifice made by Christ, surrounded by religious figures and a landscape dotted with local church towers.

Surviving Against the Odds

The painting has had a troubled history – the Calvinists nearly destroyed it; Austria's Emperor Joseph II was horrified by the nude Adam and Eve, and had the panels replaced with clothed versions (the originals are now back in place); and the painting was marched off to Paris during the French Revolution and was later stolen by the Nazis, who concealed it in an Austrian salt mine during WWII. The panel *De Rechtvaardige Rechters (The Fair Judges)*, stolen in 1934, is still missing.

Fine Art Adventures

Prepare to be dazzled

Styled like a Greek temple and topped by two winged bronzes, superb 1903 fine-art gallery **MSK** *(mskgent.be; adult/youth/ child €13/2.50/free)* introduces a veritable A to Z of great Belgian and other Low Countries' painters from the 14th to mid-20th centuries. Highlights include a happy family of coffins by Magritte, luminist canvases by Emile Claus, and Pieter Brueghel the Younger's 1621 *Dorpsadvocaat* – a brilliant portrait of a village lawyer oozing with arrogance. English-language explanation cards are available in each room.

Close by, Ghent's highly regarded Museum of Contemporary Art – or **S.M.A.K.** *(smak.be; adult/concession €18/3.50)* – is one of Belgium's largest. Works from its 3000-strong permanent collection (dating from 1939 to the present) are regularly curated to complement visiting temporary exhibitions of provocative, cutting-edge installations, which sometimes spill out right across the city.

Green Spaces in Ghent

Explore gardens, parks and lakes

Home to more than 10,000 species, the pièce de résistance of Ghent's 2.75-hectare **Universiteit Gent Botanical Garden** *(gum.gent/en/event/visit-botanical-garden; free)* is its glasshouses, which contain an impressive collection of tropical plants, subtropical plants and succulents, and offer shivering winter travellers what is effectively a free sauna. Some plants are tagged with their endangered status, a sobering note among the gorgeous greenery.

This 7700-sq-m garden and hot-garden of **De Wereld van Kina: de Tuin** *(dewereldvankina.be; adult/child €5.80/3.50)* has more than 1500 plants (plus live bird spiders) and a broader age appeal than its sister museum, the **House**. It's somewhere that kids can come to learn and have fun, while their custodians relax a little and enjoy the natural beauty of the plants and garden. The admission fee grants entry to both complexes.

Another way to sample the outdoors in Ghent is by having a swim at **De Blaarmeersen**, a lake which lies a half-hour walk west of Gent St Pieter's station. There's a kid-friendly recreation centre with water slides on the north side, but most folk just wild-swim in the lake, avoiding an entrance fee. It's a lovely, sociable spot on warm summer days. Paths loop through the trees around the lake, making this a perfect place for a stroll.

BELGIUM'S ART THEFT OF THE CENTURY

On the night of 10 to 11 April 1934, two panels were stolen from the *Mystic Lamb* altarpiece: the *Fair Judges* and *John the Baptist*. John's panel was returned the next month by the self-proclaimed thief (whose ransom demand was refused), but the *Fair Judges* is still missing, its rightful place taken by a replica. The disappearance of this panel has been the subject of countless conspiracy theories.

Several people searched for the panel throughout the years, while many others were suspected of its theft – including police officers, clerics and prominent politicians. Whether it has been destroyed, hidden or kept in private possession, the theft of the *Fair Judges* remains one of the greatest mysteries in the Belgian art world to this day.

DRINKING IN GHENT: BEST BROWN CAFES & COFFEE SHOPS

Rococo: Lit by candles, this classic late-night cafe with carved wooden ceilings is ideal for cosy midnight conversations. *9pm-late Tue-Sun* €€

Mokabon: Ghent's classic old-world coffee shop still serves old-school Belgian coffee with whipped cream. *9am-6pm daily* €

De Geus van Gent: Congenial bar-café with eclectic decor and 20 beers from the barrel: they host regular jam nights and live music. *4pm-3am Mon-Fri, from 7pm Sat* €

't Oud Clooster: This atmospheric cafe was long ago a nunnery, hence the cherub lamp-holders. Well-priced light meals presented with style. *11.30am-2.30 pm & 6-10.15 pm Mon-Sat* €€

Beyond
Ghent

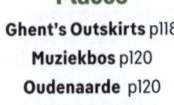

Ghent is centrally located in Flanders:
it's the perfect base for a few days'
exploring of nearby forests and small towns.

Places

Ghent's Outskirts p118
Muziekbos p120
Oudenaarde p120
Geraardsbergen p120

GETTING AROUND

From Ghent,
settlements like
Oudenaarde,
Geraardsbergen and
Aalst are easy to reach
by train: services are
frequent and efficient.
If you're looking to
go to the Muziekbos
('Musical Forest') or
other lesser-known
places around Ghent,
you may want to rent
a car (roads are well
maintained). The area
is mostly flat and very
well set up for cycling:
rent a bike in Ghent,
and transport it by
train to avoid super-
long journeys.

Ghent is the capital of East Flanders, but not the only place in
the area where you can have a good time. Boat trips beyond
the city limits afford some gorgeous views, or head to moated
castles such as Kastel Oiddonk. You'll find countless hikes and
cycling trails, with routes running through the Muziekbos or
'Musical Forest' in the Flemish Ardennes. In early April, these
rural landscapes are also the scenery for one of the biggest one-
day cycling races in Belgium: the suspenseful Tour of Flanders.
The tour runs through the appealing towns of Oudenaarde and
Geraardsbergen, both also worth a visit out of cycling season.
Another seasonal draw is the Aalst Lenten carnival, a colorful
but controversial event.

Ghent's Outskirts

TIME FROM GHENT: **20MIN** 🚗

Beyond the city centre

On fine days, canal cruisers **Rederij De Gentenaer** (p114) add
an extra 10 minutes along Ketelvaart to emerge outside the
Duivelsteen waterfront castle-house, **Geeraard de Duivelsteen**.

Originally constructed around the 13th and 14th centuries,
and reconstructed in 1595 after much pillaging, **Kasteel
Oidonk** *(2-5.30pm Sun Apr-Sep; adult/child €12/4),* replete
with moat, is considered one of the most beautiful in Belgium.

The upmarket suburban villages of **Deurle** and **St-Martens-
Latem** peter out into woodlands. A century ago, this attractive
area was home to symbolist and expressionist artists, notably
Gustave de Smet and Constant Permeke. Today the shady lanes
are dotted with galleries and upmarket rural restaurants.

 EATING AND DRINKING IN OUDENAARDE & GERAARDSBERGEN

The Preacher:
Facing the church in
Geraardsbergsen,
this unexpectedly hip
family-run cafe/bar
dishes up live music and
a wide array of beers. €

La Pomme d'Or: Tiffany-
glass windows, wrought-
iron lamps and 1930s
decor create a welcoming
feel at this Oudenaarde
brasserie-cafe. Set menus
are good value. *noon-
10pm* €€€

't Hemelrijck: A bustling
tavern with a pleasant
outdoor patio, cold local
beer and good-value pub
food. A meal here is the
reward for ascending
Geraardsbergsen's Muur.
noon-9/10pm Thu-Tue €€

De Mouterij: A homely
Belgian affair offering
alfresco dining in a
spacious Oudenaarde
garden. The menu features
grilled meats, seafood,
salads and beer. *10am-
11pm Thu-Sun* €€

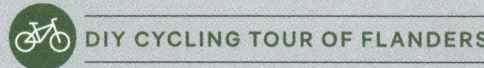

DIY CYCLING TOUR OF FLANDERS

Follow in the cycle tracks of Tour of Flanders heroes on the steep cobbled hills of the Flemish Ardennes.

START	END	LENGTH
Huise	Oudenaarde	34.5km; 3hrs

The first of many cobbled sections in the Tour of Flanders, the ❶ **Huisepontweg** connects the town centres of Wannegem and Huise, along the Castle of Wannegem-Lede.

The Tour climbs may not look like much of a challenge to spectators, but when you're standing at the foot of the ❷ **Oude Kwaremont**, it's a whole different story. At 2.2km, the Oude Kwaremont is the second-longest climb in the course. With its average slope of 4%, it's a slow burn.

Things get tough at the ❸ **Paterberg**, a short but challenging section with a maximum gradient of 20.3%; depending on the route, it can serve

as the last climb of the race. Although the ❹ **Koppenberg** is one of the most dreaded cobblestone hills, with an average gradient of 11.6%, it's rarely the decisive climb of the Tour.

To finish off, head into the medieval city of ❺ **Oudenaarde**, dubbed 'the pearl of the Flemish Ardennes' and primarily known as a dramatic finish point of the Tour of Flanders, where legends have been created.

Next it's time for a well-deserved break at the ❻ **Centrum De Ronde van Vlaanderen**. Here, you can delve into the history of the Tour of Flanders, relive Belgium's most iconic cycling moments – and have a drink in the cycling cafe.

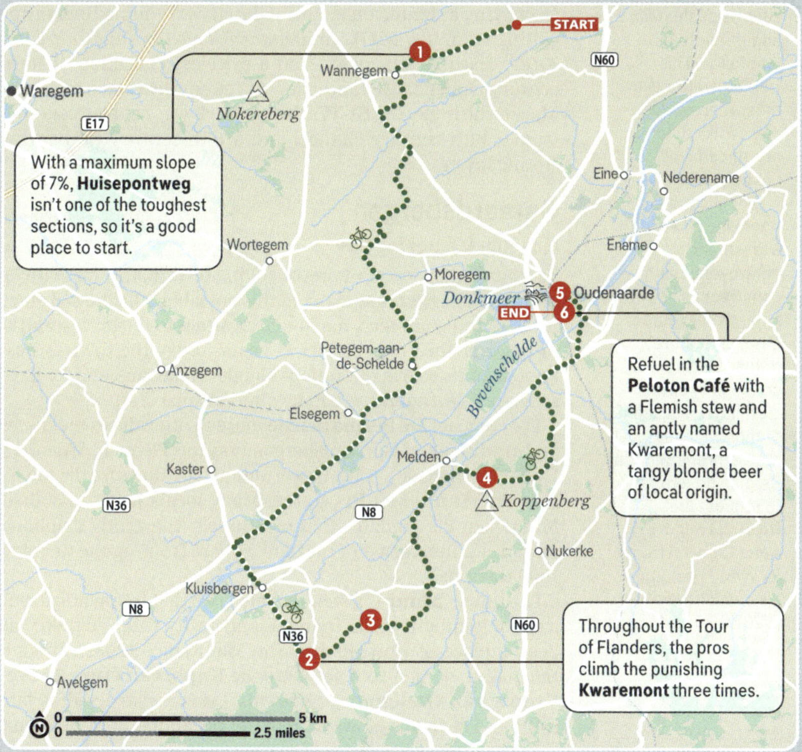

> With a maximum slope of 7%, **Huisepontweg** isn't one of the toughest sections, so it's a good place to start.

> Refuel in the **Peloton Café** with a Flemish stew and an aptly named Kwaremont, a tangy blonde beer of local origin.

> Throughout the Tour of Flanders, the pros climb the punishing **Kwaremont** three times.

THE CONTROVERSIAL AALST CARNIVAL

The Lenten carnival in the town of Aalst dates back to the Middle Ages, and is a tradition of mockery and satire: a float in the 2023 parade showed the Aalst's mayor as Big Brother, in protest against the use of CCTV.

Festivities conclude with the burning of a doll and the untranslatable 'Stoet van de Voil Jeanette' parade, when men dressed as women carry objects such as pushchairs and threadbare umbrellas. This tradition reflects a time when working-class folk couldn't afford carnival costumes.

Some carnival floats have caused widespread controversy, with comic songs about a high-profile murder case, caricatures of the Jewish community and clothing reminiscent of the KKK. This racism prompted the Belgian government to request that UNESCO remove Aalst Carnival from its World Heritage List, which it did in 2019.

Muziekbos

TIME FROM GHENT: **40MIN** 🚌

Forest walks & rides

Just northwest of Ronse is leafy **Muziekbos** (Musical Forest). In this 620-acre area of oak and beech groves, look out for wood nuthatches, black woodpeckers and buzzards. **Geuzentoren** is a folly tower from 1864, while a nearby hill served as a Gallo-Roman burial mound. You'll find hiking trails (5km to 22km), many accessible to wheelchair users, and cycling routes ranging up to 78km.

Oudenaarde

TIME FROM GHENT: **30MIN** 🚆

On your bike

In the 16th and 17th centuries, Oudenaarde was a wealthy rural town famed for its local weavers' elaborate, detailed tapestries. Today, it's brightly adorned cyclists that weave through the streets as the **Tour of Flanders** bike race finishes here. With a handful of niche museums, it's worth considering staying overnight at this very pretty and compact town. Lovers of cycling shouldn't miss the state-of-the-art **Centrum De Ronde van Vlaanderen** *(crvv.be; adult/child €7.50/6),* featuring displays on the history of the race and cycling in general. Staff can help plan your own cycling tour of the Flemish Ardennes or Flanders Fields.

Architectural grandeur

Occupying a significant chunk of the city's stunning Brabantine Gothic stadhuis, **MOU** *(oudenaarde.be/en/mou; adult/child €10/2)* features silverware and a priceless collection of 16th-century Oudenaarde tapestries. At the southwestern corner of Markt, the imposing **St-Walburgakerk** was cobbled together from a 13th-century chancel and a 15th-century Brabantine Gothic tower.

Geraardsbergen

TIME FROM GHENT: **50MIN** 🚆

Museum & a peeing boy

Surrounded by vistas of pretty, rolling terrain, the 'free city' of **Geraardsbergen** has claimed this enviable hillside spot since 1068. Trundle up steep, narrow Grotestraat to the hilltop Markt to uncover the city's historical gems. Today the town is best known for its role in the Tour of Flanders bike race, and for local speciality *Mattentaart* (a flaky almond curd tart).

The compact **De Permanensje** museum introduces the trades and traditions of Geraardsbergen and the Flemish Ardennes. Highlights include a collection of antique costumes for the town's beloved **Manneken Pis** statue. Many locals insist that their Manneken Pis predates that of Brussels: the gently dribbling fountain is in a corner of the main square fronting the turreted 1893 town hall.

The town's **Muur** is a steep cobbled rise that frequently forms a major highlight of the Tour of Flanders. It's believed there has been a place of worship atop the Muur since 1294, although the quaint, domed-roof neo-baroque **Kapel van Onze-Lieve-Vrouw van Oudenberg** *(7am-5pm)* was constructed as late as 1906. The inside glows with scores of candles lit by pilgrims.

Bruges

GABLED BUILDINGS | ARTISTIC TRADITIONS | TRANQUIL BACK STREETS

If you set out to design a fairy-tale medieval town, it would be hard to improve on central Bruges (Brugge in Dutch), one of Europe's best-preserved cities. Picturesque cobbled lanes and dreamy canals link photogenic market squares lined with soaring towers, historical churches and lane after lane of old whitewashed almshouses. Medieval Flemish painters were perhaps the first to use oil paint, kicking off a tradition that rivals that of Renaissance Italy. Bruges' galleries and museums are simply outstanding, with many boldly incorporating contemporary works into their historic collections.

For many, though, the Bruges secret is already out; during the busy summer months, you'll be sharing the magic with a constant stream of tourists in the medieval core. To really enjoy Bruges, stay one or two nights – day trippers miss out on the city's stunning nocturnal floodlighting – and try to visit midweek to avoid weekend crowds.

Marvellous Markt

The historic heart of Bruges

The heart of ancient Bruges, **Markt**, the old market square, is lined with pavement cafes beneath step-gabled facades. The buildings aren't always quite as medieval as they look, but together they create a fabulous scene; even the neogothic former post office is architecturally magnificent. The urban panorama is dominated by the 13th-century **Belfort** *(visitbruges.be/nl/ belfort; adult/child €15/13),* towering 83m above the square like a gigantic medieval rocket. There's relatively little to see inside, but it's worth the mildly claustrophobic 366-step climb for the fine views. Look out through wide-gauge chicken wire for panoramas across the spires and red-tiled rooftops towards the wind turbines and giant cranes of Zeebrugge. Visitor numbers are limited to 70 at once, which can cause queues at peak times.

GETTING AROUND

The medieval city centre of Bruges is compact and walkable: it's also a great place to explore by bike. If you're travelling from the train station, hop on city bus #1 or #2, both of which run through the city centre (you can make contactless payments on board), or take a taxi.

☑ **TOP TIP**

The best times to visit are in spring, when daffodils carpet the tranquil courtyard of the historic **Begijnhof** retreat, or outside of Christmas in winter, when you'll have the magnificent, if icy, town almost all to yourself.

continues on p124

Koningin Elizabethlaan
Ezelpoort
Klaverstr
Vlamingdam
St-Clarastr
Annuntiatenstr
Baliestr
Bidderstr
Lange Raamstr
Langerei
Pottenrei
H Losschaertstr
Jan Boninstr
St-Jorisstr
Jan Miraelstr
Hoedenmakersstr
Gouden-Handstr
Gouden Handrei
Genthof
Spiegelrei
Spinolarei
St-Annarei

39

Ezelstr
Poitevinstr
Augustijnenrei
Kortewinkel
Spaanjaardstr
Jan Van Eyckplein
Biskajersplein
Koningstr

44 **45**
32

Grauwwerkersstr
Naaldenstr
Academie-str
Kraanrei
19
17 St-Jansstr
St-Jansplein
Bromeraadstr
28

Kraanplein
43
41
St-Jakobsstr
Kuipersstr
Vlamingstr

Philipstockstr
Twijnstr
Hoogstr
Groenerei

Eiermarkt
Markt
8
26
Geldmuntstr
St-Amandstr
20 **15**
46 **2**
Belfort
35
40 **1**
Burg
4
16
12
52
Meestr
Freren Fonteinstr
25

Basiliek van het Heilig Bloed
Stadhuis
30

Zwarteleertouwersstr

38
27 **29**
Dweersstr
Zuidzandstr

Helmstr
Noordzandstr
Zilverstr
Steenstr
Simon Stevinplein
Oude Burg
Dijver
Eekhoustr
Waalsstr

Koningin Astridpark

6 **Groeningemuseum**
7 **Gruuthusemuseum**

Het Zand
Korte Vuldersstr
Mariastr
Heilige Geeststr
Goezeputstr
Guido Gezelleplein
Nieuwstr
11 **Onze-Lieve-Vrouwekerk**

33

5 **Concertgebouw**
Oostmeers
Westmeers
10
Museum Sint-Janshospitaal
50
Groeninge
Nieuwe Gentweg
Oude Gentweg

Walplein
Walstr
47
Zonnekemeers
3
18
Brouwerij De Halve Maan
Wijngaardstr
Noordstr
34
Katelijnestr

Boeveriestr
Hoefijzerlaan
14

Arsenaalstr
Sulferbergstr
Gentpoortvest
48
36
49

Koning Albertlaan
Buiten Begijnvest
Prof Dr J Sebrechtsstr
Minnewater
Minnewater Park

9 **Minnewater**

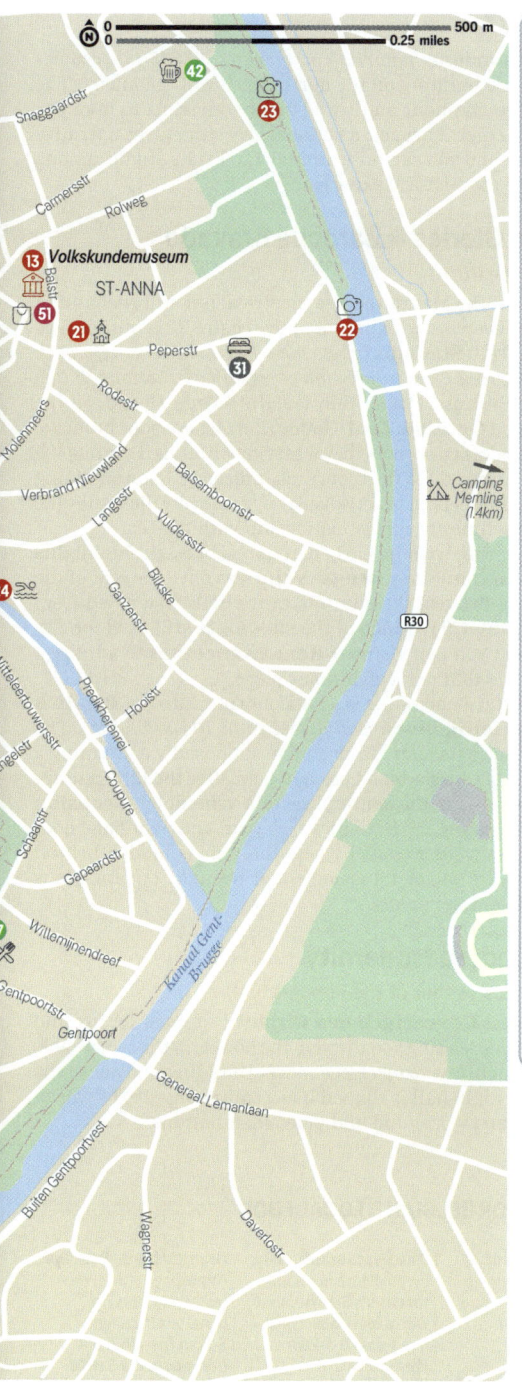

⭐ **HIGHLIGHTS**
1 Basiliek van het Heilig Bloed
2 Belfort
3 Brouwerij De Halve Maan
4 Burg
5 Concertgebouw
6 Groeninge-museum
7 Gruuthuse-museum
8 Markt
9 Minnewater
10 Museum Sint-Janshospitaal
11 Onze-Lieve-Vrouwekerk
12 Stadhuis
13 Volkskunde-museum

🔴 **SIGHTS**
14 Begijnhof
15 Bruges Beer Experience
16 Brugse Vrije
17 Choco-Story
18 Diamant-museum
19 Frietmuseum
see 12 Gotische Zaal
20 Historium
21 Jeruzalemkerk
see 21 Kantcentrum
22 Kruispoort
see 17 Lumina Domestica
23 St-Jans-huismolen

🔴 **ACTIVITIES**
24 Canal swim
see 8 Legends Walking Tours

⚫ **SLEEPING**
25 B&B Amaryllis Dieltiens
26 Dukes' Palace
27 Hotel Bla Bla
28 Hotel Patritius
29 Passage Bruges
30 Relais Bourgondisch Cruyce
31 St Christopher's Inn Hostel at The Bauhaus

🟢 **EATING**
32 Blackbird
33 Christophe
34 De Bron
35 De Stove
see 13 De Zwarte Kat
see 29 Gran Kaffee De Passage
36 One Restaurant
37 Patisserie Schaeverbeke
38 That's Toast

🟢 **DRINKING & NIGHTLIFE**
39 Café Vlissinghe
40 De Garre
41 De Republiek
42 De Windmolen
43 Le Trappiste
44 't Poatersgat

🔴 **SHOPPING**
45 Bacchus Cornelius
46 De Reyghere Reisboekhandel
47 De Striep
48 Sashuis
49 Simbolik
50 Sukerbuyc
51 't Apostelientje
52 Vismarkt

THE BRUGES MATINS

The precocious wealth and independent spirit of Bruges' medieval guildsmen brought political tensions with their French overlords. In 1302, when guildsmen refused to pay a new round of taxes, the French sent in a 2000-strong army to garrison the town.

Undeterred, Pieter De Coninck, dean of the Guild of Weavers, and Jan Breydel, dean of the Guild of Butchers, led a revolt that went down in Flanders' history books as the 'Bruges Matins' (Brugse Metten). Early in the morning on 18 May, guildsmen crept into town and murdered anyone who could not correctly pronounce the hard-to-say Dutch phrase 'schild en vriend' (shield and friend). This revolt sparked a widespread Flemish rebellion, which gave medieval Flanders a short-lived moment of independence.

continued from p121

The **Historium** *(historium.be; adult/child €26/18)* occupies a neogothic building on the northern side of the Markt. The immersive one-hour audio and video tour aims to take you back to medieval Bruges: a fictional love story gives narrative structure, and you can nose around Van Eyck's studio, among other pseudo-historic experiences.

Gothic Glories & Baroque Bravado

Around the Burg

Just east of the Markt, the less theatrical but still enchanting **Burg** has been Bruges' administrative centre for centuries. The beautiful 1420 **Stadhuis** *(visitbruges.be/en/stadhuis-city-hall; adult/children €8/4, admission covers all attractions in this section)* features a wonderfully fanciful facade. Upstairs is the astonishing **Gotische Zaal** (Gothic Hall), whose polychromatic ceiling is adorned with medieval carvings. Murals depicting the town's history add to the room's magnificence. In an adjoining room, an augmented reality display dynamically illustrates the city's sometimes perilous relationship with the sea.

Eye-catching with its early baroque gables, gilt highlights and golden statuettes, **Brugse Vrije** was once the seat of the 'Liberty of Bruges', the administrative body that ruled from Bruges (1121–1794). Much of the building is still used for city offices, but you can visit the **Renaissancezaal** to admire a remarkable 1531 carved chimney piece.

The western end of the stadhuis morphs into the **Basiliek van het Heilig Bloed** *(holyblood.com; 10am-5.15pm)*. The basilica takes its name from a phial supposedly containing a few drops of Christ's blood brought here after the 12th-century Crusades: this is the centrepiece of a venerable **Ascension Day procession** and festivities each year. The right-hand door leads upstairs to a chapel where the relic is hidden behind a flamboyant silver tabernacle and brought out for pious veneration at 2pm daily.

Unexpected Modernity

An interactive tour of the concert hall

The self-led **Concertgebouw Circuit** is a must for art and music lovers, leading you through the bowels of the remarkable **Concertgebouw** *(concertgebouw.be)* building and above the halls (the main hall is shaped like a calling mouth) by way of a superb array of sound and video installations.

 EATING IN BRUGES: BEST FOR BELGIAN & LOCAL FOOD

De Stove: A 20-seat gem where local fish, caught daily, is the house speciality. *7-9pm Fri-Tue, noon-1.30pm Sun* €€

Christophe: A chic little bistro dishing up Flemish beef stew and the like. *6pm-1am Thu-Mon* €€

One Restaurant: Tasty Flemish fare in a snug tavern-style restaurant with a leafy courtyard. *noon-2pm & 6-9pm Wed-Sun* €€

Gran Kaffee de Passage: Atmospheric old-time restaurant, serving generous local fare. *5-11pm Tue-Thu & Sun, from noon Fri & Sat* €€

DMITRY RUKHLENKO/SHUTTERSTOCK

Burg square

Step away from old Bruges and take two to three hours to deeply explore and engage with this evolving collection, from Luc Tuyman's painted angel who holds a harp on the high wall of a side corridor, to the absorbing surround sound of the *Poème electronique,* to startlingly life-size videos of performances in the space. This is a tour which allows you not to only to look and listen, but to participate. You can activate an array of steel tubes with your body to create music, tap the coloured plates of the Omni dome to release its huge spectrum of sounds and – on the roof of the building with the city as a backdrop – play carillon bells.

The Concertgebouw co-hosts the MA Festival in August, bringing an experimental approach to early music.

On the Water

Getting on – and in – the canals

An essential activity in Bruges is to see the city by water on a 30-minute **canal boat tour** *(adult/child €15/9).* Boats depart roughly every 20 minutes from jetties south of the Burg, including Rozenhoedkaai and Dijver. Each operator is essentially a branch of one or two companies regulated by the city: they all do the loop and they all cost the same.

If you're visiting the city in the warmer months, don't miss the glorious opportunity to **swim** in a Bruges canal. A section of the Coupure canal is roped off, a temporary pontoon is installed, and you can take a dip for free, with swans and boats passing in the distance. Kids congregate to jump from the pontoon, while adults can make leisurely laps up the canal. Lifeguards are on hand.

FANCY FACADES
The glorious facade of the Stadhuis in Bruges is second only to that in **Leuven** (p183) for exquisitely turreted Gothic excess.

HELP ME PICK:

Museums in Bruges

The museums of Bruges have everything covered, from the sublime (exquisite medieval art) to the ridiculous: chip museum, anyone? Some long-established museums are emerging from major re-hangs, giving a fresh take on venerable works by mixing them with the modern. As well as big-hitter museums, a number of private ventures can be found across town. Bear in mind that you won't be able to use your Musea Brugge Card at the private museums.

Museums if You Love...

Works of Art

Groeningemuseum (p128) A world-class art gallery, with a particularly strong showing of the light-filled work of the Flemish Primitives.

Museum Sint-Janshospitaal (p129) Hans Memling masterpieces and medical implements, all in the grand timbered surrounds of a 12th-century hospital. Don't miss the adjoining historic pharmacy and herb garden.

Concertgebouw Circuit (p124) A self-guided tour through the bowels of the city's modern concert hall, with outstanding auditory and visual installations along the way.

Onze-Lieve-Vrouwekerk (p129) This is not strictly speaking a museum, but we couldn't have you miss Michelangelo's beautifully sombre *Madonna and Child* (1504).

Local Life in Bruges

Gruuthusemuseum (p129) This palace-like building houses an enthralling collection of applied arts, including tapestries, lace and ceramics.

Volkskundemuseum (p130) The appealing Museum of Folk Life presents visitors with themed tableaux illustrating Flemish life in times gone by.

Historium (p124) A first port-of-call for kids, with movie-style narratives to engage them in the tangled history of the city, and fictional romances to bring it all to life.

Kantcentrum (p130) Exquisite handmade lacemaking can still be seen at Bruges' Lace Centre.

Food & Drink

Choco-Story Exhibits at Bruges' museum of cocoa and chocolate give you a quick rundown of chocolate's history in Europe. A couple of small treats along the way include a tasting at the praline-making demonstration.

Bruges Beer Experience

Explore the history of beer, the brewing process and the different types of beers in Belgium and beyond. Three tastings are included.

Frietmuseum Follow the history of the potato from ancient Inca grave sites to Belgian fryers. Perhaps more interesting is the arch-gabled 1399 building itself, first used by Genoese traders, then by local weavers.

Quirky Sights

Lumina Domestica The enlightening Domestic Lamp Museum has over 6500 artefacts relating to domestic lighting throughout history, making it the largest collection of its kind.

Diamantmuseum The idea of polishing stones with diamond 'dust' was originally pioneered in Bruges. This is the theme of this slick museum, which also displays a lumpy, greenish 252-carat raw diamond. The narrative skims a little too lightly over the racist, colonial history of diamond mining.

HOW TO

Discounts Purchase a Musea Brugge Card *(concession/adult €33/17)* for free entrance to the major museums in Bruges over a three-day period.

Buying Your Card Musea Brugge Cards cannot be purchased online: just ask for one at your first port of call.

Locations The card gives free entry to all museums operated by the city of Bruges: these constitute the big city attractions *(museabrugge.be/en)*.

When to Go Bear in mind that many sights close on Mondays. And if you're looking to avoid museum crowds, don't visit on weekends.

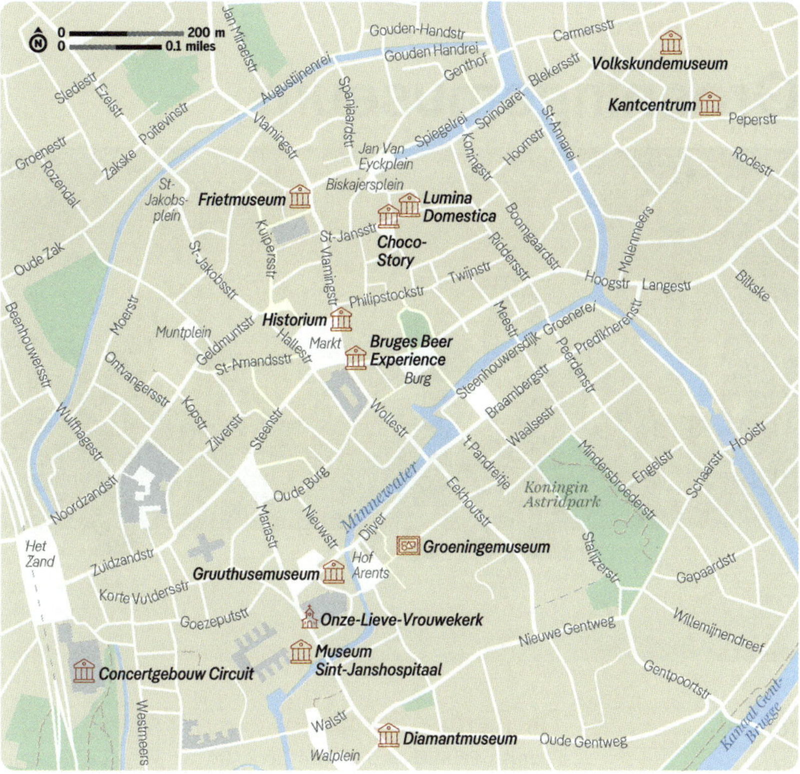

Map of Bruges showing locations including Volkskundemuseum, Kantcentrum, Frietmuseum, Lumina Domestica, Choco-Story, Historium, Bruges Beer Experience, Groeningemuseum, Gruuthusemuseum, Onze-Lieve-Vrouwekerk, Museum Sint-Janshospitaal, Concertgebouw Circuit, Diamantmuseum, Koningin Astridpark.

Free Bruges

Bruges is not the most affordable of cities, but you can still get a taste of some of its history and culture without breaking the bank.

Legends Walking Tours A series of wildly popular (and free) guided walks that are a great way to get oriented before making your own explorations of the city.

RICHIE CHAN/SHUTTERSTOCK

Minnewater

Coupure Canal In the warmer months you can swim in the Coupure Canal for free, getting up close and personal to some watery city infrastructure.

Belfort & Markt Listen out for the free summertime carillon concerts in the courtyard of the Belfort, and brass bands playing in the Markt.

Onze-Lieve-Vrouwekerk (p129) A must-visit for art lovers: sadly Michelangelo's sculpture can't be viewed for free, but the rest of the church can.

Begijnhof (p130) This complex just celebrated its 800th anniversary. You can stroll the paths around its whitewashed

buildings, and enjoy a deeply tranquil escape.

Minnewater (p130) The park surrounding the 'Lake of Love' is a gorgeous spot for a picnic: pick up some affordable fare from the local supermarket.

Vismarkt (p130) This fish market has operated since 1821 and is a great spot for people-watching and browsing the craft stalls.

Markt (p121) It costs nothing to appreciate this grand square and its surrounding architecture, watching the horses and carriages clop by.

Groeningemuseum

MATTHIAS DESMET/GROENINGEMUSEUM

PRACTICALITIES

● museabrugge.be/ en/visit-our-museums/ our-museums -and-monuments/ groeningemuseum

● 9.30am-5pm Thu-Tue

● Adult/youth €15/13

The Flemish Primitives

Flemish Primitives Jan Van Eyck, Rogier Van der Weyden, Hans Memling and Gerard David depicted the affluence and beauty of Bruges to brilliant effect. A marvellous example is the *Madonna Crowned by Angels* (1482) by the Master of the Embroidered Foliage, where the rich fabric of the Madonna's robe meets the 'real' foliage at her feet with pin-sharp detail. Van Eyck's portraits, like those of his counterparts, reflect the abundance of the city, while adding a further dimension of psychological depth. Memling's epic *Moreel Triptych* (1484) is one of the first large-scale group portraits ever painted.

1500–1600

The gallery proceeds with the work of Jan Provost, who arrived in Bruges in 1494 – the year that Memling died. His macabre *Death and the Miser* (1500) still eludes interpretation. Hieronymus Bosch's *Last Judgement* (1482) writhes with demons and monsters.

Fauvism & Flemish Expressionism

Works from the 1920s show the influence of Cubism and German expressionism on Flemish artists – most striking are Constant Permeke's earth-coloured depictions of peasant life in *The Pap Eaters* (1922). Further rooms also cover the modern period, ending with arch-surrealist Magritte.

Memling & Michelangelo

More Bruges masterpieces

In the restored chapel of a 12th-century hospital building with superb timber beamwork, the **Museum Sint-Janshospitaal** *(visitbruges.be/en/sint-janshospitaal-saint-johns-hospital; adult/child €15/7)* shows various torturous medical implements, a hospital sedan chair and a gruesome 1679 painting of an anatomy class. It also incorporates contemporary pieces such as Berlinde De Bruyckere's fallen archangel, a crumple of feathers with fragile legs emerging, and deeply moving video works that muse on illness, death and mourning. But most eyes are on seven masterpieces by 15th-century artist Hans Memling, including the enchanting reliquary of St Ursula, which looks like a miniature Gothic cathedral.

The largest of the Memlings is the triptych of *St John the Baptist and St John the Evangelist,* commissioned by the hospital church as its altarpiece. The artist's secular portrayals are just as engrossing as the devotional work, and include the delicate *Portrait of a Young Woman* (1480), in which the subject's hands rest on the painted frame of her portrait. Your ticket also allows visits to the hospital's handsome 17th-century *apotheek* (pharmacy).

The enormous 115m spire of **Onze-Lieve-Vrouwekerk** *(adult/child €8/4)* is unmissable throughout much of the city. Inside, it's best known for Michelangelo's serenely contemplative *Madonna and Child* (1504) statue, the only such work by the artist to leave Italy during his lifetime. Look out also for the *Adoration of the Shepherds* (1574) by Pieter Pourbus.

City Centre Palace

The enthralling Gruuthusemuseum

The **Gruuthusemuseum** *(museabrugge.be/en/visit-our-museums/our-museums-and-monuments/gruuthusemuseum; adult/youth €15/13)* takes its name from the flower-and-herb mixture *(gruut)* that flavoured beer before the cultivation of hops. With a romantic heraldic entrance in a courtyard of ivy-covered walls and dreamy spires, it was originally built in the 13th century; the building was transformed with Victorian Gothic panache. It comprises a marvellous warren of 17 rooms crammed with treasures, as well as a lofty studio. Room 1 features a portrait of original owner, Louis de Gruuthuse, as well as a fascinating 16th-century map of Bruges. The extraordinary oak-panelled oratory, or private chapel, was built in the 1470s for Louis and his wife to eyeball Mass at Onze-Lieve-Vrouwekerk: you can peek through a window in the oratory for a view of the church's Gothic chancel.

MADONNA & CHILD

Michelangelo's *Madonna and Child* is extraordinary in many ways, and not just for its masterful naturalism and grace. The sculpture was stolen from Bruges (and Belgium) twice. In 1794 it was shipped to Paris after French Revolutionaries conquered the Austrian Netherlands (to which Bruges belonged at the time).

Twenty-one years later, the Madonna was returned to Bruges after Napoleon's defeat at Waterloo. Then in 1944 retreating German soldiers smuggled the sculpture to Germany. A year later, it was discovered in a salt mine in Altaussee, Austria, which the Nazis used as a huge repository for stolen art – and thankfully returned to the Church of Our Lady. The Madonna's calm downcast gaze belies the drama of her history.

STOP THIEF
For more on audacious Belgian **art thefts**, see p117.

Bruges Brews

Visit the half moon brewery

Founded in 1856, though there has been a brewery on the site since 1564, the **Brouwerij de Halve Maan** *(halvemaan.be; adult/child €16/8.50)* is the last family *brouwerij* (brewhouse) in central Bruges. Multilingual guided visits depart on the hour. Alternatively, you can simply sip one of their excellent Brugse Zot (Bruges Fool, 7%) or Straffe Hendrik (Strong Henry, 9%) beers in the appealing brewery bar-café. In 2016, a 3km beer pipeline, leading to the bottling point, was installed under the brewery's cobbles; it's up to 34m below ground in parts.

Tranquil Bruges

The *begijnhof* and Minnewater

Bruges' delightful **Begijnhof** (p132) dates from the 13th century. Despite hordes of summer tourists, it remains a remarkably tranquil haven. Outside the 1776 gateway bridge lies a tempting (if tourist-priced) array of terraced restaurants, lace shops and waffle peddlers.

Peaceful **Minnewater**, surrounded by parkland, harks back to Bruges' medieval heyday. This waterway was once a dock, and ships from as far afield as Russia arrived here, laden with cargoes of wool, wine, spices and silks, then left loaded with Flemish cloth.

Lace & Windmills

Strolling the St-Anna district

The district of St-Anna provides a delightful breather from central Bruges. In the quiet back streets, you'll begin to get a sense of the city's true beauty.

The **Volkskundemuseum** *(visitbruges.be/en/volkskunde museum-folklore-museum; adult/child €8/6),* set in a *godshuis* (almshouse), features 18 themed tableaux illustrating Flemish life in times gone by. Stop at the old-style museum bar-café **De Zwarte Kat** for cheap beer and snacks. Nearby **Kantcentrum** *(kantcentrum.eu; adult/child €8/6)* displays a collection of lace; you can watch bobbin lace being made by experienced lacemakers and their students. At '**t Apostelientje** you'll find delicate authentic local lacework garments and gifts.

Beer meets art history.

DRINKING IN BRUGES: BEST PLACES FOR A BEER

't Poatersgat: A cross-vaulted cellar glowing with flickering candles. 't Poatersgat (the Monk's Hole) has 120 Belgian beers on the menu, including selection of Trappists. *3pm-late*

De Garre: Try the fabulous Garre draught beer, which comes with a thick floral head in a glass like a brandy balloon. *noon-midnight*

Le Trappiste: A specialist Belgian beer bar (26 beers on tap) in an 800-year-old vaulted medieval cellar. *5pm-midnight Mon-Sat*

Café Vlissinghe: Luminaries have frequented Bruges' oldest pub for 500 years; allegedly Rubens painted an imitation coin on the table here, then did a runner. *11am-7pm Wed-Thu & Sun, to 9pm Fri & Sat*

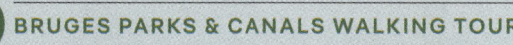

BRUGES PARKS & CANALS WALKING TOUR

START	END	LENGTH
Vismarkt	Vismarkt	3.4km; 2–3 hrs

The handsome colonnaded 1821 **① Vismarkt** (fish market) is still open for business most days. Check out pretty Huidenvettersplein, ringed with archetypal Bruges buildings.

Walk south along Jozef Suvéestraat for a few minutes until you reach local hangout **② Koningin Astridpark**, named after the Swedish wife of King Léopold of Belgium; you'll come across her bust when you reach the park. Walking through the park you'll pass a community radio station, bandstand and adventure playground. Beyond the Gothic revival Magdalen Church is scrumptious **Patisserie Schaeverbeke.**

Continue south to **③ Gentpoort**, one of the town's four medieval gateways. From here, a pleasant footpath leads through the greenery along the water's edge. Follow the path west until you reach **④ Minnewater** and its eponymous park, a scenic green space with orderly flower beds and secluded paths.

Just north of the park, Wijngaardplein, a touristy but still irresistible square, is ringed by bar-cafés. Over the little arched bridge from the square, the 13th century **⑤ begijnhof** is one of the delights of Bruges, its whitewashed buildings encircling a garden with tall trees and swathes of daffodils in spring. It's well worth visiting the church here.

One of the prettiest of this pretty city's hangout spots, **⑥ Hof Arents** features a humpback bridge and the clattering hooves of passing carriages which call here. From here, it's a short stroll back to Vismarkt.

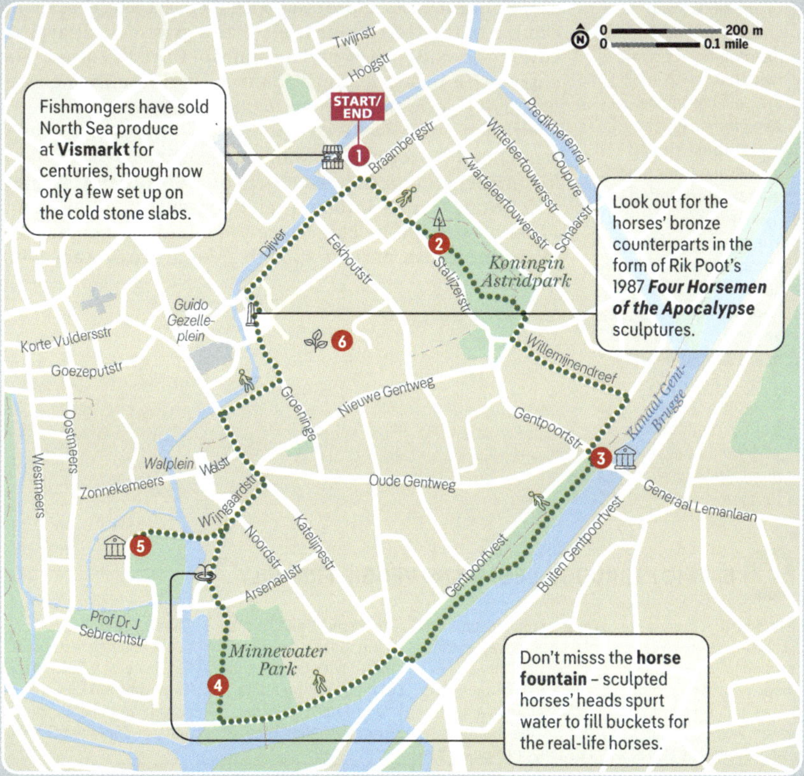

Fishmongers have sold North Sea produce at **Vismarkt** for centuries, though now only a few set up on the cold stone slabs.

Look out for the horses' bronze counterparts in the form of Rik Poot's 1987 *Four Horsemen of the Apocalypse* sculptures.

Don't misss the **horse fountain** – sculpted horses' heads spurt water to fill buckets for the real-life horses.

START/END

Twijnstr
Hoogstr
Braambergstr
Predikherenrei
Coupure
Witteleertouwersstr
Zwarteleertouwersstr schaarstr
Dijver
Eekhoutstr
Stalijzerstr
Koningin Astridpark
Willemijnendreef
Guido Gezelleplein
Korte Vuldersstr
Goezeputstr
Groeninge
Nieuwe Gentweg
Gentpoortstr
Kanaal Gent-Brugge
Oostmeers
Westmeers
Walplein
Wol str
Oude Gentweg
Gentpoortvest
Buiten Gentpoortvest
Generaal Lemanlaan
Zonnekemeers
Wijngaardstr
Noordstr
Katelijnestr
Prof Dr J Sebrechtstr
Arsenaalstr
Minnewater Park

0   200 m
0   0.1 mile

BEGIJNHOVEN

In the 12th century, large numbers of men from the Low Countries embarked on crusades to the Holy Land and never returned. Their women-folk often felt obliged to seek security by joining a religious order. However, joining a convent required giving up one's worldly possessions and even one's name.

A middle way was to become a *begijn*. These lay sisters made Catholic vows of obedience and chastity, but could maintain their private wealth. They lived in a self-contained *begijnhof*: a cluster of houses built around a central garden and church, surrounded by a protective wall. These all-female communities were self-sufficient. Most had a farm and vegetable garden and made supplementary income from lacemaking and from benefactors, who would pay the *begijnen* to pray for them.

HUNGRY_HERBIVORE/SHUTTERSTOCK

Jeruzalemkerk

Within the Adornesdomein estate is one of Bruges' oddest churches, 15th-century **Jeruzalemkerk** (*adornes.org/en -home; adult/child €10/6*). Supposedly based on Jerusalem's Church of the Holy Sepulchre, it has a gruesome altarpiece covered in skull motifs and an effigy of Christ's corpse. The entry price includes admission to a small family museum occupying several pretty *godshuizen* (almshouses).

Fortified gate-tower **Kruispoort** is an impressive isolated remnant of the former city wall; north of here are a couple of historic windmills. Eighteenth-century **St-Janshuismolen** still grinds cereals into flour and houses a small museum. From here, you'll be able to see the quaint corner café **De Windmolen**: a perfect spot to take a break and enjoy the outlook.

EATING IN BRUGES: VEGAN AND VEGGIE-FRIENDLY

Blackbird: A Bruges rarity: an all-vegan cafe serving bagels, bountiful 'happiness' bowls, pancakes, fresh juices and cakes. *9am-3pm Wed-Sat, 9.30am-1pm Sun* €

De Bron: By the time this glass-roofed restaurant's doors open, there's a queue of diners keen to get vegetarian fare from *de bron* (the source). *11.45am-2pm Mon-Fri* €

De Republiek: This is a big, buzzing modern bistro with great vegan choices on the menu. *noon-1am Wed-Sun, from 5pm Mon-Tue* €€

That's Toast: Bruges' best breakfast restaurant has gained a following for its all-day brekkies, with several vegan options. *8.30am-4pm Wed-Sun* €€

Beyond Bruges

Water is the theme of explorations beyond Bruges: an arrow-straight canal, and the dunes and ports of the North Sea coast.

Consider a bike ride from Bruges up the canal to nearby Damme, where you can drop into a tavern or browse secondhand bookstores. In coastal Knokke-Heist, golf carts and lavish SUVs rule the streets, and the restaurants are correspondingly swish: there are a couple of outstanding Michelin-starred options here. Closer to the Dutch border, Zwin Nature Park is a holiday favourite for birds from all over the world, so be sure to bring your binoculars. West of the mighty but not tourist-friendly port of Zeebrugge you'll find the quaint coastal towns of Blankenberge and De Haan. The first features a charming cottage museum; the second is an engagingly elegant seaside resort.

Places

Damme

TIME FROM BRUGES: **25MIN**

Along the canal
Charming Damme village is little more than a single street and a main square upon which the fine Gothic *stadhuis* is fronted by a statue of local 13th-century Flemish poet Jacob Van Maerlant. The village is linked directly to Bruges by a perfectly straight canal, with a cycleway on one side and a road on the other. In parts, the canal is almost completely covered by a verdant canopy.

Half the fun is getting here. The most popular way is to rent a bike in Bruges and cycle the flat 5km canal-side route. In midsummer you'll be jostling for space on the path; otherwise, you might find yourself blissfully alone.

Books & a prankster
Officially declared a Book Town in 1997, Damme has a large number of antiquarian stores and secondhand bookshops. Every second Sunday of the month, you'll find a book market on the Market Square. The **Uilenspiegel Museum** (*visitdamme.be/uilenspiegelmuseum; adult/child €6/2*) covers five centuries' worth of stories about folkloric prankster Tijl Uilenspiegel. It's in the same building as the **Visitors Centre**.

GETTING AROUND

Damme is best reached by bike, following the canal path for 5km, while Knokke is accessed via a rapid train journey from Bruges. You can get to Het Zwin by car or bus from Knokke. By far the best way to reach the run of coastal settlements west of Knokke is to take the Coastal Tram operated by **DeLijn**, a marvellously smooth and frequent service that swooshes you through back streets and at points along the seafront.

Knokke-Heist

TIME FROM BRUGES: **20MIN**

High life in Knokke-Heist

The Belgian equivalent of Saint-Tropez, Knokke has been a renowned summer destination for affluent Belgian and Dutch holiday-goers since the 19th century. Thanks to its modernist casino – the largest of its kind on the Belgian coast – Knokke became a meeting place for Belgian high society throughout the years. Today the city is still very much hot and happening, with chic fashion boutiques, flagship stores and private galleries sprawled across its wide avenues. Look out for exhibitions and events at the excellent **Cultuur Centrum** (*cultuur.knokke -heist.be*).

Belgians know the city as a gastronomic hot spot. With 35 mentions in Gault&Millau and dozens of swanky beach bars popping up during the summer, foodie visitors are spoiled for choice.

Het Zwin

TIME FROM BRUGES: **30MIN**

Belgian birdlife

About 5km northeast of Knokke, you'll find the revamped **Zwin Nature Park** (*zwin.be/en; €12/6*). It's known as an international bird airport: thousands of storks, avocets, nightingales and other birds come here every year to breed, spend the winter and forage for food. The biotopes of Het Zwin also appeal to the imagination: beach, dunes, mudflats and salt marshes will leave you feeling like you've stepped into an impressionist painting.

Zeebrugge

TIME FROM BRUGES: **30MIN**

Port of call

Initially built between 1895 and 1907, Zeebrugge's enormous artificial harbour had been in use for less than a decade when Allied forces sank ships to block its entrance, thus preventing German naval use during WWI. Further bombed in WWII, the harbour finally reopened to sea traffic in 1957. Since then it has remained Belgium's busiest port, primarily for cargo ships; you'll skirt round its dramatic cranes on the Coastal Tram.

Lissewege

TIME FROM BRUGES: **15MIN**

A village out of time

Though only 7km south of brutally functional Zeebrugge, the cute little village of Lissewege is a world away with its pretty whitewashed cottages and oversize brick church. Set in meadows 1.6km north of Lissewege, a sturdy 13th-century barn is the last

EATING IN DAMME & KNOKKE: GOURMET RESTAURANTS

De Zuidkant: Elegant Damme dining room with a dash of Mediterranean flavour. *noon-2pm & 7-9pm Mon, Tue, Fri, Sat* €€€

Sel Gris: Creativity and sophistication in a Knokke interior of 50 shades of grey, awarded a Michelin star. *noon-2pm & 7-8.30pm Fri-Tue* €€€

Boo Raan: Refined traditional Thai cuisine in Knokke that has been awarded a Michelin star. *Tue-Sat 6-11pm* €€€

Cuines 33: Compact, airy bistro in Knokke where the food is a work of art, crafted from the freshest ingredients of the day. *noon-2pm & 7-9pm Fri-Sat & Mon-Tue* €€€

remnant of the original Abdij Ter Doest, a once-powerful abbey ruined during the religious wars in 1569.

Blankenberge

TIME FROM BRUGES: **12MIN**

The smallest house in town

Belle époque Blankenberge features an Art Deco pier, wide sandy beaches and an idiosyncratic attraction in the form of **Huisje van Majutte** *(majutte.be; free)*. Originally constructed in 1272, when Blankenberge first acquired city rights, this impossibly cute fisher's cottage was rebuilt in 1775. Owners Peter and Lena have turned it into a heritage site: today it is a visitor centre and cafe.

De Haan

TIME FROM BRUGES: **30MIN**

In the footsteps of Einstein

Prim and proper De Haan (Le Coq) is Belgium's most compact and engaging beach resort. Its most famous visitor, Albert Einstein, lived here for a few months after fleeing Hitler's Germany in 1933. Several fanciful half-timbered hotels and a scattering of tasteful eateries, bakeries and shops form an appealing knot around a cottage-style former tram station, from where Leopoldlaan leads 600m north to the beach passing De Haan's distinctive circular La Pontinière park.

According to local legend, De Haan (meaning 'The Rooster') got its name because it had no lighthouse, and in fog fishers used the sound of crowing cocks to work out where the shore was.

Roam the rooster

Take a stroll around the roads that radiate to the east and west off the La Pontinière to explore the area of indulgent heritage homes. Down lanes that undulate gently through what were once wild dunes, you'll find some houses that are whitewashed and thatched, and others that are beautifully restored.

Bredene

TIME FROM BRUGES: **30MIN**

Bare all on the beach

The only seaside town where the beach isn't overshadowed by towering apartment blocks, Bredene, just west of Ostend, is a low-cost alternative to the coast's larger resort communities. Fringed by a weathered tangle of knotted sand dunes, this seemingly endless stretch of white sand is actually only 4km long, and includes a popular **nudist** section. Free from the multi-storey developments that typify the Belgian coast, Bredene Strand offers a real sense of being away from it all.

THE GUIDE

GHENT, BRUGES & NORTHWEST BELGIUM BEYOND BRUGES

THE BELGIUM PIER

The first proposal to build a pier in **Blankenberge** came from a Londoner, John Hendrey, in 1873. The city council was hesitant at the time, but an ornate cast-iron pier was eventually built in 1894. It proved to be a major attraction, but it was burned down by the Germans after a mere 20 years.

In 1933 came the second version of the pier, designed by Jules Soete – a gorgeous circular Art Deco structure with sea views, a restored walkway that stretches for 350m, and eating and drinking options. To this day, there is only one other pier on the Atlantic coast of continental Europe: in Scheveningen in the Netherlands.

EATING & DRINKING IN DE HAAN: OUR PICKS

Bistro Villa Julia: Flemish fine dining in a beautiful historical villa, with meals prepared from fresh local ingredients. *noon-2pm & 6-11pm Wed-Sun* €€€

Frituur Erly: A fancy *frituur* for fabulous fast food and *frites*. Look for the little green van opposite the tram stop. *noon-10pm* €

Moment!: Big English breakfasts as well as more traditional continental fare. There's waffles, eggs and excellent lunches too. *8am-6.30pm* €€

Strand Hotel: Get a drink from the modest Strand Hotel and watch the sun set into the sea from its glassed-in terrace. *noon-11pm* €

HELP ME PICK:

Coastal Towns and Beaches

After a period of stasis, Belgium's seaside region has regained popularity among local, French and Dutch tourists as an 'it' destination. The 65km-long coastline is fronted by wide white-sand beaches, backed by dunes and dotted every few kilometres with resort towns. Out of season many towns can feel deserted, but with its regular events and conventions, hub-town Ostend keeps a lively vibe year-round. Other top picks for coastal stays include De Haan, wealthy Knokke-Heist and Bredene.

Where to Head If You Love...

Old-World Elegance

De Haan While many coastal towns in the area have maxed out on glossy seafront apartment buildings, De Haan retains its *belle époque* architecture, much of it quaintly timbered.

Het Zoute (Knokke) The easternmost part of Knokke is the most exclusive, and a wander round the grand villas gives you a peek at the Belgian high life.

Walking

Ostend Ostend's tourist board promotes several app-guided city walks, including the Ensor walk (p141), the Marvin Gaye Midnight Love tour (p310) and an architectural heritage route. The beaches and dunes are also great for strolls.

Nieuwpoort Follow the GR5A Coastal Route from Nieuwpoort to the French border, and you'll encounter Hoge Blekker, the highest sand dune in the region, dotted with sea buckthorn.

Het Zwin Walk the 5km from Knokke-Heist through the dune polders to this marshy nature reserve with its mudflats and scrub forest.

De Haan Take the coastal route through and around town, or head inland among historic dikes and polders.

History

Nieuwpoort This venerable town was founded way back in 1163. It was badly bombed in WWII, but the market square features handsomely reconstructed gabled buildings.

Lissewege Located just inland from Zeebrugge, this enchanting little place is dotted with whitewashed polder cottages.

Ostend Just west of town, preserved WWII sea defences give a chilling insight into occupied Flanders. Take the Coastal Tram out to Atlantikwall Raversyde to explore its wartime bunkers.

Yachts, Boat Trips and Horses

Nieuwpoort This is the place to base yourself for all kinds of water sports, including sailing and boat trips.

Oostduinkerke Extraordinary heritage that just about survives: horseback fishers drag nets through the sea to catch shrimp in the shallows.

Swimming Beaches

Nieuwpoort Look out for the lifeguard stations, then fling yourself into the North Sea from the sandy beaches of Nieuwpoort.

Ostend The spacious sandy beach makes for great dips, as well as sandcastle building.

Bredene Around 250m of the long sandy strand at Bredene has been designated as a nudist beach, the only one on the Belgian coast.

Ostend boardwalk

HOW TO

When to Go
Summer sees busy beaches and bustling promenades. Year-round there may be a wind chill factor, so come prepared.

Book Ahead
Every settlement offers a wide selection of accommodation, but finding a room can be difficult in summer. Booking ahead is essential for the most popular towns.

Getting There
NMBS/SNCB operates regular 'B' trains between Brussels and Ostend; there are also rapid services to Knokke and other smaller destinations.

Getting Around
The efficient De Kusttram (Coast Tram) runs between Knokke-Heist and De Panne. It serves every town on the Belgian coast.

The Belgian Coast with Kids

Sand, sea, buckets and spades... there's plenty on offer to entrance kids holidaying on the Belgian coast.

Aside from swimming – just make sure there's a staffed lifeguard station before your offspring take to the water – you'll find a plethora of water-sports activities all along the coast, including surfing, windsurfing and kitesurfing, plus boating and sailing trips, particularly from Nieuwpoort.

Bigger kids might like to try beach kiting with large kites that catch the strong sea breezes, or sand yachting – this involves sitting in a buggy with a sail and zipping along the sands. The region specialises in wacky transportation: the promenade at Ostend buzzes with go-karts of all shapes and sizes, and quadricycles that are big enough to seat whole families.

The horseback shrimp fisherfolk at Oostduinkerke are very appealing to young ones, and there are various spots where you can arrange for beach horseriding yourself: try **Manege Sanders** just east of De Haan.

Nature-inclined families will enjoy the bird-spotting opportunities at Het Zwin nature park, looking out for migratory and meadow species, while history-loving kids can explore the bunkers at **Atlantikwall Raversyde**.

Chips, waffles and ice cream may not fulfil all your kids' nutritional needs, but cravings for the above can be answered at any of the beachfront promenades.

Ostend

GOLDEN SAND | ARTISTIC LEGACY | COASTAL FESTIVALS

GETTING AROUND

The Coastal Tram (Kusttram) has several stops in Ostend. The central sights are walkable, or hire a bike or go-kart, which are available in multiple wacky shapes. If you're coming from the centre, it's 10 minutes' walk from the ferry jetty to Fort Napoleon. Earth Explorer is 500m beyond that, near the Kusttram stop Duin en Zee.

☑ TOP TIP

Be sure to make time for a walk or buggy ride on the promenade. There's a fabulous selection of buggies and go-kart-like *kwistaxs* for hire.

Ostend is the largest city on the Belgian coast and its only truly year-round destination. Along its wide white-sand beach is a spacious promenade surveyed by an interesting mix of midrise architecture atop cosy seafront cafes with glassed-in terraces.

Always an important strategic port, Ostend has a rich history of fame, fortune, famine and hardship. It was ravaged by the Spanish between 1600 and 1604, before regrouping and reinventing itself as one of Europe's most stylish seaside resorts. Though bombing in WWII caused significant destruction to the city, Ostend has a wealth of beautiful *belle époque* and art deco architecture scattered around its residential streets.

Emerging from a period of economic decline that began when transcontinental ferry services ceased in the late 1990s, Ostend has again found its feet, with locals and visitors buzzing up and down the promenade on bikes and go-karts of every possible type. It's worth spending a night or two here to explore.

Neogothic Grandeur

Ostend's most striking historical building, **St-Petrus-&-Pauluskerk** features beautifully ornate twin spires, a rose window and a gloomy neogothic interior. It was consecrated on 31 August 1908, though it appears eons older. It's a massive, magnificent building and quite a surprise the first time you

 EATING IN OSTEND: BEST SEAFOOD RESTAURANTS

't Zeezotje: Floor-to-ceiling glass and outdoor seating. Try the Vispannetje, a trio of fish fillets topped with cheese, mini-shrimp and curry sauce. *noon-11.45pm* €€

Agua del Mar: Imaginative mussel-shell-mosaics and terrace views of the western beaches. Try scallop risotto or lobster with asparagus. *noon-9.30pm* €€€

The Catch: A changing menu featuring the freshest fish of the day. Plus some great cocktails. *6pm-midnight Tue-Sat* €€

Toi, moi et la Mer: A great seaview spot to get your shrimp croquette on, or go for catch of the day. *noon-2pm & 6-9 pm Wed-Sat* €€

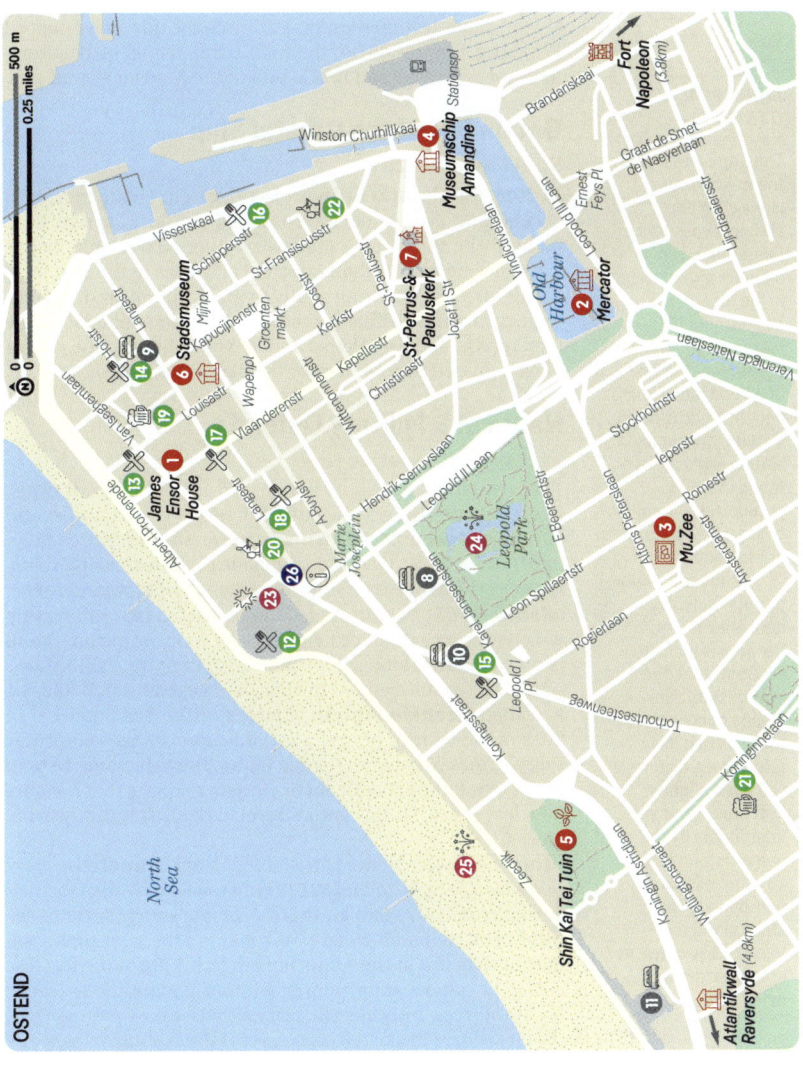

OSTEND

North Sea

HIGHLIGHTS
1 James Ensor House
2 Mercator
3 Mu.Zee
4 Museumschip Amandine
5 Shin Kai Tei Tuin
6 Stadsmuseum
7 St-Petrus-&-Pauluskerk

SLEEPING
8 De Hofkamers
9 Hostel De Ploate
10 Leopold Hotel
11 Thermae Palace Hotel

EATING
12 Agua del Mar
13 Bistro Beau-Site
14 Den Artiest
15 Frituur Franky
16 'tZeezotje
17 Tea Room Benny
18 The Catch

DRINKING & NIGHTLIFE
19 Café Botteltje
20 Lafayette Music Bar
21 Le Châtelet
22 'tKroegske

ENTERTAINMENT
23 Casino
24 North Sea Beer Festival
25 Ostend Beach Festival

INFORMATION
26 Tourist Office Oostende

139

The pride and joy of the Belgian coast is the common shrimp. Typically no longer than 5cm, the animal's importance in the local cuisine cannot be understated: Belgium consumes over half of all common shrimp caught worldwide. In Ostend, the common shrimp is most often found in shrimp croquettes – fried, crispy, salty balls of golden dough.

The second wildly popular delicacy here are oysters: the area is home to De Oesterput, the only oyster farm in the country. The oysters from this farm have a distinct salty and slightly nutty taste and are identifiable by the name Ostendaise. To sample local fish, head to the stalls along the Visserskaai, or to one of the restaurants listed here.

come upon it: it's somewhat incongruous with its surrounds. A stone 'bridge' behind the altar leads into the tiny crown-topped Praalgraf Louise-Marie, the 1859 tomb-chapel of Belgium's first queen, whose sad tale is told at the Stadsmuseum.

Get on Board the Crystal Ship

Street art in the city

In 2016, the **Crystal Ship** project began to create murals in Ostend and ever since, international and local artists have painted the town red – and every other colour imaginable. There are now more than 80 street artworks in the city, from Ensor-inspired grinning skulls to giant botanical drawings. Visit the **tourist office** for more information, download the free app Ostend City Walks and let your phone guide you, or book a guided tour on foot or by bike *(thecrystalship.be/en)*.

Nautical & Military Ostend

Set sail at this seaside town

The last Ostend trawler to have fished around Iceland (1970s) is brought to life with waxwork figures, videos and sound effects at **Museumschip Amandine** *(amandineoostende.be; adult/child €6/4)*. Highlights include the fish-freezing room. It's near the **Mercator** ship-museum *(zeilschipmercator.be; adult/child €7/5)*, a fully rigged, three-masted 1932 sailing ship which was once used for Belgian Navy training purposes and is now a nautical museum that hosts changing exhibitions.

Near the eastern end of the beach in Ostend, you'll find the so-called **Zeeheldenplein** ('Heroes of the Sea Square'). In 2012, Arne Quinze placed a set of bright orange sculptures there – *Rock Strangers* – some up to 20m tall. Some Ostend locals found the artwork out of place in a square that honours men lost at sea, while visitors revel in the Instagram-worthy pieces.

Impenetrable, pentagon-shaped **Fort Napoleon** *(fort -napoleon.be; adult/child €11/9)* is an unusually intact fortress dating from 1812, though there's comparatively little to see inside, and the audio guide covers many of the same topics you may have heard at the Atlantikwall. Drinking at the fortress cafe gets you decent glimpses without paying the entrance fee. A toll-free, fully electric ferry service takes visitors from the city centre to Oosteroever several times a day, or take the coastal tram to Oosteroever.

DRINKING IN OSTEND'S PUBS & BARS: OUR PICKS

Lafayette Music Bar: With traditional panelling and chic backlit bottles, Lafayette is hip and friendly. Fifty beers include the sweep of Trappists. *2pm-2am*

't Kroegske: There's a giant devil-fish's head on the roof of two old houses with facades covered with cartoons. Inside it's filled with bric-a-brac. *11am-2pm & 6-11pm*

Le Châtelet: This busy pub-café on Ostend's so-called 'Little Paris' corner was built in 1885: a thoroughly atmospheric place to down a beer. *11am-11pm*

Café Botteltje: In a spacious bar-café reminiscent of a British pub, you'll find around 300 different beers, including a dozen on draught. *11.30am-1am*

Ostend city & beach

Introducing Ostend

Tour the town museum

One might expect the **Stadsmuseum** *(oostende.be/ stadsmuseum; adult/child €5/2),* occupying a house that hosted Napoleon in 1798 and Belgian royals during 1834–1850, to be a little more grandiose and exciting than it is. That said, it's the best place to get an introduction to the fascinating and, at times, troubled history of a city that has served as an important gateway to Europe for centuries. Multimedia displays, artefacts and models of 'lost' buildings recount the city's former glories.

Artists in the City

Gallery and a unique house museum

Mu.Zee *(muzee.be; adult/child €12/3),* Ostend's foremost gallery, features the work of predominantly local artists. There's a significant collection by symbolist painter Léon Spilliaert (1881–1946) whose most brooding works are reminiscent of Munch.

But perhaps the artistic highlight of Ostend is the house museum dedicated to symbolist artist James Ensor. The **James Ensor House** *(ensorhuis.be; €13/6)* – the place where Ensor worked and lived for the last 32 years of his life with his manservant Gust Van Yper – has been preserved in its original state and

THE STORY OF JAMES ENSOR

Born in 1860 to an English father and a Belgian mother, James Ensor spent almost his entire life in Ostend. His mother ran a shop selling souvenirs, shells, chinoiserie and carnival items such as masks. These objects left a deep impression, and masks and skulls would often appear in Ensor's paintings.

After three years at the Royal Academy of Fine Arts in Brussels, he moved back to Ostend in 1880 and became a founding member of 'Les Vingt', a radical group of Belgian artists who rebelled against academism. Ensor became a local legend, both for his expressive canvases, which had a significant influence on the expressionist and surrealist movements, and for his daily walks around the town.

GETTING IT ON IN OSTEND

For the story of another fabled Ostend resident – **Marvin Gaye** – see p310.

OSTEND'S BEST FESTIVALS

Film Festival Ostend: New Flemish and international film releases in Jan/Feb.

Oostende voor Anker: Sailing ships, shanties, seafood and more at the late May festival.

Ostend Beach Festival: Two days of live music and partying on the beach in July.

Theater Aan Zee: A ten-day theatre and music festival held in July/August, with locations including parks and beaches as well as theatres.

Paulusfeesten: A grand music festival in August dating back to 1973 and a local favourite. It's based around St-Petrus-&-Pauluskerk (p138).

North Sea Beer Festival: Beer-lovers from far and wide flock to Ostend every August for this three-day celebration of Belgian beer and food with lashings of live music.

expanded with an interactive visitor centre. You can visit the artist's painting-lined and object-filled rooms, as well as the bizarrely appealing shop run by his parents, the jumbled contents of which greatly influenced the artist. Here you can also access the interactive, app-guided Ensor Walk of the surrounding streets.

Back Street Pleasures

Belle époque beauties and a Japanese garden

This lesser-known residential part of Ostend was once in ill repute, but savvy homebuyers have recently snapped up its wealth of utterly charming Art Nouveau/*belle époque* townhouses, restored them and transformed the neighbourhood into a very desirable part of town. Wander the narrow streets admiring the architecture's finer details, or picnic in the lovely little park. Follow Tourhoutesteenweg south of the **Casino** for about 1km until you reach Oude Molenstraat, then walk down the street admiring the facades until you reach Prinsenlaan.

Evolving since 2001, architect Takashi Sawano's **Shin Kai Tei Tuin** has faithfully reproduced a Japanese garden just blocks from Ostend's seashore. Come to wander through its 2500 sq m of refined delights or sit and observe zazen meditation.

Bunkers in the Dunes

In the bunkers at Atlantikwall Raversyde

Gripping **Atlantikwall Raversyde** *(raversyde.be/en; adult/child €10/4)* is a remarkably extensive complex of WWI and WWII bunkers, gun emplacements and linking brick tunnels created by occupying German forces. Most bunkers are furnished and 'manned' by waxwork figures, and there's a detailed audio-guide explanation. This is one of Belgium's best and most underrated war sites, but you'll need around two hours, and reasonable fitness, to make the most of the 2km walking circuit. Graphic art, both contemporaneous and modern, is used to great effect here. Take the Coastal Tram to Domein Raversijde.

Don't miss the paintings upstairs of Ostend locals.

EATING IN OSTEND: BEST CAFES, BRASSERIES & FRITUURS

Frituur Franky: Lovers of the humble fry are spoiled for choice at this chip shop. *noon-2pm & 5.30-11pm Tue-Sat, 5-10pm Sun* €

Tea Room Benny: Fabulously frozen-in-time cafe that beckons you to slide into a booth for a coffee and cake or a milkshake. *9.30am-8pm* €

Den Artiest: Casual brasserie on different levels: generous meals are barbecued in front of you. Occasional live music. *5pm-2am* €€

Bistro Beau-Site: Deco touches, a communal table, jazz on the stereo and art books. Upstairs window seats have beach views. *11am-7pm Mon, Wed & Thu, noon-late Fri-Sun* €€

Beyond Ostend

West of Ostend, the dunes, golden beaches and holiday towns of the coast continue, while inland are some quiet but engaging settlements.

Travelling west from Ostend, the first stop is jaunty Nieuwpoort, where you can swim, sail and enjoy water sports, as well as explore the town's intriguing WWI history. Just down the coast from here, Oostduinkerke still clings to its unusual fishing tradition: time your visit right and you'll see fisherfolk on horseback hunting for shrimps. Beach resort De Panne sits close to the French border, and features a cheerful promenade as well as kids resort Plopsaland. Inland from here, quietly attractive Veurne merits a wander, with its gables and spires, while Diksmuide speaks to the conflict that caused so much destruction in this region, with a startling peace tower that dominates the horizon.

Places

Nieuwpoort p143
Oostduinkerke p144
De Panne p144
Veurne p145
Diksmuide p145

Nieuwpoort

TIME FROM OSTEND: **42MIN**

Set sail on the Belgian coast

Nieuwpoort is the coast's top sailing centre, and it's home to one of northern Europe's largest marinas, the **Vlaamse Yachthaven**, with more than 2000 mooring places. Come here to gaze at the tall masts bobbing on the water, or to hook up with a skipper for local cruises, charters and, if you're a captain yourself, yacht hires. The wide 3.5km beach makes Nieuwpoort a great spot for swimming and all types of water sports, including surfing, kayaking and windsurfing.

War & reconstruction

This is also a historic place, remembered for playing a key role in WWI; local partisans thwarted the German advance by opening sluice gates and flooding surrounding low-lying land. Bombardments during the war devastated Nieuwpoort's historical townscape, but in the 1920s the medieval main square was rebuilt, including the former 1280 town hall, belfry and a sizeable church. Today, flanked by step-gabled houses, the scene looks lovely at dusk thanks to tasteful floodlighting. By day, however, the overly neat brickwork lacks the apparent authenticity of similar reconstructions in Ypres or Diksmuide.

GETTING AROUND

Most places around Ostend worth visiting are located on the Belgian coast, and easy to reach with the Coastal Tram. Find more information, download a map with the tram stops, and buy tickets at *delijn. be/en/content/ kusttram.*

Oostduinkerke

TIME FROM OSTEND: **46MIN**

Fishing by horseback

The archetypal vision of Belgium's rural North Sea coast is of *paardevissers*: shrimp fishers riding their stocky Brabant horses into the sea, dragging triangular nets through the low-tide shallows. These days, shrimp catches are minimal, but horse fishers and their Belgian Draft horses – the strongest horse breed in the world – take to the North Sea twice a week, except during the harsh winter months. They treat visitors to 45-minute fishing demonstrations and shrimp-cooking workshops. For the low-down, see *paardevissers.be*.

Outside these times, the town is a quiet alternative to the larger resorts, with one or two attractions to pique your interest; consider visiting as a day trip.

A fisher's life

Visits to **Navigo** *(navigomuseum.be; adult/child €10/4)* walk you through a genuine 19th-century fisher's cottage, teaching you about fish quotas and fisher's superstitions, then send you and your audio guide beneath a 1930s fishing shack flanked by aquariums of fish. An accompanying soundtrack of waves and shrieking gulls builds up to a four-minute storm every half-hour. The Veurne–Ostend bus 68 stops nearby.

De Panne

TIME FROM OSTEND: **1HR 23MIN**

Coastal dunes

Take time out among the grassy-topped hillocks to discover De Panne, the westernmost town on the Belgian coast: this busy beach resort started life as a fishing village set in a *panne* (hollow) among the dunes. Ice creams and promenade walks are big attractions here, and you're likely to be served in French rather than Dutch due to the proximity to the French border. Stroll west of town in winter to spot migratory birds among the sandy dunes.

Surreal De Panne

This superb **Paul Delvaux Museum** *(delvauxmuseum.com; adults/concessions €12/7)* occupies the house and studio of Paul Delvaux (1897–1994), one of Belgium's most famous surrealist artists. What appears to be a handsome Art Deco house on a quiet street belies a 1000-sq-m basement gallery full of sketches, watercolours and paintings of Delvaux's beloved nudes, trains and buildings.

WHERE TO EAT IN NIEUWPOORT, OOSTDUINKERKE & DE PANNE

Galjoen: Overlooking masts in the harbour, Galjoen is picture perfect, and the food is good too. *noon-10pm Tue, Wed, Sat & Sun, from 6pm Fri* €€€

Estaminet de Peerdevisscher: Wonderful old-time Oostduinkerke bar-café with fishers moonlighting as bar staff, and a seafaring vibe. *10am-8pm Tue-Sun* €€

Julia Fish & Oyster Bar: This acclaimed De Panne restaurant, run by female-led fishmongers Mare Nostrum, secures a supply of fresh seafood daily. *noon-3pm & 6.30-10pm Thu-Mon* €€€

Octopus: Suitably near the sea in De Panne, Octopus mixes up fresh seafood with a farm-to-table ethos. *noon- 2pm & 6.30-9pm Thu-Mon* €€€

One for the kids

Cute if unfortunately named theme park **Plopsaland** *(plopsa. com/en/plopsaqua-de-panne; €24/13.50)* is based around Belgian TV character Plop the gnome and his friends. It's a kid-pleasing world of rides, roller coasters and fun. Access by public transport is excellent: catch the Coastal Tram to Plopsaland station from anywhere on the coastal line, or take the train to De Panne station for direct pedestrian access to the park.

Veurne
TIME FROM OSTEND: **30MIN** 🚗

Quiet magic

Delightful little Veurne, just south of the Belgian coast, has a special architectural charm. Historical spires and towers peep above the picture-perfect Flemish gables that surround its quaint Grote Markt. The view is especially magical at dusk when partly floodlit. Veurne's main church is the delicately spired **St-Walburgakerk**, a spacious, heavily buttressed affair containing much-revered relics. The skull of St-Walburga is contained in a reliquary facing the entrance. A wooden fragment that was supposedly once part of Jesus' original cross is not displayed, but the story of its arrival here is the subject of local legends.

Diksmuide
TIME FROM OSTEND: **30MIN** 🚗

Peace tower power

Like Ypres, Diksmuide was painstakingly restored after total obliteration in WWI, but that's where the similarities end. Diksmuide is a quiet and pretty town, but with few attractions to entice a visit. Its resurrected Grote Markt (main square) offers a compact array of attractive traditionally styled buildings and a romantic city hall: it's hard to believe that almost everything in sight was rebuilt in the 20th century.

West of the main square, there's a pretty little river port behind which stands the striking **IJzertoren** *(ijzertoren. org; adult/child €9.50/5);* it's the town's main attraction. This colossal 84m-high 'peace' tower is at once crushingly ugly and fascinating. It's set behind the shattered ruins of the 1930 original, the mysterious 1946 sabotage of which remains controversial. The tower is probably Flanders' foremost nationalist symbol: its 22 floors house a very expansive museum related to WWI and Flemish emancipation.

THE TRENCH OF DEATH

The tranquillity of Diksmuide makes it hard to believe that this was the location of the notorious WWI Trench of Death. In 1915, the Belgian army was attempting to dislodge the Germans away from petrol tanks in Diksmuide. They constructed a trench along the River Yser, towards the fuel drums, and the Germans also began trench building.

After heavy fighting, the Belgians breached the Yser dyke, which meant that the two sides had nothing but a narrow waterway between them. Both sides dug in, fortifying their bunkers with concrete and adding gun emplacements. For three long years, a bloody and ultimately pointless stalemate ensued, and the trench system gained its sadly grisly name.

EATING & DRINKING IN VEURNE & DIKSMUIDE

't Hof van de Hemel: Quaint Veurne teahouse with wooden beams and exposed brickwork: it was once a tiny alleyway. Beer, stews, soups, steaks and tarts. *11am-10pm Wed-Sun* €€

Grill de Vette Os: Old timbers, jugs, buckets and statues of saints are crammed into this atmospheric carnivore's lair in Veurne. *noon-2.30pm & 6pm-2am Fri-Tue* €€

De Dolle Brouwers: Oerbier, a highly rated stealthy dark ale, is brewed here in a brilliantly colourful little brewery-café. *2-7pm Sat & Sun* €€

Frituur 't Klein Kasteeltje: Friendly Diksmuide purveyor of *frites*, served with dollops of homemade mayonnaise. *11am-1.30pm & 5.15-9.30pm Thu-Mon* €

Ypres

WARTIME MEMORIES | RECONSTRUCTED GRANDEUR | POPPY FIELDS

GETTING AROUND

Ypres is easy to get around on foot, but some sites are far from the centre. Flat terrain means easy cycling (except for those pesky cobblestone streets). Anyone intending to visit WWI sites around Ypres, hire a car. Or, if you're feeling athletic, you can cover the Ypres Salient by bike.

Once a bustling centre of industry ranking alongside Bruges and Ghent, it's now impossible to reference Ypres (Ieper in Dutch) without acknowledging the huge role it played in WWI. After its almost total annihilation, the town was rebuilt to its former specifications – a monumental task – to serve as a memorial to those who lost their lives here in the Great War. Its restored Lakenhalle is one of Belgium's most spectacular buildings. This now houses the sombre and reflective In Flanders Fields Museum, which brings together artefacts and testimonies to greatly moving effect. It's an unmissable introduction to cemetery visits in the region.

Ypres has become a place of pilgrimage for many. It's the gateway to the Salient (aka Flanders Fields), a bow-shaped bulge that formed the front line around town; some 300,000 Allied soldiers and up to 200,000 civilians and German troops lost their lives here.

Belgium's Grandest Building?

Visit reconstructed Lakenhalle

Dominating the Grote Markt, the enormous reconstructed **Lakenhalle** is unmissable and impressive. Its 70m-high belfry has the vague appearance of a medieval Big Ben. The original version was completed in 1304 beside the Ieperslee, a now covered-over river that once allowed ships to sail right up to the Lakenhalle to unload their cargoes of wool. These were stored beneath the high gables of the 1st floor, where you'll find the unmissable In Flanders Fields Museum.

In Flanders Fields

A museum to recall past atrocities

In Flanders Fields *(inflandersfields.be; €12/6)* contains a wealth of letters, household objects, military equipment, maps, newspapers and memorabilia pertaining to WWI. But the real stars of the show are the striking video installations illustrating how

☑ **TOP TIP**

In recent years visitor numbers from Commonwealth countries have soared, so be sure to plan your visit to the cemeteries well in advance to avoid disappointment.

families and soldiers on both sides experienced the horrors of the Great War. The audio guide *(€2 per person)* includes additional, in-depth listening points, and a story for children. Climb the restored Belfry *(€2)* for a spectacular 360-degree view of Ypres. Expect to spend at least two hours exploring the museum.

Ypres Remembers

Wander the town's wartime sights

One of Ypres' most attractive military graveyards, **Ramparts CWGC Cemetery**, a Commonwealth War Graves site, is found 1km south of the Grote Markt.

A block east, **Menin Gate** is a huge stone gateway straddling the main road at the city moat. It's inscribed with the names of 54,896 lost WWI British and Commonwealth troops whose bodies were never found.

Every night at 8pm, traffic through the Menin Gate is halted while buglers sound the **Last Post** *(lastpost.be; free)* in remembrance of the WWI dead, a moving tradition started in 1928. Every evening the scene is different; buglers may be accompanied by pipers, troops of cadets or a military band. There's usually at least 100 visitors, most with a connection to someone lost in Flanders Fields.

THE LAST POST

The Last Post originated as a bugle call that marked the end of the day for the British Army in wartime. More than 100 years later, it has come to represent a final farewell to more than 9 million fallen Allied soldiers and civilians. In recent times, the Last Post has also become a symbol of collaboration and solidarity between all nations involved in the war.

The daily event is organised by an independent non-profit called the Last Post Association, founded in 1928. The tribute has sounded 365 days a year, every year – except during the German occupation of Ypres during WWII.

Attending is free and no reservation is required. Explore ways of actively participating (such as laying a wreath) at *lastpost.be.*

CLAUDINEVM/GETTY IMAGES

Last Post performance, Menin Gate

Modern/Medieval Marvel

A grand church brought back to life

If the Lakenhalle has piqued your interest in the remarkable rebuilding of Ypres, head directly behind it to gaze at the beautifully restored soaring Gothic interior of vast **St-Maarten en St-Niklasskerk**. The building stood for eight centuries before being almost totally obliterated in WWI.

A Grand Manor

Ypres' pre-war high life

Step inside an Ypres manor house for a sense of how the city felt pre-war, at least for the privileged. The **Merghelynck Museum** *(merghelynckmuseum.be)* faithfully reproduces a French manor house dating from 1774, and it's rich in architectural and artistic interest, from the wrought-iron balcony of the rococo-neoclassical facade to the chandelier and harp of the stuccoed music room to the elegantly snug alcove bed in the Lady's Bedroom.

The catch: it's only open to the public when (irregular) guided tours are being held.

PLACES TO EAT & DRINK IN YPRES: OUR PICKS

De Ruyffelaer: Traditional local dishes served in an adorable wood-panelled interior with chequerboard floors. *11.30am-3.30pm Sun, 5.30-9.30pm Fri-Sun* €€

't Binnenhuys: The 1772 Binnenhuys survived WWI relatively intact: in the sitting room and back garden they serve coffee, cake and beer. *9.30am-6.30pm Mon & Wed-Sat, 2-6pm Sun* €

In 't Klein Stadhuis: This split-level bar-café in a quirkily decorated historical guildhall serves gigantic good-value meals, some beer-based. *11am-midnight, kitchen to 10.30pm* €€

Slowwings: Coffee connoisseur joint serving micro cold-brew, *ristretti* and more. Tables are made from old sewing machines. *10am–12.30 pm & 2–6.30pm Tue-Sun* €

Beyond Ypres

Esen
Diksmuide
Westvleteren
Woesten
Roeselare
Poperinge · Ypres · Zonnebeke
Dranouter · Menen · Kortrijk
Mesen · Mouscron
FRANCE
Tourcoing

Ypres is the perfect base to explore the Westhoek region: a verdant haven of rolling hills, historic towns and picture-postcard villages.

Prosperous **Kortrijk** was founded as the Roman settlement of Cortoriacum. It grew wealthy as a flax and linen centre, but was severely bombed by the Allies during WWII. It retains a gorgeous *begijnhof* and an important historical resonance as the venue for Flanders' defining medieval battle. The battlefield site is now Groeningheveld, a leafy park in relatively central Kortrijk marked by a 1906 pseudo-medieval gateway and the triumphant Groeninge Statue featuring a gilded woman unleashing the Flemish lion.

Poperinge is one of the loveliest towns in Flanders, with a pretty townscape and a number of historical WWI-related sites. It has less of the tourist crush and the heaviness of nearby Ypres and the Salient.

Places

Kortrijk p149
Poperinge p152

Kortrijk

TIME FROM YPRES: **30MIN**

The historic centre

Kortrijk's curved central square, the **Grote Markt**, is scarred by insensitive 20th-century constructions, but the slightly leaning, multi-spired brick *belfort* (belfry) provides an attractive focus, and the restored 1421 Historisch Stadhuis (former town hall) building has a fine ornate facade dotted with stone mini-spires and niche statues.

Small but utterly delightful, the enclosed **begijnhof** is as charming a cluster of whitewashed old terraced houses as you could hope to find. Enter through a portal tucked behind Café Rouge (p152) and admire the 1682 turreted mansion at Begijnhof 27. Designed for single women, the complex was founded by Johanna of Constantinople way back in 1238: her statue can be seen near the entrance. The last member of the community died in 2013, and the buildings were restored and now provide affordable housing.

St-Maartenskerk is a noble 83m tower that adds finesse to the Kortrijk skyline. It belongs to this mostly 15th-century Gothic church, built on the site of St-Eloi's 7th-century chapel.

continues on p152

GETTING AROUND

The towns of Kortrijk and Poperinge are well connected to Ypres by frequent and efficient train services. Cycling is a popular way of getting round the region, and car hire gives your travels flexibility.

The Ypres Salient

During WWI, the Ypres Salient was an arc around the city where many major battles were fought. It was an important element of the Western Front, and today, the Ypres Salient is a signposted, 70km-long car route – or 36km-long cycling route – past several historic cemeteries, museums and monuments. These are a few key stops, but you can find an overview of the entry points and more information in the Ypres Tourist Office.

❶ Ypres

Prepare for your trip with a visit to Ypres' In Flanders Fields Museum.

The Drive: From Ypres Station, head north towards Haiglaan. Take the first exit on the first roundabout, then the second exit on the next. Essex Farm Cemetery is on your right, just after the bridge.

❷ Essex Farm Cemetery

In 1915, Canadian doctor John McCrae – who wrote "In Flanders Fields" – had a shelter dug out here to care for the first victims of German gas attacks. That shelter grew into Essex Farm Cemetery. McCrae's poem acted as a powerful incentive for the Allied war effort and turned the poppy into a symbol of sacrifice.

The Drive: From here, drive west on Noordhofweg for about 800m. Turn left on Veurnseweg, then left onto Noorderring (the N38). After 4km, turn right onto Moortelweg, then immediately left on Brugseweg. Next, turn right on Roeselarestraat for 4.5km. Turn right on Schipstraat, then next left on Vijfwegestraat for Tyne Cot Cemetery.

PHILLIP KRASKOFF/SHUTTERSTOCK

Tyne Cot Cemetery

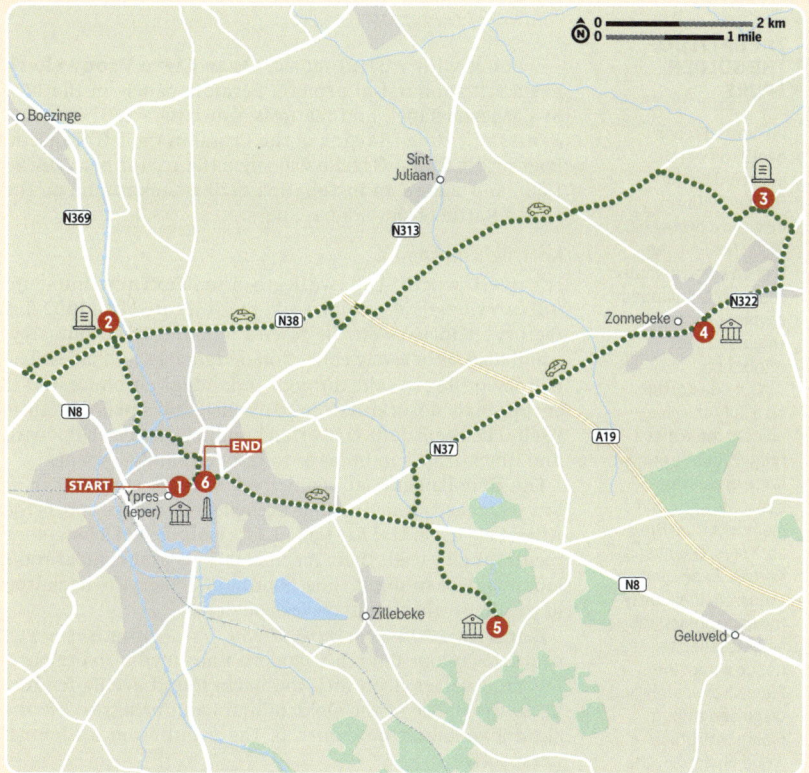

③ Tyne Cot Cemetery

If you only visit one WWI cemetery, make it Tyne Cot. With almost 12,000 soldiers buried here – more than 8000 of them unidentified – it is the world's largest Commonwealth war cemetery, with endless rows of white headstones and harrowing stories at the visitor centre.

The Drive: Head southeast on Tynecotstraat, then left on Passendalestraat. At the roundabout, turn right. Continue on Roeselarestraat (the N332), then go straight at the next roundabout. Take the first left on Berten Pilstraat. Pacchendaele Museum is to your left.

④ Passchendaele Museum & Memorial Gardens

Next up is Passchendaele Museum, this time specifically focused on the Third Battle of Ypres – also known as the Battle of Passchendaele. This 1917 battle caused over 500,000 casualties and became a symbol of the futility of war.

The Drive: Head west on Ieperstraat (the N332) and take the third exit on the roundabout onto Briekestraat (the N37). Continue on Briekestraat for 3.5km, then turn left on Begijnenbosstraat. Turn left on Meenseweg, then immediately right on Canadalaan. Hill 62 is at the end of the street.

⑤ Hill 62

Hill 62 served as an observation point during the war and is now home to the Sanctuary Wood Museum. The adjacent garden feels like a different world, with its well-preserved trenches, shell craters and narrow underground passages.

The Drive: Head back north on Canadalaan, then turn left on Meenseweg (the N8). At the roundabout, continue straight. Turn left on Frenchlaan.

⑥ Menin Gate

The Menin Gate ends the Ypres Salient route. Every night at 8pm, The Last Post honours the fallen.

continued from p149

Echoing with wistful music, **Onze Lieve Vrouwekerk** has a gilt sunburst altarpiece, heraldic panels in the 1373 St-Catherinekapel, and features Van Dyck's 1631 painting *Kruisoprichting* (Raising of the Cross) in the left transept. Poet-priest Guido Gezelle was once the pastor here (1872–1889) and there's an installation giving background on the fabled Battle of the Golden Spurs.

Kortrijk's museums

It's well worth the walk to the **Texture** museum *(texturekortrijk.be; adult/child €8/6),* located in a 1902 flax factory. It focuses on the town's flax and linen industry; you'll also see a lovely collection of damasks and laces. The history of flax is told through individual accounts and is surprisingly absorbing: you can touch and smell the fabric itself. The beautifully converted building uses flax chipboard and linen drapes in homage to the museum's content.

The **Broeltorens**, an iconic pair of three-storey fortress towers, guards a picturesque arched stone bridge across the River Leie in central Kortrijk. Last reminders of a long-gone medieval city wall, their machicolations and conical roofs look magical in night-time floodlights when the backdrop of mediocre apartments is less obvious.

Kortrijk 1302 *(kortrijk1302.be; free)* promises seven centuries in one day: this modern multimedia 'experience' museum delves deep into the background events leading up to the Battle of the Golden Spurs and brings to life the significance and outcomes of the event from a Flemish perspective.

Poperinge

TIME FROM YPRES: **8MIN** 🚆

Hop into pops

For centuries, the Poperinge area has produced the quality hops required for Belgium's beer industry, and it remains a magnet for beer lovers. During WWI, Poperinge was just out of German artillery range, and it became a posting and R&R station for Allied soldiers heading to or from the Ypres Salient. English troops, remembering Poperinge for its many entertainments and doubtless too for its brews, referred to the town fondly as 'Pops'.

THE BATTLE OF THE GOLDEN SPURS

Flanders' French overlords were incensed by the Bruges Matins massacre of May 1302. Philip the Fair, the French king, promptly sent a well-equipped cavalry of aristocratic knights to seek retribution.

Outside Kortrijk on 11 July, this magnificent force met a ragged, lightly armed force of weavers, peasants and guild members from Bruges, Ypres, Ghent and Kortrijk. Expecting little from their lowly foes, the horseback knights failed to notice a trap: the Flemish townsfolk had disguised a boggy marsh with brushwood. Snared by the mud, the heavily armoured French were quickly immobilised and slaughtered, their golden spurs hacked off and displayed as trophies. The event became a potent symbol of Flemish resistance, and to this day, 11 July is celebrated as Flanders' 'national' holiday.

PLACES TO EAT & DRINK IN KORTRIJK: OUR PICKS

Café Rouge: French-style shuttered facade and a bold semi-minimalist interior; the terrace fills a tree-lined square behind the *begijnhof. 11am-9pm Tue-Sun* €€

't Mouterijtje: Spacious brasserie with bare brickwork and red steel beams; a good range of beers, fish dishes and signature dish *côte-à-l'os* (rib roast). *5pm-midnight Fri-Tue* €€

Gainsbar: Beer specialist bar with a youthful upbeat vibe. Some rare beer gems, including occasional draught masterpieces from Dupont and Struise. *noon-1am Tue-Thu, 2pm-2am Fri-Sun* €

Viva Sara: Kortrijk coffee house with its own brand of chocolate (Viva Laura) and confectionery (Viva Lena). *8am-6.30pm Mon-Fri, 9am-6pm Sat* €

Wander into imposing Sint-Janskerk to see the 'miraculous' little Virgin-and-Child statuette, which reputedly brought a stillborn child to life in 1479.

Wartime injustice

Though English troops nicknamed it 'Good old Pops', Poperinge had a more sinister side – it was a place of execution for wartime deserters. Hidden behind a red door in the north side of the stadhuis, you can still see a chilling original shooting post and the stone-walled **Death Cell** *(9am-5pm)*, where deserters spent their last night. Brochures in the cell explain in some detail the era's injustices, accompanied by an audio recounting of the 1917 execution of 17-year-old soldier Herbert Morris.

Hop museum

Once the municipal centre for weighing and storing hops, the 19th-century Stadsschaal now houses the distinctively scented **National Hopmuseum** *(hopmuseum.be; €7/4),* where you'll learn more about hops than you'd ever want to know. The simple attached bar-café serves several local brews; the building was once home to Dirk Frimout, Belgium's first astronaut.

Historic house

Talbot House *(talbothouse.be; €12/7)* is an unusually light-hearted WWI attraction. Reverend Philip 'Tubby' Clayton set up the Everyman's Club here in 1915 to offer rest and recreation for WWI soldiers regardless of rank. The main 1790 townhouse has barely changed since; the garden is a charming oasis. Visits start with a modest exhibition (accessed from Pottestraat) where photos, quotes and videos remind visitors of Tubby's sharp gallows humour. End the visit with a free cup of English-style tea in the kitchen.

WESTVLETEREN TRAPPIST BEER

When Westvleteren 12 was declared to be the world's best beer in 2005, isolated Trappist brewery **Abdij Sint-Sixtus** was inundated with press and visitors, all in search of the twice-fermented dark ale with its irresistible nut and raisin notes. In response to the frenzy, the monks declined to increase production, saying, 'We make the beer to live but we do not live for beer.'

The architecturally unremarkable abbey where the legend is brewed is located north of Poperinge down a web of tiny lanes; it is closed to visitors but there's a bar-café (see below) for tastings. You can't take bottles away; purchasing a case is only possible by reserving weeks in advance online (the abbey's infamously overloaded 'beerphone' was replaced in 2019).

EATING & DRINKING IN & AROUND POPERINGE

Hotel Amfora: A step-gabled frontage and traditional bar-restaurant that doesn't disappoint. *noon-9pm Thu-Mon* €€

Deca Brewery: One of the only places you can buy takeaway beers by respected local boutique-brewer Struise. *2-6pm Tue-Fri, 1-4.30pm Sat* €€

In de Vrede: This abbey pub is the only place in the world where you can be (virtually) sure of tasting the incomparable West-vleteren 12, often cited as Belgium's greatest beer. *noon-8pm Sat-Wed* €€

Restaurant Pegasus: A very upmarket affair. While mains are presented as nouvelle cuisine, extra sides are there for those who prefer old-cuisine Belgian-sized portions. *8am-11pm Tue-Sat* €€€

Places We Love to Stay

€ **Budget** €€ **Midrange** €€€ **Top End**

Ghent
MAP p112

Uppelink € Within a classic step-gabled canal-side house, the showstopping attraction at this super-central hostel is the unbeatable view of Ghent's towers from the breakfast room.

Ecohostel Andromeda € Sleep on a reed-sprouting 'recycled' barge with a small open-top conversation deck. The boat's canal-side moorings are 600m northwest of Oude Begijnhof.

De Draecke € Behind a pseudo-medieval facade facing a picturesque willow-lined central canal lies this recently renovated and spotless (though slightly institutional) HI hostel.

Simon Says €€ Get in quick to snap up one of two fashionably styled guest rooms located above their well-patronised, chilled-out coffee shop in a fabulous part of town. It's the brightly coloured Art Nouveau house on the corner.

Big Sleep €€ The three guestrooms of this friendly B&B in an attractive 1890s townhouse have high ceilings and private showers but shared toilets.

ApartGent Apartments €€ Book in advance for these wildly popular fully self-contained apartments. They're spacious, stylish, central and with great weekly and monthly rates.

1898 The Post €€€ This beautiful boutique offering is housed in Ghent's spectacular twin-turreted former post office. Dark and moody in a wonderful way, with great design at every turn.

Hotel Harmony €€€ Luxuriously heaped pillows, fine linen, Miró-esque art and swish modern colours lie beneath the 18th-century beams of this old-meets-new beauty; rooms 30 and 31 share a wonderful panorama of Ghent's spires.

Bruges
MAP p122

St Christopher's Inn Hostel at The Bauhaus € This backpacker village incorporates a hostel, apartments, a nightclub and a little chill-out room.

Passage Bruges € This small hotel has stylish, large and well-priced rooms. Located at the end of a small alleyway, they are also very quiet.

Camping Memling € Quiet campground in St-Kruis where pitch prices assume two adults. Get off bus 11 at Vossensteert and walk back 400m towards Bruges.

B&B Amaryllis Dieltiens €€ Old and new art fills this lovingly restored classical mansion, which remains an appealing real home run by charming musician hosts. Superbly central yet quiet.

Hotel Patritius €€ Enter this proud 1830s townhouse through the carriageway and past a bar-lounge. Up the historical spiral staircase, 16 guest rooms vary in size and style.

Hotel Bla Bla €€ A shuttered and step-gabled building given an elegant makeover, with parquet floors, modern artworks and soothingly pale rooms. Excellent buffet breakfast.

Relais Bourgondisch Cruyce €€€ This luxurious little boutique hotel occupies a part-timbered medieval house that's been tastefully updated and graced with art, antiques, Persian carpets and fresh orchids.

Dukes' Palace €€€ This large-scale five-star hotel is imposingly tall with a Disneyesque turret. It partly occupies the Prinsenhof building, Bruges' 15th-century royal palace.

Ostend
MAP p139

Hostel De Ploate € This HI hostel is smart, modern and minimal with no curfew, super-helpful and friendly staff, and a great location.

De Hofkamers €€ Rooms are all different but play on romantic pseudo-antique themes; some have four-poster beds. All have a safe, fridge and kettle.

Leopold Hotel €€ A variety of room types in a range of layouts and sizes, from tiny (and cheap) to something a bit more fancy. It's not a swanky hotel, but has a classy feel.

Thermae Palace Hotel €€€ The beautiful, beachfront Thermae Palace is ageing gracefully and it retains appeal for folks seeking that old-school Euro-beach-resort vibe.

The Belgian coast

De Peerdevisser € This 34-room HI hostel in Oostduinkerke has 138 beds, but outside the summer months it's blissfully quiet. It's situated near the dunes just a short walk to the ocean.

Duinezwin Camping € This family-friendly campground in Bredene has good facilities, tidy sites and a convenient almost beachfront location.

Auberge des Rois – Beach Hotel €€€ This tried and true De Haan beachfront hotel has fanciful rooms and excellent service, though it may be a bit old-school for some.

Manoir Carpe Diem €€€ This cosy yet indulgent little De Haan hotel is set on top of a knoll amid the finest local villas on a quiet street.

La Réserve €€€ Even though the property isn't directly on the beach, Knokke's fanciest digs are undoubtedly impressive, with opulent interiors, wide balconies and top-notch service.

Veurne

't Kasteel en 't Koetshuys €€ This delightful 1907 red-brick mansion features high ceilings, old marble fireplaces and stripped floorboards, creating a lovely blend of classic and modern, all immaculately kept.

Auberge de Klasse €€ This comfortable three-room B&B retains more of its 18th-century structure than you'd guess from the outside. The interior is heaped with soft furnishings and frilly linens.

Ypres   MAP p147

Yoaké B&B €€ Smart two-room B&B attached to a hip wellness centre. Great breakfasts and a warm welcome.

Ariane Hotel €€ This peaceful, professionally managed large hotel has a designer feel to its rooms and popular restaurant. Wartime memorabilia dots the spacious common areas.

Main Street Hotel €€€ Jumbling eccentricity with historical twists and luxurious comfort, this is a one-off that oozes character. The breakfast room has a Tiffany glass ceiling.

Kortrijk

Hotel Messeyne €€ This grand 1662 townhouse's beamed high ceilings and original fireplaces meld with stylish contemporary decor and immaculate rooms.

Center Hotel €€ Attractively modernised rooms at reasonable prices above a subtly fashionable bar with handy 24-hour reception.

Poperinge

Het Wethuys €€ On the Watou village central square, you'll find this charming historical bar-café with attractive B&B rooms. It also offers St-Bernardus Tripel on draught.

Hotel Amfora €€ While its step-gabled frontage and bar-restaurant (p153) are traditional in style, the rooms here have been upgraded with a muted modern look.

ARTERRA/PHILIPPE CLEMENT/UNIVERSAL IMAGES GROUP VIA GETTY IMAGES

Thermae Palace Hotel, Ostend

*Researched by
Mark Elliott*

Antwerp & Northeast Belgium

CENTURIES OF CREATIVITY, CONTINUED CUTTING EDGE

Dynamically 21st century yet oozing with historical splendour and cultural creativity, Antwerp is just the best known of many fascinating destinations in northeastern Belgium.

Vibrant and multifaceted, the forward-looking city of Antwerp sits astride the Brussels–Amsterdam railway and demands that visitors take note. The rest of this region, however, is like a Christmas pudding: richly full of delights yet it somehow tends to get forgotten, as everyone's already had their fill by the time dessert rolls around.

The northeast is culturally part of Flanders, though nitpicking linguists point out that local dialects of Dutch are technically classified as Brabantine (Antwerp and Leuven) and Limburgish. Their distribution roughly fits with the historic duchies of Brabant and Limburg that preceded Burgundian rule in the 15th century. These names live on as provinces, though Antwerp has long since become a province in its own right, as befits the economic powerhouse of Flanders and one of Europe's foremost ports.

Lier and Mechelen are memorable gem cities and the region has some of Belgium's loveliest historic *begijnhoven*. Western Brabant (Hageland) and southern Limburg (Haspengouw) are predominantly rural with rolling hills, orchards and vineyards producing many of Belgium's rapidly improving wines as well as fruit and the sugar that historically made Tienen prosper. Tongeren has a rich Gallo-Roman history while wealthy Hasselt is known for its *jenever* (Flemish gin). Despite an industrial heritage, the Genk area also retains forest parks and is great for cycling.

ERIK A.JV/SHUTTERSTOCK

THE MAIN AREAS

ANTWERP
Trailblazing mix of art, history and contemporary cool. **p162**

MECHELEN
The grandest city you've probably never heard of. **p178**

LEUVEN
Student vibes in the Cambridge of Belgium. **p183**

For places to stay in Antwerp & Northeast Belgium, see p193

TRAVELLING2BPRECISE/SHUTTERSTOCK

Left: Brabo Fountain, Antwerp (p163); Above: Antwerpen-Centraal train station (p174)

Antwerp, p162
Medieval meets 21st-century in this centre for fashion, diamonds and art ranging from homeboy Rubens to Berchem's explosion of street art.

Mechelen, p178
Historically Belgium's religious centre, this inviting city has several of the country's most impressive churches in a very appealing cityscape with some fascinating museums.

Leuven, p183
Bubbling with student life and graced with one of Europe's most flamboyant town halls, Leuven is a logical launching point for touring vineyards, orchards and historic cities further east.

Goes

Yerseke

Bergen-op-Zoom

Breda

Baarl
Herto

Westerschelde

NETHERLANDS

Terneuzen

Hulst

Lillo

Hoogstraten

Brecht

E19

N14

Westmalle

Oostmalle

Turnhout

N49

E34

Stekene

Antwerp
(Antwerpen)

E34

Sint-Niklaas

Bazel

Boechout

Herentals

Albertkanaal

E17

Tems

Lier

E313

Puurs

Boom

Nete

E19

Willebroek

N10

Buggenhout

Canal de Willebroek

Mechelen

Werchter

Aarschot

Scherpe
heu

A12

Aalst
(Alost)

Meise

Vilvoorde

E314

Rillaar

Affligem

Zottegem

Ninove

E40

BRUSSELS

E40

Leuven
(Louvain)

N3

Tienen
(Tirlemont)

Brakel

Geraardsbergen
(Grammont)

N8

R0

Tervuren

Hoegaarden

Linkebeek

Lessines
(Lesen)

Halle
(Hal)

E19

N5

Waterloo

Wavre
(Waver)

Jodoigne
(Geldenaken)

Ath
(Aat)

Enghien
(Endingen)

Canal Bruxelles-Charleroi

Nivelles
(Nijvel)

Soignies
(Zinnik)

La Louvière

0   20 km
0   10 miles

Find Your Way

Antwerp, Mechelen and Leuven are all easy short hops from Brussels, with Leuven especially handy for Brussels Airport. Antwerp is an obvious stop en route to Amsterdam.

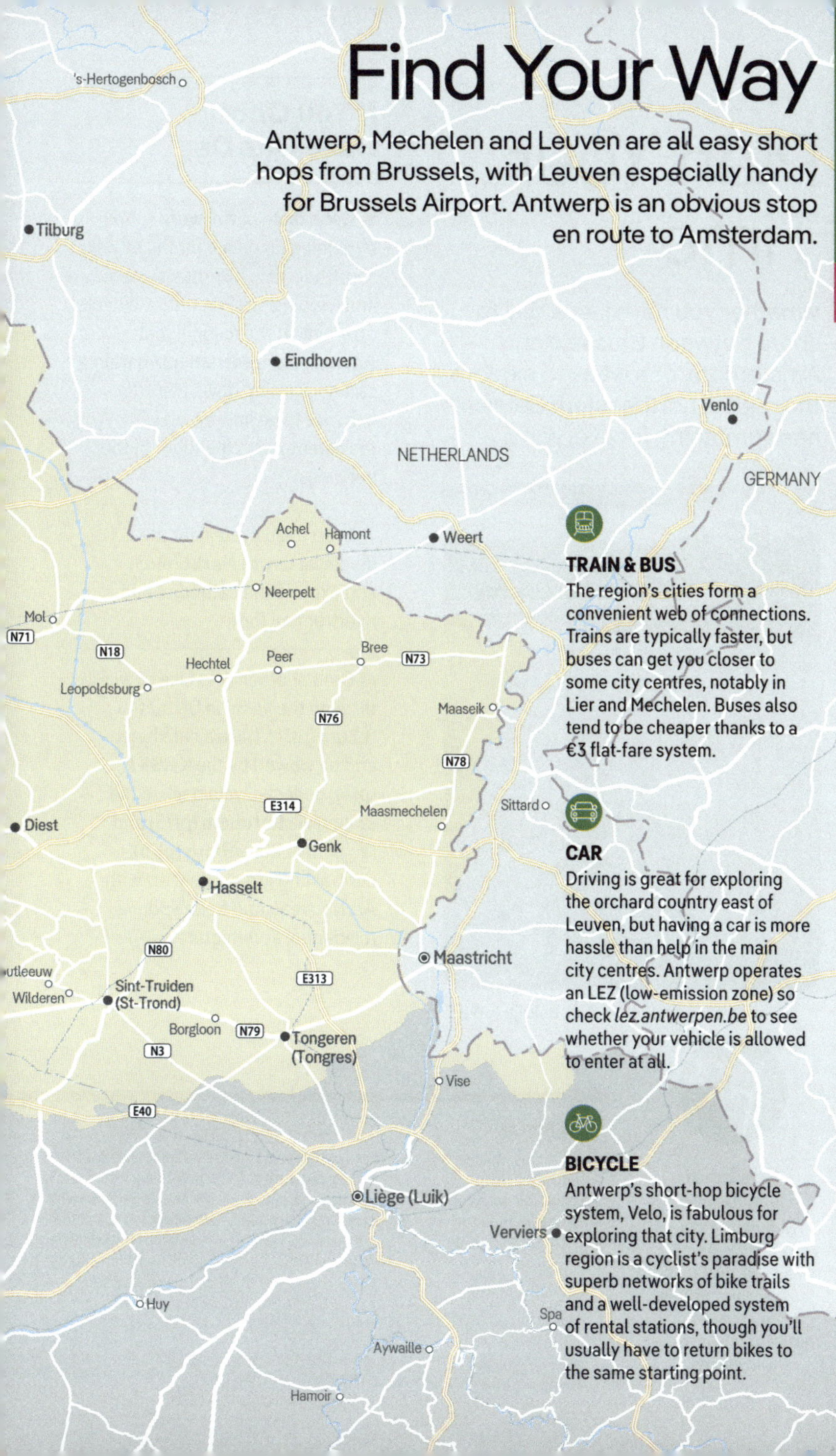

TRAIN & BUS

The region's cities form a convenient web of connections. Trains are typically faster, but buses can get you closer to some city centres, notably in Lier and Mechelen. Buses also tend to be cheaper thanks to a €3 flat-fare system.

CAR

Driving is great for exploring the orchard country east of Leuven, but having a car is more hassle than help in the main city centres. Antwerp operates an LEZ (low-emission zone) so check *lez.antwerpen.be* to see whether your vehicle is allowed to enter at all.

BICYCLE

Antwerp's short-hop bicycle system, Velo, is fabulous for exploring that city. Limburg region is a cyclist's paradise with superb networks of bike trails and a well-developed system of rental stations, though you'll usually have to return bikes to the same starting point.

159

Plan Your Time

Whether you have just a day to spare between Brussels and Amsterdam, or a week to explore the region, northeastern Belgium has something for everyone.

ARTUR DEBAT/GETTY IMAGES

'Cycling through Water', Bokrijk (p191)

If You Only Have One Day

● Get a taste of **Antwerp** (p162) by signing up online for the city's short-hop Velo bike-hire system and jumping straight onto a bicycle on arrival at the magnificent **Antwerpen-Centraal** (p174) train station. Cycling down Meir, it's hard not to be impressed with the ostentatious grandeur of the buildings.

● Drop the bicycle near the medieval **Grote Markt** (p163) and explore the cathedral and riverfront on foot.

● Grab another Velo bike to wiggle through the Fashion District to **'t Zuid** (p174), have a cafe lunch and be wowed by the **KMSKA** (p174) gallery. Cycle back to the station via **Berchem** (p175) and residential **Zurenborg** (p175), contrasting great street art with Art Nouveau and *belle époque* residential architecture.

Seasonal Highlights
Summer sees an extraordinary plethora of cultural and music festivals and virtually every quarter of Antwerp organises its own events.

FEBRUARY
Though far less folkloric than at Binche or Stavelot, the carnival at **Tienen** includes an impressive float parade.

APRIL
A mass of blossoms transform the pretty **Haspengouw** orchard region around Borgloon into a giant work of natural art.

MAY
On the weekend before Ascension Day, Mechelen's **Hanswijk Procession** is a solemn religious parade that follows a fun-filled public party.

Four Days in & Around Antwerp

● Take longer exploring **Antwerp** (p162), adding in a visit to the immersive **Chocolate Nation** (p170), an amusingly interactive tour of the **De Koninck Brewery** (p175) and learning more about diamonds at **DIVA** (p167). Cycle around the **Het Eilandje** (p166) regeneration area, survey the cityscape from the top of **MAS** (p166), and admire Zaha Hadid's curiously discordant **Havenhuis** (Harbour House; p167) building.

● At night don't miss sampling a good selection of the city's characterful bar-cafés, both city-central classics like **Oud Arsenaal** (p172) and off-beat mould-breakers like **Bar Paniek** (p167).

● Spend part of one day making an excursion to **Lier** (p176), one of Belgium's loveliest smaller cities with a quaint *begijnhof* and unusual clock tower.

If You Have More Time

● **Mechelen** (p178) is a city that rewards at least an overnight stay to enjoy the subtle lighting that adds atmosphere to its cathedral tower and beautiful central square.

● Take a look at **Leuven** (p183) and experience the hubbub of the collection of pubs that make up 'Europe's longest bar' (p185). With a car, a full day is enough to fleetingly visit impressive central squares at **Tienen** (p190), **Zoutleeuw** (p190) and **Sint-Truiden** (p190) en route to **Tongeren** (p188) with its Roman roots.

● If possible allow time en route to discover some mesmerising art installations in orchards around **Borgloon** (p187). Loop north to the prosperous 'gin-city' of **Hasselt** (p189), then jump on a bicycle at **Bokrijk** (p191) to explore the greenery beyond.

JULY

Belgium's biggest music festivals bring pop and rock to **Werchter** near Leuven and electronica to **Tomorrowland** at Boon.

AUGUST

At 9pm on 15 August, candles replace all electric light in Aarschot for **Sint-Rochusverlichting** (p192) celebrating a 1667 miracle: the town avoiding plague.

OCTOBER

Hasselt celebrates its gin-making traditions in the **Jeneverfeesten**. At 4pm on the Saturday, water turns to gin as the little Borrelmanneke statue 'miraculously' spouts *jenever*.

NOVEMBER & DECEMBER

Antwerp hosts a magical **Christmas market** on the Grote Markt. Leuven's **Kort Film Festival** screens around 120 international short-form movies.

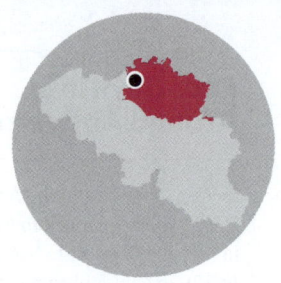

Antwerp

ART | FASHION | ARCHITECTURE

☑ TOP TIP

The app-based **Antwerp City Pass** *(antwerpcitypass.be; 24-/48-/72-hours €45/55/65)* allows entry to over 20 key attractions plus free public transport. It might make sense if you're visiting Chocolate Nation, De Ruien and De Koninck Brewery. However, almost all other Antwerp museums are included in the all-Belgium MuseumPass *(museumpassmusees. be; €64.95)*, which lasts a whole year.

Belgium's second city is also its capital of cool, a fashion hub and world-leading diamond trading centre, yet it retains an exquisite medieval heart. By the 16th century, Antwerp had taken over from Bruges as one of Europe's main trading ports, opening the world's first specially built stock exchange. From the 1560s, iconoclasts, the Dutch Revolt and the inquisition devastated the place, exacerbated later by a blockade of Antwerp's port. Skilled workers and international trade fled north (hence Amsterdam's rise). Still, the world's first newspaper was produced here in 1606 and Rubens hung around to paint baroque masterpieces. Once the port blockade finally ended in 1863, wealth quickly returned and by the 1920s Antwerp was important enough to host the Olympic Games and build Europe's first skyscraper. WWII destroyed much and decimated the significant Jewish population, but Antwerp rebounded, and today few cities have a more optimistic 21st-century vision.

Medieval Marvels

MAP P164

Antwerp's antique heart

Other than Europe's first skyscraper (the 1929 Boerentoren), central Antwerp's architecture remains relatively low rise, so that the 16th-century belfry of **Onze-Lieve-Vrouwekathedraal**

 GETTING AROUND

Beautiful Antwerpen-Centraal is the main train hub and the nearest station to the old city centre. Antwerpen-Berchem is a possible alternative for the Art Nouveau area of Zurenborg. Antwerpen-Zuid is marginally nearer Het Zuid. Antwerp has a well developed bus and tram system, the trams being known as 'pre-metro' when

tunnelling underground. However, the easiest way to get around the main sights is generally using the Velo short-hop bicycle-hire system *(velo-antwerpen.be/en)*. Bike pick-up and drop-off stands are plentiful and the system is unusually easy to use, though always double-check that the bike has been properly returned after each hop.

Onze-Lieve-Vrouwekathedraal

majestically dominates the cityscape. Ornately magnificent, the 123m tower rarely fails to prompt a gasp of awe, and it has a habit of popping into view from all kinds of intriguing angles. The cathedral itself is a Gothic masterpiece that took 169 years to finish (1352–1521).

The small streets around the cathedral are abuzz with cafe life, with bars also spilling onto the main market square, **Grote Markt** – a beautiful cobbled space lined on three sides by classic step-gabled medieval-style merchant houses. Behind the Brabo Fountain is the **Stadhuis**, Antwerp's 1565 city hall with a statue-topped palatial facade that blends Flemish and Italian styles. Inside is a fascinating, map-rich free exhibition about the city's development and ambitious plans for the future.

Outside, a summer-only **tourist 'tram'** *(touristram.be/eilandje -old-harbour),* disguised as a 1930s limousine, provides 40-minute guided tours around Het Eilandje. However, there's lots to see by simply walking the cobbled lanes nearby. A good start is strolling down to **Het Steen**, Antwerp's dinky but photogenic castle dating from 1200. It contains a tourist office and free-access viewpoint along with the **Antwerp Story** *(visit.antwerpen .be/en/info/the-antwerp-story-en; adult/child €7/5),* an 11-room museum-experience introducing the city. Outside, spot **Lange Wapper**, a humorous statue of a tall folkloric 'peeping Tom' figure showing off his codpiece to two diminutive onlookers.

BRABO AND ANTWERP'S HAND SYMBOL

Antwerp's gorgeous Grote Markt is focused on a bronze **fountain-statue** of a man holding a huge, disconnected hand that he's about to fling into space.

This is Brabo, a Roman warrior who, according to legend, defeated a fearsome giant who had controlled a bend of the Scheldt, forcing passing ship captains to pay an extortionate toll. Brabo killed him and symbolically chucked his hand into the river. Though etymologists have a much more prosaic theory, popular folk culture says that the name Antwerpen derives from this act of hand throwing – *hand werpen.* Today *Antwerpse handjes* (little Antwerp hands) have become a city trademark, turning up in all manner of guises, from De Koninck beer glasses to chocolates and souvenir jewellery.

The alley also hosts the better-known restaurant Anthony Van Dijck.

 EATING IN CENTRAL ANTWERP: OUR PICKS

MAP P164

Elfde Gebod: Belgian classics served in an ivy-clad medieval masterpiece with astounding interior of angels, saints and sacrilege. *noon-10pm* €€

InVINcible: Get social, sitting shoulder-to-shoulder at the kitchen counter watching show-chefs create seasonally changing dishes. *noon-1.30pm & 6.30-10pm Mon-Fri* €€€

Fiera: Like a musically jazzed up Cambridge college formal, set in the world's oldest stock exchange building. Gastronomic food or fancy cocktails. *noon-11pm* €€€

't Hofeke: Adorable, lively little restaurant tucked into a medieval hideaway. Menu ranges from shrimp croquettes to duck in port wine. *noon-3pm & 6-10pm* €€

CENTRAL & NORTH ANTWERP

Enlargement

See Enlargement

HIGHLIGHTS
1 Chocolate Nation
2 Grote Markt
3 Onze-Lieve-
   Vrouwekathedraal

SIGHTS
4 Brabo Fountain
5 De Handelsbeurs

6 De Ruien
see 6 DIVA
7 Het Steen
8 MAS
9 Red Star Line Museum
10 Rubens Statue
11 Sint-Annatunnel
12 Snijder-Rockoxhuis
13 Stadhuis

14 Statue of Lange Wapper
15 St-Carolus-
   Borromeuskerk
16 St-Jacobskerk
17 Vlaeykensgang

ACTIVITIES
18 Tourist 'tram' Het
   Eijlandje route

19 Waagnatie

● **SLEEPING**
20 De Witte Lelie
21 Hotel Julien
22 Hotel O
23 The Ash
24 U Eat & Sleep

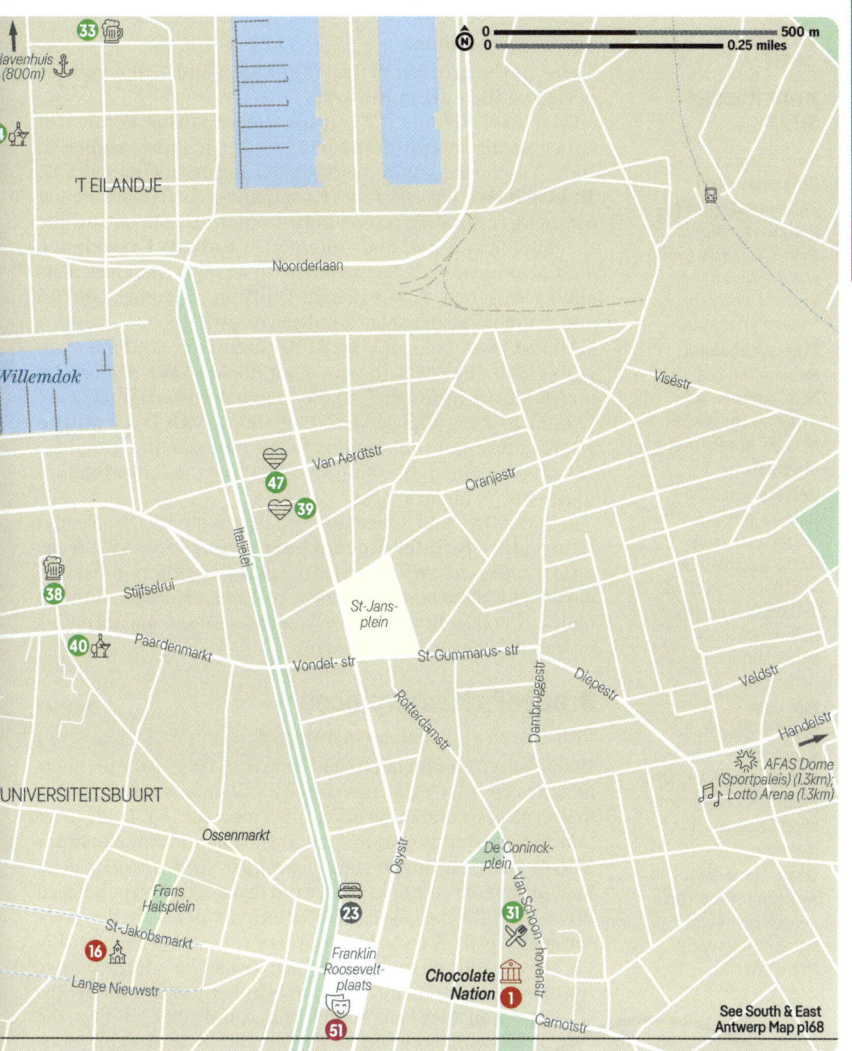

'T EILANDJE

Noorderlaan

Willemdok

Viséstr

Van Aerdtstr

47

39

Oranjestr

38

Stijfselrui

St-Jans-plein

40

Paardenmarkt

Vondel-str

St-Gummarus-str

Italiëlei

Rotterdamstr

Dambruggestr

Diepestr

Veldstr

Handelstr

AFAS Dome
(Sportpaleis) (1.3km);
Lotto Arena (1.3km)

UNIVERSITEITSBUURT

Ossenmarkt

De Coninck-plein

Frans
Halsplein

23

St-Jakobsmarkt

16

31

Chocolate
Nation

1

Lange Nieuwstr

Franklin
Roosevelt-plaats

Oltstr

Van schoon-hovestr

Carnotstr

51

See South & East
Antwerp Map p168

lavenhuis
(800m)

33

EATING
25 Elfde Gebod
26 Fiera
27 InVINcible
28 Jam
29 Marcel
30 Msemen
31 Potala Kitchen

32 't Hofeke

**DRINKING &
NIGHTLIFE**
33 ABC (Seef)
Brewery & Cafe
34 Bar Paniek
35 Batavier
36 Bonaparte

37 Cafe Beveren
38 Café Hessenhuis
39 Club Random
40 Cousteau
41 De Kat
42 Den Bengel
43 Den Beulebak
see 42 Den Engel
44 Normo

45 Pelikaan
46 't Waagstuk
47 The Boots
48 The Yellow Window

ENTERTAINMENT
49 De Muze
50 Den Hopsack
51 Opera House

Artistic Pedigree

MAP P164 & P168

van Dijk and Rubens

Three of the greatest artists of the 16th and 17th centuries perfected their art in Antwerp.

Peter Paul Rubens (1577–1640), whose **statue** dominates Groenplaats, moved here in 1609 after lengthy studies in Italy. The house-studio he designed is now the memorable **Rubenshuis** *(rubenshuis.be)*. Its museum section is undergoing a massive restoration project until around 2027 but meanwhile the site offers a half-hour interactive **Rubens Experience** *(adult/concession €12/8; closed Wed)* to set the scene, and tickets allow access to the flower-rich garden. Numerous other galleries and churches also display a Rubens or two.

Almost as famous, the artist Antoon (later Anthony) van Dyck (1599–1641) was the son of an Antwerp silk dealer who honed his art in Rubens' studio long before becoming court painter to King Charles I of England. A **van Dyck statue** wearing posing britches adds to the monumental grandeur of Leysstraat/Meir, the main street linking the central station to Antwerp's historic heart.

Both van Dyck and Rubens are well represented at the splendid 17th-century **Snijder-Rockoxhuis** *(snijdersrockoxhuis.be; adult/under-26 €10/6)*, a richly endowed gallery-museum, partly within the house of Rubens patron and former Antwerp mayor Nicolaas Rockox. Here you can also see masterpieces by Van der Weyden and Breugel.

MORE RUBENS SITES

Sint-Carolus Borromeuskerk: Rubens designed the baroque interior of this 1621 church, giving worshippers a very visceral foretaste of heaven's delights.

Sint-Jacobskerk: Rubens' tomb is here, adorned with a painting he made himself. In advance, obviously.

Waterpoort: The Rubens-designed 'water gate' once led to 't Zuid's inner harbour. It was filled in the 1960s and is now a park, so don't expect boats docking here now.

Museum Plantin-Moretus: Paintings by Peter Paul Rubens and books by his brother Philip, with illustrations by the master.

Onze-Lieve-Vrouwekathedraal: This central cathedral is home to four early Rubens works.

Breugel's Masterpieces

MAP P168

16th-century surrealism in Antwerp

Dutch-born Pieter Breugel the Elder (c 1525-1569) made his home in Antwerp from 1555, and the city still houses several of his masterpieces, notably his brilliantly grotesque 1561 *Dulle Griet (Mad Meg)*. That is usually kept at the magnificent **Museum Mayer van den Bergh** *(museummayervandenbergh.be/en)*, founded by collector Fritz Mayer van den Bergh who purchased Breugel's works cheaply in the later 19th century when they were considered of dubious taste. Fritz was significant in popularising his oeuvre and the museum, which looks like a 16th-century townhouse, was actually built in 1904 by his mother to house the collection after Fritz's early death. Until 2029, however, the museum is closed for a total refit. Instead, exhibitions plan to display key canvasses, including *Mad Meg*, at the nearby **Maagdenhuis** *(maagdenhuis.be; adult/under-26 €10/6)*, a former 16th-century orphanage/refuge, now a fascinating and at times poignant museum.

MORE MASTERS

The Brussels **Old Masters Museum** (p57) has more than 50 works by Rubens, churches in both Aalst (p120) and Mechelen (p178) have more Rubens creations, while Mechelen's **cathedral** (p178) has an altarpiece by van Dyck.

Maritime Foundations

MAP P164

Het Eilandje and Antwerp's port regeneration

At the heart of the regenerated docklands zone **Het Eilandje** is the distinctive 10-storey **MAS** (Museum aan de Stroom; *mas.be; adult/under-26 €10/5*). At first glance it looks as though great chunks have been chopped out of its sides. There are several museum floors designed around big-idea themes using a barrage of media. However, there are also several little-heralded free-to-visit spaces including sweeping city views from a top-floor **panorama point** reached via 10 escalators. Quicker to access on Floor 2 is **A Glimpse of the Collection** which stores unused treasures from city museums with a few selected items on show.

About 700m north of MAS, the **Red Star Line Museum** *(redstarline.be; adult/under-26 €10/6)* considers the human stories of some two million people who emigrated to North America using ocean liners from Antwerp. Opposite, **Waagnatie** *(waagnatie.eu)* is an expo centre that holds May's big food festival **Antwerpen Proeft** *(proeft.be)*.

Another 600m north, port museum **Haven Wereld** is due to open in 2026. Its collection of historic boats is visible as you cycle on towards **Havenhuis**.

The World's Biggest 'Diamond' MAP P164

Zaha Hadid's Flemish masterpiece

Antwerp's most adventurous piece of contemporary architecture is the extraordinary **Havenhuis** (Harbour House). The work of the late maestro architect Zaha Hadid (1950–2016), it looks as though a diamond-faceted UFO has landed on top of a giant historical mansion. It's a working office so you can't go upstairs, except by occasional **tours** *(experienceantwerp. be)*. However, the building's exterior is endlessly Instagramable and the floor of the public area inside displays a giant photo that helps you understand the sheer enormity of Europe's second-largest container port whose area is as big as the whole of Antwerp's populated zones.

Best Friends Forever? MAP P164

The world's diamond trading centre

The majority of the world's uncut diamonds pass through Antwerp, via exchange buildings along Hoveniersstraat and Schupstraat. However, these short, heavily guarded streets are oddly dour and banal. For a far more interesting introduction to the industry, visit **DIVA** *(divaantwerp.be; adult/under-26/child €12/8/free),* an engaging contemporary museum of diamonds and silverware. It has recreations of some of the world's most famous diamonds and a whole series of interactive exhibits, pullouts and touch-screens.

continues on p170

ANTWERP'S PORT HISTORY

Historically ships would sail down the wide river Scheldt, offloading at sheltered riverside docks right in the city centre. Antwerp suffered a massive blow following 16th-century Dutch-Spanish wars, when treaties closed the Scheldt to all non-Dutch ships. From 1797, temporarily Napoleon ignored such trifles and had the docks rebuilt.

Once the blockade was fully removed in 1863, business surged and by the late 19th century Antwerp was the world's third-largest port after London and New York. In the 20th century the city adapted quickly to the arrival of far bigger container ships and tankers, creating giant canal docks and vast, specially designed wharfs well north of the centre. Older port basins became Het Eilandje's prime redevelopment land.

EATING & DRINKING IN HET EILANDJE: OUR PICKS MAP P164

ABC (Seef) Brewery & Cafe: The fashionably dishevelled Seef brewpub also serves tasty beer-based meals. *noon-11pm Sun-Thu, to 1am Fri & Sat* €	**Batavier:** Traditional brown cafe with a terrace facing MAS. An upstairs dining room serves Flemish classics including grey-shrimp croquettes. *11am-late* €	**Marcel:** Classic gastronomy with impressive wine selection in an atmospherically historic former seamen's chapel. *noon-2pm Mon-Fri & 6-9pm Mon-Sat* €€€	**Bar Paniek:** Chaotic former warehouses transformed into a ramshackle pub by an artists' collective. Well chosen beer selection. *4-11pm Mon-Fri & 11am-11pm Sat-Sun*

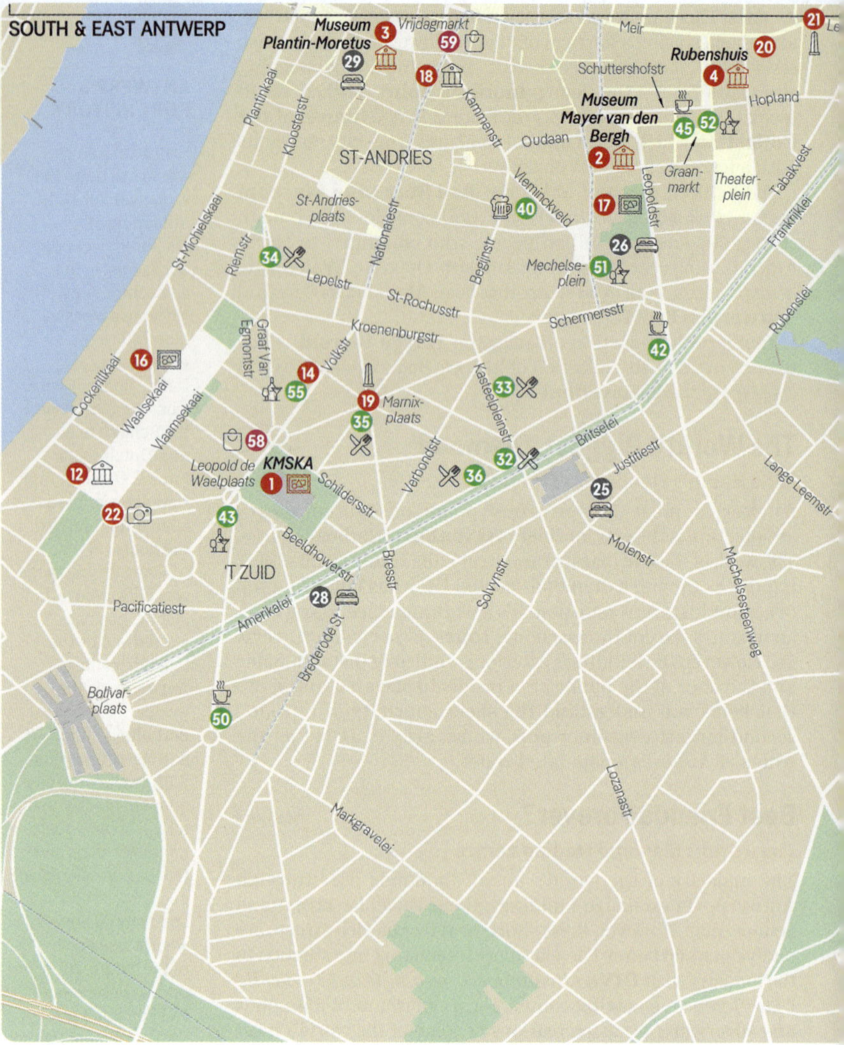
SOUTH & EAST ANTWERP
Museum Plantin-Moretus
Vrijdagmarkt
Meir
Rubenshuis
Schuttershofstr
Hopland
Museum Mayer van den Bergh
Oudaan
Kammenstr
Plantinkaai
Kloosterstr
ST-ANDRIES
St-Andries-plaats
Nationalestr
Vleminckveld
Leopoldstr
Graan-markt
Theater-plein
Tabakvest
Frankrijklei
St-Michielskaai
Riemstr
Lepelstr
St-Rochusstr
Begijnstr
Mechelse-plein
Schermersstr
Kroenenburgstr
Graaf Van Egmontstr
Volkstr
Rubenslei
Cockerillkaai
Waalsekaai
Vlaamsekaai
Marnix-plaats
Kasteelpleinstr
Verbondstr
Britselei
Justitiestr
Lange Leemstr
Leopold de Waelplaats
KMSKA
Schildersstr
Beeldhouwersstr
'T ZUID
Bresstr
Solvynsstr
Molenstr
Mechelsesteenweg
Pacificatiestr
Amerikalei
Brederode St
Bolivar-plaats
Lozanastr
Markgravelei

HIGHLIGHTS

1 KMSKA
2 Museum Mayer van den Bergh
3 Museum Plantin-Moretus
4 Rubenshuis
5 Zoo Antwerpen

SIGHTS

6 23-35 Transvaalstraat
7 Antwerpen-Centraal
8 De Twaalf Duivelkens
9 De Vier Seizoenen
10 Dive
11 'Flower' Houses
12 FOMU
13 Graffiti Streets
14 Help U Zelve
15 Les Mouettes
16 M HKA
17 Maagdenhuis
18 MoMu
19 Schelde Vrij Monument
20 Stadsfeestzaal
21 Van Dyck Statue
22 Waterpoort
23 Zurenborg

SLEEPING

24 A-Stay
25 Bed, Bad & Brood
26 Botanic Sanctuary Hotel
27 Boulevard Leopold
28 Hotel Rubenshof
29 Motel One
30 YUST Antwerp

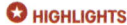

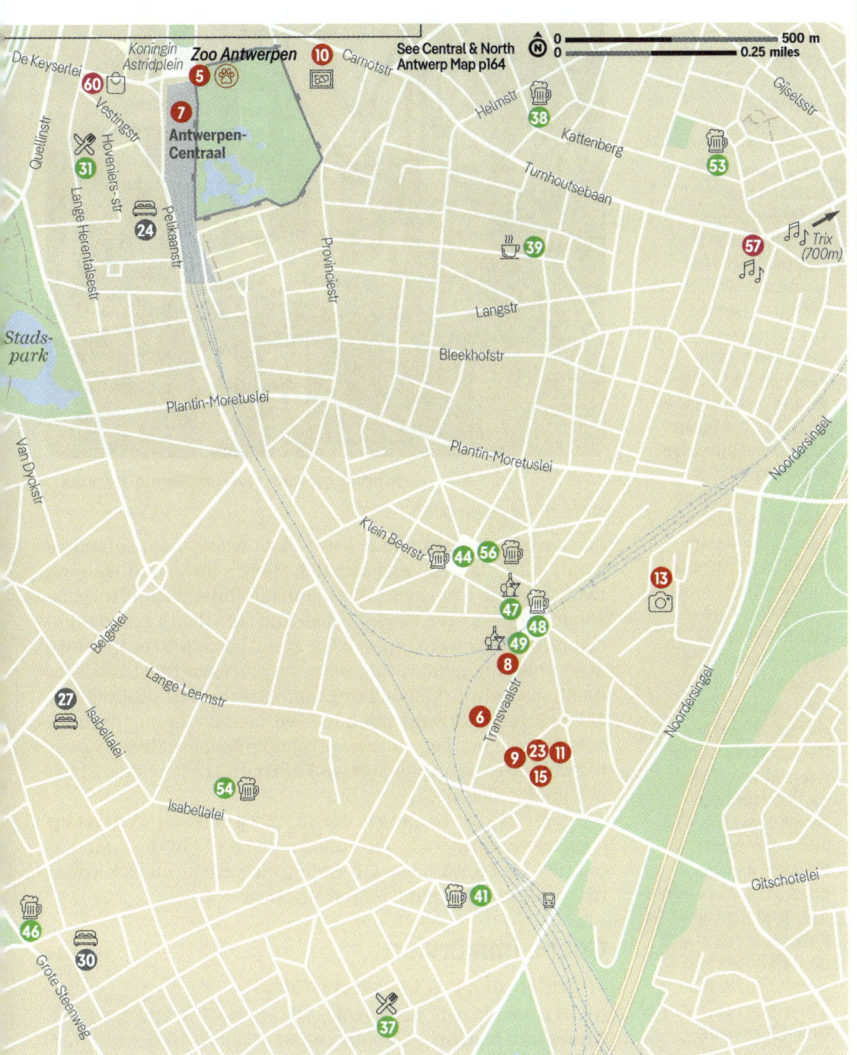

— map of Antwerp & Northeast Belgium

Map labels visible:

De Keyserlei
Koningin Astridplein
Zoo Antwerpen
Carnotstr
See Central & North Antwerp Map p164
0   500 m
0   0.25 miles
Quellinstr
Vestingstr
Hovenierstr
Helmstr
Kattenberg
Gijselsstr
Antwerpen-Centraal
Turnhoutsebaan
Lange Herentalsestr
Pelikaanstr
Provinciestr
Langstr
Trix (700m)
Bleekhofstr
Stads-park
Plantin-Moretuslei
Plantin-Moretuslei
Noordersingel
Van Diyckstr
Klein Beerstr
Belgielei
Lange Leemstr
Transvaalstr
Isabellalei
Noordersingel
Isabellalei
Gitschotelei
Grote Steenweg
Grote Steenweg

DIAMOND DEALERS

Trust is key to diamond trading. It was Antwerp's decision to ban the sale of counterfeit stones in 1447 that eventually led the city to become the global centre handling 80% of the world's uncut stones by 2022. That figure has since dipped due to EU boycotts of Russia over Ukraine: Moscow now sells its diamonds through Dubai. But Antwerp remains the world leader and a great place to shop for genuine diamonds.

Jewellers are concentrated just west of Antwerpen-Centraal train station. A dozen are officially certified for your peace of mind as 'Antwerp's Most Brilliant'. If you've purchased diamonds from a non-certified Antwerp store, you can still have them authenticated with a free appraisal by **Orsini Diamonds**.

Printing presses, Museum Plantin-Moretus

UWE ARANAS/SHUTTERSTOCK

continued from p167

Start in a darkened room to learn about where diamonds come from, both 'natural' and created: there's an incredible ring made entirely from synthetic diamond. Enter a vault to learn about the 4Cs (carat, clarity, colour and cut), then a grand salon displaying tableware through the ages. Videos tell the life story of an 1820s diamond cutter, show the processes that transform rough stones into diamond rings and examine 21st-century uses of blockchain authentication to keep 'conflict diamonds' from entering the market. In the workshop room, use the eye-glass to examine extraordinary stone 5 in Tray 6.111: it's cut as a bust of King Baudouin.

If you want to learn more, **Experience Antwerp** *(experienceantwerp.be/en)* runs guided tours of the diamond district. Or **DIVA** has a QR code from which you can load a free self-guided version onto your phone.

Cocoa Immersion

MAP P164

Spoonfuls of joy at Chocolate Nation

Allow a couple of hours to enjoy the engrossing and extensive **Chocolate Nation** *(chocolatenation.be; adult/student/under-12 €20/18.50/14.50),* the self-described 'world's largest Belgian

'Miss Hessenhuis' nights from 9pm, 3rd Sunday of each month.

DRINKING IN ANTWERP: LGBTQI-FRIENDLY

MAP P164

Café Hessenhuis: A 16th-century warehouse turned 'Embassy of Freedom' bar. Friendly starter venue where DJs rev up the vibe quite early. *4pm-1am Tue-Sun*

Bonaparte: Inclusive DJ-led party nights and karaoke with drag events and parties on the Grote Markt. *9pm-3am*

Club Random: Popular gay club with live DJs, drag acts, chilling couches, video lounge and cruising area. Special events for Pride weekend. *11pm-6am Fri-Sun*

The Boots: Notorious full-on fetish club. Read the dress code, and if you choose to come naked, wear shoes – the right kind of shoes. Sign up before arriving. *Fri-Mon*

chocolate museum'. Arriving here feels like you're entering a cinema but at times the visit is more like wandering through Willy Wonka's factory with stylised whirring of gears and pumping of pistons. These help simulate the creation processes, explained from the growth of cacao plants to the shaping of pralines. Let a humorous holographic choco-chef make you a surprise, then descend into an old-world candy shop where you learn about the history of Belgian chocolatiers, gaining plenty of extra detail by waving your audio guide in suitable spots. After seeing gigantic choco-sculptures, look through windows into a production room where chocolates are being made (for sale in the museum shop) and do an interesting true-or-false chocolate quiz: spoiler alert, yes, chocolate is toxic to dogs. Your reward is a spoon with which you can taste 10 different types of liquid chocolate and see if you agree with the tasting notes. The fascinating Ruby chocolate's raspberry-like notes are not due to added essence but thanks to the unusual if highly secretive method of processing.

Print Pioneer
MAP P168

The world's oldest surviving presses

Printing was the 'internet of the 16th century', a new technology that upended society by making knowledge and conspiracy theories available to a mass audience. Antwerp was at the forefront of the revolution. In a building that was a print shop from the 1550s, **Museum Plantin-Moretus** (*museum plantinmoretus.be; adult/under-26/under-18 €12/8/free*) retains half a dozen antique presses, including two that are the oldest still in existence anywhere. Several others remain in working order, giving great insights into the technology's development, and there's much more to see in this UNESCO-listed museum. The medieval building is memorable in itself, with its gilt-leather 'wallpaper', 1622 courtyard garden and 1640 library, not to mention the fabulous collection of paintings.

Cafe Crawling
MAP P164 & P168

Central Antwerp's drinking culture

The medieval centre is awash with traditional brown cafes, timeless old-fashioned pubs noted for their atmospheric interiors. Visiting a selection is a very agreeable way to absorb Antwerp's kaleidoscopic character. Right on Grote Markt is **Den Engel**, filling a 16th-century guild house and aped by copycat **Den Bengel** next door, with old-school DJ parties

BEST LESSER-KNOWN ANTWERP CURIOSITIES

De Handelsbeurs: The world's first stock exchange (1531) was rebuilt in fabulous neogothic style in 1872. Since 2019 it has served as an events venue, meaning getting in can be hit and miss.

De Ruien: Wellington boots are provided for this fascinating 90-minute tramp through the network of sewer tunnels and underground passageways beneath old Antwerp. Three tours daily (*ruien.be; over-16/10-16 years old €19/12*).

Vlaeykensgang: Picturesque 1591 passageway winding past medieval houses off Pelgrimstraat.

Sint-Annatunnel: Walk beneath the River Scheldt through this 1930s tiled foot-tunnel for novel views back over the Antwerp skyline from Linkeroever.

Stadsfeestzaal Exuberant shopping mall within a 1908 neoclassical exhibition hall with gilded detailing.

DRINKING IN ANTWERP: BEST FOR COFFEE
MAP P164 & P168

Normo: One of the original experimental barista havens is fanatical about sustainably sourced beans brewed in a wonderfully ramshackle setting. *8.30am-7pm Mon-Sat*

The Yellow Window: Caffeine comfort with sofa seating in a quiet corner of the medieval centre. English-style scones available too. *10am-6pm Wed-Sat*

Kolonel Koffie: House-roasted beans and a laptop-friendly ambience in a former petrol station in the partly gentrified 'new Zuid'. *8am-6pm Mon-Sat*

Caffènation: Sip delectable coffee on a street terrace facing the grandiose triangular 1879 building that was the national bank untill 2014. *8am-5pm Mon-Fri, from 10am Sat-Sun*

some nights. **De Kat** is calm with mirrored panelling. Other classics include **Pelikaan**, **De Duifkens** and the wonderful locals'-favourite **Oud Arsenaal**, little changed since 1924. For regular live jazz, don't miss triple-level **De Muze**. Then, weekends only, there's uncompromisingly local **Cafe Beveren**, the absolute antithesis of contemporary style with its Wurlitzer jukebox and 1937 DeCap organ.

Further south, **Bierhuis Kulminator** is a unique specialist for tasting aged rarities, but you might have to convince the owner that you're enough of a beer lover to 'deserve' entry. Nearby **Korsåkov** serves its own brews and has a scruffy-chic vibe. It's one of several choices on Mechelseplein where street terraces bubble with conversation till late on a summer's evening.

Northeast of the centre beware of the oppressively testosterone-heavy three-street red-light district around Verversrui. Beyond, however, **'t Waagstuk** is a delightful find on super-pretty Statswaag while nearby student favourites like **Cousteau** entertain with music from cheesy 1970s hits to live jazz on Tuesday nights.

Sartorial Style
MAP P168

Sint-Andries, Antwerp's fashion district

In the late 1980s, Antwerp exploded unexpectedly as a global fashion leader following daring, provocative shows in London and Paris by half a dozen fashion graduates from Antwerp's Royal Academy. They soon became known as The Antwerp Six. Dries Van Noten, the group's most commercially prominent figurehead, has his Antwerp flagship store in a 19th-century 'flatiron' building, **Het Modepaleis** (*driesvannoten.com*). This, along with nearby **MoMu** (*momu.be; adult/under-26/child €12/8/free),* Antwerp's cutting-edge fashion museum, forms the axis of the compact Sint-Andries fashion district. An unusually concentrated selection of designer boutiques, streetwear shops, end-of-line discounters, upmarket vintage stores and more mainstream labels are to be found in surrounding streets, notably Steenhouwersvest, Lombardenvest and Kammenstraat. Note that some designers have decamped to 't Zuid, notably **Ann Demeulemeester** (*anndemeulemeester.com*).

Venerable Zoo
MAP P168

A temple garden for animals

Antwerp Zoo (*zooantwerpen.be/en; adult/student/under-12 €34.50/32.50/27.50)* is one of the world's oldest, but has a good reputation for wildlife preservation programmes.

 EATING IN ANTWERP: BUDGET PICKS ———————————— MAP P164 & P168

Jam: Fresh, imaginative cafe (and terrace) serving flavour-packed snack-lunches inspired by world travels. *11am-6pm Thu-Mon* €

Potala Kitchen: Simple but great-value Tibetan, Chinese and pan-Asian meals, most under €10. On the station area's 'Chinatown' strip. *noon-10pm Thu-Mon* €

Msemen: Moroccan stuffed puff pastries served with mint tea and tasty harira soup in an invitingly light, bright interior or rear garden. *11am-7.30pm Tue-Sun* €

Aahaar: The €12 buffet of authentic Indian vegetarian food is a budget traveller's delight. Good mango lassis, though scores zero for decor. *noon-3pm & 5.30-9.30pm* €

Het Modepaleis

It's right beside Antwerpen-Centraal station, entered between grand, statue-topped gateposts that date from its first opening in 1843. While enclosures have been enlarged to fit contemporary norms, some 19th-century structures remain, including an 'Egyptian temple'. Save €2 with an online ticket. You can get a taster look inside the Flamingo Square section for free.

Digital Masters

MAP P168

Dive into art

Aimed at 'museum-shy' younger audiences, multi-sensory **Dive** *(divenow.be)* wants to immerse you in the artistic world of a specific painter. The featured artist changes every six months: Klimt, Monet, Dali and Magritte so far. A visit starts in the artist's imagined 'home' decked with reproductions of their canvases. So far, so normal. Upstairs, however, you enter a giant all-black room into which are projected swirling 360° evocations of their art on walls, floors and the 10m-tall ceiling. After 30 minutes, a second VR experience follows.

Check opening dates as the venue is also used for other events, notably doubling as the music/party venue **Woom** *(we.are.woom)*.

BEST VENUES FOR ENTERTAINMENT

AFAS Dome (Sportpaleis): Belgium's biggest concert arena (23,000 seats) has recently hosted Dua Lipa, Andrea Bocelli, Santana and Lady Gaga. Widely known as the 'Sportpaleis', it was renamed in September 2025.

Lotto Arena: The Sportpaleis' sister venue (capacity 8000) hosts tennis and basketball events, rock acts (in 2025 Morrisey, Marilyn Manson), comedy shows (Ismo) and variety/dance.

De Roma: Alternative cinema plus concert venue for indie artists past and present. 2025 names included Kim Deal, Morcheeba, Stereo MC's.

Trix: Four-in-one venue hosting party- and festival-style gigs. Recording studio too.

Opera Ballet Vlaanderen: The 1907 opera house is a spectacular venue for Opera Ballet Flanders, which also puts on shows in Ghent.

THE GUIDE

ANTWERP & NORTHEAST BELGIUM ANTWERP

🍸 **DRINKING IN BORGERHOUT: OUR PICKS** ———— MAP P168

Cafe Mombasa: Cycle-themed cafe with superlative beer choices. Perfect spot during May's Borgerrio street festival. *3pm-1am Tue-Sun*

Bakeliet: Stylish neighbourhood local made distinctive with old enamel signs, 1950s decor and a 1964 jukebox. Jazz gigs some weekends. *Tue-Sun times vary*

Plaza Real: Ragged cult shop-bar founded by a member of indie-band dEUS. In summer, de Steeg in the passageway beside takes over. *8pm-late Wed-Sat*

Bar Caju: Stylish corner cafe on Borgerhout's most memorable square. Convivial for breakfasts, decent barista coffee or a glass of wine. *9am-4pm Wed-Sat*

AROUND ANTWERPEN-CENTRAAL STATION

To appreciate the full magnificence of arriving at **Antwerpen-Centraal** train station, take the exit through the upper/north level. To head into the city from the station, walk west down **Leysstraat** and **Meir** past some of Antwerp's most impressively grandiose 19th-century architecture. Should you head east, however, you'll find yourself in the highly multicultural inner suburb of **Borgerhout**. It's somewhat rough-edged but Borgerhout's **Districtshuis** is architecturally impressive. Side streets have a small scattering of great bar-cafés while main streets feature authentic Turkish teahouses, African groceries, and shops selling Moroccan cookies.

Palace of Art

MAP P168

Antwerp's blockbuster gallery

The neoclassical frontage of the enormous **KMSKA** (kmska. be; adult/under-26/under-18 €20/10/free) is matched by a marvellous collection spanning most eras and displayed in two very contrasting styles. A grand ornamental stairway maintains the original 19th-century grandeur leading into the Old Masters section, though there's lots of sly humour in the hangings: a Magritte tucked amid 18th-century landscapes, a canvas of a drunk person displayed at a distinctly tipsy angle. In stark contrast, the upper Modern Masters levels use a disorientating gloss-white environment that leaves you feeling weightless. Belgian modernist painters are prominent. Can you find the singing buttocks? On Thursdays (September to June) the gallery stays open untill 10pm, often with pop-up bar and music.

KMSKA is the heart of the attractive 't Zuid district. Other great artistic spaces here include **FOMU** (fomu.be; adult/under-26 €6/3), an excellent photography museum, and **MHKA** (muhka.be /en; adult/under-26 €14/8), a gallery presenting ever-changing, often provocative contemporary art exhibitions. A short walk from KMSKA is a plethora of buzzing restaurants and bars.

Refined and Lively

MAP P168

Pre-war architecture in 't Zuid

The quarter around KMSKA is unpoetically nicknamed **'t Zuid** (the South). Built from the 1870s, it hosted World Fairs in 1885 and 1894 during an era when Antwerp's port finally enjoyed resurgent prosperity after nearly 300 years of blockade. The 1863 'liberation' of the Scheldt River is commemorated by the 20m-high **Schelde Vrij Monument**, symbolically festooned with broken chains and topped with a trident-wielding Neptune. It forms the photogenic centrepiece of cafe-ringed Marnixplaats from which eight streets radiate. One passes a Steiner School in the 1901 **Help U Zelve building**. Originally HQ for the Socialist Party, the building is adorned with sinuous wrought ironwork, curved windows and a mosaic of rural workers, in the nude!

Their winter special is stoemp, Belgian potato-vegetable mash.

 EATING & DRINKING IN 'T ZUID: OUR PICKS ———— MAP P168

Eetcafe Chocola: Fairy lights twinkle on the tree-shaded tree terrace; whacky informal Tim Burton-esque interior. Salads, fish dishes and wine. *11am-11pm Mon-Sat* €	**De Broers van Julienne:** Enticing townhouse venue for a candlelit vegetarian dinner or veranda lunch. *noon-7.30 Sun-Thu, to 8.30pm Fri & Sat* €€	**Patine:** Lively and informal, this wisteria-fronted 'wine bistro' has a popular street terrace and mussels on the menu in season. *11am-1am*	**Chatleroi:** Atmospherically grungy bar with DJ sets at weekends or live music on Thursday nights. *4pm-late Mon-Fri, 2pm-late Sat & Sun*
Ta-nnin: An 'Urban Street Winebar' making good wine more accessible to a younger audience. Tree-shaded terrace, excellent nibbles. *5-11pm*	**Het Gerecht:** Hard to beat for a multi-course Franco-Belgian lunch with gastronomic flair and professional service. *noon-4.30pm Tue-Fri & 7pm-12.30am Thur & Fri* €€€	**Fiskebar:** Antwerp's classic place for seafood on Marnixplaats. Stick to the weekday fixed menus to keep prices in check. *noon-3pm & 6-10pm Wed-Mon* €€	**Ciro's:** Nostalgic restaurant with mid-20th-century decor and quality traditional Flemish food. The 'Black Beauty' dish is what you may have guessed. *noon-10pm Wed-Sun* €€

The Classic Bolleke

Visit De Koninck Brewery

Three years older than Belgium itself, **De Koninck Brewery** *(adult/student €18/16)* produces a refreshing brown ale that has become an iconic symbol of Antwerp, served in a *bolleke* (little bowl) glass that is so distinctive that it has become synonymous with the beer. Production is now done elsewhere but self-guided visits around the old brewery in Berchem are entertainingly designed. Start, beer in hand, with videos and interactive screens telling the story of Antwerp, the beer and the brewing process. Walk past a winding cacophonous series of screen walls illustrating the bottling lines, then reach a De Koninck combi-van. Hop inside for a 'ride', then pour yourself a Triple d'Anvers taster. Enjoy that while sitting in the 'Plaisante Hof' bar where animated portraits good-humouredly tell the story of feisty Josephina de Koninck and how the brewery somehow got through the war. After perusing the pre-1995 brewing area, end the tour with a quick quiz that checks whether you were paying attention. There's a (very small) prize for each winner.

The De Koninck complex also includes a hip, music-heavy bar and tasting space, plus baker, cheese maker, chocolate shop and butcher, whose cuts can be sampled at the fragrant Black Smoke barbecue restaurant and rooftop terrace. With beer-based sauces, of course.

Century of Changing Tastes

Zurenborg and Berchem: Art Nouveau to street art

Developed between 1894 and 1914, **Zurenborg** is a wealthy inner suburb famed for its fine array of *belle époque* and Art Nouveau houses, notably in the 'Golden Triangle' formed by Cogels Osylei, Transvaalstraat and Waterloostraat. Spot a selection of beauties by bicycle, then repair for refreshment to one of the cafe-ringed squares, **Dageraadplats** or **Draakplaats**. Directly east of the latter in utter contrast you'll find Krugerstraat and Minckeleresstraat, Antwerp's '**graffiti streets**', potentially grim but brilliantly repainted every summer during the **Zommer Fabriek street art festival** *(zomerfabriek.be)*. There's masses more street art in the surrounding Berchem district, with walking and cycling routes suggested on Instagram *@streetartcities,* and guided tours are offered by **Street Art Antwerp** *(streetartantwerp.com).*

HOUSE-SPOTTING IN ZURENBORG

23-35 Trans-vaalstraat: Together these seven houses create the impression of a single Greek temple.

De Twaalf Duivelkens: Transvaalstraat 59-61. 1900 chalet-style house nicknamed for the 12 devils of its humorous balcony.

Les Mouettes: Waterloostraat 39. Modest but featuring curls of wrought-iron balcony and a lovely central mosaic of seagulls and the Flemish coast.

'Flower' Houses: A series of houses along Cogels Osylei featuring floral motifs, notably **Iris** at No 44 and **Sunflower** at No 50.

De Vier Seizoenen: Four matching houses facing off across the corners of Waterloostraat and Generaal Van Merlenstraat are enlivened with mosaic-work depicting the four seasons, hence their collective name.

DRINKING & EATING IN BERCHEM & ZURENBORG

Spéciale Belge Taproom: Microbrewery pub in the arty PAKT zone where old metalworking factories have become studios and cafes. *4-11.30pm Mon-Fri, 2pm-2am Sat* €

Den Draak: Charming 'straight-friendly' cafe bar which is an epicentre of Pride afterparties but normally low-key by day. *4pm-late Tue-Sat, noon-1am Sun*

ZeeZicht: The most atmospheric bar around tree-shaded Dageraadplaats, with many other dining choices and play areas for children. *noon-11pm*

Vitis: Cosy former corner shop turned family restaurant with an emphasis on foraged ingredients. Majority of dishes are meat-free. *4-8.30pm Wed-Sun & 11.30am-2pm Sat & Sun* €€

Beyond
Antwerp

Lier and Turnhout both have magical historic cores. And who knew that printing playing cards could be so interesting?

Places

Lier p176
Turnhout p177

In the 14th century, the Duke of Brabant offered the townsfolk of Lier the chance to host Flanders' first great university. They refused and chose a livestock market instead. So while students went to Leuven, Lier became a backwater and its people were dismissively nicknamed *schapekoppen* (sheep-heads) for their economically disastrous decision. However, Lier retains a special historical charm, brought to public notice through the work of local writer Felix Timmermans (1886–1947), whose 1916 novel *Pallieter* recast the townsfolk as life-loving bohemians.

Like Lier, appealing Turnhout has a lovely *begijnhof*, but its fame rests as home to leading global game-maker Cartamundi and the town styles itself as the world's playing-card capital.

Lier

TIME FROM ANTWERP: **15MIN**

A unique timepiece

Around 20km southeast from Antwerp, historic Lier lives life at a slower pace. A 15-minute stroll from the station, cross the outer canal and continue down the main shopping street to the fine **Grote Markt** with its fine step-gabled shop-houses and 1369 UNESCO-listed **belfry**. Attached is a proud town hall building with chandeliers, spiral stairs and painting-filled room that hosts the **tourist office** *(visitlier.be)*.

Stand amid the flowerboxes of the Aragonstraat bridge for a beautiful perspective on **St-Gummaruskerk**, a huge Gothic church that commemorates Lier's famously hen-pecked 8th-century founder St-Gummarus, who saved a child from a python's mouth and made rain with a stroke of his staff.

The town's most iconic feature is the **Zimmertoren**, an eccentric 1930 timepiece shoehorned into a partly 14th-century tower. It's photogenically over-endowed with dials, zodiac signs and a globe on which the Congo remains forever Belgian. Daily at noon, a procession of figures – including Belgium's first kings – emerge briefly, though the effect is a little underwhelming and the clock looks better in afternoon light. Next door, the **Zimmermuseum** *(adult/under-16 €5/2)* allows horology fanatics to check out the mechanisms and observe a second, even more elaborate 1935 astronomical Wonder Clock by the same creator. The ambitious **Stads Museum Lier** *(stadsmuseumlier.be; adult/ student €4/3)* is an engrossing museum-gallery that includes a

GETTING AROUND

Trains to Turnhout via Lier depart from both Antwerpen-Centraal and Antwerpen-Berchem stations. An intriguing way to reach the Dutch city of Breda is via Baarle-Hertog, a disconnected exclave of Belgium within the Netherlands which might not have much in the way of visual beauty but is a weird geographical patchwork that forms the world's most complex international border. Start with bus 46 from Turnhout, then swap onto Dutch bus 375.

Zimmertoren, Lier

1900 pre-Raphaelite-style canvas by Isidore Opsomer showing Jesus hanging out in Lier.

However, Lier's real charm comes from wandering around the idyllic **begijnhof** and enjoying the canals, whether by boat, on foot, or at a waterside cafe terrace.

Turnhout

TIME FROM ANTWERP: 1HR

Quite a card

Historic Turnhout has a sturdy moated **castle** (now the courthouse), an utterly gorgeous 17th-century **begijnhof** *(free, museum section adult/child €5/3)* and a loveable local museum, **Taxandria** *(taxandriamuseum.turnhout.be; adult/student €5/3)*. However, the city's claim to fame is as home to the world's biggest producer of playing cards. If that doesn't sound much like a tourist attraction, try visiting Turnhout's engrossing **Speelkaartenmuseum** *(speelkaartenmuseum.turnhout.be; adult/child €5/3)* which illustrates the exacting technical precision required to create cards that are faultless enough to prevent cheating. Admire 21st-century technological advances including UV-sensitive inks for clarity in low light. Learn how history judged the morality of card games: a guillotine recalls French revolutionary times when anti-royalist sentiment went as far as to remove kings and queens from the pack. Perhaps the most impressive exhibits are still-operable 19th-century printing presses and a vast steam-powered drive-wheel.

BEST ANTWERP DETOURS

Lillo: A tiny old hamlet at the far northern end of Antwerp's vast port, accessed by De Waterbus river ferries from Antwerp's Steenplein. Lillo's quaintly old-fashioned Poldermuseum opens Sunday afternoons.

Verbeke Foundation: Belgium's wackiest contemporary art endeavour occupies an indoor-outdoor 12ha former industrial site off the A11 highway between Antwerp and Bruges. *verbekefoundation. com/en; adult/ student €13/10*

Hoogstraten: Home to a small *begijnhof* and dominated by a soaring brick belfry, it was laboriously rebuilt after being dynamited by retreating Nazis at the end of WWII.

Westmalle: Beside the main Antwerp-Turnhout road (bus 410), you can't visit Westmalle Abbey, but its famous Trappist beer is served across the road at Café Trappisten.

Menu includes Flemish stews and horse steaks.

DRINKING IN LIER & TURNHOUT: OUR PICKS

Sint-Gummarus: Historic brown cafe in Lier with enamel signage, barrel urinals and a good beer selection. Summer terrace tables face the canal. *10am-late*

Harvey & Hayes: Artisan cheese maker and cute tearoom in the historic Gulden Hooed shophouse building in Lier. Try a Liers Vlaaike, the local pastry. *9.30am-5.30pm Wed-Sun*

De Ranonkel: Great street-corner Turnhout pub near the city castle with panel-walled interior and ample outdoor seating. *10am-late Mon-Sat, from 6.30pm Sun*

Bar Muza: Modernist Lier cafe-restaurant hidden away in the gardens between the cathedral and youth hostel. *11.30am-10.30pm Mon-Fri, from 9am Sat & Sun*

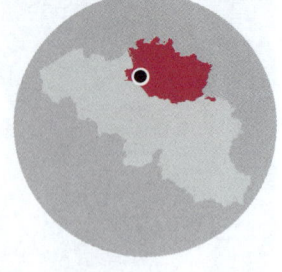

Mechelen

CHURCHES | FOLKLORE | BEER

GETTING AROUND

The main Mechelen train station is a 20-minute walk south of the Grote Markt. Mechelen-Nekkerspoel is about half the distance, but only a limited number of services stop there, notably to/from Antwerp. Bus 1 links the two stations via the city centre, which is otherwise mostly pedestrianised. Bus 5 from Mechelen station links to Technopolis.

Mechelen (Malines in French) is an unexpected treasure trove of medieval architecture, a gorgeous central square, great museums, and an astonishing selection of splendid churches as befits the seat of Belgium's Catholic primate (archbishop equivalent). From 1473, Mechelen became the administrative capital of the Burgundian Low Countries under Charles the Bold and, later, of his feisty widow Margaret of York (sister of England's King Richard III), whose palace is now repurposed as the Stadsschouwburg theatre. Mechelen's courthouse building has been repurposed from a different former palace, that of Margaret of Austria (1480–1530), who developed an especially glamorous court culture encouraging science, literature and the arts. Margaret's ultrapowerful nephew, Holy Roman Emperor Charles V, moved the capital back to Brussels after her death, but Mechelen continued to reinvent itself and remained important enough that in May 1835 it became the destination of continental Europe's very first passenger steam-train service (from Brussels).

Mechelen's Catholic Heart

Sint-Romboutskathedraal, the city's foremost religious wonder

Rising 97m above Mechelen's majestic Grote Markt, the 15th-century tower of **St-Romboutskathedraal** (St-Rombouts Cathedral) is an iconic landmark that you'll find variously framed down gently curved medieval streetscapes. It looks even better at dusk, with clever lighting emphasising the detail and giving the step-gabled houses and restaurants of Grote Markt even more pizzazz. Inside the cathedral is a 1723 monumental pulpit and a 1630 crucifixion scene by Van Dyck (p166). Allow around an hour if you want to climb

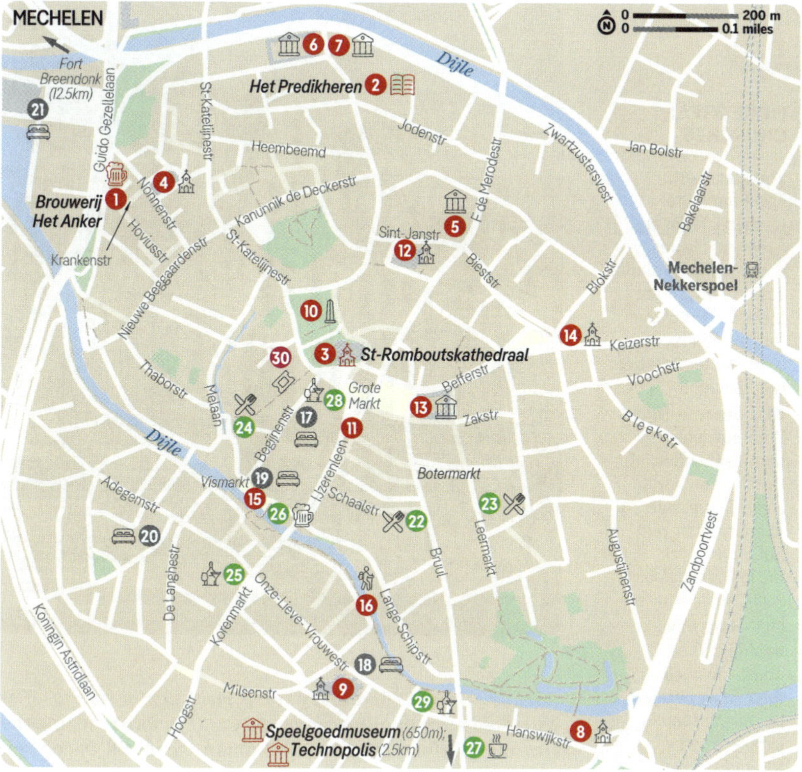

MECHELEN

Fort Breendonk (12.5km)

Brouwerij Het Anker

Het Predikheren

St-Romboutskathedraal

Grote Markt

Vismarkt

Botermarkt

Mechelen-Nekkerspoel

Speelgoedmuseum (650m);
Technopolis (2.5km)

0 — 200 m
0 — 0.1 miles

⭐ **HIGHLIGHTS**
1 Brouwerij Het Anker
2 Het Predikheren
3 St-Romboutskathedraal

● **SIGHTS**
4 Begijnhofkerk
5 Hof van Busleyden
6 Kazerne Dossin
7 Museum of Deportation
& Resistance

8 OLV-Hanswijkbasiliek
9 OLV-over-de-Dijle
10 Opsinjoorke Statue
11 Schepenhuis
12 Sint-Janskerk
13 Stadhuis
14 St-Pieter-en-Paulkerk
15 Vismarkt

● **ACTIVITIES**
16 Dijlepad

● **SLEEPING**
17 3 Paardekens
18 Dusk till Dawn
19 Hotel Vé
20 Martin's Patershof
21 Van der Valk Hotel

● **EATING**
22 De Margriet
23 De Vleeshalle
24 Graspoort

● **DRINKING &
NIGHTLIFE**
25 Antverpia
26 De Gouden Vis
27 Lief
28 Unwined
29 Zapoi

● **ENTERTAINMENT**
30 De Maan

🍴 **EATING IN MECHELEN: OUR PICKS**

De Vleeshalle: Former meat market turned food hall with a dozen stalls offering assorted cuisines. Buzzy youthful vibe. *11am-9pm Tue-Sat, to 8pm Sun* €

Brasserie Het Anker: The brewery's tasting room is great for beers but also serves filling meals including hearty Belgian stews. *noon-9pm, bar 10am-11pm* €€

Graspoort: Imaginative multi-course 'new world' fusion dinners in an atmospheric secret alley, half engulfed by foliage yet close to the Vismarkt. *7-9pm Tue-Sat* €€€

De Margriet: The courtyard of a historic monastery beckons for brasserie-style meals, particularly asparagus or mussels when in season. *11.30am-8.30pm Mon-Sat* €€

MORE GREAT CHURCHES

Sint-Janskerk: Towering white-washed interior and a remarkable Jesus-and-shepherds pulpit. To (virtually) rotate the paintings of the Rubens altarpiece, use the interpretative touch-screen.

OLV-over-de-Dijle: Breathtakingly huge Brabantine Gothic church with a very impressive interior and its own Rubens triptych, the 1619 *Miraculous Fish Catch*.

OLV-Hanswijk basiliek: This dome-crowned three-wing basilica has an unusual circular interior, a Paradise Lost pulpit and an octagonal floor stone commemorating the pope's 1985 visit. It's home to a 10th-century Madonna that's the centrepiece of Mechelen's greatest religious pageant, the Hanswijk Procession.

St-Pieter-en-Paulkerk: Spacious interior with whitewashed Corinthian columns and lots of gilt detail.

Begijnhofkerk: Baroque masterpiece with a 'God the Father' relief atop the front gable.

the 538 steps of the **belfry** *(visit.mechelen.be/ascent-of-st-rumbolds-tower; adult/under-26 €8/3)*. Before reaching the viewing platform you'll see a human treadmill once used to bring up building materials, plus the impressive array of 49 bells that play carillon concerts in summer. Capacity is limited so book ahead, especially in peak holiday season, and check the weather forecast first.

Family Playtime

Fun and nostalgia for all at the Speelgoedmuseum

A great rainy-day family standby is Mechelen's toy museum, **Speelgoedmuseum** *(speelgoedmuseum.be; adult/under-13 €17.50/12.50)*. There's also a vast selection of hands-on game activities for children young and old, as well as a nostalgic collection of toys and dolls of various epochs. The museum optimistically attempts to address four semi-philosophical questions about the nature of play. To understand what's happening, use your wristband to unlock numerous interactive panels and audio-stories, helpfully presented in the language you selected on entry. If you're overwhelmed, there's a tactile snooze-zone for unwinding. Opened in 2024, this very contemporary museum is hidden away near the parking pay station in the bowels of Mechelen station, itself a long-term construction site.

CATARINA BELOVA/SHUTTERSTOCK

Cafes on IJzerenleen street

Nazi Nightmares in Mechelen

Tragic Holocaust memories

A block north of the simple Tinèlle garden and Mechelen's prize-winning new library, **Het Predikheren**, is a whitewashed former military building called **Kazerne Dossin** (*kazernedossin.eu; free*). Push open the door marked 'memorial' and you enter a low-lit, black-walled room where klezmer (Jewish folk) music plays and you find yourself watched by a series of disconnected eyes. In case you hadn't realised, this was the transshipment point for dehumanised victims of the WWII Nazi occupation, where over 25,000 Jews and 354 Roma were reduced to statistics before being loaded onto freight trains and sent to death camps in Poland. Only 1273 returned.

The memorial not only honours the dead but reminds us that many of the Belgian Jews had themselves arrived as victims from earlier repressions further east. Photos and videos

WHY I LOVE MECHELEN

Mark Elliott, Lonely Planet writer @markbekaz

Mechelen is impressively adept at repurposing its incredible stock of historical buildings. A once derelict 1652 monastery became **Het Predikheren**, voted one of the world's best new libraries of 2021. Part of the **De Maan** performance venue was recycled from a 13th-century chapel. Hotels have reused another old church, **Patershof**, and a monumental 1920s swimming pool, **Van der Valk**.

In the mid-1990s, I remember **Vismarkt** being grubby and down-at-heel, but now it's a charm-filled square of buzzing terraced cafes. The once-putrid Dijle River and canal are now clean and you can walk on water (well just above it) strolling the **Dijlepad** boardwalk footpath.

 DRINKING IN MECHELEN: OUR PICKS

Zapoi: Artily alternative twist on the classic Belgian cafe, with occasional improv nights. Gouden Carolus range of beers on tap. *11am-1am Mon-Sat, 4-11pm Sun*

Lief: Spacious barista coffee shop serving breakfasts, home-made lemonades, salads and a blackboard of daily specials. *9am-4pm Wed-Mon, food until 2.20pm*

De Gouden Vis: Lively, downmarket hangout despite the wonderful Art Nouveau touches and little balcony area overlooking the river. *11am-late Mon-Sat, from 1pm Sun*

Unwined: Imaginative wine bar with weekly changing open-bottle specials and hidden garden seating. *5-11pm Mon-Thu, noon-11.30pm Fri & Sat, 3-9pm Sun*

Mechelen's landmark brewery, **Het Anker** (p179), forms an incongruous addition to the little streets of the city's Grote Begijnhof. But it is heir to a beer-making tradition started here by the *begijns* themselves in 1369. Het Anker beer names are interesting for historico-cultural references relating to Mechelen's past.

There's a well-crafted blonde called **Manneblusser** meaning 'moon extinguisher' – that's been a self-mocking nickname for Mechelen townsfolk since 1687, when cloud-diffused moonlight above the cathedral tower was mistaken for a fire that they tried to put out.

The **Gouden Carolus** range references Holy Roman Emperor 'Golden' Charles V.

Ambrio is based on a recipe that was supposedly Charles' favourite ale.

Hopsinjoor is a hoppy pun on Opsinjoorke.

---

illustrate carefree scenes of pre-occupation life in the 1930s. Then clicking typewriters and confiscated IDs recall how the oppressors made killing a blandly administrative process.

To learn more, cross the road to the extensive **Museum of Deportation & Resistance** *(kazernedossin.eu; adult/student €12/5)*, housed in a tall, starkly austere whitewashed building designed by celebrated Belgian architect Bob Van Reeth.

If this hasn't proved harrowing enough, more WWII horrors await 12km northwest at **Fort Breendonk** *(breendonk.be/en; adult/under-18 €12/9)*, a haunting moated prison fort that was used as a Nazi internment camp.

Look Out for Opsinjoorke

The city's folkloric anti-mascot

Opsinjoorke is Mechelen's lewdly cackling folkloric anti-mascot whose reputation for wife-beating is ceremonially punished by tossing him in the air during Mechelen's biggest celebration, the **Hanswijk Cavalcade**. However, as that's only held every 25 years (next in 2038), you'll need to watch videos of the event online or in the glorious **Hof van Busleyden** *(adult/under-26 €15/13)*, the city museum, nicknamed a 'house of humanism'. That's also where the stout, ugly-faced original doll 'lives'. Alternatively you can meet his younger brother at the tourist office, housed in the magical **Schepenhuis** *(visit.mechelen.be/en)*. Looking like a small fantasy castle, it dates from 1288 and has served as the council/parliament for the Burgundian Netherlands from 1473.

A giant garish-yellow **Opsinjoorke statue**, weighing over a ton, acts as a children's playground attraction in the grassy open space fronting St-Romboutskathedraal. A smaller statue in front of the splendid **Stadhuis** (city hall) shows Opsinjoorke in full flight. And the figure appears in various guises in the unpretentious local pub that's slyly named **Antverpia**. An 18th-century feud between Mechelen and Antwerp was exacerbated in 1775 when the doll was stolen by Antwerp folk. When recovered, its previous name Sotscop (Foul Bridegroom) was swapped for Op-Sinjoorke, a diminutive form of 'Signor' (Spanish gentleman) as Antwerpers were mockingly known at the time.

Science Unveiled

Discovering real-life magic at Technopolis

'Everything starts with Wow' is the premise behind **Technopolis** *(technopolis.be/en; adult/child €27/22)*, which aims to imbue science with a sense of awe and excitement. One of Belgium's first truly interactive technology museums, it remains a big draw thanks to regular reinvestment in new digital experiences and awareness of developing trends. Although it's aimed primarily at children and teenagers, it's engrossing for all and you'll need the best part of a day to do it justice. Bus 5 from platform 12 leaves every 30 minutes from Mechelen station. By car it's easily accessed 2km south of town near the E19 highway.

Leuven

STUDENT VIBE | ARCHITECTURE | BREWING

Lively Leuven (Louvain in French) elegantly combines history and fun, and being less than 25 minutes by train from central Brussels, offers a tempting alternative base from which to visit the capital. Until the mid-14th century, Leuven was a major cloth-making centre. It declined after a bloody dispute between the townsfolk and the Duke of Brabant's nobles which led many weavers to flee, but rebounded as its university rapidly became a magnet for Europe's foremost scientists and thinkers. Today it's still home to Flanders' foremost university and with some 25,000 students in residence between mid-September and June, there's always loads going on. Also based here is the world's biggest brewing conglomerate, including the Stella Artois brewery. Though the city suffered horribly in both world wars, somehow Leuven's phenomenally intricate 15th-century Stadhuis survived almost intact, and there's also an unusually well preserved former abbey set in gardens at the southern edge of town.

Gothic Spectacular

The lucky Stadhuis

Leuven's incredible 15th-century **Stadhuis** (ex-city hall) is an architectural wedding cake flamboyantly overloaded with terraced turrets, fancy stonework and colourful flags. A phenomenal 235 statues were added in the mid-19th century, each representing a prominent local scholar, artist or noble from the city's history. During WWII a falling bomb scoured part of the facade but miraculously failed to explode, so what you see today is the original stonework. The interior has several outlandishly lavish rooms including a pseudo-medieval Gothic Hall, but a huge renovation project is planned to last until 2029, so don't count on getting inside before then.

GETTING AROUND

Leuven bus and train stations are a 15-minute stroll from the Stadhuis straight along Bondgenotenlaan. Pedestrianisation means it's best to park at one of the train station car parks. Buses 14 and 15 link the station to Abdij van Park. Arenburg Castle is a 15-minute walk from Heverlee station, a 5-minute train hop from Leuven. Trains to Brussels Airport take less than 15 minutes, starting from 5.07am, making Leuven a good overnight option before an early flight. For Mechelen, buses are cheaper than trains and depart more centrally.

☑ **TOP TIP**

Visiting on a Tuesday or Wednesday maximises your chances of hearing the university belfry's 63-bell carillon ring out across the city with tunes that could be anything from a Scarlatti sonata or Evita show-song to Guns N' Roses' 'Sweet Child o' Mine'.

LEUVEN

De Hoorn (500m)

Stella Artois (800m)

200 m
0.1 miles

Vismarkt

Smolders-plein

Grote Markt

Stadhuis

Oude Markt

Monseigneur Ladeuzeplein

Hogeschool-plein

Hoover-plein

Pater Damiaanplein

St Antoniusberg

Stadspark

Begijnhof Hotel (200m)

Arenburg Castle (1.7km); Dwaaltuin (2km)

Abdij van Park (1.1km); Abbey Church (1.3km); Parcum (1.3km)

Zwarte Zusterstr

★ **HIGHLIGHTS**	**6** Sint-Antoniuskapel	**12** Leuven City Hostel/	**18** Lukemieke
1 Oude Markt	**7** Sint-Donatuspark	Hotel Ladeuze	**19** Mamaye
2 Stadhuis	**8** Sint-Michielskerk	**13** The Fourth	**20** Raffat
● **SIGHTS**	**9** St-Pieterskerk	● **EATING**	● **DRINKING &**
3 Grote Begijnhof	**10** University Central	**14** Bar Bao	**NIGHTLIFE**
4 Klein Begijnhof	Library	**15** De Werf	**21** De Blauwe Kater
5 M Leuven	● **SLEEPING**	**16** Domus	**see 20** Noir Koffiebar
	11 De Pastorij	**17** Leuven Central	

Flemish Last Supper

Treasures of St-Pieterskerk and M Leuven

If the northwest frontage of the 1425 **St-Pieterskerk** *(free)* looks unfinished, that's because Leuven's unstable subsoil forced builders to abandon plans for a 170m-high tower. However, the interior is lavished with priceless artworks, most notably *Het Laatste Avondmaal*, a triptych by Leuven-based Flemish Primitive artist Dirk Bouts. Finished in 1467, the work is a landmark in art history, remarkable for placing Jesus' last supper in a typical Flemish Gothic dining hall. Panels have been 'lost' several times. During WWII, Nazis hid them in an Austrian salt mine, where they were found by the US Army in 1945. Now this is one of 12 church masterpieces that you can experience much more viscerally if you rent one of the clever interactive iPads *(adult/student €5/3)*. Alternatively, the same information is imparted by a hi-tech but less user-friendly VR experience *(€12)*. These visitor aids are conceived by Leuven's foremost art museum, **M Leuven** *(mleuven.be; adult/under-26 €12/5, 10am-4.30pm Mon-Sat, from 11am Sun)*, in whose main venue a superb collection gains enormously from clever thematic curation, counterpointing, for example, 16th-century Flemish Primitive canvases with religious statues and contemporary installations.

Something Brewing

Beer in Leuven

Wander into the **Oude Markt** square any night in the university term time (September to June) and you'll find a surging mass of happy drinkers whose chatter and whoops reverberate around the baroque gables. Dozens of side-by-side pubs here are collectively nicknamed 'Europe's Longest Bar'. Meanwhile, Leuven is home to AB InBev, the world's biggest brewing group. You'll need to prebook to join a two-hour tour of their vast flagship **Stella Artois Brewery** *(breweryvisits.com; tour €17.50)*, usually weekends only. Alternatively, just drink a *pintje* at Stella's precursor location, **De Hoorn** *(8am-11.30pm Mon-Fri, from 11.30am Sat)*. It no longer brews beer but the 2012 regeneration includes a cafe-restaurant complete with the old copper mash-tuns. Don't like Stella? **Domus** pre-empted the microbrewery trend decades ago, while **De Blauwe Kater** *(11am-2am)* has over 100 beers and free blues or jazz gigs on term-time Monday nights.

CHURCHES & COSY CORNERS

Grote Begijnhof: An idyllic village-like area of around 100 red-brick houses on cobbled lanes and canals. It feels like a film set when lantern-lit at dusk.

Klein Begijnhof: Cute, one-street mini-*begijnhof* with neatly whitewashed houses.

Sint-Michielskerk: Enormous baroque church with a trompe-l'œil stand-in for a tower. Accidentally bombed by Allies in 1944 and still not fully restored, but there's a new 7-tonne organ based on a 1779 original.

Sint-Antoniuskapel: The 1960s chapel is the last resting place of Father Damien (1840–89), Belgium's missionary saint. Damien's work with Hawaiians affected by leprosy was the basis of the 1999 Hollywood movie *Molokai*.

Sint-Donatuspark: Popular student picnic spot containing sparse remnants of a historic city wall.

EATING & DRINKING IN LEUVEN: OUR PICKS

De Werf: Eccentric student classic with tables spilling out into Hogeschoolplein. Popular for back-to-basics fare or a drink. *9am-9pm Mon-Fri* €

Leuven Central: A full-on expression of Belgian-ness designed to feel like a classic brown cafe. *9.30am-midnight Mon-Fri, 10.30am-2am Sat, 1pm-10pm Sun* €€

Noir Koffiebar: Craft barista coffee roastery with a graffiti-cool interior and terrace tables that spill beyond the pavement to the street. *8.30am-5.30pm* €

Domus: Flemish favourites make a good accompaniment to the house-brewed beers in what feels like a heavy-beamed old-English pub. *11am-10pm Tue-Sun* €€

185

Irrepressible University

Flanders' foremost educational institute

In late afternoon light, gaze across the cobbled expanse of Monseigneur Ladeuzeplein. With heraldic details and a soaring belfry, the square's centrepiece looks like a medieval cloth hall, but it's the **central library** of what's now called the **Katholieke Universiteit van Leuven** (KU Leuven). A university was first founded here in 1425, after Lier decided it would prefer livestock to students. It soon became one of Europe's most highly regarded educational centres, attracting free thinkers such as cartographer Mercator and Renaissance humanist Desiderius Erasmus. However, in WWI the library was burned by German troops, causing an international outrage. A massive postwar effort led by US schools and colleges funded the building's reconstruction. Then in WWII the Nazis repeated the atrocity.

The story of its double rebuilding is the main thrust of over-detailed guided visits *(visitleuven.be/universiteitsbibliotheek -toren; adult/student €10/8)* on Sunday at 11am. You might prefer a self-guided belfry-tower visit *(adult/student €8/6),* which gives the key facts through photo exhibits on each of six levels as you climb 289 narrow spiral steps to the view balcony. On Tuesday *(7pm)* and Wednesday *(1pm)* the bells play carillon concerts. Listen for free from the square or pre-purchase a *beiaard* ticket and sit with the bell-player at an organ-like console. The library reading room allows peep-in visits at weekends and holidays.

Monastic Survivor

Gaze up at Parcum

At the southern edge of Leuven lies a green oasis of calm ponds, trees, cycle paths and the remarkably well preserved **Abdij van Park**, a vast walled abbey complex into whose grounds you're free to wander. Incense still wafts from services at the impressive **abbey church** *(free).* The astonishing stucco ceilings in the abbey's refectory and library somehow survived the revolutionary destructions of the 1790s and are now highlights of visiting the museum section **Parcum** *(adult/student €12/10):* you can use mirrors and lie-on-to-look-up divans to help you appreciate the details. An entry ticket also lets you visit changing exhibitions that counterpoint religious imagery from the abbey's collection with intriguing contemporary artworks: in 2025 the theme was 'ecstasy', comparing Catholic 'mystical jubilation' with the feelings of dancing at a rave.

CHANGE COMES IN WAVES

In 2025, Leuven celebrated the 600th anniversary of its university-city status by installing *Kunst- en Wetenschapsroute*, a walking route linking 16 new works of outdoor contemporary art and subtitled in English *And So, Change Comes in Waves*. Many of the artworks are so subtle you need the guide pamphlet to realise that you're actually looking at them.

The route starts in the attractive parkland campus around **Arenburg Castle**, where **Dwaaltuin** is the latest monumental artwork by Gijs Van Vaerenbergh (p187). As yet it's just a monumental steel superstructure, but over coming years the various planted creepers will grow up around the rust-coloured frameworks, creating a circular labyrinth of cascading foliage.

There's wine, a fancy cocktail menu, but no beer.

 EATING IN LEUVEN: INTERNATIONAL

Bar Bao: Snack meals under €10, notably stuffed bao-buns weaving together a satisfying mixture of tastes and textures. Spacious with rear yard. *noon-10pm* €

Mamaye: In a beautiful medieval building, the atmosphere is trad cafe-style, food is Ethiopian (plus pastas), wine is mostly Portuguese. *11am-2pm & 5-9pm Thu-Mon* €€

Raffat: Dazzling colours, punning menus and a tear-jerking dedication are all part of the show as you share Pakistani-fusion creations. *5.30-10pm Wed-Mon* €€

Lukemieke: Serving vegetarian delights for over 50 years in a discreet townhouse with a rear garden. *noon-2pm & 6-8pm Mon-Fri, closed mid-Jul-mid-Aug* €€

Beyond Leuven

Don't be blinded by the brilliance of Antwerp, Mechelen and Leuven: there's a lot more to see in the less famous smaller cities of northeastern Belgium.

The region east of Leuven offers a plethora of quick-visit attractions, and some great outdoor wanders including the pretty, orchard-rich countryside around Borgloon where some memorable public art lies hidden. However, as none of the individual sights tend to make it into top-10 listings, relatively few foreign tourists come this way, and those who do rarely see much more than Tongeren and its excellent Gallo-Roman Museum. A car is handy for the many lesser attractions, but less so in the busy, wealthy city of Hasselt, centre of the *jenever* (gin) industry since the 17th century. To the east is Bokrijk, probably Belgium's best open-air museum along with a botanical garden and some highly imaginative quirks for walkers and cyclists.

Borgloon

TIME FROM LEUVEN: 1HR 🚗

Ephemeral chapels

Doorkijkkerkje *(24hr, free)* is one of Belgium's most magical sights: especially at sunset, the shape-shifting mirage of a 'chapel' seems to dissolve from the spire down as you approach. Known in English as *Reading Between the Lines*, it's a 2011 structure by contemporary artist Gijs Van Vaerenbergh built through the clever use of well-placed rusty slats. The nearest parking is a layby at Km 11.6 on the N79 (just outside Borgloon), from which it's a 10 minute (800m) walk.

It's just one of several conceptual art installations hidden amid the orchards and fields of this pretty, undulating region that's fun to explore by bike.

Some 1200m south of Doorkijkkerkje, stroll around Bollenberg Hill to find **Twijfelgrens**. From most angles, this rural sculpture looks like just a wavy line of rusty iron. However, when viewed from a specific point, the line arranges itself into a piece of cursive script, the Flemish for 'Doubtful Border'. Less visually successful is the **Landmark Romeinse Villa**, a series of sculpted 'seats' evoking Roman villas, intended to celebrate the route of the former Cologne–Boulogne Roman road that passed this way between Tongeren and Tienen. Some 6km due west along that old Roman Road, **Zwevende Kapel** is a tiny 'floating' chapel made of wooden faggots. Photos seen from the west will baffle a viewer's sense of perspective. But if you approach from the east you'll see that it's actually suspended over the void of a small slope.

GETTING AROUND

Hasselt is well connected by train to Brussels (via Diest), Antwerp (via Lier and Diest), Leuven (via Tienen and St-Truiden) and Liège. A car is useful for touring the orchards and castles. Bicycle rental is particularly well organised in the Limburg region: search *fietsverhuurpunten* for details. If you're heading to the Netherlands, there are buses to Maastricht from both Hasselt and Tongeren.

CASTLES AROUND BORGLOON

Kasteel van Ordingen: A Relais & Château linked five-star castle hotel with Michelin-starred restaurant, ideal for a romantic stay.

Château de la Motte: Another moated beauty that doubles as a hotel. Its tavern brasserie serves Motte beer and typical local cuisine, but without castle views.

Kasteel Hulsberg: Gated and completely private, but an imposing sight spied from outside as you drive the eastbound on N79.

Kasteel Rijkel: This medieval castle has been on sale for several years. Unoccupied since 2004, it's falling into disrepair but is still priced at almost €3 million. Ponder your offer in the local cafe.

Château Looz: The hotel section looks very pretty viewed from the south across the moat, but there's a banal modern extension and the brasserie-restaurant is looking a tad dated.

DVPHOTOWORLD/SHUTTERSTOCK

Statue of Ambiorix, Tongeren

Sweet saviour

For 150 years the Borgloon area has been famed for fruit production. From the 1880s, when it was hard to preserve apples and pears, much of the harvest was turned into a thick syrup, which was popular as a spread before marmalade and chocolate pastes took over after WWII. It's hard to believe that in 1936 alone, one Borgloon factory was producing 1400 tonnes of such syrup. Following a kind of Flemish reality TV show, the last such factory was preserved and now forms the **Stroopfabriek Museum** (*stroopfabriek.be; adult/child €8/1*), a fascinating, tri-lingual 'fruit experience' that tells the history of fruit syrup with multi-sensory games, historic equipment and a new mini-factory that has revived the industry in a small way. It doubles as a tourist office, sells local wines (now more profitable than syrup) and rents bikes (best to prebook on *fietsparadijslimburg.be*).

Tongeren

TIME FROM LEUVEN: 1½HR

The original Asterix?

Despite the 'down-with-Caesar' efforts of Belgium's Gallic hero Ambiorix, what's now Tongeren developed as Atuatuca Tungrorum, a prosperous Roman settlement on the Cologne–Bavay road. It retains several significant sections of the Roman city wall, and Tongeren sees itself as Belgium's oldest city. By the 4th century, it was also one of the Low Countries' earliest Christian bishoprics. Learn more at the **Gallo-Roman Museum**

DRINKING FROM LEUVEN TO TONGEREN

Den Venetiaen: Enamel signs, wooden board floors and a classic central bar island make this Hoegaarden local a great place to sip the white beer where it was born. *10am-1am Wed-Mon*

Wilma: Super-central cafe with a social conscience, fresh soups, barista coffee and hoppy beers facing Tienen's Groot Markt. *10am-4pm Tue, Wed & Sun, to 11pm Fri, 1pm-11pm Sat*

De Lakenhalle: Archetypal old-time Belgian bar-café in the historic building facing Zoutleuw's famous church. Small back-yard terrace behind. *5pm-10pm Wed-Sat, 11am-9pm Sun*

Wilderen Brouwerij: Buzzing modern brewery/distillery-cafe in a slightly hidden half-timbered barn at Wilderen, 3km west of central Sint-Truiden. *1pm-9pm Tue-Sun, weekends only Oct-Mar*

(galloromeinsmuseum.be; adult/student/child €8/5/1) which starts down a long dark tunnel, taking you to 500,000BC and walking you back through history from stone-age flint axes to a 7th-century AD gold brooch. Thousands of original artefacts are supplemented with interviews, timeline video maps, quizzes and touch boxes that make it child-friendly. You're nearly two-thirds of the way through when you reach Ambiorix. A highlight here is a seven-minute film that dramatises his daring if ungentlemanly battle tactics.

An iconic **statue of Ambiorix** stands on the Grote Markt facing **Onze Lieve Vrouwebasiliek**, Tongeren's Gothic central church which has its own archaeological museum, **TeSeUm** *(adult/senior/under-26 €6/5/1),* allowing you to see vestiges of Roman houses and the original 4th-century church. Various combination tickets also get you into the church treasury, up the bell tower and into the cloister. Before leaving Tongeren, don't miss strolling down to the riverside via the pretty **begijnhof** area.

On Sundays Tongeren's large **antiques market** attracts people from far and wide.

Hasselt

TIME FROM LEUVEN: **35MIN**

Hasselt has plenty to keep you interested, including the architecturally disjointed **Kathedraal Sint-Quintinus**, a large **Japanese Garden** *(visithasselt.be/nl/japanse-tuin; adult/student €7/1),* a **fashion museum** *(modemuseumhasselt. be; adult/under-26 €8/3)* in a former monastery, and **Het Kunstuur** *(hetkunstuur.com/hasselt; €22; closed Jun-Aug),* which repurposes the elegant former city hall as an intimately immersive art space. But its claim to fame is *jenever.*

Heritage in a glass

Prosperous Hasselt might look sedate but on the third weekend of October, the city erupts into party mode for the annual **Jeneverfeesten**. It celebrates *jenever,* the Flemish juniper-based spirit that locals don't want labelled as gin, despite the drinks' obvious similarities. And whatever you do, don't call it *genever* – that would be Dutch. At 4pm on the Saturday, a miracle occurs: the water pouring from the little statue-fountain of a barrel carrier, the **Borrelmanneke**, turns briefly to *jenever.* Sexual equality is assured on Sunday when his female equivalent, the **Borrelvreuke** on Capucienenplein, repeats the feat at 1.45pm.

Year-round, the city's most engaging attraction is similarly booze related: the **Nationaal Jenevermuseum** *(jenevermuseum.be; adult/under-26 €7/3),* in a beautifully

TONGEREN'S PLUCKY HERO

As the sun sets on the main square of Tongeren, Belgium's oldest city, it silhouettes a curious statue of a muscular, moustachioed figure. This is Ambiorix, one of the inspirations for the Beefix character in Asterix cartoons. Semi-mythical Ambiorix was a chieftain of the Gallic Eburones tribe. In 53 BCE he led a brief revolt against Julius Caesar's Roman rule in the Tongeren region. It was a failure and had been largely forgotten by historians until the 1830s. However, when newly founded Belgium was in need of national heroes, Ambiorix became the perfect choice – a plucky underdog whose campaign reputedly led Caesar to call the Belgians 'the bravest of all the Gauls'.

 EATING & DRINKING IN TONGEREN

De Pelgrim: Small brown cafe in a very picturesque 17th-century step-gabled building in the heart of the romantic *begijnhof* area. *10am-8pm Wed-Sun* €

Stoemp: Modernised Belgian cafe serving *stoemp* (veg-potato mash), salads, soup and gnocchi dishes. *11am-9pm Fri-Tue, bar to 11pm* €€

Infirmerie: Upmarket brasserie-style menu served in a 1701 stone building with waterside terrace. *5-9.30pm Wed-Fri, from 11.30am Sat & Sun* €€

Magis: Behind a caryatid frontage, Michelin-starred garden lunches aren't quite as wallet-busting as you might presume. *noon-1pm Wed-Fri & 7-8pm Wed-Sat* €€€

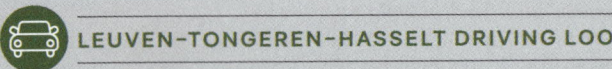

LEUVEN–TONGEREN–HASSELT DRIVING LOOP

This appealing driving tour from Leuven will likely take a day each way plus however long you stay in Tongeren and Hasselt.

START	END	LENGTH
Leuven	Leuven	Two days

First stop 25km southeast of Leuven is **①** **Hoegaarden**, synonymous with the unfiltered wheat beers brewed here. Brewery visits are for prebooked groups only, but you can taste the beers at cafes on Gemeentplein with its floral bandstand and Belgium's largest rococo church.

Directly north, **②** **Tienen** (Tirlemont in French) grew rich on sugar and has a fair scattering of beautiful old architecture, including two phenomenal churches. Driving east, **③** **Zoutleeuw** is famed for St-Leonarduskerk, a UNESCO-listed Gothic church with a fanciful tower reminiscent of a galleon's crow's nest. The town hall, opposite, has pre-Raphaelite murals and a traditional cafe.

In **④** **Sint-Truiden** (St-Trond in French), the western half of the main market square is used as a car park, so to see the UNESCO-registered belfry at its most impressive, look from the east across a shallow pool beside Cosmo Cafe. Continue past the castles and art-surprise orchards around **⑤** **Borgloon** to wonderful **⑥** **Tongeren**. After visiting Tongeren's Gallo-Roman museum (p188), head for **⑦** **Bokrijk** and **⑧** **Hasselt**.

After exploring lovely old **⑨** **Diest**, stop briefly at the Catholic pilgrimage town of **⑩** **Scherpenheuvel** with its basilica and Lourdes-style gift shop of religious knick-knacks. Stroll around appealing **⑪** **Aarschot** and then return to Leuven via **⑫** **Horst castle**, a rural moated beauty.

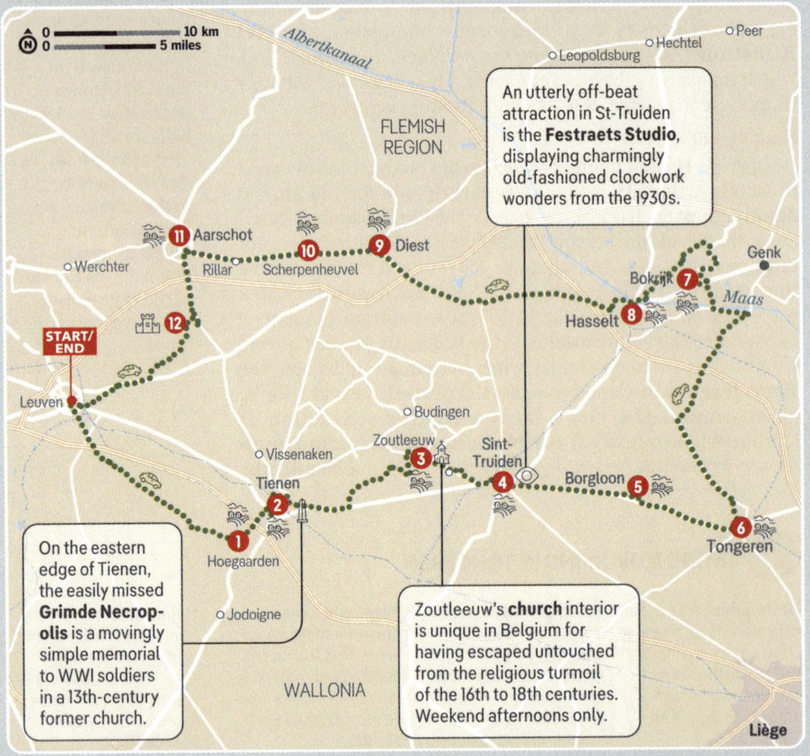

Map labels:

0 — 10 km / 0 — 5 miles

Albertkanaal

FLEMISH REGION

○ Peer
○ Hechtel
○ Leopoldsburg

⑪ Aarschot   **⑩**   **⑨** Diest   Genk
○ Werchter   Rillar   Scherpenheuvel   Bokrijk **⑦**   Maas
   ⑫   Hasselt **⑧**

START/END

Leuven
○ Vissenaken   ○ Budingen   Zoutleeuw **③**   Sint-Truiden   Borgloon **⑤**
Tienen **②**   **④**
①   Tongeren **⑥**
Hoegaarden
○ Jodoigne

WALLONIA

Liège

> An utterly off-beat attraction in St-Truiden is the **Festraets Studio**, displaying charmingly old-fashioned clockwork wonders from the 1930s.

> On the eastern edge of Tienen, the easily missed **Grimde Necropolis** is a movingly simple memorial to WWI soldiers in a 13th-century former church.

> Zoutleeuw's **church** interior is unique in Belgium for having escaped untouched from the religious turmoil of the 16th to 18th centuries. Weekend afternoons only.

restored 19th-century distillery which still produces around 1000 bottles a year. While it's interesting to learn all about the art of Flemish distilling, what makes the museum even more fun are the interactive screens asking visitors questions about drinking habits. Answers to the 'How many can you drink?' game might seem optimistic. Finish the tour with a free shot of the '*jenever* of the week' in the atmospheric museum cafe-shop.

Bokrijk

TIME FROM LEUVEN: **65MIN**

Nostalgic open-air wandering

You could easily spend most of a day appreciating **Bokrijk Openluchtmuseum** (Bokrijk Open-Air Museum; *bokrijk. be; adult/under-13 €17/3; closed Nov- Mar*), one of Europe's largest open-air museums. A wealth of historic buildings have been salvaged, reassembled and renovated here since 1958, from thatched cottages to grand mansions, chapels to windmills, and much more. The setting is super-photogenic, spread through 550ha of beautiful green space with mature trees and traditional farm crops under cultivation – the hemp field is marked 'not drugs' in case you were confused/ tempted. Check the online calendar for hands-on activities and workshops. It's just 10 minutes by train from Hasselt. If driving, all-day parking costs €5.

Cycling through water

The region around Bokrijk is criss-crossed with foot- and cycle paths. Some routes have been made all the more intriguing by imaginative bike-friendly constructions. The best known lets you feel like Moses parting the waters at **FDHW** (Fietsen Door Het Water) aka 'Cycling Through Water' where the trail crosses 'through' a lake at eye level thanks to a half-sunken concrete gully track. It's just beyond the northwest edge of the Openluchtmuseum on well-marked cycle paths (blue rectangles).

April to October, bicycles can be rented (*fietsparadijslimburg. be; per day €15*) from Bokrijk's eastern 'Kasteel' Car Park 1, with a self drop-off system allowing you to return your cycle up until 9.30pm. Without a bicycle, FDHW can be reached on foot using a 4km loop walk around the Bokrijk perimeter (follow the yellow rectangles). Or it's just a 15-minute stroll from a handful of **parking spots** at the sharp corner of Bokrijkseweg and Zavelvennstraat.

TOP MUSIC FESTIVALS

Pukkelpop: Major international festival famed for having hosted Nirvana pre-*Nevermind* but also for a freak tornado tragedy in 2011. Festivalgoers get free train tickets to nearby Kiewit from any Belgian station.

Rock Werchter: Belgium's biggest cross-genre music festival kicks off in late June/early July. Shuttle buses depart from Leuven station. Among 2025 acts were Linkin Park, Iggy Pop and De La Soul.

Tomorrowland: One of the world's foremost celebrations of electronic dance music, held late July in a wide natural amphitheatre at the De Schorre provincial park 15km south of central Antwerp.

Desertfest Antwerp: This multicity cacophony of heavy rock and psych-metal comes to Trix in Antwerp one weekend in mid-October.

BorgerRio: Carnivalesque one-day celebration of multicultural beats in Antwerp's Borgerhout district. Free, mid-June.

 EATING & DRINKING IN HASSELT

King Kong Coffee: Friendly, characterful caffeine-lovers' paradise that's hard to beat for barista brilliance. *10am-5pm Thu-Sat, from noon Sun* €

In de Kleine Hal: Classic, unpretentious dark-beamed beer-cafe with a terrace right beside the Kathedraal Sint-Quintinus. *10am-8pm Tue-Sat, from 2pm Sun* €

De Levensboom: Gourmet vegetarian cuisine in a very discreet townhouse. One-time winner of Belgium's Best Vegan restaurant award. *6-10pm Wed-Fri, 5-10.30pm Sat* €€€

't Genoegen: Refined 'gastro bar' dining in a modernist white-on-white decor that contrasts with the 1652 brick exterior. Seasonal menus, minimal choice. *6-11pm Wed, 6pm-midnight Thur-Sat* €€€

Nature walks

Directly north of Bokrijk, it's delightfully calming to stroll in the **Arboretum** *(free)*. Some 2.5km west is the inspirational **Domein Kiewit** *(hasselt.be/nl/domeinkiewit; free),* an expansive parkland full of animals both domestic and wild. It's focused on helping young people appreciate sustainability and get more actively involved with the natural world.

Diest

TIME FROM LEUVEN: **35MIN** 🚗

Begijn again

Between Leuven and Hasselt, the handsome town of Diest is one of Flanders' undiscovered delights. The star attraction is the 1252 **St-Katharinabegijnhof**, one of Belgium's most soothingly beautiful *beguinages*. It's a picturesque five-street village-within-a-town with lovely antique houses, baroque portal, art studio/gallery and a former chapel repurposed as a bar-café. Just outside the *begijnhof* are the remnant bastions of the Vaubanesque former fortifications, overlooked by the **Lindenmolen** windmill. West of the *begijnhof*, shopping street Koning Albertstraat is colourfully decked in heraldic flags and leads to the cafe-ringed Grote Markt with a gigantic church, **St-Sulpitiuskerk**, and a museum in the town hall.

Aarschot

TIME FROM LEUVEN: **30MIN** 🚗

Martyr city

Aarschot, west of Diest, is another of those appealing Flemish towns that is rarely on tourists' itineraries despite a good scattering of classic step-gabled houses, great bars and an atmosphere that's become much more serene since the pedestrianisation of the city centre. If you are near here on the evening of 15 August, don't miss the **Sint-Rochusverlichting**. At 9pm the town centre turns off all electric lamps and is totally illuminated by candles until midnight. The custom started in the 17th century to give thanks to patron saint St Rochus for miraculously sparing the town from the Black Death. It expanded considerably in the mid-19th century and nowadays most people take part.

DRINKING & SNACKING BETWEEN HASSELT & LEUVEN

De Kapel: Ultra-simple cafe-bar in a historic chapel-house with tables spilling onto the lawns of Diest's beautiful *begijnhof. 11am-7pm Wed-Sun* €	**Bij Het Bazeke (Bij de Baas):** Ultra-traditional Belgian brown cafe in Diest that is so intimate that your arrival will likely raise eyebrows. *hours vary* €	**In de Beiaard:** Stylish dining in one of Diest's most attractive corners. A medieval canon points at the windows. *11.30am-2.30pm Fri-Sun & 5-9.30pm Thu-Sat* €€	**Den Hagelander:** A showcase for local wines along with excellent food served beside a mini vineyard in Rillaar, 7km west of Scherpenheuvel. *11am-11pm Wed-Sun* €€
Kop of Munt: Quirky brasserie-cafe hidden away in an antique building in Aarschot. Primarily Belgian food or just a drink. *5-10pm Thu-Mon* €€	**Brasserie Kombinné:** Belgian classics, steaks, croques and salads in a stylishly reworked Aarschot cafe. *11am-2pm Thu-Sun & 5-10pm Wed-Sun* €€	**'s Hertogenmolens Brasserie:** Aarschot cafe-restaurant in a painstakingly restored 16th-century watermill. *11am-10pm Sun-Fri, 5pm-11pm Sat* €€	**Het Wagenhuis:** Drink or dine facing the drawbridge and moat of the picture-perfect medieval rural castle at Horst. *11.30am-8.30pm Wed-Sun* €€

Places We Love to Stay

€ Budget   €€ Midrange   €€ Top End

Antwerp
MAP p164 & p168

The Ash € Big, functional hostel with good kitchen, bar and a handy location for the station. Can overheat in summer.

Hotel Rubenshof € Basic rooms in a large 1890s 't Zuid mansion whose talking-point feature is the fabulous Art Nouveau dining room.

A-Stay € The vibe of a great hostel with common area, sociable bar-café, washing machines, but comfortable, hi-tech rooms trumping those of many pricier mid-range hotels.

Bed, Bad & Brood €€ Comfortable B&B in a 1905 *belle époque* townhouse with high ceilings and eclectic furniture. Two-night minimum stay.

YUST Antwerp €€ Stylish midrange hotel incorporating a luxury contemporary hostel close to De Koninck Brewery.

Hotel O €€ Moody, with bold reproductions of 17th-century artworks and an unbeatably central location with oblique views of the cathedral.

Motel One €€ Don't let the name fool you: this stylish, 21st-century hotel is right in the St Andries fashion district of town, not out on the highway.

Boulevard Leopold €€ Discreet, personable B&B evoking Antwerp's 19th-century glory days with curiosities and museum-worthy antiques.

Hotel Julien €€€ Boutique hotel in a grand, central mansion oozing suave,
understated elegance. Lots of designer detail and a fab roof-terrace.

De Witte Lelie €€€ Behind a 16th-century facade, this highly distinctive design hotel has some startling artistic statements and a courtyard garden.

Botanic Sanctuary Hotel €€€ Fifteenth-century monastery reborn as a breathtaking five-star wonder with two Michelin-starred restaurants.

U Eat & Sleep €€€ Subtle, fashion-conscious boutique hotel facing the water in Het Eiland.

Mechelen
MAP p179

3 Paardekens € Bare-bones rooms and app-activated automated reception, but very central, with a perfect cathedral view from the breakfast terrace.

Dusk till Dawn €€ Two sleek B&B rooms in a fine 1860s townhouse originally built for the Lamot brewing barons.

Hotel Vé €€ Artistic hotel on Mechelen's liveliest nightlife square retaining elements of the building's former role as a fish smokery.

Martin's Patershof €€ Fashioned out of an 1867 monastery with an altar in the breakfast room.

Leuven
MAP p184

Leuven City Hostel/Hotel Ladeuze € Small, low-key 'grown-ups' hostel with games lounge and quality kitchen. Budget hotel rooms too.
De Pastorij €€ Super-central guesthouse where the decor is less the attraction than the very personable welcome.

Begijnhof Hotel €€ Business-style rooms in a garden off the inner ring road, backing onto the charming Groot Begijnhof area.

The Fourth €€ Super-central in a photo-perfect historic building that's the fourth incarnation of a 1479 guild house.

Borgloon & Tongeren

De Pastorei € Charming rural guesthouse and social-inclusion project with locally sourced breakfast fare, honesty bar, AC and very comfortable beds.

Boutique Hotel Caelus VII €€ A stone's throw from Tongeren's main square, this delightful seven-room property fills a former hat shop with antique and antique-style furniture.

Hasselt & Bokrijk

Roerdomp Hostel € There's a state-of-the-art new HI hostel near Hasselt train station, but this simple, rustic alternative is ideally located for exploring Bokrijk.

't Hemelhuys €€ Charm-filled boutique hotel right in the heart of Hasselt's most appealing quarter.

B&B Maison Mairie €€€ Grand villa-castle in spacious grounds with outdoor pool and easy parking. It's beside the N20 in Wimmertingen, 7km south of Hasselt.

GUYON21/SHUTTERSTOCK

For places to stay in Wallonia, see p254

Above: River Meuse (p224); Right: Binche Carnival (p217)

THE MAIN AREAS

WATERLOO
From battlefield
to Eurovision icon. **p200**

MONS
Come and say hello to
Doudou the dragon. **p206**

NAMUR & DINANT
Fortress capital with a
shiny new cable car. **p222**

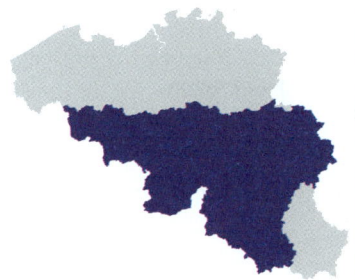

Researched by
Mark Elliott

Wallonia

BELGIUM'S FRANCOPHONE SOUTH

From the Waterloo Battlefield to post-industrial Charleroi, independent-minded Liège to fort-dominated Namur, plus the great outdoor playground of the Ardennes.

Wallonia is a place of contradictions. It is Belgium's outdoorsy rural underbelly but also the home to cities whose heavy industries brought the country wealth before it decayed into an economic malaise during the 1980s. The carnivals are wild (Binche in particular), the mindset humorous and the language a form of French that amuses visitors from France. There's also a series of distinct Walloon languages, though they're now almost purely folkloric. In addition, German is spoken in the Eastern Cantons, which only became Belgian as Berlin's reparations for WWI.

Though scarred by 20th-century eyesores, Liège was once an independent prince-bishopric and has complex historical layers that reward patient discovery. Sports-

minded folks are drawn to the forests and riversides of the Ardennes with family-friendly adventure parks, hiking, kayaking, biking and even skiing a few days a year. Spa is the original spa, and nearby is the racing circuit that's home to the Belgian Formula 1 Grand Prix. There are fortresses galore, from medieval castles to grand châteaux and more recent fortifications. The biggest dominate Namur, Dinant and Huy. If it weren't for Flanders outshining with medieval standouts like Bruges and Ghent, more tourists might flock to Wallonia's historic hot spots like Mons and Tournai. And there's plentiful fascination in the region's industrial heritage, from mine visits at Blégny to the world's biggest canal lift at Strépy. Bonne route!

| **BOUILLON** | **SPA** | **LIÈGE** |
| The castle that launched a crusade. **p227** | The town that gave water treatment its name. **p237** | Patchy brilliance full of understated eccentricity. **p245** |

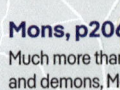

Mons, p206
Much more than its world war angels and demons, Mons is one of Belgium's underrated cultural gems with a crazy dragon-slaying festival to boot.

Waterloo, p200
Napoleon's last battlefield has a plethora of engaging attractions, both old and contemporary, and it's just an hour south of Brussels by bus.

Ghent
(Gent)

BRUSSELS ✪

Leuven
(Louvain)

Menen
(Menin)

Kortrijk

Oudenaarde

Ronse
(Renaix)

Flobecq

Geraardsbergen
(Grammont)

Halle
(Hal)

Wavre
(Wave

Mouscron
(Moeskroen)

Lessines
(Lesen)

Enghien
(Endingen)

Braine
l'Alleud

Waterloo

Tourcoing

Schelde

Silly

Louvai
la-Neu

Armentières

Roubaix

N48

N60

Ath (Aat)

N55

N6

Ottignies

N7

Nivelles
(Nijvel)

Genappe

N4

Lille (Rijsel)

Leuze-en-
Hainaut

Soignies
(Zinnik)

E420

Gembloux

Tournai
(Doornik)

Le Roeulx

A54

Ligny

La Bassée

E42

A16

Mons

Havré

La Louvière

Spy

Carvin

E19

Quiévrain

Quévy

Binche

Charleroi

Châtelet

BICYCLE
La Roche-en-Ardenne is the mountain-biking capital of the Benelux region. It has some good road-biking routes too, while there's plenty more in the Haute Fagnes area, with many riders basing themselves at Malmédy.

Valenciennes

Bavay

N6

N40

N55

Thuin

N5

Erquelinnes

N53

Ham-sur-Heure

Jeumont

Berzee

Laneffe

Maubeuge

Beaumont

Boussu-lez-
Walcourt

Florenn

N97

Lacs de
l'Eau
d'Heure

Philippeville

N53

Rance

N40

Mariembourg

Chimay

N99

CAR
In contrast to much of Flanders, having a car is a great advantage in Wallonia where many of the attractions are rural and/or awkward to reach by public transport. Free parking is common.

PUBLIC TRANSPORT
Train connections are fine for Mons, Liège, Verviers, Namur and Tournai. There's a regular bus to Waterloo from Brussels and river-buses are a pleasure in Namur and Liège.

Couvin

N5

Momignies

N99

Brûly-de-
Pesche

Fuma

Hirson

Abbaye Notre
Dame de
Scourmont

FRANCE

Charleville-
Mézières

Find Your Way

Wallonia covers 55% of Belgium's territory but has only 31% of the population, so it's not surprising that attractions tend to be more widely scattered than those of Flanders, with transport links less comprehensive.

Rethel

Namur & Dinant, p222

Wallonia's capital has a lively cultural vibe and an urban cable car that can whisk you to the top of its signature fortress-citadel.

Liège, p245

Beneath a crusty post-industrial exterior, the sprawling city of Liège reveals multiple layers of historical intrigue and self-deprecating humour.

Spa, p237

Underlined by UNESCO listing since 2021, Spa is one of the world's foremost mineral springs towns, as well as the launch pad for discovering Belgium's moorland 'Fagnes'.

Bouillon, p227

Especially magical in evening floodlights, this riverside castle town has talking-point crusader connections and is also a great starting point for summer kayaking trips.

Aarschot

Tienen (Tirlemont)

Sint-Truiden (St-Trond)

Jodoigne (Geldenaken)

A3 E40

N80

Namur (Namen) N90

A15 E42 Maas

N92

Annevoie

Anhée

Dinant

Houyet

Givet

E411 A4

N95

Vresse-sur-Semois

Rochehaut

Sedan

Maastricht

NETHERLANDS

Ében-Émael Fort

Tongeren (Tongres)

E313

Vise

Herstal

Blegny

A3 E40

Liège

Amay

Huy

Modave

N63

Hamoir

Durbuy

N4 N97

Ciney

Barvaux

E25

Hotton

Marche-en-Famenne

Rochefort N86 Waha

Han-sur-Lesse

Champlon

N89

Euro Space Center

St-Hubert N4

Redu

Libramont

E25 A26

Paliseul

N89 Bertrix

Neufchâteau

Bouillon

Florenville

Villers-devant-Orval

Virton

Aachen

Kelmis

Welkenraedt

Eupen

Euskirchen

Verviers N68

Vesdre Pepinster

Theux

Spa

A27

Malmédy Bütgenbach

Coo Stavelot Waimes

Trois Ponts Amblève

Vielsalm St Vith

N68

GERMANY

La Roche-en-Ardenne

Houffalize

Clervaux

Bastogne

LUXEMBOURG

Martelange

E25 A4

Arlon

LUXEMBOURG CITY

N87

Pétange

Longwy

Esch-sur-Alzette

GERMANY

Thionville

Saarlouis

0 50 km
0 30 miles

Plan Your Time

Wallonia's sights tend to be more spread out than those of Flanders, while hilly terrain and sparser populations mean limited transport, making planning more important here.

Exhibition of Waterloo battlefield (p200)

RICHARD BAKER / IN PICTURES VIA GETTY IMAGES

If You Only Do One Thing

● Easily visited as a day trip from nearby Brussels, the **Waterloo Battlefield** (p200) was the site of Napoleon's famous defeat, one of the bloodiest days in European history. There is loads to learn, whether you know nothing about it or are an aficionado wanting to scope out each of the battle's secondary skirmish points.

● In summer there are several daily costumed 'demonstrations' held at the base of the gigantic conical mound that makes the site instantly recognisable from miles away. The main museum **Mémorial 1815** (p200) is incredibly professional, with an immersive 3D film experience in which you really feel you're in the midst of the fighting.

● Finish the day with a meal and beers at the battlefield farmstead **Brasserie de Waterloo** (p202).

Seasonal Highlights

Much is seasonal: July and August are event-packed while much closes down completely from November to April.

FEBRUARY

Carnival fever hits. On Mardi Gras, the top spot is **Binche** (p217), but the day before there's a contrastingly light-hearted alternative in **Eupen** (p242).

MARCH

Later than most carnivals, long-nosed Blancs Moussis are the stars of the **Laetare** pageant at Stavelot, three Sundays before Easter.

MAY

For a week in late May or early June, Mons erupts as St George fights Doudou the dragon in the raucous madness of the **Lumeçon** (p209) on Trinity Sunday.

A Long Weekend in the Ardennes

● Belgians seeking fresh air and family-friendly escapes from Brussels tend to strap their bikes on the roof and drive down to the Ardennes. Different destinations cater for different interests.

● Mountain bikers make a beeline for **La Roche-en-Ardenne** (p233) or **Malmédy** (p241), while families might be more interested in the adventure activity outfits at **Durbuy** (p233) or **Coo** (p242). For indulgent relaxation, head to the original spa at **Spa** (p237) and unwind in the thermal baths.

● For a place that combines visual history, clever lighting, falconry displays and leisurely kayaking, it's hard to beat the crusader-linked castle town of **Bouillon** (p227). For better prices, take your 'weekend' during the midweek. From October to Easter, much closes down.

Nine Days in Western Wallonia

● Having arrived by plane at 'Brussels South' airport near dystopian **Charleroi** (p218), rent a car and drive via **Nivelles**, with its Romanesque masterpiece church (p204) to Waterloo (p200). Stay two nights, visiting the Napoleon-linked battlefield sites. Then drive via the 'giants' town of **Ath** (p211) to stay in Roman-rooted **Tournai** (p213) with its spectacular cathedral and fine Grand-Place.

● On day five, drive through 'beer villages' (p213) en route to multi-faceted **Mons** (p206). Spend two days exploring the city's prehistoric and historical sites, WWII history and Van Gogh connections. Then visit the remarkable boat-lifts on the **Canal du Centre** (p216) and the mask museum of carnival-obsessed **Binche** (p217). Sleep in or near undiscovered **Thuin** (p217) before returning the car to Charleroi.

JUNE

Reconstructions of the **Battle of Waterloo** (p203) see hundreds of costumed 'soldiers' battle it out. Scale and dates vary each year (can be early July).

JULY

During the days surrounding the **Belgian Grand Prix**, all accommodation for miles around Spa and Stavelot will be booked solid.

AUGUST

A week of entertaining drunken craziness in Liège's **Outremeuse quarter** (p249) culminates on 15 August with fireworks, puppets and giants.

DECEMBER

WWII-era military vehicles are a major part of the parade for Bastogne's **Nuts Weekend** celebrating the city's 1944 survival.

Waterloo

NAPOLEON'S LAST STAND | BATTLEFIELD BOOZE | COSTUMED DRAMAS

Stand beside a huge bronze lion atop a grassy artificial pyramid-shaped hill and gaze out across peaceful green fields that slope gently away to the south. It's hard to imagine that on 18 June 1815 this was the scene of butchery – 32,000 deaths – and the inspiration for ABBA's Eurovision hit song. Had Wellington and Blücher not stopped Napoleon's rapidly expanding 'come-back' army here, the whole of European history would have been quite different. Though known to all as the Waterloo Battlefield, technically Waterloo itself is the next town north, now a suburban satellite town for Brussels commuters. Central Waterloo has a station, great tourist office, museums and a plethora of restaurants and bars. However, the main battlefield experience is around 5km south with an impressive visitor centre and that distinctive Lion's Mound (Butte du Lion), which is a visual landmark for miles around. For aficionados, a variety of other battle-related sites lie within a few kilometres.

Site of Napoleon's Downfall

The 1815 battlefield experience

As you enter the main battlefield site **Mémorial 1815** (*waterloo1815.be; adult/under-18/under-10 €24/12/free),* you appear to be descending into the earth. Collect a lanyard to facilitate multimedia quizzes and connect to the internal wi-fi to access *visit.io* on your smartphone for written and spoken extra coverage. Suitably equipped, the museum section then explains the Battle of Waterloo's historical context from the Enlightenment to the rise of revolutionary France. Then a parade of life-sized soldiers leads you to a 3D film – an intense experience in which you feel really in the thick of the fighting. Then there's a whole lot more about the battle and its repercussions: don't miss the animated schematics of each skirmish, watched beneath a Montgolfier balloon.

WATERLOO

0 ———— 100 m

Ave Claire
Drève des Dix Mètres
Venelle des Trois Sapins
Chaussée de Bruxelles

14
Musée Wellington
R de la Station
15
3
R François Libert
R de la Chapelle Royale
5

Enlargement

Drève des Dix Mètres
See Enlargement
0 ———— 1 km
0 ———— 0.5 miles
WATERLOO
Waterloo
R de la Station
Ave Reine Astrid
Domaine d'Argenteuil
Parc Communal Jules Descampe
Boulevard de la Cense
R de l'Infante
Chaussée de Tervuren
13
Drève Richelle
10
Chaussée de Bruxelles
Chemin des Noces
Chaussée Bara
Drève Richelle
Chemin de l'Infante
JOLIBOIS
R Sainte-Anne
R du Ménil
R Victor Hugo
Chaussée de Louvain
Rue du Ménil
R Coleau
R Baty Gigot
Parc Bourdon
R Pergère
MONT-SAINT-JEAN
Chaussée d'Alsemberg
R du Ménil
Chaussée Reine Astrid
Chaussée de Mont-Saint-Jean
Museum Mont-Saint-Jean
4
11
BRAINE-L'ALLEUD
Braine-l'Alleud
Route du Lion
Mémorial 1815
12
9
2
7
Route du Lion
R Longue
Chaussée de Nivelles
6
Chaussée de Charleroi
BELLE ALIANCE
Parc du Paradis
Boulevard de l'Alliance
Parc du Cheneau
R Longue
Route de Praumont
Hougoumont 1 8
Dernier Quartier Général de Napoléon (2.8km);
Musée de la Bataille de Ligny (25km)
Prussian Monument, Plancenoit (1km)

⭐ **HIGHLIGHTS**
1 Hougoumont
2 Mémorial 1815
3 Musée Wellington
4 Museum Mont-Saint-Jean

🔴 **SIGHTS**
5 Chapelle Royale
6 Lion's Mound
7 Panorama de la Bataille

⚫ **SLEEPING**
8 Gîte Ferme d'Hougoumont
9 Hotel 1815
10 Van der Valk Hotel Waterloo

🟢 **EATING**
11 Brasserie de Waterloo
12 Le Boucher de Maximus
13 Le Commercio
14 Lou Soleou

🔵 **INFORMATION**
15 Waterloo Tourist Office

LIGNY: TWO DAYS BEFORE WATERLOO

In 1815, Napoleon was in a hurry. His 124,000 men could outnumber the roughly 106,000 Anglo-Dutch-Hanoverian allies under Wellington as long as they didn't work together with another 117,000 Prussians approaching from the east. On 16 June 1815, at Ligny near Charleroi, Napoleon believed he had defeated the latter, with the Prussian general, 72-year-old Field Marshal Blücher, left half crushed for hours beneath his dead horse. Had Blücher expired at Ligny, rather than bathing his wounds with rhubarb, garlic and schnapps, Waterloo would have ended differently.

The memorabilia-filled **Musée de la Bataille de Ligny** tells the tale, and also covers the pre-Waterloo skirmish between Napoleon and Wellington at nearby Quatre Bras.

Still within Mémorial 1815, continue to the contrastingly old-fashioned **Panorama**, a circular diorama of the battle painted in 1912. It comes complete with sound effects and foreground models of fallen troops and horses. You can also climb the iconic **Lion's Mound**, a memorial erected in the 1820s at the request of the Dutch king whose son had been injured while assisting Wellington in the battle here. The 28-tonne lion is accessed up 226 precipitously steep steps and surveys wide views across the battlefields. At the mound's base, you might find a pair of costumed soldiers performing 'animations' – ie demonstrations of canon- and musket-shooting, battlefield surgery and drill practice on a changing roster (check the day's timetable).

Hougoumont Farmstead

The sub-battle site that saved Wellington's skin

Mémorial 1815 tickets include entry to **Hougoumont**, 1.2km west of the main site. Valiant defence of this classic fortified farm proved pivotal in robbing Napoleon of a decisive flanking manoeuvre. The highlight of a visit here is in the antique barn where a very impressionistic if slow-moving 20-minute film is projected onto hi-tech swivelling panels. The film starts hourly on the half-hour, but only a few times daily in English, so check timings for this and for a guided tour with a costumed soldier, which adds some insights and shows bullets found nearby. Peep into the chapel whose original wooden Christ was scorched but not destroyed on the battle day, only to be stolen in 2011. When recovered, it had lost a leg.

The walk to Hougoumont across the battlefield is on public footpaths for which no ticket is required. It's also possible to drive, or use the shuttle 'train' (free for ticket holders), which departs roughly every 20 minutes from noon.

Blood & Booze

Waterloo's Mont St Jean farm

Over 62,000 men were injured at Waterloo. Many of the British and Dutch were taken to the fortified 18th-century farmstead at **Mont St Jean** for treatment of the most brutally rudimentary form. In the farm's former chapel, a fascinating little **museum** *(fermedemontsaintjean.be; €5)* outlines pre-anaesthetic interventions and a stomach-turning video explains types of wounds typically inflicted by different

EATING IN WATERLOO: OUR PICKS

Lou Soleou: A good-value taste of the South of France, notably through Provençal pizzas. Booking advised. *noon-2pm Tue-Fri & 6.30-10pm Tue-Sat €€*

Le Commercio: Cosy, long-term favourite for Franco-Belgian food in a newly located retro-cafe style interior. *6.30pm-11.30pm Wed-Mon €€*

Brasserie de Waterloo: Bistro fare plus beers and spirits created on the premises in this family-friendly battlefield farmstead. *11am-11pm Wed-Sat, 10.30am-7pm Sun €€*

Le Boucher de Maximus: Though overlooking the battlefield, the carnivorous grill feasts attract locals as much as tourists. *noon-2pm & 6.30-9.30pm €€*

weapons. Get tickets from the shop section of the fabulous brewery-distillery **Brasserie de Waterloo**. Museum tickets are free if you also do a brewery tour *(3pm Wed-Sun, €15)*.

Wellington Museum & More

Heading into downtown Waterloo

Today Waterloo is a suburban satellite town. However, back in 1815 it was a rustic village huddled around the copper-domed **Chapelle Royale**, a still-impressive 1609 baroque church built to bribe God into giving the Spanish King Philip III a male heir. The densely wooded Forêt de Soignes, then considered dangerous for travellers, came right up to what is now the **L'Amusoir** restaurant. Before and after the battle, Wellington stayed opposite the church in what was then a coaching inn. It's now the **Musée Wellington** *(museewellington.be adult/student; €10/8)*. One of the prize exhibits is the original folding table at which he sat to write a victory note. It was the fact that this letter was addressed from Waterloo that gave the battle its abiding name (technically the battlefield actually lies within neighbouring Braine-l'Alleud). The museum's well-designed QR-code audio guide is informative without being overly long, and cleverly self-aligns with a projection (room 14) that very visually shows the various troop movements as the battle progressed. Don't miss the wooden prosthetic limb of Lord Uxbridge, made to replace his leg that had been shattered during one of the cavalry charges.

Beside the church, accessed via the **Waterloo Tourist Office** *(waterloo-tourisme.com)*, is a smaller, free museum about Waterloo town, housed in an 1829 presbytery.

Le Caillou

Napoleon's last HQ

Napoleon's last lodgings were around 4km south of Mont St Jean at **Le Caillou**, a former farm commandeered by aide-de-camp General Gourgaud. Now it is the **Dernier Quartier Général de Napoléon** *(dernier-qg-napoleon.be/en; adult/under-18 €5/3)*, a museum displaying one of the emperor's 1804 folding camp beds, as well as the original tables at which the pre-battle war council met. Around 35 minutes of audio guide is particularly enjoyable for the 'voices' of various French characters describing their roles on that fateful evening. And how Bonaparte ignored their advice.

Driving back to Waterloo, you could loop through **Plancenoit village** where a **monument** commemorates the ultimate sacrifice made by 6700 Prussian soldiers. Brutal skirmishes here importantly diverted some of Napoleon's energy away from the main battlefield, giving just enough breathing to Wellington's troops who could thus hold out until more Prussians arrived to relieve them.

WATERLOO BATTLES REPLAYED

In late June 2025, over 2000 men dressed up in early-19th-century military costumes and replayed scenes from the 1815 battle beside the Lion Mount. Reconstructions on this scale take place every five years, with a grandstand erected for ticketed onlookers and a running commentary. Still in character, the 'soldiers' camp overnight at La Cailliou (Napoleonic) and Hougoumont (allies), and a visit to these 'Bivouacs' (also ticketed) is nearly as interesting as the battle show.

In the four years between big reconstructions, smaller ones take place, show-fighting around the gates of Hougoumont with around 200 or so participants. The exact weekend (in late June or early July) depends on Belgian holidays, not the battle's anniversary.

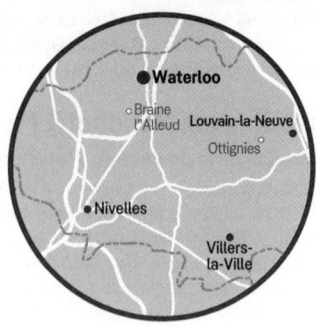

Beyond
Waterloo

Easy, free parking makes Waterloo a
sensible alternative base to Brussels if
you're visiting northern Wallonia by car.

Places

Nivelles p204

Louvain-la-Neuve p205

Villers-la-Ville p205

GETTING AROUND

Trains between
Brussels and
Charleroi go via
both Waterloo and
Nivelles, though only
the slower trains stop
at Waterloo. Louvain-
la-Neuve is on a spur
line with trains from
Brussels travelling
via Ottignies. That's
where you change for
a train to Villers-
la-Ville, though the
station at Villers
is 2km from the
abbey ruins.

If driving to Louvain-
la-Neuve, you can
park for free beside
the N250 around
500m north of the
Hergé Museum, then
use the woodland-
footpath accessways.

The undulating fields of southern Brabant are often
overlooked by foreign visitors concentrating on the greater
drama of the Ardennes or the medieval architecture of
Belgium's gem cities. But there's a lot to discover, including
great former monastery churches, little-known castles in
pretty landscapes, and golf courses tailored to a wealthy
Brussels-periphery population. The city of Nivelles was once
one of the region's foremost abbeys, and its centrepiece is an
imposing 11th-century Romanesque church. Contrastingly
lacking any historical pedigree, Louvain-la-Neuve (L-L-N)
was founded as a campus town after 1968 riots led Leuven's
famous university (p186) to split along linguistic lines. L-L-
N's layout is a baffling pedestrian maze, but there are two
remarkable museums that you shouldn't miss.

Nivelles

TIME FROM WATERLOO: **17MIN**

The grandeur of Ste-Gertrude

Dominating Nivelles' Grand-Place is the 11th-century
Collégiale Ste-Gertrude *(free)*, one of Belgium's most
impressive Romanesque churches. Look up on the hour
to see a 2m-tall mechanised gilt warrior figure dangling
precariously from the southern turret and hammering out
the time. Inside, beyond enormous unadorned arches, is
the silver *châsse* (reliquary casket) of 7th-century founder
Ste-Gertrude, plus the 15th-century chariot used to carry it
during Nivelles' principal procession *(late-Sep/early-Oct)*.
Another fascinating time to visit is Whit Monday when the
whole Grand-Place is transformed into a full-blown livestock
market.

Taste a unique Nivelles' speciality

Textured somewhere between pizza and quiche, and flavoured
with fragrant green chard, *tarte al djote* is Nivelles' modest
culinary speciality. There's even a specialist fraternity of
bakers who are specially qualified to make them. Try a small
takeaway version from loveable historic bakery **Le Chant du
Pain** *(6am-5.30pm Mon-Sat)* on Rue du Géant, which still
uses wood-fired stoves to bake its various breads.

Louvain-la-Neuve

TIME FROM WATERLOO: **30MIN** 🚗

Honouring a great cartoonist

The inventive, modern yet touchingly nostalgic **Hergé Museum** *(museeherge.be; adult/child €12/5)* celebrates the multitalented creator of comic-strip hero Tintin. You'll need well over an hour to peruse the original materials, watch the various videos and cover all 25 chapters of the QR-code-activated app-based guide: bring earphones for the best experience so you can simultaneously watch the pictures and listen on your phone. The museum's abstract glass-and-concrete architecture is an attraction in itself, filled with multi-storey geometrical forms and slashed through with a central 'light chasm'. Great gift shop.

The other Louvain

Louvain-la-Neuve also has an enviable university collection. In a triangle of 1970s brutalist concrete, **Musée L** *(museel.be; adult/over-60/under-26 €8/6/3)* houses priceless collections that were bequests made by university supporters. The result is a mind-boggling ride from contemporary art to paleontology and historic measuring machines to African tribal art. There's a Picasso engraving, two Delvaux paintings and a very thought-provoking video discussing the development of scientific thought and 21st-century-era doubts about identity. The 6th (top) floor is especially inspired, counterpointing themed objects from utterly different eras.

Villers-la-Ville

TIME FROM WATERLOO: **25MIN** 🚗

Music in the ruins

Nestled attractively in a wooded dell lie the atmospheric ruins of **Villers-la-Ville Abbey** *(villers.be/en; adult/student/under-12 €10/8/4)*, once one of Belgium's biggest monastic complexes. QR-coded audio guides on your phone help bring the very extensive site to life. There are game-based options for children, but best of all is late-August's *Nuit des Chœurs (nuitdeschoeurs.be)* or other enchanting outdoor concerts.

TINTIN AFTER NEARLY A CENTURY

Along with Hercule Poirot, quiff-headed boy-reporter Tintin remains the most famous Belgian who never 'lived'. Tintin's adventures with loveable dog Snowy, hard-of-hearing Professor Calculus and crusty old salt Captain Haddock have sold over 270 million copies since 1929. Blistering barnacles! Creator Hergé didn't want other writers to take on the character after his death, so no new albums have been released since 1986. Yet some four million copies a year still sell in dozens of languages.

Tintin figurines, T-shirts and postcards remain enormously popular and in 2011, Stephen Spielberg brought Tintin to Hollywood audiences. In 2023, an original black-and-white Hergé sketch, drawn in 1942 for *Tintin in America*, sold for €2.16 million.

Try the disarmingly drinkable Ste Gertrude 7.5% triple on tap.

 EATING & DRINKING BEYOND WATERLOO

Le Bistro de l'Abbaye: Self-brewed beers or trout with quinoa in vaulted cellars beside Villers-la-Ville abbey's ticket office. *11am-7pm daily May-Sep, Wed-Sun only Oct-Apr* €

L'Air du Temps: Gastronomic rural farmstead 20km southeast of Louvain-la-Neuve that gets two Michelin stars for veg-friendly creativity. *7-8.30pm Tue-Sat* €€€

Maurice le Limonadier: Cosy Nivelles wine bistro with a cuisine that gives some of the Franco-Belgian favourites an Asian fusion twist. *noon-2pm & 6-10pm Tue-Sat* €€

Le Palais du Hublon: A who's who of local and national brews in five inter-connected cellar rooms. Central Nivelles, yet almost invisible at street level. *noon-1am*

Mons

MUSEUMS | DRAGONS | VAN GOGH

GETTING AROUND

Mons' modernist new **train station** finally opened in December 2024, nine years late. Fast trains link to Brussels (45 mins via Soignies), Charleroi (30 mins) and Tournai (30 mins). Ouigo budget trains to Paris North run three times daily (2¼ hours, from €10). The city centre is walkably small. Parking is tough right in the historic core, but easier to find south of the centre, with free places available beyond the Boulevard Albert-Elisabeth, within a 15 minute walk of the Grand-Place. The tourist office rents bicycles (per day €10/20 standard/ electric, return by 5.15pm)

☑ **TOP TIP**

The **Mons Card** *(24-/48-hours €18/26)* can save money if you plan to visit more than a couple of museums, plus you get bicycle hire included. But double-check opening days and note that some museums are free anyway on the first Sunday of each month.

Handily located for visiting western Wallonia's many intriguing if commonly overlooked attractions, Mons itself hosts four UNESCO-listed features, including one of Europe's most memorable festivals. European city of culture in 2015, it remains a pleasantly attractive place despite a brutal history of battles and de-industrialisation. The medieval city developed around the hilltop site of a Roman *castrum* (fortified camp) and for centuries it was the capital of the powerful county of Hainaut. From the 18th century, the surrounding Borinage region became one of Europe's foremost coal-mining areas, with Van Gogh among many visitors to be appalled by miners' working conditions. In WWI it was at the Battle of Mons that the British army had its disastrous first engagement with German forces. Some 4000 men escaped, miraculously aided by an apparition of the 'Angels of Mons' – or so they believed. NATO's command-operations HQ, SHAPE, is 5km north of town.

Towards the Bells

Views from Mons' belfry

On the highest point of the town, partly ringed by remnant fortifications, the **belfry** *(beffroi.mons.be; adult/senior/under-12 €9/6/free)* is a focal point that marks out Mons from miles around. There are great views without climbing it, but paying for entry gets you a lift to the 5th floor with even finer panoramas and touch-screen view identifiers. You can continue up to see the workings of the thumping clock mechanism. Then part way down again, watch CCTV images of the bells and play on-screen games. Beware that entry tickets are not sold in the belfry itself but in the **Maison des Patrimoines**.

Mons Through all the Senses

Culture, art and traditions at CAP

Techniques of contemporary art engage with a rich historical-cultural collection at the very unusual **CAP gallery** *(adult €9-16*

MONS

Grand Hornu (14km);
Maison Van Gogh
de Colfontaine (15km);
Marcasse Mine ruins (15km)

26

14

15

R des Dominicains

R des Compagnons

R du 11 Novembre 1918

R de Nimy

R Verte

Musée du Doudou **3**

6

R Neuve

R du Gouvernement

Cimetière Militaire de
Saint-Symphorien (6km);
Havré castle ruins (6km);

Silex's (7km)

9

10

32

Grand-
Place

R Claude de Bettignies

17

11

R des Sars

18   Belfry

5

30

8

20

Parc du Château   **1**

16

12

23

24

27

R d'Havré

34 Place
Léopold

7

R des Clercs

13

28

R du Chapitre

Square
St-Germain

25

R de la Chaussée

29

R de Hautbois

R de la Réunion

R de la Coupe

R de la Clef

Maison Van Gogh,
Cuesmes (2km);
Paturages former
train station (6.5km)

R des Fripiers R de Houdain

Grand Rue

R Notre-Dame

R de la Halle

R des Capucins

21

R des Archers

Bvd Dolez

R de Bouzanton

22

Porte des
Guérites

R Achille Legrand

R Larir

33

R des Chartriers

2

Mons
Memorial
Museum

Jardin de
la Grande
Pêcherie

19

R de la Trouille

R des Arquebusiers

0   200 m
0   0.1 miles

4

⭐ **HIGHLIGHTS**
1 Belfry
2 Mons Memorial Museum
3 Musée du Doudou

🔴 **SIGHTS**
4 Anciens Abattoirs
5 Artothèque
6 CAP
7 Collégiale
   Ste-Waudru
8 Grand-Place
9 Hôtel de Graty

10 Jardin du Meyeur
11 'Le Sinche'
12 Lucie & the
    Butterflies
13 Maison des
    Patrimoines (belfry
    ticket office)
14 Mumons
15 Mundaneum
16 Musée François
    Duesberg
17 Ruelle Cesar
18 Small tower

⚫ **SLEEPING**
19 La Maison de la
    Duchesse de la Vallière
20 L'Olivier
21 Mons Dragon House
22 St Martins
    Dream Hotel
23 Youth Hostel

🟢 **EATING**
24 Henri
25 Origines
26 Osmose

🟢 **DRINKING &
NIGHTLIFE**
27 Café de la Joie
28 Citizen Fox
29 Ginger & Rosemary
30 Jolicoeur
31 La Lorgnette
see 31 L'Excelsior
32 Modjo
33 Tearoom Le Paddington

🔴 **SHOPPING**
see 28 Mons Où Venir

🔵 **TRANSPORT**
34 Train Station

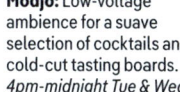

🍸 **DRINKING IN MONS: OUR PICKS**

Modjo: Low-voltage ambience for a suave selection of cocktails and cold-cut tasting boards. *4pm-midnight Tue & Wed, 11.30am-2am Thu-Sun*

La Lorgnette: Rock-vibe pub with a decent range of brews but specialising in a whacky drink that mixes Bush beer with ignited hot alcohol. Quite a show! *1pm-late*

Citizen Fox: Venture through the alfresco courtyard to find this buzzing party-pub with craft beers, pool table and international food menu. *noon-late*

L'Excelsior: Classic Belgian bar-café with wood panelling, stained-glass frontage and zinc-brass table-tops. Grand-Place terrace, St-Feuillien on tap. *9.30am-11pm*

HEART OF MONS

This short but inspiring walk reveals some of central Mons' most appealing viewpoints and 'secret' cut-throughs.

START	END	LENGTH
Train Station	Grand-Place	1.5km, 45 minutes

From the controversial new **1** **train station** (p206), walk past the **2** **Musée François Duesberg** (p210) and **3** **Lucie & the Butterflies**, a giant statue of a kneeling girl in faceted steel. Look inside Mons' foremost church, **4** **Collégiale Ste-Waudru**, then continue climbing past **5** **Maison des Patrimoines** (p206) on attractive Rue des Clercs, doubling back past the discordant **6** **youth hostel** and up the Rampe du Château. Emerge at the magnificent, UNESCO-listed **7** **belfry** (p206) for views across town.

In the northwest corner of the castle plateau site, an unlikely looking passage leads through a small reconstructed **8** **tower** and down a stairway via **9** **Ruelle Cesar** onto Rue Bervoets. Almost directly opposite, what looks like a private lane is Passage Victor Hugo, a walkway that emerges through a 19th-century former school called **10** **Hôtel de Graty** onto Rue d'Enghien. Turn right, then swiftly left at No 20 on a path leading into **11** **Jardin du Meyeur**, a 'secret' garden at the back of which is the **12** **Musée du Doudou**. On the southeast side of the garden, take a vaulted 'tunnel' into a wisteria-decked courtyard, then emerge onto the **13** **Grand-Place**. The superstitious can score a wish by rubbing the head of **14** **'Le Sinche'**, a small metal monkey statue mounted on the gateway of the City Hall.

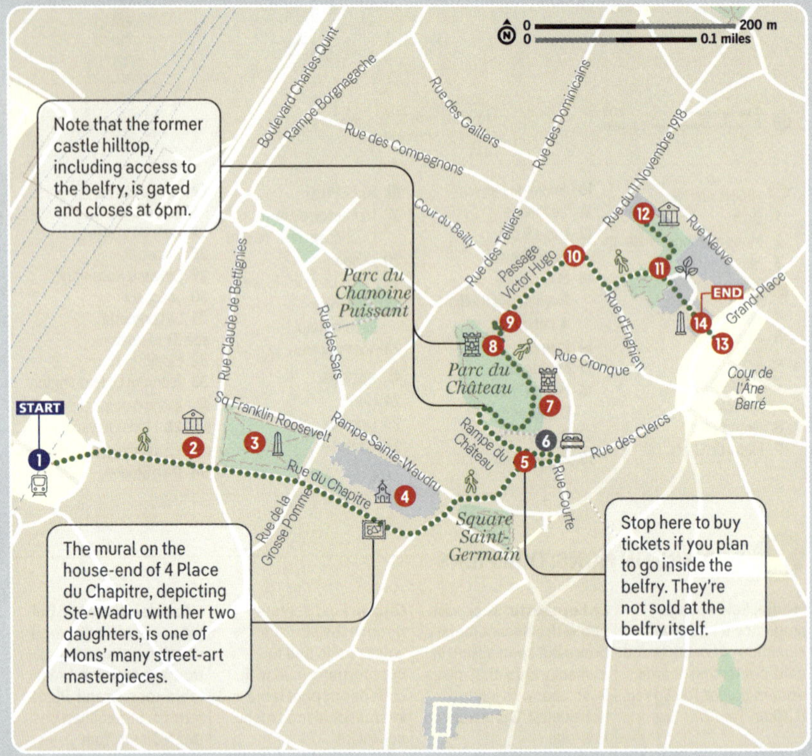

Note that the former castle hilltop, including access to the belfry, is gated and closes at 6pm.

The mural on the house-end of 4 Place du Chapitre, depicting Ste-Wadru with her two daughters, is one of Mons' many street-art masterpieces.

Stop here to buy tickets if you plan to go inside the belfry. They're not sold at the belfry itself.

according to exhibition). Daring curation and an extravagant wealth of contrasting exhibition spaces allows evocations of the city and its varied legacies through regularly changing exhibitions that appeal to all of the senses using not just light and sound but also tactile and even smell-based discoveries. The medicinal garden behind is a free-to-access oasis.

Chasing the Dragon
Doudou and the Lumeçon

Assuming you can't be in Mons for the UNESCO-recognised **Ducasse**, get a flavour of events from a video in the nave of the **Collégiale Ste-Waudru**, a superb 15th-century Gothic church. The video screen is behind the cherub-encrusted **Golden Coach** that carries the saint's relics around during the festival. To see just how much effort is required, visit the **Musée du Doudou** *(adult/senior/under-12 €9/6/free),* hidden in an attractive courtyard-garden behind the city hall. Dedicated to the Ducasse, the museum asks 'What is a dragon?', ponders whether St George was a 'megalo-martyr' and provides an immersive experience capturing the testosterone-fuelled feats of the Car d'Or.

Once you know what he looks like, you'll start noticing references to Doudou's globular green form all across town, in the Doudou-shaped shelving at the **Mons Où Venir** souvenir shop, or the Doudou tail overhanging the cash desk in restaurant **Henri**, for example.

No More War
Remembering a history of suffering

After the lighthearted fun of Doudou, it comes as a bit of a shock to see at the **Mons Memorial Museum** *(musees-expos.mons.be; adult/student €9/6)* just how many horrors the city has endured. The first five sieges are dispensed with swiftly, but the harrowing tales of WWI leave the visitor feeling shellshocked; even the 'Miraculous Angels of Mons' story is retold in a brooding video with a sombre twist. Just when you're ready for some light relief, it all happens again in WWII. Tragic history. There's lots to read (four language options), well chosen personal testimonies, superb day-by-day animated war maps, and memorably understated artefacts, like a post used for executions and the bronze head of Göring ripped off a statue and thrown on the ground. At last something positive.

THE DUCASSE

Mons' seven-day **ducasse** (festival) reaches fever pitch on Trinity Sunday, eight weeks after Easter. In the morning, the remains of Mons' patron saint, 7th-century miracle-worker Ste-Waudru, are paraded around town on a heavy 1782 'Golden Coach' cart in the **Procession du Car d'Or**. Then at lunchtime the sounds of drums and chanting crescendo as people pack the Grand-Place for the **Lumeçon**. This mock battle pits St George and his Chinchins (soldiers in 18th-century dress) against a green-painted wickerwork dragon called **Doudou**, supported by a gang of bladder-wielding devils. The most daring spectators surge forward at the end, attempting to grab hairs from the dragon's long, dangerously flailing rigid tail.

Speciality is pork 'berdoulle', smothered in thick mustard-onion-tarragon dressing.

 EATING IN MONS: OUR PICKS

Osmose: Chef Sandro d'Antonio's elegant take on Franco-Belgian cuisine, with a particular reputation for fish and seafood dishes. *noon & 7pm Tue-Fri* €€€

Chez les Filles: Comfort food and gastronomy in a cosily intimate shop-house on the main dining street. *noon-2.30pm Wed-Sun & 6.30-10pm Wed-Sat* €€

Origines: Effortlessly stylish mod-French dining that won't break the bank. Upstairs restaurant above an open kitchen. Enter from a tiny side alley. *noon-2pm Wed-Fri & Sun, 7-9pm Wed-Sat* €€

Henri: Regional Belgian home-cooking that's been a local favourite since 1956. Lunch plates €8.50, cash only. *noon-2pm daily & 6.30-9pm Wed-Sat* €

Mundaneum: Displays a pre-electronic informatics system so ingenious that UNESCO calls it the 'first model of a search engine'.

Artothèque: A former convent chapel full of objects from various museum basements: use interactive screens to locate and learn more about them.

Musée François Duesberg: Eclectic collection of gilded clocks, dazzling porcelain and silver coffeepots from 1775 to 1825.

Anciens Abattoirs: Art-and-craft space that also hosts September's Festifood food fair.

Mumons: Mish-mash university collection of old maps, scientific equipment, art and curiosities.

Historic Holes
Mining in the stone age

Silex's (*musees-expos.mons.be; museum adult/student/child €6/4/2*) is one of the most obscure UNESCO World Heritage Sites anywhere: it's essentially just a hole in the ground near Spiennes village, 7km southeast of Mons. In fact, this was a major Neolithic flint-mining site, and its existence revealed the degree to which cooperative mining and long-distance trade was a thing in the stone age. Sign boards around the site give extensive background and a small modern museum shows how the flint was knapped into durable tools. If you want to descend 10m down a ladder to look inside, that is only possible at 2pm on weekends; book well ahead by phone through **Visit Mons** (*065-335580; €14, max 12 people*).

To make an interesting loop by car from Mons, you could additionally stop briefly in Havré to admire its spectacularly shattered, moat-ringed **castle** (*free*) and visit the peacefully rural WWI military cemetery at **St-Symphorien**, where both the first and last Commonwealth casualties of WWI are buried beneath mature trees. Unusually here, roughly equal numbers of German and British graves lie almost side by side.

Van Gogh & the Brutal Borinage
Echoes of industrial glory

In 1879, young Vincent Van Gogh was led by intense religious convictions to the Borinage mining area around Mons. Aiming to live like Jesus, he gave away all he had to workers who suffered in dismal conditions, before turning to art. The **Maison Van Gogh, Cuesmes** (*adult/student €4/2*) where he lodged is now a small museum that explains more. The far-from-idyllic surrounding area has several other Van Gogh–related sites (p214) that you could explore by bicycle partly using a RAVeL cycle route between Mons and the former **Paturages Train Station** that Vincent would have used.

Not all miners endured conditions that were quite as awful as those that Van Gogh observed at Marcasse Mine. In the 1830s, a 'model village' was built for colliery workers 12km west of Mons with neatly laid out cottages and a neoclassical oval of more grandiose central buildings. This has been preserved and UNESCO-protected as **Grand Hornu**, a cultural centre and contemporary art space with changing exhibitions.

MORE RAVeL CYCLING ROUTES

RAVeL (*Réseau Autonome des Voies Lentes; ravel.wallonie.be*) is Wallonia's vast network of cycle paths. They are easy to ride, having been built along old railway lines and canal towpaths. Another example is the riverside route between Namur and Dinant (p224).

DRINKING IN MONS: BEST CAFES

Tearoom Le Paddington: Vintage floral & gingham cafe for tea, scones and home-baked cakes. *11am-6pm Tue-Fri, from 1pm Sat*

Jolicoeur: Micro barista-cafe showcasing superb house-roasted beans named for stations on the Montreal metro. *8am-6pm Wed-Fri, from 10am Sat*

Ginger & Rosemary: Spacious family-run coffee-sipping space with a good selection of breakfast and brunch options. *8.30am-4.30pm Thu-Sun*

Café de la Joie: A range of healthy teas as well as pancakes and homemade coffee ice cream, with the chance of live gospel music. *11am-3pm & 6-9pm Tue-Sat*

Beyond Mons

The Borinage is full of post-industrial fascination while beyond lie rural brewing villages, great carnival towns, venerable Tournai and plenty of rural peace.

The coal mines of the Borinage region fuelled Wallonia's 19th-century industrialisation. However, fortunes reversed after the 1970s and nowhere is a starker symbol of dystopian decay than the intriguing former steel city of Charleroi. Some sites have been museum-ised and the region has a remarkable network of historical canals with UNESCO-listed boat-lift contraptions. Further afield lie some unexpectedly pretty rural areas and country estates. The city of Tournai is a historical charmer, Binche hosts Belgium's most unforgettable carnival, while Ath's lesser-known 'Giants' and Lessines 'Penitents' are surreal. Further south, things get ever more rural, with outdoor activities aplenty in the 'Pays des Lacs' and charming villages around attractive castle-and-beer town Chimay.

Enghien
TIME FROM MONS: 45MIN 🚌
Historic break
If you're in need of a quick break while driving between Brussels and Tournai/Lille, a lovely option is Enghien (Endigen) with its selection of cafes, small historic core and a fine park with formal gardens, woodlands and lakeside strolls. Parking is free and it's just a couple of kilometres off the highway.

Ath
TIME FROM MONS: 35MIN 🚆
City of giants
The appealing historic city of Ath comes alive on the fourth weekend of August with a series of parades featuring distinctive giants (p212). These towering wicker-framed figures, over 4m tall, have a complicated semi-religious symbolism that's explained in

 GETTING AROUND

Tournai and Charleroi are connected by train to Mons and Brussels. If heading for Lille, France, using the Ouigo service from Mons or stopping in Tournai and then taking the local hopper can prove cheaper than taking the direct high-speed Brussels–Lille train. Without wheels, reaching most of the other sights beyond Mons will be frustrating, though it's possible to reach Binche and Couvin by train. Excellent RAVeL cycle paths follow several former railway lines.

ATH'S GIANTS' WEEKEND

Friday night (4th weekend of August) The 'trousers' of the main giant-figure, Goyasse (Goliath), are ceremonially burnt as a form of stag party!

Saturday
'Wedding day' for Mr & Mrs Goyasse. The giant couple process to Église St-Julien for their nuptials, stopping partway to do a little dance. Goyasse (who is 'Goliath' after all) briefly meets 'David', who symbolically defeats his evil side with a well-thrown ball flung at his underbelly. Everyone cheers, then the party continues.

Sunday
The full giants' parade. Characters joining the Goyasses include a two-headed eagle and a horse called Bayard ridden by four small children. It's so heavy that it takes 16 people inside to make it walk.

Ath's **Maison des Géants** (*maisondesgeants.be; adult/senior €8/7*). The museum mixes in town history and an impressive art collection that includes an original Breughel. It's housed in an Art Nouveau house entered via the hidden rear garden.

Ath's decent **Gallo-Roman Museum** (*espacegalloromain.be/ en; adult/under-26 €6/5*) is strong on explaining archaeology and features preserved Roman boats.

Temples of zoology

Home to some 7000 animals, **Pairi Daiza** (*pairidaiza.eu; adult/ child €48/42, parking €11*) distinguishes itself from other major zoos through its imaginative enclosures: remnants of a historic abbey are genuine, while East Asian temples and an African stilt village are flights of fancy. Allow a full day to do it justice.

Lessines
TIME FROM MONS: **50MIN**

Medicine, folklore & faith

Had you been suffering from suspected plague in medieval Belgium, your best hope would likely have been getting scared out of your wits by a 'doctor' in a bird-beaked mask.

 EATING & DRINKING AROUND MONS: OUR PICKS

Taverne St-Géry: In Aubechies, this is one of rural Belgium's most authentic village pubs. Bookings are recommended for meals. *6pm-9pm Sat & Sun €€*

Trolls & Bush: Highly professional Pipaix pub-brasserie with pond-side summer seating attached to the BeerStorium. *10am-10pm €€*

Café de la Brasserie: Yes, there's a town called Silly. And yes, they brew Silly beers. Try them at the unrepentantly local bar-café beside the brewery. *10am-11pm €*

Quai n°4: There are buzzing brasserie bar-cafés round Ath's main square but for creative gastronomy it's hard to beat this one. *noon & 7pm Wed-Sat €€€*

SANTIAGO URQUIJO/GETTY IMAGES

Tournai Cathedral

Such a costume is just one of many fascinating exhibits at **Hôpital Notre-Dame à la Rose** *(notredamealarose.be; adult/student/under-12 €13/10/5),* a museum that helps you viscerally appreciate just how basic medical knowledge once was. You'll need a minimum of 1¼ hours to zip around this very rare surviving example of a medieval convent-farm-hospital complex, even if you skip sections of the rather pedestrian audio guide. Highlights include a painting-decked refectory, a reconstructed 1715 infirmary, grandiose chapel and 1860s pharmacy where the accompanying video employs a chilling horror-movie vibe.

You don't need a ticket to wander round the hospital's lovely herb garden. Stroll up towards the town hall and notice the chap sitting on a bench wearing an upside down bowler hat – a **statue** of surrealist artist René Magritte, who was born in Lessines.

Tournai

TIME FROM MONS: **35MIN**

Be dwarfed by Tournai's Notre Dame

While Tournai has a splendid triangular Grand-Place and Wallonia's oldest municipal **belfry**, the city is nicknamed the 'city of five spires' for the unusual fistful of towers on the city's gigantic centrepiece **Cathédrale Notre Dame de Tournai** *(cathedrale-tournai.be; free).* The interior architecture is a textbook comparison of styles. The side apses and recently restored 12th-century nave are solidly Romanesque. However, the 13th-century choir is a fine example of early Gothic. Some soaring pillars bend disconcertingly, but scaffolding and protective cladding hide much of the choir pending long-term repairs. This only partly detracts from the imposing effect.

WEST WALLONIA BREWS

Brasserie à Vapeur: Tiny, antique and highly experimental, this family business in Pipaix village maintains the last surviving steam brewery anywhere. Brew days are something to behold, but rare: check dates in advance *(vapeur. com).* Cafe opens 10am-6pm Fri-Sun.

Dupont: Synonymous with Belgian Saison ales, Dupont's brewery dominates Tourpes village. Book online *(brasserie-dupont. com; €12.50)* for tours, visit their brew-shop, or sample the beers at **La Forge,** Tourpes' local cafe/lunch-bar.

Dubuisson: A moated former castle site near Pipaix today hosts Dubuisson's 21st-century interactive beer experience, **BeerStorium** *(discover.dubuisson. com/en adult/student €9/7).* That includes a VR bar-room, discovery games and 'the world's smallest micro-brewery'. The slick brasserie-restaurant offers taster-size beer portions.

VAN GOGH SITES AROUND MONS

Maison Van Gogh, Colfontaine: As a wannabe pastor, Vincent shared the outhouse of this basic cottage at Colfontaine/ Wasmes in 1879 when he first arrived in the area. The house is only open by appointment; tel 0492 760303.

Marcasse Mine ruins: On arrival, Van Gogh was shocked to find workers 'living' in galleries 700m underground at this mine. The site was later used as a set for the 1955 Kirk Douglas movie *Lust for Life*. Though now in ruins, some mine buildings are appealingly graffitied with Van Gogh–related images and cared for by a local trust.

Artothèque, Mons: Displays *Les Bêcheurs*, a Van Gogh etching made during his Borinage period.

Entry is beneath the fine rose window and giant organ from the Place de l'Évêché or more intriguingly via a minor door on the west side from the little square where a group statue shows a saint, fascinated by Mary breastfeeding her baby Jesus.

On the northeast corner, **Carré Janson** is a 'smart centre' planned to open in 2026 with a cathedral-viewing belvedere and a multi-sensory experience of an 'other Tournai' mixing history and fantasy. Nearby, look inside the **Tourist Office** where a gilded reflective panel creates intriguing reflections of the spires, and a very professional 30-minute cinema-quality film *(€4)* outlines city history.

Tournai's historical fortifications

An intriguing aspect of Tournai is finding fragments of fortifications from so many eras. At **Pont des Trous**, a wall segment first bridged the River Escaut/Schelde here in the 13th century. Dynamited in WWII, its rebuilt central arch was widened in 2022 to facilitate river transport. **Tour Henri VIII** is a round tower dating from Tournai's brief stint as an English town, 1513–1519. The **Citadelle** is a 17th-century mega-pentagon of Vauban fortifications that has now almost vanished; remnants lie in a military area. However, two Sunday afternoons a month in summer, you can visit the site's underground remnants. Free, but book ahead via *visittournai.be*. **Tour St-Georges & Tour du Cygne** are isolated remnants of the 1202 city wall. **Fort Rouge** is a 12th-century tower 'rediscovered' in 1998, now heavily renovated and used as an occasional art space.

Beloeil & Aubechies

TIME FROM MONS: **45MIN** 🚗

Baroque indulgence of Beloeil

The **Château de Beloeil** *(chateaudebeloeil.com; adult/child €12/6, park-only €6/3)* palace-mansion is so grand that it's nicknamed Belgium's Versailles. It faces an artificial lake and vast manicured park laid out in 1664, while inside you'll find a four-poster bed made for Marie Antoinette: did she really need a canopy that high?! A dozen rooms are so lavishly furnished that it can feel like you're on a film set – as indeed you are: many Belgian movies have used the chateau as a backdrop.

Time travel at Archéosite

Rewind a millennium or two at the fascinating **Archéosite** *(archeosite.be; adult/student/under-13 €13/11/5)* where you can throw yourself into a recreated 'settlement' of ancient dwellings

---

EATING IN TOURNAI: OUR PICKS

Grains de Folie: Merrily upbeat lunch corner for inexpensive meals made with organic and locally sourced ingredients. *11.30am-2.30pm Mon-Sat* €

L'Éléphant Blanc: Great Thai food in an adorable little square behind the Grand-Place. Tiny rear garden. Lunch deals except Saturdays. *noon-2pm & 7-9.30pm Tue-Sat* €€

Chez Marie: Enticing for its high-ceilinged 1930s-style decor. Blackboard menus offer fair-priced, beautifully cooked classics. *noon-3pm Mon & Thu-Sat, plus 7-9pm Fri & Sat* €€

La Petite Madeleine: Modern gastronomic fare in an atmosphere that's suave but not stuffy, with summer garden seating. *7-9pm Wed-Sat & noon-2pm Thu-Fri & Sun* €€€

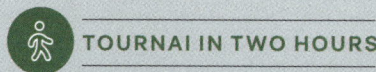

TOURNAI IN TWO HOURS

This quick stomp introduces you to central Tournai's loveliest spots. Allow longer if you're going to visit the museums en route.

START	END	LENGTH
Palais de Justice	Notre Dame cathedral	3km, two hours

Free two-hour disk parking is available in leafy streets southeast of the ❶ **Palais de Justice**, an imposing 1879 court building. Walk northwest to Place Reine Astrid for an enticing ❷ **viewpoint** of spires ahead. A formal park leads past the ❸ **City Hall** to Tournai's most memorable museum, the ❹ **Museé des Beaux-Arts**, a Horta-designed building whose superb collection includes works by Monet, Rubens and Van Gogh.

Cut through small lanes past the sprawling ❺ **Military History Museum** and the modest ❻ **Tour St-Georges**, one of two surviving towers from the 1202 city wall. Emerge near the ❼ **Halle aux Draps** whose grand facade originally dates from 1611: it collapsed in 1881 but

was rebuilt identically in the 1890s. From here, a photogenic feast of colourful guild-banners frame a panorama across the ❽ **Grand-Place** towards the cathedral and the UNESCO-listed ❾ **belfry**, Belgium's oldest.

Walk through the peaceful garden Sq Roger Delannay, past the 14th-century tower turned mini exhibition-space ❿ **Fort Rouge**. On Rue des Carmes there's a fine vista of ⓫ **Église St-Jacques**, a marvellous medieval church with an incongruous African mask collection. Head for the river and with luck you'll see the ⓬ **lift bridge** in action as huge barges slide by. Then return past the ⓭ **Academy of Arts building** and the ⓮ **tourist office** to the ⓯ **cathedral** (p213).

Adding an extra 15 minutes to the walk from Église St-Jacques, you could visit the iconic **Pont des Trous**, where a section of city wall bridges the river.

While some areas of Tournai have lost most of their shops, a section of **Rue du Courtrai** features several creative boutiques.

The intriguing, round-ended building that forms the foreground as you look up Place Reine Astrid is the **Conservatoire de Tournai**, a school of performing arts.

Rond Point de l'Europe
Pont des Trous
Schèldt (Escaut)
R de l'Arsenal
Q Sakharov
Q des Salines
R de la Planche
R St-Bruno
R du Château
Ave Leray
Blvd des Nerviens
Pl Verte
R du Sondert
R Campin
R du Becquerelle
R du Bourdon
R du Cygne
R Piquet
R des Carmes
R Blandinoise
R Claquedent
Blvd Leopold
Pl de Lille
R Perdue
Grand-Place
R Dame-Odile
R Clé
Q du Maître Poisson
Q St-Brice
R du Pont
R St-Brice
Pl P E Janson
Pl St-Pierre
R des Chapeliers
R des Frères Rimbaut
Blvd des Frères Rimbault
R Roc St-Nicaise
R As-Pois
R du Ballon
Pl R Astrid
R Tête d'Or
R des Jésuites
R St-Martin
R Fauquez
Pl Palais de Justice

END

START

0   200 m
0   0.1 mile

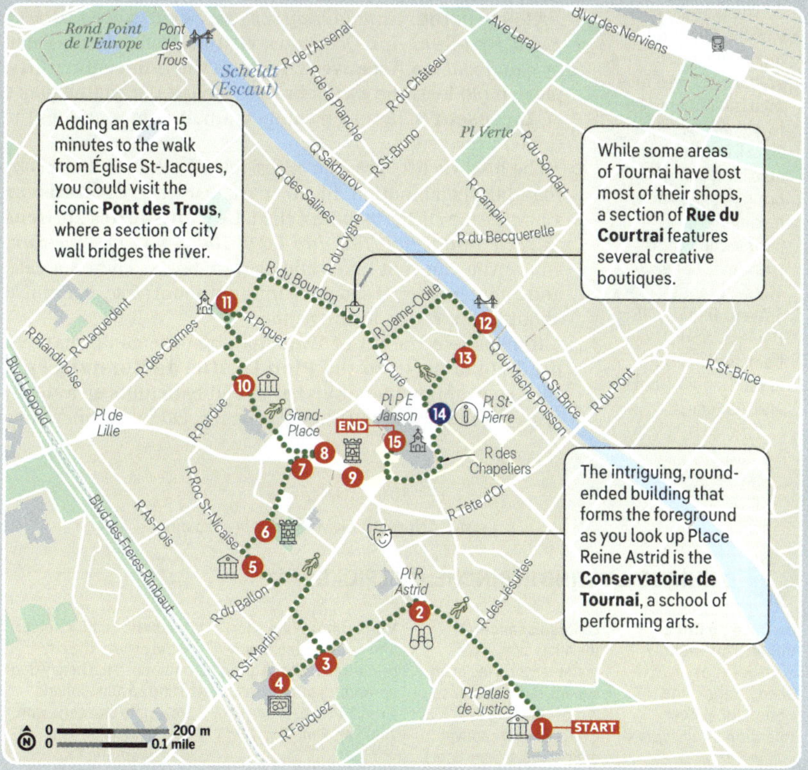

WAFFLE IRON POLITICS

From the 1960s until 1988, official Belgian policy was to ensure parity of government infrastructure spending between Wallonia and Flanders. This approach was nicknamed 'Waffle Iron Politics': after all, a Belgian waffle must be equally crisp on both sides. However, in some cases, whole projects appeared to have been created simply to use up allocated funding.

The craziest case was the Charleroi metro, with four stations of line 5 fully built but left unused for decades (until 2026). But there are also long lists of bridges to nowhere, meaningless intersections and pointless tunnels. These 'Grands Travaux Inutilles' (Big Useless Works) have been documented in tragi-comic books and videos.

and workshops. Rather than concentrate on one epoch, it provides tasters of Neolithic, Bronze Age, Iron Age and Gallo-Roman eras, helping you imagine how life might have been in all these periods. An initial 30-minute video (English option) gives an overview of the site.

Ideally time your visit for a summer Sunday afternoon when, from 2pm, volunteer craftsfolk in period costumes demonstrate the activities and industries of the various eras and musicians perform. It's in attractive little Aubechies village, 7km northwest of Belœil.

Strépy-Thieu
TIME FROM MONS: **25MIN** 🚌

Barging over the Walloon Hills

The **Canal du Centre** links the rivers Meuse/Maas and Escaut/Scheldt. At Thieu, 10km east of Mons, it has to deal with a daunting height differential of 73m. In the 19th century this was achieved using four wrought-iron ship-lifts *(ascenseurs)* that are now UNESCO-listed. They still work, but since 2002 they've been bypassed by the world's single biggest ship-lift, **Strépy-Thieu**. It operates seven or eight times daily, and it's fascinating (and free) to watch from a view-walkway. You can also visit the interior *(adult/concession €10/8);* look down on the engine room, watch a multilingual construction video and peruse exhibitions about inland navigation and container transport.

A 2½-hour **tour** *(canalducentre.be/en; adult/under-12 €18/13, 10am Wed-Sun, Apr-Oct)* takes visitors from Strépy-Thieu by canalboat via **Ascenseur 4** (one of the 19th-century lifts) plus an old lock and swing-bridge, to visit the engine house of **Ascenseur 3**. Return by mini-'train'. A 2pm tour does the same in reverse.

The historic lifts are also accessible by road, or (better) by road-bike combination. Ideally park just west of **Ascenseur 1** at a group of 1940s huts called **Le Cantine des Italiens** *(bicycle rental half/full day €6/8; 10am-4.45pm, Tue-Sun)* where you can rent bikes and electric boats. There's a cafe, and an interesting if shocking mini-museum *(free, in French)* about immigration to the region.

To complete the set of Wallonia's historic canal marvels, head 20km north to the **Plan Incliné de Ronquières**, a 1968 contraption that drags barge-and-bath units up a steady gradient rather than lifting it vertically. Oddly mesmerising.

Garlic-rich meals and €8 four-beer tastings.

DRINKING & EATING IN BINCHE: OUR PICKS

Du Coté de Chez Boule: This friendly little gem has an Art Deco interior, and a good local beer selection. *10am-8pm* €

La Renaissance: Of the many similar bar-restaurants on the main square, La Renaissance is most thoroughly overloaded in carnival memorabilia. *8am-11pm* €

Vinissimo: Wine shop and good-value lunch-restaurant with seating spreading out onto the Grand-Place. *10am-9pm Tue-Sat, 9am-7pm Sun* €

Brasserie La Binchoise: At the base of the city walls, push the heavy door to find an atmospheric brew-pub/brasserie with tree-shaded garden. *11am-10pm Wed-Sun* €€

Morlanwelz

TIME FROM MONS: 30MIN

The understated treasure trove of Mariemont

As a place to unwind, few places beat the **Domaine de Mariemont** parkland near La Louvière, full of mature rare trees and lawns dotted with statuary, including a Rodin. Only semi-visible ruins remain of what the Austrian Hapsburgs once considered their second most beautiful palace (after Schönbrunn). A later mansion built by the Warocqué family burnt down in 1960. However, their astoundingly rich collection was saved and is now displayed in the **Musée Royal de Mariemont** *(musee -mariemont.be/en; free)*. Ranging from stone-age tools and Greco-Roman vases to lots of Tournai porcelain, the treasures make you forgive the ugly 1975 centrepiece building.

Binche

TIME FROM MONS: 25MIN

Home of the ultimate Carnival

Nowhere does carnival like Binche. The town is so firmly associated with excess that Binche is considered a possible root of the English term 'binge'. Come on Shrove Tuesday to meet the iconic **Gilles de Binche**: male figures all dressed alike in clogs and straw-padded colourful suits decorated with heraldic symbols.

Outside Mardi Gras, make do with excellent **MuMask** *(mumask.be; adult/student €8/7)*, a museum in two parts. The first half focuses on Belgian carnivals: act as Gilles, playing an orange-throwing game and donning clogs to try stomp-dancing. To understand why you're doing this, ideally start the visit where you're supposed to finish it with the wordless movie that shows the main events of Binche's UNESCO-honoured big day. The museum's other half, totally revamped in 2025, is an interactive presentation of exquisite masks and costumes from Africa, South America and Melanesia.

Next door, the modest **Centre de la Dentelle** *(free)* celebrates Binche's historic role as a lace-making centre, allowing you a fascinating hands-on opportunity to discover just how laborious an art that is.

Thuin

TIME FROM MONS: 45MIN

The hanging gardens of Belgium

Surprise! Belgium has its own **hanging gardens** *(free)*, terraced steeply down from the ridge-top heart of Thuin (pronounced 'twa') where there's a tourist office beside the UNESCO-listed 1638 **belfry** *(beffroidethuin.be; adult €5)*.

BINCHE ON CARNIVAL DAY

At dawn on Shrove Tuesday, 'brotherhoods' of Gilles clomp into Binche's Grand-Place shaking *ramon* stick-bundles to symbolically sweep away winter. After beer-and-oyster breakfasts, they briefly don eerie green-eyed masks and perform ring-stomp 'dances' before being invited into the city hall.

After a lengthy interlude when everyone seeks lunch and a clean toilet, up to 1000 Gilles reassemble. Wind allowing, they march across town wearing enormous ostrich-feather headdresses, intermittently lobbing oranges from little wicker baskets into the increasingly inebriated crowd. Don't even think of hurling one back: getting hit by an orange is meant to be interpreted as a metaphorical blessing – but only when it's thrown by a Gilles.

EATING & DRINKING IN THUIN: OUR PICKS

Casa Nostra: Excellent baguette sandwiches from €3.50 and Italian snacks served behind an Art Nouveau–style shopfront. *10am-3pm Mon-Fri* €

Bagù: Inventive cuisine in a townhouse just across the Biesmelle River from Thuin's hanging gardens. *7-9.30pm Wed-Sat* €€

Café Au Beffroid: Local boozing crowd despite a perfectly framed belfry view from upper-front windows. Roll the dice and maybe win a free drink. *3pm-midnight* €

La Grange des Légendes: Snacks and quality local meals at the Distillerie de Biercée in an atmospheric fortified farm at Ragnies. *11.30am-10pm Thu-Sun* €€

The gardens are a patchwork of mostly private sub-plots, best appreciated from the cobbled alley that starts by tunnelling through the **Posty Arlequin tower**. Sadly some lower gardens have gone to seed and most shops on the potentially magical **Grand Rue** are empty.

Historic Thuin

There's more life in the lower town near the River Sambre where the **Maison de l'Imprimerie** *(adult/infant €7/free)* displays an irreplaceable collection of printing machines from the 19th and 20th centuries in a former school building. Most are still in working order. Thuin also has a great **tram museum** *(museedutramvicinal.be; €5)* and on Sunday you can ride one of their historic trams on a nostalgic trundle to nearby Lobbes, dominated by the gigantic **Collégiale Saint-Ursmer**, a former abbey-church originally dating from the 9th century.

Monastic memories at the Abbaye d'Aulne

Ivy, shrubs and birdsong seem to be reclaiming much of the **Abbaye d'Aulne**, an extensive rural monastic complex left mostly in romantic ruins since the anti-religious wake of the French Revolution (1794). Unlike busy Villers-la-Ville (p205) you might find you are the only visitor here. Much is cordoned off due to unsafe masonry, but do tunnel through to the Jardins section (info-points 11-14) for the best view of the shattered church section. Two intact buildings are now used as events venues and just outside the walls are a brasserie, hotel, cafe and minigolf. It's 7km northwest of Thuin.

Charleroi

TIME FROM MONS: **30MIN**

Post-industrial adventures

A Dutch newspaper once rated Charleroi the World's Ugliest City. They have a point. Grim industrial and post-industrial debris sits amid a confusing spaghetti of grey expressway overpasses. But the dystopian setting makes a fabulous canvas for an explosion of street art: dereliction and banality mix with odd elements of historical class to make Charleroi a photographer's dream. To truly embrace the realities, you could join one of Nico Buissart's bruising **Charleroi Adventure** *(charleroiadventure.com)* 'urban safaris'. Alternatively. take the metro to Providence, epicentre of the worst (or best?)

Meet Charleroi's version of the Binche Gilles here around 4am on Mardi Gras.

 DRINKING & EATING IN CHARLEROI: OUR PICKS

Brasserie du Quai 10: Within a theatre/cinema complex, food here is a creative step up from most of the competition in central Charleroi. *noon-9.30pm €€*

Café du Musée: If you're visiting the Musée de la Photographie, its cafe serves generous salads at prices that are as minimal as the park-facing decor. *10am-3pm Tue-Sat €*

Chez Duché: Compact restaurant popular since 1993 for traditional French food and that Charleroi classic: horse steak. *noon-2pm Tue-Fri & 6.30-9.30pm Tue-Sat €€*

Les Templiers: 'Carnival' pub with Trappist beer on tap and more atmosphere than the surviving handful of cafes on the main central squares. *10am-11pm Tue-Sat, 11am-8.30pm Sun*

USLATAR/SHUTTERSTOCK

Église Saint-Christophe, Charleroi city centre

of the industrial horrors, where you could attend a very alternative concert at **Rockerill** *(rockerill.com)* in a former foundry building. Or if you rate fascinating philosophical conversation and arty absurdity above conventional comforts, you could sleep next door at **Ghostel** up four flights of stairs in a banal former office building turned private art space. But you'll need spoken French to really make the most of it.

Mining memorial

Le Bois du Cazier *(leboisducazier.be; adult/senior/child €9/8/5)* is a former coal mine that became infamous when a 1956 disaster killed 262 mostly immigrant workers (136 of them Italians). You'll need over 90 minutes to do justice to the full visitor experience here: don't skimp on the €1 audio guide – the cleverly-scripted conversational approach makes the museum section far more compelling. A 17-minute cinema-show outlines Wallonia's industrial rise and fall, and can be played in English on request. The visit culminates with another 15-minute video (with four-language earpieces) giving eyewitness accounts of the tragedy. Includes entry to a sub-museum of glassware such as an Egyptian flask from 1300BC (no English explanations).

Picture perfect

Charleroi's excellent **Musée de la Photographie** *(museephoto.be; adult/student €8/4),* in a far southern suburb, unveils a great collection of cameras and provides a trilingual chronological development of photographic subject matter over two centuries. As the curators are keen to underline, given the billions of images that exist, such an endeavour is like setting up 'an aquarium in an ocean', but the archive allows extensive searches and there are interesting temporary exhibitions (extra charge).

CHARLEROI AIRPORT CONNECTIONS

Belgium's budget airline hub, sometimes misnamed 'Brussels South', is actually on the northern outskirts of Charleroi. Flibco *(flibco.be)* runs direct buses to Brussels Midi station every 20 minutes except late night *(€18.90, 55 minutes),* along with 12 daily services to Mons, 10 to Luxembourg via Arlon, and 10 more to Antwerp via Brussels Zaventem Airport.

If you want to head into Charleroi, take bus A1, but there are also local buses to train stations at Luttre (on the line to Brussels via Waterloo) and Fleurus (with direct services to Leuven via Ottignies). All three bus routes run twice hourly from around 4am until 11pm and add €6 to the cost of a rail ticket to/from anywhere in Belgium.

OTHER MINES

Le Bois du Cazier is remarkable for its tragedy, but if you prefer to go underground in a mine, consider heading instead to **Blégny** (p251, Liège) where you descend in an original lift, or to **Rumelange** (p271, Luxembourg), an iron ore mine with access by mini-train.

The most interesting 'Parcour decouverte' section lacks English explanations, but the dark room, camera obscura cubicle and camera design diagrams are all fairly self-explanatory.

LAND OF LAKES

Look on a map and you'll notice a geographical protrusion of Belgium sticking a green 'boot' into the Avesnois hills of France. Combining slivers of both Hainaut and Namur provinces, this area has sensibly decided to work across provincial boundaries as a way to highlight the region's gentle charms, which go well beyond the l'Eau de l'Heure lakes for which the region is now dubbed **Pays des Lacs** (Land of Lakes).

There are 3500km of marked trails for walkers and cyclists, notably the 235km Grand Traversée route linking a dozen free-camping 'bivouac' sites that are completely inaccessible by road. The Pays des Lacs' tourism outfit (*lepaysdeslacs.be/en*) produces a brilliant free map.

Chimay

TIME FROM MONS: **1HR** 🚗

Pretty principality of beer

Chimay was – and remarkably remains – its own principality. Popular French-born Princess Élisabeth de Chimay died in 2023 aged 97 and her son Philippe is the 22nd prince. Their fairy-tale **castle** (*chateaudechimay.be; entry €12.50*) hides in plain site behind low gates at the western end of the picturesque town centre. Visits are allowed by tour most days in summer (French or Dutch language) but only rarely outside the holiday period.

Chimay's compact historic centre is a delight to explore anyway. The attractive main square has cafe terraces, a gin cave and a souvenir shop touting the world-famous Chimay Trappist beer. It's actually produced 9km south at the 1850 **Notre-Dame de Scourmont**: you can visit the abbey's startlingly all-white church interior but not the brewery. Instead backtrack 1km to the **Espace Chimay** (aka Auberge de Poteaupré; *chimay.com*), an ever-expanding cafe-shop-playground complex serving all things Chimay. All five styles of Chimay beer are available in (rare) draught form and in manageably small 18cL taster measures. Order a four-beer set with cheeses to qualify for free entrance to the attached Chimay Experience, with videos and interactive screens telling the beer's story. Otherwise that's €5.

Bird- & fish-watching at Virelles

Near Virelles, 4km northeast of Chimay, wetland ponds are rich in both bird- and aquatic life. Waterfront **Aquascope** (*aquascope.be*) has a free information room and access to a bar-terrace overlook, but if you pay (*adult/child €10/6*) there's also a film about wolves in Belgium and access to 2km of walking trails whose highlights are a raised bird-watching tower (look for storks) and a unique half-submerged passage from which you can spot fish, amphibia and insect eggs in/on the pond waters. Binoculars and electric bicycles are available for rent.

 EATING IN THE PAYS DES LACS: OUR PICKS

L'Absolu: Atmospheric stone tavern with tables spilling onto a lamp-lit cobbled lane in photogenic central Couvin. *11.30am-10pm Wed-Fri & Sun, from 6.30pm Sat* €€

Cafe-Restaurant Le Montjoie: Slow but friendly Treignes restaurant-pub serving slow-cooked pork cheeks in Chimay stew. Batin beers on tap. *11am-10pm Thu-Sun* €€

La Bonne Auberge: Loveable family restaurant in Nismes with a decades-long reputation for good, honest regional food. *11.30am-9pm Fri-Wed* €€

Poul & Boul: Facing Place Léopold, this convivial Chimay favourite uses all local sources for its meatballs, fishballs and roast chicken. *noon-2.30pm Wed-Sun & 6-9pm Tue-Sun* €€

Lacs de l'Eau d'Heure

TIME FROM MONS: **50MIN**

Lakeland water sports

'Welcome to Walifornia', gushes **The Spin** *(thespin.be),* a water-fun hub on Lake Féronval where you can learn water-skiing or practise wakeboard jumps while being dragged round by overhead wires. Mid-teens can throw themselves down the Xtrem Tower to be flung out of a chute-jump into the lake. Children aged 10+ can work their way around the multi-faceted Aquapark. And parents can watch, beer-in-hand, from waterside perches. It's a great atmosphere on a sunny summer weekend, even if you just come to watch (free). Yet this is just our favourite of several centres around the dam-linked reservoir lakes known as the **Lacs de l'Eau d'Heure**, where possibilities include kayaking, jet ski, sailing, parachuting, zip-wires, bouncy castles *(parcducrocodilerouge.be)* and stunt biking *(naturaparc.be).*

Mariembourg

TIME FROM MONS: **1HR**

Steam down the Viron Valley

Mariembourg is the starting point for the 14km enthusiasts' railway **CFV3V** (Chemin de Fer à Vapeur des Trois Vallées; *cfv3v.eu).* A few times daily at weekends, trains chug through attractive landscapes to Treignes, stopping long enough for you to peruse a rail museum before returning. One or two runs use steam engines (see online timetable). Even if you don't ride one, the engine movements at Mariembourg station are interesting to watch.

Those who are not rail fans driving a similar route could also stop at arguably more attractive Vierves-sur-Viroin, and in loveable Nismes, which has boating ponds, a watermill tourist office and, on the hill high above, shattered limestone formations known as the **Fondry des Chiens**. They're not quite 'Belgium's Grand Canyon', as sometimes dubbed, but they're worth a 15-minute look around.

Brûly-de-Pesche

TIME FROM MONS: **1¼HR**

WWII surprise in the woods

In May 1940, the inhabitants of little Brûly-de-Pesche were bundled out of their homes by Hitler's staff. The area was turned into a command complex from which to direct the blitzkrieg on France. Beside Hitler's specially built Bavarian style chalet, a solid-concrete box-bunker provided a short-term shelter in case of bombardment or attack. This small **Bunker d'Hitler** *(bdp1940.be; adult/child/under-12 €6.50/6/4.50; closed Nov-Mar)* is now the centrepiece of an hour-long visitor experience starting from the village inn. It's still a cafe but now also part-exhibition where you collect an audio guide, which explains context and tells stories of local victims. There's another museum section before the bunker itself, and a re-creation of a resistance dugout.

BEST OF PAYS DES LACS

Beaumont: Walk 300m south of Beaumont's cafes and sandwich shops to find the five-storey Tour Salamandre, last remnant of a once majestic fortress. Napoleon overnighted in Beaumont four days before Waterloo.

Lompret: Tiny hamlet with cafe-restaurant, perched church and farmstead-turned-hotel in an idyllic little river valley.

Phillipeville: Between 1659 and 1815 Philippeville was a completely encircled, ultra-fortified exclave of France. The walls have long gone but the characteristic city plan remains and the tourist office *(cm-tourisme.be)* organises fascinating guided walks through the fort's souterrains (subterranean passageways).

Couvin: The sloping Grand-Place looks pretty at dusk, with lights of changing colours illuminating the church.

Vierves-sur-Viron: The soaring castle towers look especially intriguing as you approach on the road from Nismes. Not open to the public, but two cafe-bars sit on the square near its entry gates.

Namur & Dinant

FORTRESSES | STRAWBERRIES | SAX

GETTING AROUND

If you don't want to use the cable car, bus 3 links Namur station to Rondpoint Thonard high on citadel hill. The tiny summer Namourette river ferries are fun but not enormously practical as A-to-B transport options. Much more useful is the Li Bia Velo *(www.libiavelo. be)* short-hop bike-hire system, with well-made bicycles and plenty of drop-off/pick-up stations.

☑ TOP TIP

Parking is free on the citadel hill but be careful not to leave your car in the Terra Nova lot after 6pm when the gates lock. Also be aware that short sections of citadel pathway close in the evening and that the souterrains only have one or two English language tours *(daily at 2.30pm, plus 12.30pm on weekends and holidays).*

Wallonia's 'capital' has a gently picturesque old town core and some great museums. Commanding the confluence of two great rivers, the Meuse and Sambre, the centre is utterly dominated by tree-dappled layers of a vast if austere citadel that was once one of Europe's mightiest fortresses. It was supposed to be impregnable but French King Louis XIV managed to take it in 1692, having sent his master strategist and military architect Vauban as a spy to find weak spots. Vauban himself was then tasked with updating the bastions. Namur is now a buzzing student centre and home to the parliament of Wallonia. Up the Meuse, the wealthy riverside suburb of Wépion is famed for its strawberries. Half an hour further, Dinant crouches photogenically beneath its own austere fortress and sees itself as the home of the saxophone.

Inner Citadelle

Key sights on the citadel hill

The **Citadelle de Namur** covers a whole hillside. For some visitors, the main attraction is simply enjoying the many great viewpoints. Or riding the cable car up to **Le Pavillon** *(le-pavillon.be; partly free, VR experiences €7-12)*, an exhibition space focused on cutting-edge digital culture. To learn more about the city's history and the fortress in particular, it's worth starting a visit at the **Terra Nova visitor centre** *(citadelle. namur.be; adult/student €6/5)*. Audio guides cover the key features, though if you speak French, there's a lot more to learn from the swirling information boards. Take the time to sit beside the 3D map of Namur in the 1750s to listen to short but well-told diary-style stories of four historical figures giving insights into 18th-century Namur.

With a Citadelle Pass *(adult/student €18/16)* you can also visit part of the **souterrains**, a fascinating web of dripping tunnels into which the fortress moved the majority of its key installations in more recent iterations. You'll need to join a guided tour which shows you some 500m of the tunnels, including never-tested 1939 gas-proof bunkers, and explains clever Vauban architectural

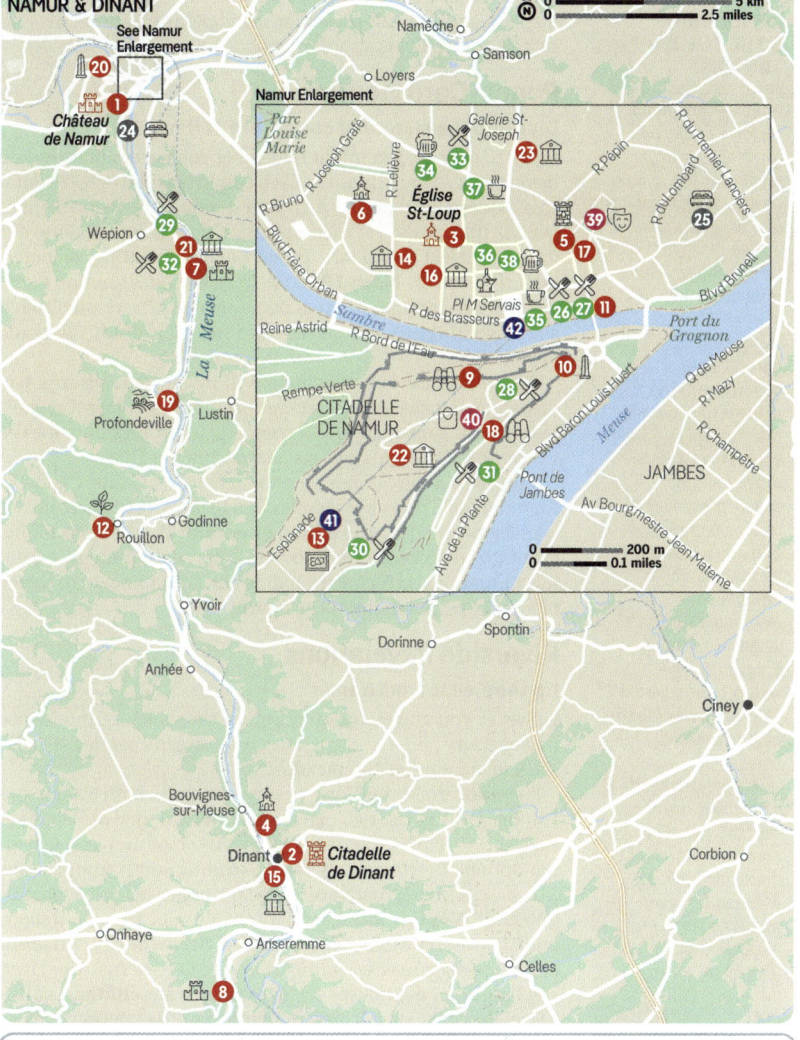

NAMUR & DINANT

NAMUR & DINANT

See Namur Enlargement

Namêche
Samson
Loyers

Château de Namur

Namur Enlargement

Parc Louise Marie

Galerie St-Joseph

Église St-Loup

R.Bruno
R.Joseph Grafé
R.Lelièvre

R.Pépin
R.du Premier Lanciers
R.du Lombard

Wépion

Pl M Servais
R des Brasseurs
R Bord de l'Eau

Port du Grognon

Reine Astrid
Sambre

Profondeville
Lustin

CITADELLE DE NAMUR

Blvd Frère Orban

Rempe Verte
Esplanade

Pont de Jambes
Ave de la Plante

Q de Meuse
R. Mazy
R.Champêtre

JAMBES

Blvd Baron Louis Huart
Meuse
Blvd Brunell

Av Bourgmestre Jean Materne

Rouillon
Godinne

Yvoir

Dorinne
Spontin

Ciney

Anhée

Bouvignes-sur-Meuse

Dinant
Citadelle de Dinant

Corbion

Onhaye
Ariseremme
Celles

0   5 km
0   2.5 miles

0   200 m
0   0.1 miles

tricks. Guides help bring the past to life using audio-visual displays and 3D wall projections. Temperatures hover around 13°C (55°F) so dress appropriately.

Punch-Card Memories

Dive into the history of computers at Nam-IP

If you're over 65, you might remember computers that worked using stacks of punch cards. Each carried just 80 bytes of data, so a modern 3MB phone-snap would require the equivalent of over 39,000 cards. Yet each card was hand-punched. Find out for yourself just how laborious that was at fascinating computer-history museum **Nam-IP** *(nam-ip.be/en; adult/senior €8/6)*. Punch the codes that spell your name, then run the result through a still-working reader and see from the print-out if you made any mistakes.

The 1980s desktop computers will make some visitors feel nostalgic, but the star attraction is an 1884 contraption built by Herman Hollerith's C-T-R company to process data for the US census. The company was a forerunner of IBM.

Nam-IP is in the campus area about 2km west of the Citadelle. En route you'll probably pass through Place Wiertz where there's a bushy-bearded **statue of King Leopold II**, infamous for his crimes in the Congo. Despite notice boards threatening legal recriminations, principled vandals have been known to throw blood-red paint bombs at the figure.

Riverside Revelations

Up the Meuse from Namur

However you travel, meandering up the valley of the Meuse makes a very pleasant excursion, passing scenic sections of cliff, settlement, garden and meadow.

There are cruises and kayak-rental options in both Namur and Dinant. Or link the two places on **RAVeL 5**, one of Belgium's easiest cycle paths – 32km of flat, mostly smooth riverside with the option of returning by train. Heading south from Namur ,you pass Namur's youth hostel and the upper-market suburban village of **Wépion** (7km), with its restaurants, ice-cream shops and strawberry stalls; there's even a **Strawberry Museum** *(museedelafraise.com; adult/student €6/5)*. Across the river, spy luxurious old houses including a private **château** called 'Dave'. Continue south through **Profondeville** which makes an intellectual pun on its name by inserting 'profound' philosophical aphorisms into carved pavement slabs. Consider a short detour to the beautiful gardens of **Annevoie** *(annevoie.be; €12, closed mid-Nov-Mar)*. If you're flagging, there's a train station across

 EATING IN NAMUR'S CITADELLE & WÉPION: OUR PICKS

Le Fief de Namur: Combines gin distillery, bar and restaurant with inventive twists on Belgian classic meals. *10am-10pm Wed-Sat, 10am-6.30pm Sun* €€

Le Panorama: Opened in 1925 but revamped as a stylish modern brasserie; worth the slightly elevated prices for truly fabulous views. *11am-10pm* €€

Le Lodge: Busy riverside brasserie at Wépion's northern edge serving hearty portions of Belgian standards. Lovely views, decent draught beers. *11.30am-10.30pm* €

L'O à la Bouche: Bookings are essential for this Wépi-on gastronomic treat, especially at lunch when the two-course option costs just €38. *noon-1.45pm & 7-9pm Tue-Fri* €€€

NAMUR'S CITADEL & CENTRE

Strolling ever downhill, discover the key attractions and viewpoints of the citadel, ending up in central Namur's café-culture zone.

START	END	LENGTH
Téléphérique (cable car)	Place Marché aux Légumes	3km, two hours

Take the **1 Téléphérique** (cable car) to the **2 Station Citadelle**. Look at the latest digital art installations at **3 Le Pavillon** (p222), then stroll down to the **4 Terra Nova visitor centre** (p222). A footpath bridging two sections of the fortress leads to the **5 Guy Delforge** perfume shop with a small free museum plus longer tours if you prebook. The carpark opposite doubles as a **6 panoramic viewpoint** looking southeast across the Meuse. Cars on the Rte Merveilleuse loop the loop near here but pedestrians can walk down more directly, passing an excellent **7 city viewpoint** and **8 observation point** that survey central Namur. Provided it's not too late (footpath gates close 8pm, or 5pm

Oct-Mar), you can descend past the **9 Golden Tortoise** to the Pont du Musée and wander into the city centre past the **10 Halle al'Chair**, a 1590 building originally housing the guild of butchers. It's now the tourist office. Across the Place d'Armes, pass **11 Palais des Congrès** (aka La Bourse), a renaissance-style former stock-exchange building that's now a congress centre, and head for the grand 19th-century **12 Théâtre**. Cut back through an arched passageway past the **13 belfry**. Explore the city's commercial centre, ending up with a well deserved drink at one of the countless terrace-bars on leafy **14 Place Marché aux Légumes**.

The Beffroi is a 1388 stone tower converted into a belfry in 1746. It's pockmarked with WWII scars from when central Namur was 'accidentally' bombed by US planes.

Beside a statue of beloved local composer Nicolas Bosret hides a tiny stone seat. Here a 'Roi des Menteurs' (King of Liars) is crowned during September's amusingly drunken festivities, the Fêtes de Wallonie.

The Fief de Namur gin distillery has a tempting cafe-restaurant.

0 200 m
0 0.1 miles

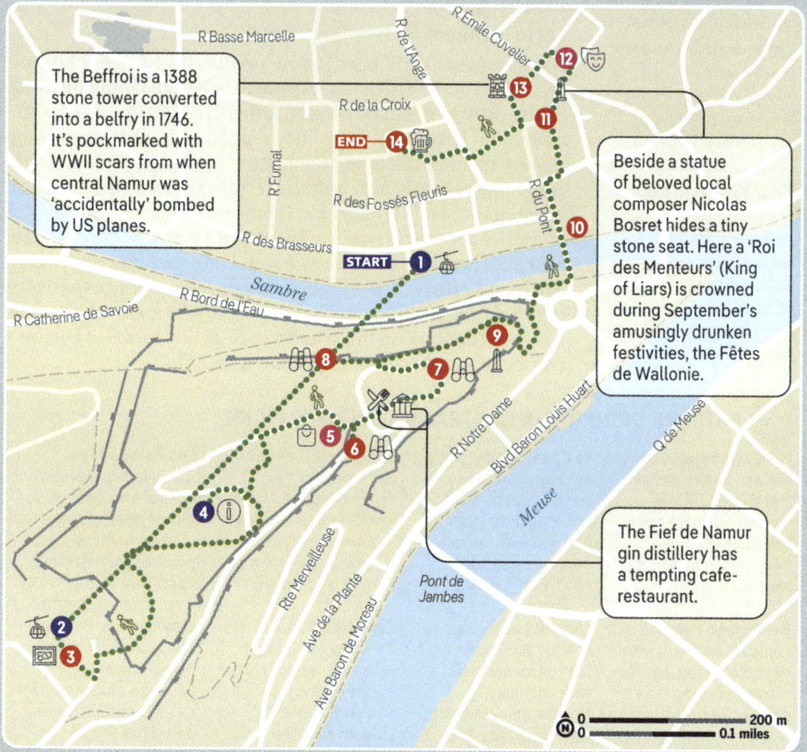

BEST MUSEUMS
& CHURCHES

Église St-Loup:
(eglise-saint-loup.be; free) Imposing baroque church with purple marble columns and complex ceiling tracery. Baudelaire called it a 'sinister and gallant marvel'.

TreMa: *(museedes artsanciens.be; adult/ student €5/2.50)* Masterpieces by Wallonia's medieval artists displayed in an 18th-century mansion.

Les Bateliers: *(lasan.be; free)* Decorative arts museum, archaeological collection, contemporary gallery and performance space with hidden formal garden.

Cathédrale St-Aubain: *(free)* A vast 1767 neoclassical exterior. Inside are paintings by Jacques Nicolaï, a follower of Rubens.

Musée Félicien Rops: *(museerops.be, adult/ under-12 €5/free)* Rops was a Namur-born artist with a warped penchant for illustrating erotic lifestyles and the macabre.

the Meuse in the pretty little town of **Yvoir**. Or you could pedal on another 6km to take in the grand renaissance **Château de Freÿr** *(freyr.be; adult/student €10/8)* with its own fabulous formal gardens.

If you're kayaking, the most popular route is not on the Meuse itself but descending the **River Lesse** from Houyet or Gendron to **Anseremme** where the rivers meet.

Fortress Sax
Power and creativity in Dinant

Viewed across the Meuse, the town of Dinant is a very striking sight. A disproportionately huge Gothic church with a 16th-century bulbous spire appears almost flattened against a cliff. On top of that, a vast, unadorned 1818 citadel-fortress, the **Citadelle de Dinant** *(citadellededinant.be; adult/under-12 €13/11)* looms menacingly. Entrance fees include a cable-car ride and an engrossing series of museum exhibits ranging from immersive historical timelines to weapon collections, a WWI trench mock-up and a 'Dutch Kitchen'.

Back down by the river there's lots of Sax. Adolphe Sax, that is. The creator of the saxophone grew up in Dinant, and colourful sculptures featuring the instrument dot the city centre in his honour. There are over 25 on the **Charles de Gaulle Bridge** alone.

Moving Beer
Leffe in Dinant

World-famous Leffe beer is now produced in Leuven but has its origins at the still active **Abbaye de Notre Dame de Leffe** at the northern end of Dinant. Other than for mass, or tours at 3pm on Saturdays, the abbey remains closed to ensure the monks' quiet religious contemplation. However, right opposite is the marvellously atmospheric restaurant **Le Confessional**, which serves Leffe with meals. On the other side of town, another former convent is now the **Infiniti Resorts 'Merveilleuse' Hotel**, where the bar serves many Leffe variants and where **Maison Leffe** *(€15)* is a highly interactive museum experience telling the beer's life story. Even for those who are not Leffe fans, it's worth coming up this way for spectacular views of Dinant's cityscape – best seen in afternoon light.

 EATING & DRINKING IN CENTRAL NAMUR: OUR PICKS

Mr Wu Noodles: Choose rice or noodles, protein and sauce, and in five minutes you have a very basic but filling meal from €6.50. *11am-9pm Mon-Sat* €

Le Casa: The decor wins no prizes, but hearty, inexpensive portions of Senegalese food pair well with similarly genuine *bissap* drink. *noon-9pm Tue-Sun* €

Cagette: Self-describing as a *cave à manger*, experimental blackboard food offerings anticipate flavour explosions enjoyed with 'natural' wines. *6-10pm Wed-Sat* €€

Les Potes au Feu: Creative 'bistronomic' gastronomy. Set course dinner menu changes regularly to harness seasonal produce. *7-9pm Mon-Fri & noon-2pm Wed & Fri* €€€

Barnabeer: Paradise found for beer fans with 46 brews on tap that you can sample in sizes as small as 15cL. *11am-1am*

Limoni: Two facing antique shopfronts beckon for cocktails, wine and tasty Mediterranean nibbles. *noon-11pm Mon-Sat*

Cafe Nomade: A classy homewares frontage hides this 'secret' barista coffee/brunch lounge with river views. *10.30am-2.30pm Thu-Mon*

Lloyd Coffee Eatery: Spacious modern coffee house which is also handy as a lunch spot for salads and light meals. *8am-8pm*

Bouillon

HISTORY | KAYAKING | LIGHT SHOWS

The inviting small town of Bouillon is dominated by a great stone dragon of a castle lurking along a ridgetop, high above a curl of the Semois River. By day it's attractive if brooding. At dusk it's utterly gorgeous with sensitive floodlighting creating reflections in the river. From April to November, several additional night-time projections around town add to the appeal of staying overnight here.

Either side of Bouillon, the Semois cuts deep valleys and eccentric curls of considerable scenic beauty. The most famous vista is across the Tombeau de Geant, where an almost perfect river loop is best appreciated from an isolated viewpoint down the dead-end Rue Moulin du Rivage at Botassart (11km from Bouillon). However, much more popular and equally gorgeous are the views from Rochehaut (18km), which is a vibrant little tourist hub of its own with fine walks and plenty of family activities.

Crusading Questions
Bouillon's take on its most famous son

To understand the background to old Bouillon and Godefroid's crusade (p228), start a visit at the **Bouillon Medieval Experience** within a 17th-century former convent building. This kicks off with an impressively immersive 25-minute multimedia experience comprising four contrasting but evocative settings. Sit around a magic well to learn about Godfroid, hear about the feudal system in a candle-lit castle chamber, then follow the course of the first crusade in subsequent scenes. Upstairs, the more standard museum section covers a potpourri of subjects, from castle design, to life in the convent, to words in French that come from Arabic. Return earphones at the giftshop where you can dress up in medieval costumes and wield a soldier's axe for fun photos.

GETTING AROUND

Bouillon is small enough to walk pretty much anywhere. Gradients are steep so you might prefer the P'tit Train, a tourist 'train' running a few times a day. However, it's more a sightseeing tour than a form of transport. Public transport to Bouillon is limited by weekday-only bus from Libramont *(45 minutes, 10 per day)*, a station stop for trains between Namur and Luxembourg. Other than the school bus, reaching Rochehaut or other villages requires sturdy boots or your own wheels.

☑ **TOP TIP**

To visit the castle, the Medieval Experience and the Maison Ducal, you'll need to buy a multi-ticket *(adult/child €12/6)*. From April to November, the cost rises to €16/12, but that also includes night-time second entry to the castle for an impressive sound-and-light show.

CRUSADING GODFREY?

In 1096, Godfroid (Godfrey) de Bouillon sold the great castle of Bouillon as a way to fund his rag-tag Crusader army. It took three years to reach the Holy Land, with crusaders slaughtering thousands of Jews in towns across Germany en route and another 40,000 Muslims and Jews upon finally breaching Jerusalem's walls in 1099. Bouillon's museums insist that these massacres were committed by the independent People's Crusade, not by Godefroid, who is portrayed as more noble in his crusade. Ultimately victorious, Godefroid was offered the title 'King of Jerusalem' but settled instead for 'Defender of the Holy Sepulchre'. He died a year later, but his brother Baudouin reigned on, keeping the Holy Land 'Belgian' a while longer.

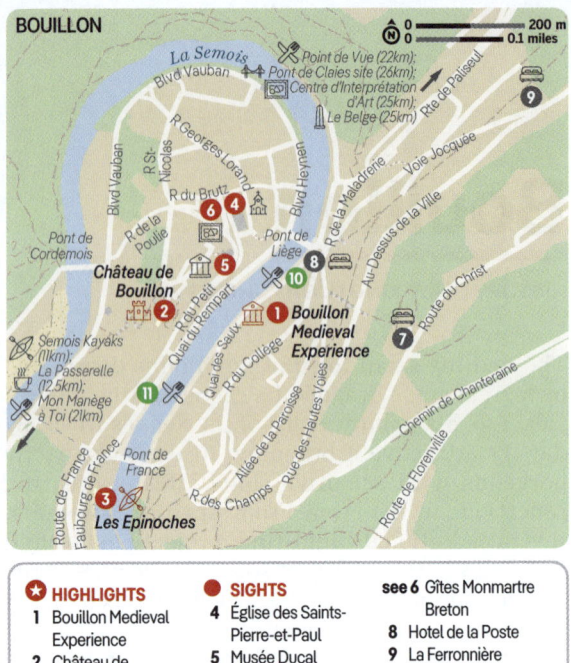

BOUILLON

⭐ **HIGHLIGHTS**	● **SIGHTS**	**see 6** Gîtes Monmartre
1 Bouillon Medieval Experience	4 Église des Saints-Pierre-et-Paul	Breton
2 Château de Bouillon	5 Musée Ducal	8 Hotel de la Poste
3 Les Epinoches	6 Quartier de Bretagne	9 La Ferronnière
	● **SLEEPING**	● **EATING**
	7 Auberge de Jeunesse	10 BOM
		11 O'Tableau

Fabulous Fortifications

Bouillon's magnificent castle

The town's unquestioned centrepiece is the **Château de Bouillon**. The site has everything you might wish for in a semi-ruined medieval castle: dank dripping tunnel passages, musty half-lit cell rooms, rough-hewn stairwells and many an eerie nook and cranny to discover. Plus there are off-beat surprises like maturing cheeses and a calligraphy mini-museum. The 45-minute falconry displays are excellent, usually held three times daily March to October and included in the multi-ticket price.

While you could drive up to the plateau and the castle entrance, it's more interesting to walk, crossing the river on the Pont de Liège, climbing past the **Église des Saints-Pierre-et-Paul** and cutting through the atmospheric **Quartier de Bretagne**, a short lane of quaint old houses with a memorial to local writer/printer Maurice Pirotte (1913–2013). Pop into the **Musée Ducal**, a somewhat haphazard museum telling the fascinating story of Bouillon over two historic houses.

After dark, the castle and old town take on a new aspect with atmospheric illuminations augmented at certain times by a series of projections at five different sites.

River Life

Enjoying the Semois by water or road

Several companies offer kayaking, each using a different section of river. By choosing Bouillon-based **Les Epinoches** *(kayak-lesepinoches.be)* you start with road transport upriver to a choice of three put-in points, then paddle back *(1½, three or six hours)*. Finish dramatically approaching the great bulk of Bouillon's castle, and you won't need to wait for slower kayakers to arrive before you head to the pub.

By car you'll likely make a beeline for **Rochehaut**, a buzzy little tourist honeypot surveying a gorgeous curl of the River Semois far below. Rochehaut's central stone-built buildings host tavern-cafes, a bakery, and a bustling brewery-restaurant. There's a choice of walks, an animal park and, at weekends, ponderous horse-cart rides that descend to pretty **Frahan-sur-Semois** hamlet and loop back having forded the river. Frahan is also a potential pick-up point for kayakers with **Semois Kayaks** *(semois-kayaks.be)* and has an almost comically basic old cafe, **La Passerelle**, near the river.

The road from Rochehaut continues via **Alle** and **Mouzaive** to **Vresse-sur-Semois** where there's an important **art gallery** *(fondation-chaidron.com; afternoons only)* and, inexplicably, a full-size reconstruction of Belgium's first steam locomotive, the 1835 **Le Belge**. Across the river, Vresse becomes Lafôret where, 500m down an unpaved track from the church, is the **Pont de Claies** site. Most of the year there's nothing to see other than a pretty riverside, but in July Belgium's last seasonal footbridge is erected here by placing hazel-weave onto log stilts embedded in the river.

OUTDOOR PURSUITS

Another main centre for kayaking is **La Roche-en-Ardenne** (p233) where paddling is often combined with mountain biking. Other major outdoor centres include **Coo** (p242) and **Durbuy** (p233), with a wide range of family-oriented activities.

BEST WALKS FROM ROCHEHAUT

Panorama Terrace: Stroll along Rochehaut's view terrace with panoramas over Frahan far below set in a perfect loop of the Semois.

Frahan and Back: Straightforward 20-minute descent to Frahan on a mostly slate-cobbled woodland lane. Cross the Semois on a 1928 footbridge with Monet-like water scenes to La Passerelle, a very basic cafe.

Promenade des Echelles: A 2.5-hour circuit following red signs marked 43. Its later section features several vertiginous climbs on ladders, some enclosed in tubes of protective ribbing where hiking poles and big bags will prove encumbrances. Walking in the suggested clockwise direction means you'll climb rather than descend the most appealing but potentially slippery rocky scramble sections.

🍴 EATING IN BOUILLON & SEMOIS VILLAGES

Point de Vue: Magnificent Rochehaut valley views are the draw but there's a wide range of snacks, meals and locally brewed beers. *10am-10pm Thu-Tue €€*

BOM: International menu, cocktails and something of a modest hipster vibe. The summer riverside terrace has great castle views. *noon-10pm Wed-Sun €€*

Mon Manège à Toi: Idyllic riverside spot in Mouzaive-sur-Semois, accessed by a footbridge across impressionistic waters. *noon-2.30pm Fri-Mon & 6.30-9pm Fri-Sun €€*

O'Tableau: Great seasonal Belgo-French meals on a menu that changes every two weeks; at the riverside base of the Bouillon castle crag. *11.30am-2.30pm & 6-10pm Fri-Wed €€*

Beyond Bouillon

If you're mobile, the central Ardennes area has enough forests, caves and walking routes to keep you busy for weeks.

Places

Orval p230

Redu p230

Rochefort & Han-sur-Lesse p232

Durbuy p233

La Roche-en Ardenne p233

Bastogne p235

GETTING AROUND

This part of Belgium can be frustrating to visit if you don't have your own wheels, though some centres can be reached by public transport. Durbuy is 4km west of Barvaux station on the Liège–Jemelle line. The nearest train stations to La Roche-en-Ardenne are Marloie and Melreux, from which there are bus connections. Bastogne has modest bus links to Namur, Luxembourg and Liege , as well as to Libramont station.

Come for the fresh air and outdoors activities; stay for castles, caves and WWII sites that abound in this deep green land of hills and forests. If you're just driving to Luxembourg on the E411, 'book-village' Redu makes a handy part-way stop with great art and a very special space experience. Regional tourist hubs each have their specialities: Durbuy for family activities, La Roche-en-Ardenne for cyclists, Rochefort and Han for cave-visits and Bastogne for memories of the WWII Battle of the Bulge, which so heavily affected much of the region.

Seasons are important here. By late summer, much of the rural tourism infrastructure starts to close down and between November and Easter many activities stop entirely.

Orval

TIME FROM BOUILLON: **35MIN**

A Trappist pilgrimage

Glowing magically in soft afternoon light, **Notre Dame d'Orval** is one of Belgium's best known abbeys. Dating from 1132, the original buildings were wrecked in 1793 but the picturesque ruins were preserved with a newer, active monastery built much later from the same golden sandstone, a giant Madonna and Child carved distinctively into its west wall. It was only finished in 1948, partly funded by the sale of charity postage stamps. The spiritually minded can make retreats here, but most visitors just explore the **ruins section** *(orval.be; adult/senior/child €8/6/3),* which includes the monastic herb garden, an 18th-century pharmacy room, the grave of King Wenceslas (1337–83) and a museum focused on the abbey's famous Trappist beer. You can't visit the brewery but you can taste the nectar it produces at the abbey's unsophisticated tavern, **À l'Ange Gardien** *(10.30am-6.30pm Thu-Tue; closed Jan).* Their crisp, hoppy 4.5% Orval Vert draught beer is available nowhere else.

Redu

TIME FROM BOUILLON: **30MIN**

Astronaut for the day

Do you have the physical and mental aptitude to go into space? Find out at the unforgettable space-themed **Euro Space Center** *(eurospacecenter.be; adult/youth €34/30),* which offers several hours of highly experiential interest, including over

CLEMMTRAVEL/SHUTTERSTOCK

Notre Dame d'Orval

40 minutes of immersive space introduction and 25 minutes of further stargazing in a planetarium. The 'normal' entry fee includes a Moon and Mars walk in which a sprung-arm seat reduces apparent gravity. If you dare, winch yourself up the 'Freefall slide' and let go. Some more advanced astronaut training contraptions, including the disorientating Space Axis spinner, are reserved for people doing residential 'Minitrip' missions, which include a night at the attached 'Galactic Inn'.

Midweek, the main centre is usually full with school groups, so plan to come at weekends or school holidays. However, the 'Cosmic Valley' gardens *(free)* behind are accessible any time. There you get an eye-opening sense of the scale of the solar system by walking all the way to Neptune past scaled representations of the planets. Venus never seemed so close to Earth! Also peruse model rockets from 1944's V2 rocket-bomb to NASA's 2021 Space Launch System.

Ground-breaking gallery in 'book-town'

Ever wondered what's the difference between rococo and neoclassicism? The superb gallery **Mudia** *(mudia.be; adult/ under-25/child €15.50/12.50/8.50)* explains such nuances using its collection of 300 priceless paintings (from Breughel to

You can eat your own picnic here if you buy a €3 drink.

THE CASTLE SAVER

Michel Koch lives in a castle that he shares with guests.

OK so you pay, but very little considering the classical grandeur of the place and the included breakfast served at a long candle-lit table overlooking a sweep of lawns and cow-mown meadow. Breathing new life into once-neglected historic buildings is, he insists, a passion. Working with the **Fondation Demeures et Chateaux** *(fondationdemeureset chateaux.be),* Michel spent several years revitalising **Château de Laclaireau** outside Virton, creating B&B rooms and meetings options to help fund the astronomical heating costs: the priceless Napoleon III furniture demands constant temperatures. Since 2024 he's worked similar magic upon the **Château de Porcheresse** (p254) between Redu and Bouillon.

✂ DRINKING & EATING AROUND REDU: OUR PICKS

Voyager Café: Cafeteria at the Euro Space Center where one of the tables is lit by jet nozzles of a mock spaceship. *11am-2.30pm* €	**Le Fournil:** Super-friendly stone-walled hotel-restaurant in Redu, specialising in food cooked with Orval beers. *noon-2.30pm & 6.30-8.30pm Wed-Sun* €€	**Le Moulin de la Dîme:** Belgian classics, 'tapas' and quiches on the terrace, plus a shop for artisanal products made with self-milled flour. *noon-2pm & 6.30-9pm Tue-Sun* €€	**Brasserie Les 4 Lunes:** Charm-filled B&B/auberge serving meals and St Feuillien beers near a moated castle in Lavaux Ste-Anne. *noon-3pm Mon & Thu, to 8pm Fri-Sun* €€

BEST CAVE VISITS IN THE GEOPARK

Grotte de Lorette: Majestic. Over 600 steps.

Grotte de Han: *(grotte-de-han.be; adult/child under-11 €29/22)* Great for stalactites, glitzy presentation and additional family activities, but pricey and heavily commercialised.

Grottes de Hotton: *(grottesdehotton.be; adult/child €14/11)* Naturally sculpted grottoes sprout pretty stalagmites and weird 'eccentrics', and there's a dramatically narrow, 37m-high subterranean chasm. One-hour visits involve 700+ steps.

Grottes de Remouchamps: *(lesgrottes.be; adult/child €20/14)* Few stalactites and limited depth but you get punted down Europe's longest underground river.

Kandinsky and Picasso) as well as clever interactive displays that bring works alive. The touch-me Hieronymous Bosch tableau is worth the entrance fee alone to see what Pythoneque motions each of the nightmarish figures will make.

Mudia is in Redu village, famous for its annual mid-April **book festival** and home to a few bookshops, cafes and artsy cottage industries.

Rochefort & Han-sur-Lesse

TIME FROM BOUILLON: **50MIN** 🚗

Going underground

Rochefort is a gently appealing castle town set in the undulating landscapes of the **Famenne-Ardenne UNESCO Global Geopark**. This extensive area has several impressive cave systems, most famously at nearby **Han-sur-Lesse** (p236). For a more personal experience, it's hard to beat Rochefort's own **Grotte de Lorette** *(grotte-de-lorette.be/en-GB; adult/ under-12 €13.50/9).* Half-lit stairways hint magically at the main cave's great vertical depth (65m) and there's a memorable revelation of its full majesty at the end. For any cave experience, prebook a tour slot, expect numerous steps, and dress assuming temperatures of around 12°C, which feels cold in summer, warm in winter.

Roman demos & family fun

To explore the region, consider renting bicycles from **Cycle Sport** near Rochefort's imposing statue-fronted church. Just 2km east, child-focused **Malagne** *(malagne.be; adult/child €8/6.50)* is a peaceful Gallo-Roman archaeological site that's most interesting on the third Sunday of July when it comes to life with costumed demonstrations.

Otherwise, head 12km north to **Domaine Provincial de Chevetogne** *(domainedechevetogne.be; €16),* a 550-hectare country park that's a godsend for families. In summer, the ticket includes a nature museum, petting zoo, various play parks, boating, swimming pool, themed gardens and a whole raft of other activities. From mid-October most activities stop, but the park becomes free and remains good for walking.

Back in Rochefort, several cafes serve signature Rochefort Trappist beers, though you can't visit the brewery-abbey. At 2pm in July and August, guided walks access the ruined section of the otherwise private castle, **Château Comtal** *(chateaurochefort. be; €5),* led by a fancifully costumed guide. Cash only.

EATING IN ROCHEFORT: OUR PICKS

Bella Italia: Convivial and inexpensive for wood-fired pizza. The drinks menu lists the full range of Rochefort Trappist beers. *noon-3pm & 6-10pm Tue-Sun* €

Couleur Basilique: Youthful Rochefort bistro with people-watching street terrace. Short, wide-ranging menu mixes international elements in salads and snacks. *noon-2pm & 6-10pm Thu-Tue* €€

Ardelle: Just six tables in a period house where Virginie & Martijn cook for you as though it was a private dinner party. Prebook and arrive at 7.15pm for a 7.30pm start. €€€

L'Incontournable: Set menus, including a Michelin Bib Gourmand option, favour duck, monkfish and seasonal specialities like asparagus. *noon-2pm & 6.30-8.30pm Thu-Sun* €€€

Durbuy

TIME FROM BOUILLON: 1HR 🚗

Family fun in the 'world's smallest city'

Durbuy is a photogenic little knot of cobblestone alleys, grey-stone buildings, cute craft shops and hotels aimed at the seasonal flood of summer tourists. Originally people visited Durbuy for its novelty value: a claim to being 'the world's smallest city' due to a quirk of 14th-century bureaucracy. These days, the green and pleasant valley still has a lot of charm out of season and makes a convenient restaurant-rich base to return to when touring the region. In mid-summer there's a vast array of activities organised by **Adventure Valley** *(adventure-valley.be/en)* whose main site is at Rome, 2.5km south across a hill from central Durbuy. Options include ziplining across lakes, 'free-fall' jumps, climbing adventures and a wide range of indoor games in case the weather turns nasty. Various all-in passes are available but some activities are sold separately, including **Le Labyrinthe** *(adult/child €19/17, Jul–early Oct)*, a cornfield maze with annually changing theme, concerts and shows.

La Roche-en Ardenne

TIME FROM BOUILLON: 50MIN 🚗

Cycling hot spot

Arrive at night in **La Roche-en-Ardenne** and what will strike you is the town's artfully floodlit **Château Féodal** *(chateau delaroche.be; adult/child €10.50/8.50)*, 11th-century castle ruins that are best appreciated from opposite **Hotel Le Chalet** on the road from Hotton. Come to La Roche on a summer's day, however, and you'll notice something else: all that lycra.

La Roche-en-Ardenne is Belgium's pre-eminent centre for mountain biking. It's a key stop along the 160km **Transardennaise** long-distance route and until 2024 was home to 10 editions of the BeMC (Belgian Mountain Bike Challenge). Steep trails and roads offer gritty challenges along with plenty of scenic variety. From October to March, check carefully for temporary trail closures due to hunting *(coeurdelardenne.be/en/hunting-information)*.

At **Panache Hotel** *(bikesleep.be)* you can repair and rent mountain bikes (basic, full-suspension and e-bike options), all with helmet, technical support and route suggestions. Panache also organises twice-monthly social rides and bike-friendly accommodation. **Ardn Bike'n'Bed** *(ardn-bnb.be)* offers secure indoor bike storage and cleaning facilities for guests at its cyclist-friendly gite-rentals.

OFF-BEAT FESTIVALS IN WALLONIA

Nuts Weekend, Bastogne: WWII commemoration on the second weekend of December with a notable parade featuring restored armoured vehicles of the era.

Sabat des Macralles, Vielsalm: On 20 July, witches briefly take over Vielsalm, telling semi-comical stories in impenetrable Walloon dialect to their general secretary Grand Maître Belzébuth (the devil). Fireworks round out the evening. Next day there's a blueberry festival.

Procession des Pénitents, Lessines: On the night of Good Friday, hooded figures march around Lessines (p212) carrying flaming torches, symbolically confessing their sins. No, they're not KKK members.

Bénédiction des animaux, St Hubert: On 3 November, people bring their animals to the basilica at St Hubert for a priest's religious blessing. Honestly!

EATING & DRINKING IN DURBUY: OUR PICKS

Aux 10 Clefs: Snacks, sandwiches and hearty Belgian/Ardennes home cooking in a family-run, farmhouse-style place that's also a great value B&B. *9am-9pm €*

Les Racines: Feisty back-alley pub and blues bar whose enjoyably rough edges makes it quite different from anything else in town. *Thu-Sun hours vary €*

Govinda's: Vegetarian Indian thalis and vegan snacks at the Krishna-run Radhadesh castle-retreat centre, 4km away. *noon-6pm Tue-Sun €*

La Canette: Buzzing atmosphere for French-inspired bistro food in a cosy interior filled with old signs, tools and assorted memorabilia. *6-11pm Fri-Tue & noon-5pm Sun €€*

LA ROCHE'S FEMALE PHANTOM

She's on a two-storey mural beside Quai Son. She's a fountain-statue near the post office. And on summer nights at 10pm, a 20-minute projection sees her ghost flying around the outer castle walls. Meet Berthe, as much a symbol of La Roche as the town's (very serious) WWII sufferings. In popular myth, Berthe's father was a 10th-century count who bartered her hand (plus inheritance) to the winner of a joust. Unexpectedly her dashing favourite lost to a diminutive, disguised underdog.

After a bloody wedding night, Berthe was murdered, her body found thrown from the castle ramparts. Her mystery 'husband' had in fact been another woman, the jilted ex-fiancée of Berthe's main suitor. Berthe was collateral damage.

FRANKYDEMEYER/GETTY IMAGES

Le Herou

For masochistic road bikers, the classic congratulatory selfie is beside the 498m signboard at the top of the muscle-burning **Col Haussire**, 6km north of La Roche.

In late August or September, cyclists come from across the globe for the 172km road race **Velomediane** *(velomediane. com/en)*, often nicknamed the 'Criquielion' to honour its founder.

Folon and the wonder of Waha

The 11th-century **Église Saint-Étienne** in Waha village, between La Roche and Rochefort, is a Romanesque church remarkable for cartoon-naive style stained glass windows. Added in 2004–5, these were the last major works of one of Belgium's greatest late-20th-century artists, Jean-Michel Folon (1934–2005). Even if you don't recognise his name, Folon's distinctive artistic universe might be familiar. His soft watercolours have featured on British postage stamps, his statues star in a Florence rose garden, and his design sensibilities were an inspiration to Apple's Steve Jobs. The Folon Foundation *(fondationfolon.be)* preserves 6000 works at the Château Solvay estate on Brussels' southern periphery, curates exhibitions and maintains an online collection.

 ## EATING & DRINKING IN LA ROCHE: OUR PICKS

La Chine: Chinese and Thai-lite food is filling rather than creative but castle views are superb. Bargain lunches. *noon-2.30pm & 5.30-10pm Thu-Tue* €

Signé Jeanne: The most professional of a gaggle of brasseries that all serve pretty much the same Belgian tavern staples. Spacious terrace seating. *10am-10pm Fri-Wed* €€

L'Apero: This compact family restaurant cooks Ardennes food promising that all ingredients are home peeled, cut, and cooked with love. *11.30am-2pm & 6-9pm Tue-Sun* €€

Le Quai Son: Once a pop-up riverside beach-bar, now a full-blown cafe-restaurant but still with that great waterfront terrace. *11am-9pm Tue-Sun* €€

Pleasures of the Ourthe

Like the Semois around Bouillon (p227), the River Ourthe between La Roche and Houffaize carves eccentric loops through the Ardennes.

On the most famous, **Le Herou** is a viewpoint atop a rocky scarp. It's just 450m walk from a parking area near Nadrin, but not designed with health and safety in mind. One challenging hike continuing from here involves descending or ascending a steep rocky slope using a handheld chain.

On another roadless river loop nearer to La Roche sits the stone-age settlement site of **Le Cheslé**. Along with Le Herou, it's on the first day of the 106km **Escarpardenne Hike** *(visitardenne.com/fr/les-routes-touristiques/escapardenne)* heading into Luxembourg.

The Cheslé section of the Ourthe features on kayak trips with **Outdoor Centre** *(outdoor-centre.be/en)*, starting with a minibus transfer from **Les Merlettes** (2km east of La Roche) to the put-in near Nisramont. Alternative kayak routes and a panopoly of other outdoor activities are offered by both **Ardenne Adventures** *(ardenneaventures.com/en)* and **BrandSport** *(brandsport.be/en)*.

Bastogne

TIME FROM BOUILLON: **45MIN** 🚗

Remembering the Bulge

For most visitors, Bastogne is all about the Battle of the Bulge. The town's central square features a US M4 **Sherman Tank** and a **tourist office** *(bastogne-tourisme.be)* that rents bicycles, handy for reaching the main sights which are further out.

Some 2km east, the **Mardasson American War Memorial** is shaped as a sombre circle within a five-pointed star. Fernand Léger, better known for his cubist paintings, created Protestant-, Catholic- and Jewish-themed mosaics for the cave-like chapel-crypt beneath. The memorial is free to visit but parking costs €5.

The excellent **Bastogne War Museum** *(bastognewar museum.be; adult/senior €22/19)* tells the battle's story using imagined voices of witnesses and participants. An engrossing 15-minute 3D film creates context presenting Germany's early attacks as though to a press conference. There are theatrical audio-visuals, well-displayed memorabilia and lots of buttons to press, accessing moving personal recollections. Particularly impressive is the **Generations 45** section, entered via a film-set style representation of a shattered street and telling the

SURRENDER? 'NUTS!'

On 16 December 1944, with the Allies surging towards Berlin, Hitler launched a last-gasp counter-attack across the snow-bound Ardennes. The surprise move quickly created a long westward 'bulge' in the front line, leading to the nickname 'the Battle of the Bulge'.

Northern Luxembourg and most of the Belgian Ardennes fell to the Germans within a week, but Bastogne held out valiantly thanks to the US 101st Airborne Division whose defence of Bois Jacques (p236) would later be immortalised in two episodes of *Band of Brothers*. On 22 December, with Bastogne surrounded, the US commander General Anthony McAuliffe was invited to surrender. His now famous answer came as a single word: 'Nuts!'

 EATING & DRINKING IN BASTOGNE: OUR PICKS

Brasserie Lamborelle: Cosy, brick-and-beam cafe-restaurant whose house brew, Airborne, is served in a ceramic helmet. *5-11pm Wed, from 11am Thu-Sun* €	**Wagon Leo:** Built around a parked tram-car, Leo is now a grand brasserie-hotel with food that ranges from Liège meatballs to oysters and lobster. *10.30am-9.30pm Tue-Sun* €€	**Le Nuts:** Nostalgic pub that's almost a museum of WWII pictures. Wide lunch menu and themed Friday night 'rock dinners'. *11am-11pm Fri-Wed, to 3pm Mon* €	**Le Saint Germain:** Contemporary French cuisine in a suburban setting with garden terrace, slightly out of centre. *noon-2pm Tue-Fri & 6.30-9pm Tue, Wed, Fri & Sat* €€

BEST BASE IN THE CENTRAL ARDENNES

While Bouillon is a great place to stay, it's worth considering at least one other base if visiting the Central Ardennes for a few days.

Han-sur-Lesse & Rochefort: At night the tour crowds leave, so Han-sur-Lesse is peaceful, but Rochefort has more personality, is more of a 'real town' and has a far greater variety of dining.

Durbuy: Can be painfully overloaded during summer weekends, but midweek off-season prices drop and it feels enjoyably cosy.

La Roche-en-Ardenne: Scenic as a location but dining choices are limited.

Bastogne: Has the region's most urban vibe, but if you're not a WWII nostalgia fan, its appeal is limited.

very contrasting stories of what happened after the war to two ex-combatants. Unmissable.

Note that the widely publicised multi-ticket option *(adult/senior €27/24)* includes the Bastogne War Rooms and is vastly cheaper than paying for both separately, though for many visitors the main museum is enough.

Bois Jacques

A crucial 'Battle of the Bulge' confrontation took place in **Bois Jacques**, a pine-wood near Foy, 5km north of Bastogne. Remarkably some 'foxhole' depressions dug by the US 101st Airborne are still vaguely visible. Access is included with Bastogne War Museum entrance: scan your ticket to open the un-staffed gate. Using the special app (yes, the forest has wi-fi!), costumed soldiers appear virtually on your phone, acting out battlefield episodes amid the trees. Great idea, but only semi-successful in reality.

The nuts barracks

A second group of WWII attractions sit around 1km northwest of central Bastogne in the former Camp Heinz barracks. The **Bastogne Barracks Museum** *(bastogne-barracks.be; adult/under-19 €12/9)* has an impressive collection of WWII era tanks and vehicles. Some are wrecks awaiting repairs, others have been brought back to life and are parked in two big museum hangars, displayed with brooding music, the smell of grease and videos featuring former commanders.

Directly south, the **Bastogne War Rooms** *(adult/senior €17/15)* is where McAuliffe penned his 'Nuts!' response. A lavish series of interactive battle-plan tables has been created here, but the target audience is die-hard war buffs and the impressive levels of detail can feel overwhelming for casual visitors. Downstairs it takes four slow-moving projected videos before an actor version of McAuliffe finally says the magic word, 'nuts'.

Enter another world at Air-V

Air-V *(air-v.net/en)* gives the family something really fun to do while granddad goes nuts in the Nuts Room. The name is a Francophone pun on VR, and if you want to stick to WWII themes, you can watch a clever 20-minute VR documentary on the Battle of the Ardennes *(€9)* using original cine-footage merged with artistic fills and contemporary scenery. There's also a fabulous series of other VR games, multi-player virtual escape rooms, simulators and a six-seater virtual roller-coaster ride with 80 variant adventures.

ARDENNES BATTLE SITES

The Battle of the Bulge was just part of a snow-hampered Ardennes-wide conflict in winter 1944, and several other important museums cover the same subject notably in **La Roche-en-Ardenne** (p233), **Ettelbruck** (p270), **Diekirch** (p270) and **Wiltz** (p270).

Spa

WELLNESS | WATER | MOTOR-RACING

Yes, the English word spa really does come from the name of this classic Ardennes health resort. Wellness remains big business while Spa's bigger industry today is bottling those precious mineral waters for the mass market. You can still drink some of the lightly sulphurous spring water at several original sources, notably within the 1880 octagonal-fronted Pouhon Pierre-le-Grand. That building was named after Russian Tsar Peter the Great, who credited a 1717 visit to Spa for his miraculous liver cure. That led to the resort's sudden surge of international fame. It was nicknamed the 'Café of Europe' in the 19th century, popular with writers including Victor Hugo and Alexandre Dumas, while 20th-century star guests included Albert Einstein. A good scattering of neoclassical architecture and statuary remains from that golden age.

For motor-racing fans, Spa is synonymous with the particularly scenic Belgian Grand Prix course at Francorchamps, some 12km southeast.

The spa at Spa

A half-day of relaxation

The **Thermes de Spa** *(thermesdespa.com; €32 for three hours)* is the city's contemporary spa centre, located on the hilltop directly above the town centre. It's an indulgent complex of indoor and outdoor baths, hammams & saunas (choice of naked or 'textile' zones) and many massage and therapy rooms. The centrepiece is

☑ **TOP TIP**

Even if you're not a motor-racing fan, check the Spa-Francorchamps events schedule: during major races, hotel accommodation is packed. On F1 race days, regional traffic gridlocks and F1 fans are advised to use special shuttle buses operating to the course from a dozen cities in Belgium, Luxembourg, Netherlands and Germany. The cheapest is from Verviers.

GETTING AROUND

Spa has two relatively central train stations, **Spa** and tiny **Spa-Géronstère**, at the end of a spur line from Verviers *(25 minutes)*. Change at Pepinster for Liège. The route of the former line to Stavelot is now a paved cycleway.

Central Spa is walkably small but you'll want wheels for visiting outlying attractions.

SpaForest near Les Thermes offers bicycle hire.

Free parking is relatively easy to find in town. Les Thermes is 5km by road from Place Royale but only 500m on foot *(15 minutes)*. Or take the **funicular** *(€1.50 each way)*.

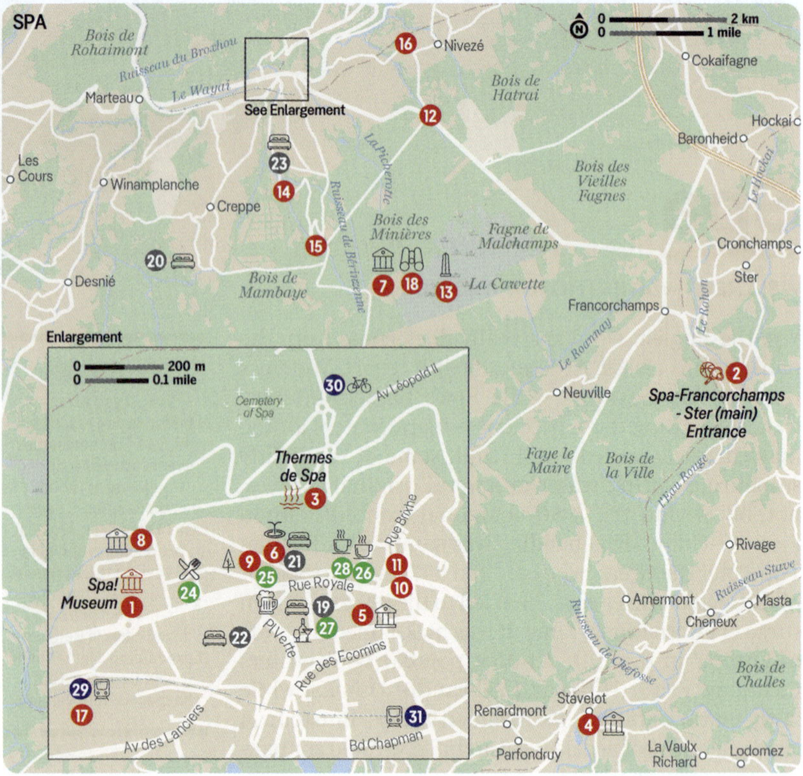
SPA
Bois de Rohaimont
Ruisseau du Brochou
Marteau
Le Wayai
See Enlargement
16
Nivezé
0 2 km
0 1 mile
Cokaifagne
Bois de Hatrai
12
Hockai
Baronheid
Les Cours
Winamplanche
23
14
Creppe
La Picherotte
Ruisseau de Bérinzenne
Bois des Vieilles Fagnes
Le Hockai
Bois des Minières
Fagne de Malchamps
Cronchamps
20
15
7
18
13
La Cawette
Ster
Desnié
Bois de Mambaye
Francorchamps
Le Rohon
Le Roannay
Enlargement
0 200 m
0 0.1 mile
Cemetery of Spa
30
Av Léopold II
2
Neuville
Spa-Francorchamps - Ster (main) Entrance
Thermes de Spa
3
Faye le Maire
Bois de la Ville
L'Eau Rouge
Rue Brixhe
8
6
21
9
28
26
11
Rivage
Spa! Museum
24
25
Rue Royale
10
Ruisseau Stave
1
19
5
Amermont
Masta
Cheneux
27
22
Pl Verte
Ruisseau de Chefosse
Rue des Ecomins
Bois de Challes
29
17
31
Renardmont
Stavelot
4
Av des Lanciers
Bd Chapman
Parfondruy
La Vaulx Richard
Lodomez

HIGHLIGHTS
1 Spa! Museum
2 Spa-Francorchamps - Ster (main) Entrance
3 Thermes de Spa

SIGHTS
4 Abbaye de Stavelot
5 Casino
6 Fontaine Marie-Henriette
7 Musée de la Forêt et des Eaux
8 Musée de la Lessive
9 Parc de Sept Heures
10 Pouhon Pierre-le-Grand
11 Pouhon Prince de Condé
12 Puhon Sauveniere/Groesbeek
13 RAF bomber crash monument
14 Source Barisart
15 Source de la Géronstère
16 Source du Tonnelet
17 Spa Monopole
18 view-tower

SLEEPING
19 Les Bains de Spa
20 Manoir de Lébioles
21 Van Der Valk Hotel, Spa
22 Villa des Fleurs
23 Villa Grand Maur

EATING
24 L'Art de Vivre
see 16 Le Tonnelet
see 11 Rest'O des Amis

DRINKING & NIGHTLIFE
see 10 Boteye
25 Des Bobolines
26 Gio Cafe
27 Les Bains Foyer Bar
28 Little Arthur

TRANSPORT
see 6 Funicular - lower station
29 Spa train station
30 SpaForest
31 Spa-Géronstère Train Station

DRINKING IN SPA: OUR PICKS

Boteye: Youthful cocktail and beer bar facing the Pouhon in the 1775 Hotel de Suede building. *5-10pm Wed-Sun*

Des Bobolines: Both an expansive steak house but also a fun bar with 'beach' style terrace serving a range of self-brewed beers. *11am-8.30pm*

Les Bains Foyer Bar: Worth the price of a drink to soak up the majesty of murals and mouldings in this UNESCO-listed building. *noon-10pm*

Gio Café: Barista coffee, lunch sandwiches and wraps in the 1769 Hotel d'Ireland building on an intimate square full of cafe terraces. *8.30am-5pm Tue-Sat*

a giant, light-filled pool with tall glass windows to contemplate the view. No phones, cameras or children under 15 are allowed inside. Prebooking is advised, and almost essential if you want specific treatments. Some Spa hotels will let guests borrow their bath towels to save you the Thermes' €4 towel-rental fee. The fun way to arrive from town is by a little funicular *(€3 return)* from beside the **Van Der Valk Hotel**, whose guests have their own dedicated carriage so they can go straight up in their bathrobes.

Soaking up Spa's Architectural Heritage
Highlights of a central stroll
The city's most magnificent example of neoclassical architecture is the 1868 former spa building, now gloriously transformed into **Les Bains de Spa**, a grandiose hotel complex. Consider drinking at the bar here, if only as an excuse to enjoy the spectacularly lavish interior details.

Also imposing but with a more faded grandeur are the two buildings next door, a cultural centre and the 1908 portico-fronted **casino**. Spa has been attracting gamblers since 1763, and you can continue the betting tradition at this latest incarnation (ID check and free temporary membership), but the gloomy interiors have little architectural charm.

For something prettier, head to the **Parc de Sept Heures**, where restoration has brought back to life the wrought-iron Galerie Leopold II, built in 1878 to shade genteel strollers from the sun.

Value of Water
Pondering Spa's raison d'etre
Spa Monopole is a major business, bottling 500 million litres of water a year from three local spring sources. Statuettes of the company's leaping clown mascot pop up all around town. You can't visit the factory but you can taste (much more heavily mineralised) waters from several historic springs and fountains both in town and in the surrounding hills (p240).

To learn more about the development of water therapies and business visit **Spa! Museum** *(spamuseum.be; adult/under-25/under-12 €5/4/1)*. Nearby is a sweetly naive museum of laundry, the **Musée de la Lessive** *(museedelalessivespa.be; adult/under-16 €4/2)*, open only Saturday and Sunday afternoons.

Some 5km south at Berizenne, the **Musée de la Forêt et des Eaux** *(berinzenne.be/musee; adult/child €7/4)* is an upland nature centre underlining the importance of the ecosystem in

MARIE-HENRIETTE

For centuries Spa has attracted celebrities – from Beethoven to Bowie, Dickens to Hemmingway. Both Napoleon and Wellington were visitors. One of the most regular residents, however, was Queen Marie-Henriette (1836-1902), the feisty Hungarian-born wife of Belgian King Leopold II. Their marriage, never happy, essentially collapsed after Leo blamed Marie-Henriette for the death of their son... and continued his open adultery.

So while Leo was busy planning dodgy colonial adventures in Africa, she would avoid boredom by riding horses across the Ardennes. The last years of her life were spent almost entirely in Spa, staying in the 1862 building that's now the **Spa! Museum**. Her old stables are still preserved, albeit only accessible to visitors on the second weekend of each month.

The lemon-meringue pie is deliciously tart.

EATING IN SPA: OUR PICKS

Le Tonnelet: Locally sourced gourmet menus served in a 19th-century wrought-iron pavilion on the outer edge of town. *noon-1.30pm Fri-Tue & 6.45-8.30pm Fri-Mon* €

Rest'O des Amis: Mixing Belgian brasserie and Italian culinary influences to create a locals' dining favourite in the heart of Spa. *11.30am-9pm Wed-Sun* €€

Little Arthur: Cosy cafe with piled cushions, William Morris wallpaper and a selection of dessert tarts and quiches. *9am-6pm Fri-Tue* €

L'Art de Vivre: Sedate, white tablecloth ambience for fine Franco-Belgian cuisine that has a certain gourmet flourish. *noon-2pm Fri-Sun & 6.30pm-9pm Wed-Sun* €€€

CLASSIC SOURCES OF SPA WATER

Pouhon Pierre-le-Grand: The classic. Its grand 1880 pavilion now doubles as tourist office and exhibition centre.

Pouhon Prince de Condé: 1849 subterranean spring-house now partly topped by a mini Louvre-esque glass pyramid. Occasional art space.

Fontaine Marie-Henriette: Fountain at the base of the funicular.

Source de la Géronstère: Set in gardens of a mill-style tavern, it's the prettiest spring-fountain but is currently dry.

Source du Tonnelet: In a dainty wrought-iron rotunda from 1884 with water tasting less ferric than most. Delightful restaurant next door has similar architecture.

Puhon Sauveniere/ Groesbeek: Forest springs with mini temple-like portal beside a rural restaurant east of town.

Source Barisart: Modernist spring-fountain.

JENS MOMMENS/SHUTTERSTOCK

Formula 1 Belgian Grand Prix, Spa-Francorchamps

safeguarding water supply. Nearby there's a seven-storey **view-tower** *(free),* and from there you can walk across the boggy **Fagne de Malchamps** through cotton grass, bilberry, dwarf oak and yellow broom. A major section is on raised boardwalks as you reach a feather-shaped **monument** commemorating the crew of an RAF Lancaster bomber that crashed here in April 1944.

Belgium's Motor Racing Hub

Grand Prix at the Spa-Francorchamps

Belgium's Formula 1 Grand Prix is held at the **Spa-Francorchamps** *(spa-francorchamps.be)* circuit. Nicknamed the 'toboggan of the Ardennes', it's often cited as a favourite with drivers. The setting is beautiful, rolling through the wooded hills and forests between Spa and Stavelot. And you don't have to brave the Grand Prix's huge crowds and startling entry costs to visit. There are dozens of other races: events at the course occur more or less daily from mid-March to mid-November. Some, like the widely famed **24-heures de Spa** GT race, attract big audiences. Other speciality meets have comparatively modest entry fees, or none at all. For less than the price of an F1 Gold Grandstand spectator-seat ticket, you could pilot your own vehicle around the course on a **Public Driving Experience** *(from €135),* available a few days a year: helmet and briefing mandatory. Motor-racing fans who want to see the paddocks, podium and race-control room can join a 1½-hour **guided tour** *(adult/child €15/8)* that runs several days a month in season. For all of the above, book well ahead.

When there are no ticketed events (check the events calendar), parking charges at the Ster main entrance are usually dropped and pedestrians and cyclists are able to explore sections of the course on the **Balade du Centenaire**, a series of paths that link 10 giant helmet creations, each with QR codes, collectively telling the story of the course. Within the vast **former abbey** at nearby Stavelot, one of several museum sections displays a fine collection of racing cars and motorcycles.

Beyond Spa

Spa is a good launch pad to explore an area of comparative wilderness ringed by towns with distinct traditions and great carnivals.

South of Spa, the Haute Fagnes constitute Belgium's highest upland plateau with signature moorlands edged by forests and attractive valleys, all offering fine opportunities for walking and cycling. Politically, much of this area forms the so-called Eastern Cantons, presented to Belgium by Germany in 1918 to make amends for WWI. It includes Belgium's officially German-speaking area. While Eupen feels distinctly Germanic, some other major towns are French-speaking, notably Malmédy, which is a popular base for outdoors types.

North of Spa it's only as you start to get close to Liège that the patchworked woods and hilly fields start showing signs of past industry and mining. Near this dividing line, Limbourg is historic and pretty. Though rather bedraggled, the once-wealthy textile city of Verviers has its charms too.

Places
**Malmédy &
the Fagnes** p241
Coo p242
Eupen p242
Limbourg p243
Verviers p244

Malmédy & the Fagnes

TIME FROM SPA: **30MIN** 🚗

Exploring Belgium's Moorland Landscapes

Malmédy has an impressively large **cathedral** in whose former cloisters there is a quietly moving museum, **Malmundarium** (*malmundarium.be; adult/student/under-13 €6/5/3*), which mourns the demise of the town's tanning and paper-making industries. However, the crowds who fill Malmédy's cafes are mostly walkers and cyclists exploring the **Hautes Fagnes** ('High Fens'), an upland plateau of swampy heath criss-crossed with walking paths. Some of the footpaths use boardwalks, allowing a greater sense of proximity to the environmentally unique sphagnum peat bogs.

In some countries the Fagnes area might not gain much attention, and some of the signature bogs appear to be drying up and sprouting shrubs. Nonetheless, this is Belgium's largest nationally protected reserve and the nearest the country has to wilderness. It encompasses the nation's highest point – the **Signal de Botrange**, marked by a 1954 stone tower. For lots of background information, **Botrange Nature Centre** (*botrange.be*), 1.4km further south, is a good starting point. Its museum section explains the Fagnes' evolution, fauna and traditional crafts, electric bikes are available to rent (book ahead), and there are tractor-pulled *char-à-banc* wagon tours. A kilometre back towards Ovifat, the ever-popular

GETTING AROUND

Verviers is a stop for fast trains running Brussels–Leuven–Liège–Eupen and for slower services to Liège-St-Lambert, Spa and Aachen (Germany). Buses 724 or 725 from Verviers get you to Dolhain, from which Limbourg is a 15-minute uphill walk. Bus 745 links Malmédy to Trois Ponts train station on the Liège–Luxembourg line. A few very limited bus routes cross the Fagnes.

RAVeL route 44A is a well-paved cycle route between Spa and Stavelot.

brewery-cafe **Peak Beer** (*11am-8pm Wed-Sun*) provides useful laminated walking maps for seven different routes.

Some of the best short walks start from the large car park at the lonely **Baraque Michel** restaurant, beside which lies the tiny 1830 **Chapel Fischbach**. The chapel is highly unusual, topped by a lantern that originally acted as an inland lighthouse to help guide people crossing the featureless moors in the dangerous days before paved roads or GPS. Across the main road, a footpath signposted to Eupen passes two grey-stone pillars from 1839 that once marked the Belgian–Prussian border. After walking around 700m, you reach one of the Fagnes' most appealing boardwalk sections.

Coo

TIME FROM SPA: **25MIN** 🚗

Sport & family fun

Tiny Coo (pronounced 'Koh') first became modestly famous as home to Belgium's tallest 'waterfall', a 15m artificial affair created when 18th-century monks dammed the River Ambleve. These days it's a family-fun destination. While the kids enjoy **Plopsaland Ardennes** (*plopsa.com/en/plopsaland-ardennes; adult/child from €25/16*), a mid-sized amusement park with around 20 attractions, adults and teens can join **Coo Adventure** (*coo-adventure.com*) for all manner of outdoors activities, from caving to paragliding to short rides in a Ferrari.

Unusually for the rural Ardennes, Coo has a handy train station with half-price 'discovery' rail tickets available for those with Plopsa Coo online prebookings. All-day car parking costs €12.50.

Eupen

TIME FROM SPA: **35MIN** 🚗

Belgium's most German town

Spared significant bombing in WWII, Eupen has retained some fine older buildings plus there's a vibrant arts scene. However, it's most intriguing for being the 'capital' of Belgium's German-speaking community whose **Parliament** (*pdg.be*) is here. You're welcome to visit: the free exhibition room is all in German but with a detailed accompanying book in English answering many a question you might have about the strange set-up, and the changing nature of borders.

Try the slow-cooked jambonneau (pork knuckle) with mustard sauce.

 EATING & DRINKING IN MALMÉDY & EUPEN: OUR PICKS

Ratskeller: Buzzy Germanic tavern atmosphere with brasserie food and Tongerlo, as well as Eupener, beers on tap. *9am-11pm daily, kitchen until 9pm* €

Au 3 Bis: In Eupen, push the heavy carved door and enter a world of chandeliers, black-washed interiors and Belgo-German cuisine. *noon-2.30 Tue-Fri & 6-9pm Thu-Sat* €€

Le No Name: Casual Malmédy bistro whose changing menus might include pork in Calvados, Ardennes croquettes or fruity chicken curry. *noon-2pm & 6-9pm Thu-Mon* €€

Â Vî Mâm'dî: Usually the liveliest terrace on Malmédy's central square, with wide-ranging menu including trout, kidney and Ardennes fare. *11am-10pm Fri-Wed* €€

Limbourg village

Stadtmuseum Eupen *(stadtmuseum-eupen.be; adult/ student €5/4)*, the appealing city museum, focuses significantly on weaving in Eupen's 18th-century golden age, but on the top floor (audio-guide track 20) you'll learn more about the region's complex geopolitical oscillations and how it has affected citizens. For example, post-WWII citizens required certificates attesting to their perceived loyalties during the war: without a 'good' report, getting a job was near impossible, at least until the system was repealed in 1951. The beer bottle contains coffee for reasons you'll discover.

Limbourg

TIME FROM SPA: **25MIN** 🚗

Wallonia's prettiest village?

One of Belgium's most delightful historic villages, old **Limbourg** is raised on a promontory with a long, central square that's very roughly cobbled and lined by picturesque 18th-century houses. The former town hall hosts **L'Arvô** *(limbourg-tourisme.com),* a tourist information office providing a synopsis of Limbourg's valiant history, and a free upstairs gallery which often has excellent exhibits. Across the square, **Brasserie St Georges** *(5-9pm Thur, 11am-9pm Fri-Sun)* is a superb old-world bar-cafe.

Families might prefer **La Gileppe** *(gileppe.com/en),* a 5km walk (or 9km drive) southwest of Limbourg. Ranged around a famous dam are various outdoor activities, most memorably a fun set of zipwires in the trees. You can also rent bikes to circumnavigate the reservoir lake or take the free lift to the top of the view tower with its **Panoramic Restaurant**.

CLASSIC ARDENNES WALKS

Ninglingspo: The 3km each-way Balade de Ninglingspo *(ovatourism.be)* gently climbs a pretty woodland valley from Sedoz, criss-crossing a stream on 20 wooden bridges. It's tame if attractive to bridge 15. Beyond that, upper *bains* (tiny erosion-carved basins) are accessed via narrower paths with a few minor scrambles.

Drouet: Rather than simply returning the same way, make the Ninglinspo into a more strenuous loop using blue-route 21 via the Drouet Viewpoint (another 3.6km).

Reinhardstein: In the valley below Reinhardstein's austerely spooky medieval castle, forest paths include a 40-minute 'cascade loop'.

Robertville: Extend a Reinhartstein walk with routes taking in the Robertville Dam and reservoir.

Baraque Michel: From Baraque Michel restaurant, get a brief taste of the Fagnes or trek right across the moors to Eupen.

Karin Breuer from Stadtmuseum Eupen shares some peculiarities about the Germanophone area of Belgium.

German dialects?
Almost every village has its own. For Eupen there's even a printed dictionary. Notably we use mixed French-German terms like Plattes Wasser for still water (rather than Stilles Wasser in standard German).

Special foods?
Reisfladen, a tart that looks like a quiche but is actually filled with set rice pudding. Eupener Platz is a brioche bread with pearl sugar and raisins.

Drinks? Eupener beer! However, that's now brewed by Haacht and we have many micro-breweries. My favourite is called Néau, the old French name for Eupen.

Verviers

TIME FROM SPA: **25MIN**

Chocolate time

Vervier's biggest draw is **La Chocolaterie Darcis** *(darcis. com/chocolaterie)*. You can simply taste delicious Darcis chocolates, macaroons and pastries in the cafe. Or pick the hour-long museum experience *(adult/under-12 €8/6)*, walking through a Mayan temple, getting seasick on Hernán Cortés' galleon and visiting a 19th-century cocoa parlour, before sniff tests, quizzes and a 10-minute video tour of Mexican plantations. Explanations of modern chocolate making and a three-praline tasting round things off. Last entry 4.30pm.

City of water & textiles

Verviers often gets a bad rap not helped by the catastrophic floods of 2021, which unravelled many of the efforts to pull the former wool-processing city out of its post-industrial depression. However, amid sometimes chaotic streetscapes there is some grand architecture with several patchily genteel neighbourhoods, notably around **Place Albert Premier**. The back story of Verviers' weaving heritage is told at the **Centre Touristique de la Laine et de la Mode** *(ctlm-verviers.be; adult/senior €6/5)*, a textiles museum in the 19th-century former Bettonville Mill. One section maps out the history of cloth and clothing from Neolithic furs via Crusader capes to 1930s garter belts. Another delves into the city's roots as a textile centre with some well-preserved industrial equipment.

Dotted around the city centre, notably along the riverside Rue Jules Cerexhe restaurant strip, you can find several other remnant chunks of historical machinery. The **tourist office** suggests several self-guided city walks, some available as free audio tours via *bestofverviers.be*.

Serves classic Ostend-style *Waterzoi* (creamy seafood stew).

 DRINKING & EATING IN VERVIERS: OUR PICKS

Gorgées Bar à Boire:	Spirit of 66:	Bistro Vino:	L'Entract:
Around 170 beers (many local) with inexpensive pasta meals. Classic decor for the indigo walls. *9am-11.30pm Mon-Fri, from 3pm Sat*	Since 1985 one of Belgium's foremost venues for live rock, blues and boogie music. Intimate, standing only, drinks by token. *hours vary*	Laid back, river-facing wine cafe also offering a blackboard of tasty mini-plates that might include escargots, oysters or asparagus salad. *5-10.30pm Wed-Sat* €€	The atmosphere is Toulouse-Lautrec's Paris; the food favours high-class Belgian brasserie favourites. Bookings advised. *noon-2pm & 6-9pm Wed-Sat* €€

Liège

URBAN CONTRASTS | FOLKLORE | MAIGRET

The sprawling city of Liège is like a living architectural onion, with layer upon layer of history lying beneath a craggily scarred façade. You couldn't call it beautiful, but scratch the surface and there's masses to discover in a city that for 800 years was independent and run by a lineage of prince-bishops. From the 19th century, reimagined Liege prospered as a dynamic centre of industry – you can find grand remnants from the glory years in the city's plethora of good-value museums, and in attractive areas such as La Bovarie, which harks back to 1905 when the city hosted a World's Fair. However, there's also plenty of gruesome post-industrial heritage along with miserable post-WWII architectural blandness in the vast conurbation (total population over 700,000). This can't stop the proudly free-spirited citizens from expressing a strong sense of self, typically humorous and disarmingly friendly. No Belgian city bubbles with more *joie de vivre.*

Light Up the Mountain

Deciding not to climb the Montagne de Bueren

'Thank you for visiting without screaming' requests neat graffiti in multiple languages as you approach the **Montagne de Bueren**. It's one of the world's most daunting public stairways, 374 steps rising vertiginously behind Rue Hors Chateau. At dusk on the first Saturday of October, this remarkable sight is transformed into a twinkling beauty during the **Nocturne des Coteaux**, when some 20,000 candles are lit on the steps. A series of free concerts and fireworks add to the atmosphere.

Having Instagrammed the stairway (but without climbing it), veer left on an alleyway leading to a group of medieval buildings now containing **Brasserie {c}**, and a network of intriguing footpath-steps accessing city overlook viewpoints.

Other tiny alleys leading off **Rue Hors Chateau** give hints of Liege's medieval heritage. The loveliest are **Impasse de la Vignette** and especially **Impasse de l'Ange/Couronne**, which meet at a delightful hidden garden and host the city's long-running 'secret' restaurant **Le Thème**.

continues on p248

GETTING AROUND

Dazzling Liège-Guillemins (p251) is the main long-distance, high-speed train station, with national and international connections. If you're arriving and want the historic city centre, Liège-St-Lambert station is a more convenient place to alight, though you might need to change at Guillemins. The city's 12km, 23-station tram system finally opened in April 2025, usefully linking Guillemins to the Opera, Pl St Lambert and the Grand Curtius area, continuing eventually to Liège Expo. At the south, the terminus is the football stadium where Standard Liège play. In summer it's fun and inexpensive to use the river ferries (p252).

LIÈGE

R Pierreuse

Montagne de Bueren

R des Anglais

R Fond St-Servais

R Pierreuse

13
3

15
36
43

Cour des Mineurs

Musée de la Vie Wallonne 2

16

Féronstrée

R du Palais

R de Féronstrée

Liège-Palais

R Agimont

Pl des Bons-Enfants

8

10

Pl St-Lambert

18

Pl du Marché

R du Pont

41

En Neuvice

31
48

La Bat

R de Bex

3
19

21
28

24

Place Saint-Lambert

R Gérardrie

47

R Léopold

22

38

34

45

Mont St-Martin

25

R Basse Sauvenière

Opéra

Pl Verte

R St-Gangulphe

Pl St-Étienne

R Souverain Pont

R de la Cathédrale

Pont des Arches

27

Pl Xavier Neujean

R de la Casquette

R G Clémenceau

Pl Saint-Denis

6

R de la Régence

Meuse

Quai sur-Meuse

Quai de Gaulle

R Pont d'Île

L'ISLE

R de l'Université

R de la Cathédrale

30

Centre-ville

Footbridge

Sauvenière

37

Blvd de la Sauvenière

R du Pot d'Or

46
35

Pl de la Cathédrale

R Charles Magnette

9
44

23

Pl Cockerill

R sur la Fontaine

R Pont d'Avroy

5

39

R Bonne Fortune

R St-Paul

R des Clarisses

Quai Roosevelt

R St-Gilles

Pont d'Avroy

R Hazinelle

Pl St-Paul

R du Méry

R des Croisiers

Quai EVan Beneden

49
14

Blvd d'Avroy

Pl des Carmes

Ave M Destenay

Château de Jehay (23km);
Château de Modave (37km);
Fort de Huy (38km)

Tour Paradis (1.3km);
YUST Liège (1.4km);
Liège-Guillemins
Train Station (1.7km)

La Boverie
(1km)

Maison de la
Métallurgie (800m);
Musée des
Transports en
Commun de
Wallonie (1.1km)

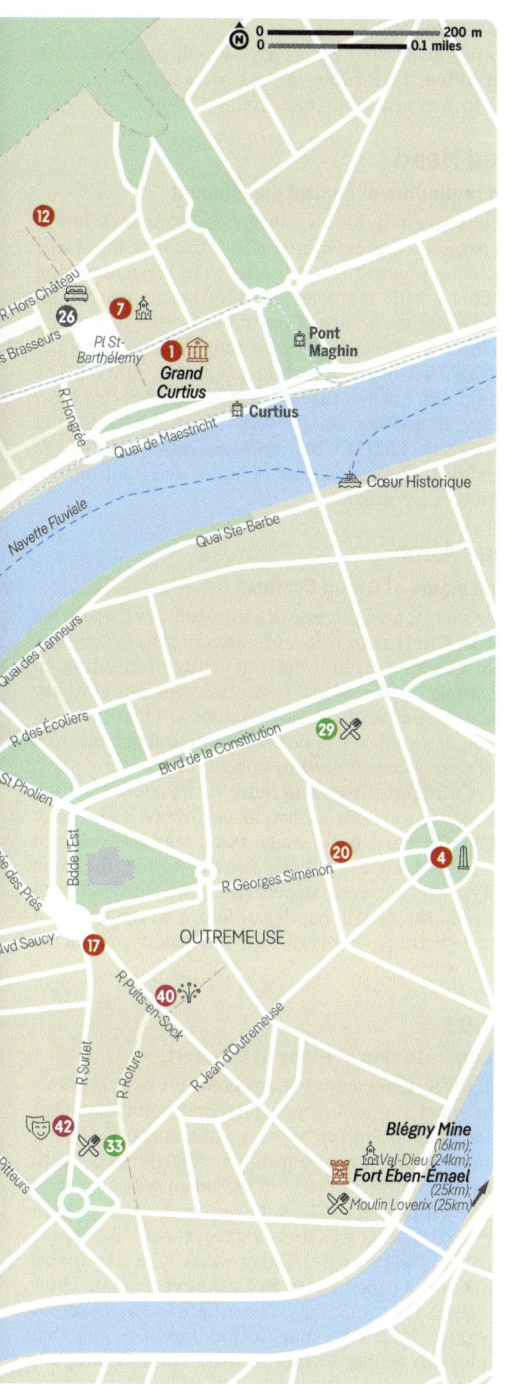

⭐ **HIGHLIGHTS**
1 Grand Curtius
2 Musée de la Vie Wallonne

🔴 **SIGHTS**
3 Archéoforum
4 Bust of Simenon
5 Cathédrale St-Paul
6 Collégiale Saint-Denis
7 Collégiale St-Barthélemy
8 Église St-André
9 Emulation/Maison Renaissance
10 Former Palace of
   the Prince-Bishops
11 Giant Simenon Mural
12 Impasse de la Vignette
13 Impasse de l'Ange/Couronne
14 Institut Zoologique
15 Montagne de Bueren
16 MULUM
17 Outremeuse
18 Place du Marché
19 Place St Lambert
20 Rue Georges Simeon
see 14 Science Museum and Aquarium
21 Seated Statue of Simenon
22 Simenon's Birth House
23 University of Liège

⚫ **SLEEPING**
24 Hotel Neuvice
25 Hôtel Sélys Liège
26 N° 5 Bed & Breakfast

🟢 **EATING**
27 ¡Toma!
28 Amon Nanesse
29 Côté cour – Côté Jardin
30 La Grand Poste
31 Le Bistrot d'en Face
32 Le Thème
33 Métisses

🟢 **DRINKING & NIGHTLIFE**
34 Aux Olivettes
35 Blaes
36 Brasserie {c}
37 Chez Moi
38 Fragrances
39 Le Pot au Lait

🔴 **ENTERTAINMENT**
40 Festival Outremeuse
41 Lou's Bar
42 Musée Tchantchès
43 Nocturne des Coteaux
44 Théâtre de Liège

🔴 **SHOPPING**
45 La Batte Weekly Market
46 Passage Lemonier
47 Wattitude

🔵 **INFORMATION**
48 Tourist Office

🔵 **TRANSPORT**
49 Pôle Fluviale

247

continued from p245

Before going much further, it's also worth dropping into the **tourist office** *(visitezliege.be/en),* set within what was originally a 16th-century butchers' hall.

A Severed Head
Mummified reminders of capital punishment

In a beautifully adapted cloister-convent, the **Musée de la Vie Wallonne** *(viewallonne.be; adult/concs €7/5)* is thematically chaotic but still arguably the best museum in Liège. Covering every aspect of local life, it ambles amiably from ancient Mosan metalwork to nostalgic photos of traditional street games and 1960s room interiors. However, in a specially darkened chamber is the ghoulish show-stopper. An original guillotine. And yes. The mummified human head of the last man to have felt 'her kiss'.

A block away in another antique building, you have to ring the doorbell to access **MULUM** *(adult/concession €2.25/1.25).* It's a wonderfully obscure museum of lamps and lighting, but openings are very irregular.

Ambitious Aims
The museum magic of Grand Curtius

In the former mansion-warehouse of a 16th-century Liège arms dealer, **Grand Curtius** *(adult/senior/under-26 €9/5/free)* is a large, scatter-gun museum optimistically attempting to explain the whole history of art. It stresses religious statuary and interweaves stories of Liège-born artists. Then there's a vast collection of antique weapons from samurai armour to a rapier sword that once belonged to Rubens.

Nearby, the **Collégiale St-Barthélemy** *(adult/senior €3/2)* is a church with twin Saxon-style diamond-facet towers. It's far older than its red-and-cream exterior suggests, for reasons explained by the 12-minute video. Even if you don't go inside, the noon carillon is delightful and you can peer through a slit-window to glimpse the remarkable 1118 baptismal font, a world highlight of Mosan art depicting in high relief the Christianisation of the Greco-Roman world.

Lost Riches
Under the concrete skin of Place St Lambert

Around 705, CE St-Lambert was murdered in Liege. Miracles linked to the martyr would attract pilgrims as important as Emperor Charlemagne. Built on the spot, St-Lambert's Cathedral eventually became the power centre for a quasi-independent territory ruled for eight centuries by independent prince-bishops, until they were toppled in the 1789 Révolution Liégeoise. Anti-religious fury by that stage was so strong that townsfolk voted to demolish the fabulous cathedral. Today, where it stood remains a bleak, blank space called **Place St Lambert** that somehow symbolises Liège's contradictions. The square is overlooked by one of the world's largest secular Gothic buildings, but that potentially glorious former **Palace of the Prince-Bishops** is

---

☑ **TOP TIP**

The €18 Liège Visit Pass allows entry to a dozen city museums over a 48-hour period for less than the price of buying separate entrances for just three, ie Grand Curtius, La Boverie and Archéoforum. You can only buy it at the **tourist office**.

CAFÉ LIÉGEOIS

The sundae known world-wide as *café liégeois* combines ice cream with coffee, vanilla milk and possibly a shot of spirit. **Le Bistrot d'en Face** has won competitions for producing the city's best (€11). However, despite the name, it doesn't actually originate in Liège. In fact it was created in pre-WWI Paris as an evocation of the suave tastes of Hapsburg Vienna. The original name was thus Café Viennois.

However, in 1914, when Germany invaded neutral Belgium, Paris reacted angrily by changing many Germanic names. Liège was honoured for heroically managing to stall the Kaiser's advance towards France for 12 all-important days. More traditionally linked with Liège is *pékèt*, Wallonia's version of gin.

used as a courthouse and can only be visited by tour on the first Sunday of the month *(free; prebook on provincedeliege.be)*.

Fortunately, beneath the square, multiple archaeological layers are revealed in the **Archéoforum** *(archeoforumdeliege. be; adult/senior €6/5)* including prehistoric elements and considerable remnants of a Roman villa. A rather pedestrian iPad-led commentary is delivered in thickly accented English, but it's a curiosity to 'watch' St Lambert's murder and to use VR 'binoculars' (point 13) to see 1000 years of evolution of the now long-gone cathedral.

Going Local

A Sunday in Liège

The best way to really sample Liégeois culture is through the mid-August mayhem of the **Outremeuse festival**. However, second best is to come on a Sunday. Start your day snacking your way around the big weekly market **La Batte** *(8am-2pm)*, with stalls along the riverside quays. Watch a folkloric puppet show at **Musée Tchantchès** *(10.30am Sun, Oct-Apr)* – not that you'll probably understand much. Then join locals singing their hearts out at the time-warp *café chantant* **Aux Olivettes**, accompanied by a pianist. Finally, ramp up the music after 4pm with a live mini-gig at **Lou's Bar**, a tiny blues-rock pub nearby.

Golden Bust

St Lambert's saintly skull

Though St Lambert Cathedral was demolished in 1790, the 15th-century **Cathédrale St-Paul** *(cathedraledeliege.be; free)* was soon promoted to cathedral in its place. There's some beautiful stained glass, old and new. But the real gem is a gilded bust of St Lambert, a grandiose reliquary designed in 1512 to encase the top of the saint's skull. You can see it on the 2nd floor of the cloisters in the **treasury** *(adult/senior €8/6)*. Doubts as to the authenticity of the relic were put to rest in 2024 when the skull received an autopsy which allegedly 'proves' that the unfortunate owner of the head really did die of a lance blow to the head, fitting the myth of St Lambert's demise.

The treasury hosts intimate classical-music concerts at 6pm most Saturdays for not much more than the price of a regular entry ticket.

Award-winning *café liégeois* available to non-diners between 3pm and 5pm.

MEET TCHANTCHÈS

Liège's mascot and oldest 'citizen' is a big-nosed wooden puppet called Tchantchès (pronounced chan-chay), who is an integral part of the culture in **Outremeuse**, the island section of Liège that lies across the river from the city centre and which declares 'independence' every August in a series of raucously entertaining, off-beat celebrations. These partly celebrate Tchantchès' 'birth' on 15 August 760, a humorous 'miracle' that's a thinly veiled biblical satire.

The fact that Tchantchès has a penchant for getting riotously drunk on *pékèt* (local gin) can't detract from his good heart, typifying the free spirit of the Liégeois. You can hear his full 'life story' in thickly accented Walloon-French through puppet shows at the **Musée Tchantchès**.

 EATING IN LIÈGE: OUR PICKS

Métisses: Convivial atmosphere for *mafe* (Senegalese peanut stew) and grilled fish in an 18th-century house at the heart of Outremeuse. *6-10.30pm Tue-Sun & 12.15-3pm Wed & Thu €*

Le Bistrot d'en Face: Old-style rural French food served in a candlelit 16th-century building. Not for vegetarians. *noon-3pm Wed-Fri & Sun, 7-9.30pm Wed-Sun €€*

Le Thème: Prebook a themed, multicourse dinner in this 'laboratory for dreamers', tucked away in one of the old city's prettiest dead-end lanes. *7-10pm Tue-Sat €€*

¡Toma!: Thomas Troupin's 'immersive cuisine' that gives Belgian classic food a Michelin-starred gourmet makeover. Thoroughly seasonal. *noon-2pm Tue-Fri & 7-9pm Tue-Sat €€€*

TOP EXPERIENCE

Fort Ében-Émael

In the 1930s it took six years to build what was then the world's largest military fort. With some 5km of passages cut 25m into the rock of a domed hillside, the only exterior sign that **Fort Ében-Émael** existed was a series of observation domes and casemates hiding heavy guns in 2.5m-thick concrete housings. It was considered impregnable. Yet on 10 and 11 May, 1940, it fell in just hours to German special forces arriving by glider. Blitzkrieg had begun.

EDWIN BUTTER/SHUTTERSTOCK

TOP TIPS

● Standard guided tours in English run four times on weekends only: 11.15am and 1.45pm on Saturdays and Sundays.

● In a historic mill across the canal from the entrance, **Moulin Loverix** (*11am-6pm Wed-Sun*) serves coffee, cold beers and huge pancakes.

● Bus 76 comes from Liège, but the site is closer to Maastricht, Netherlands.

PRACTICALITIES

● fort-eben-emael.be

● self-guided tour adult/under-14 €12/9

● guided-tour €17/12

● 10am-5pm, last entry 2.30pm

The full monty

Paying for an excellent guided tour is ideal, but you'll need decent fitness as you'll likely climb 20m-plus of metal steps to visit one of the casemates. Here big guns remain in place, some almost ready to fire, others left in shreds from the German 'hollow charges' that slammed through the housings in 1940. On standard tours there's no turning back once you've started (2 to 2½ hours). Private tours offer extra flexibility.

The self-guided tour

Without joining a tour, you'll still see plenty of exhibits, mini-museum sections and much of the clever engineering that provides ventilation. You won't see guns or climb to casemates. The 12-minute background film is available in English. Other details are currently in French and Dutch, but a downloadable app has English summaries/translations. Allow about 1¼ hours.

A free taster

If time is limited, you can still get a significant taste of the place by walking from the car park to the pay desk and back through a long subterranean tunnel: there are several interesting room exhibits en route (no charge). Also, directly left of the entry tunnel, a footpath climbs steeply and takes you through woodlands past the exteriors of a few defensive domes and concrete casemate structures. No ticket required.

Extreme Architecture
The modern masterpiece of Guillemins train station

Liège-Guillemins is not the city's most central train station but it's the main railway hub and one of Belgium's most jaw-dropping architectural statements of the 21st century. It's worth coming just to enjoy the sweeping arcs of this 2009 Santiago Calatrava masterpiece from various angles. The surrounding regeneration area is most notable for the **Tour Paradis**, a blue glass skyscraper. You can't go up, but for a perfect view down onto the station's curves, head to the 7th-floor roof bar of the **YUST** hostel.

Art & Gastronomy in the Park
Discovering La Boverie

Set amid goose ponds and contoured lawns, the domed façade of **La Boverie** looks like a 19th-century country house. In fact, it was originally built for Liège's 1905 World Fair and is now a superb art gallery. A **full ticket** *(adult/senior/under-26 €15/12/10)* includes inventive contemporary exhibitions, while the **permanent collection** *(adult/senior/under-26 €5/3/free)* is quite inspiring enough, proceeding swiftly from 16th-century altarpieces to a who's who of 20th-century painting. There are works by Pissarro, Picasso, Kokoschka, Chagall, Monet, Gauguin, Leger and even some curvaceous cubism by Le Corbusier, better known as a brutalist city planner. Belgian greats Magritte, Ensor and Emil Claus are represented, and there's a brilliant 1890 realist canvas by Constantin Meunier.

For five days over the Pentecost weekend (late May/early June) thousands of gastronomes visit La Boverie park for **Liège Foodie Fest** *(epicuriales.be)* to sample taster plates created by renowned Belgian chefs, some of them Michelin starred. Free entry; food payments by pre-chargeable wristband.

Sights & Sounds of the Coal Seam
A moving descent into Blégny mine

It's the sheer deafening roar of machinery that hits hardest when you're deep inside the **Blégny coal mine** *(blegnymine .be/en; adult/over-60/under-13 €16/14/11.20)*, albeit graciously only in very short bursts for demonstration purposes. The initial descent is also a memorable experience, in little cage lifts that would originally have been crammed full. Superstitious miners put their lives in the hands of God through Ste-Barbara whose

SIMENON IN LIÈGE

Prolific Liège-born author Georges Simenon (1903–89) is most famed for his 76 Inspector Maigret crime novels. On average, he churned out a book every 120 days, moved house 33 times and still had time to have 10,000 sex partners. Or so he claimed. Liège places with Simenon connections include:

Simenon's birth house: Rue Leopold 24, now the *L'Art de Plaire* fashion shop.

Seated Statue: On Place Maigret. Evokes the 1952 novel *Maigret et l'Homme du Banc*.

Bust of Simenon: Stares down Rue Jean-d'Outremeuse. His pipe often gets stolen.

Giant Simenon Mural: At 18 Rue de Pitteurs.

Rue Georges Simeon: Fine 1890s and Art Nouveau houses. Simenon lived at No 25 during 1905–1911.

Try typical boulettes, Liège meatballs in raisin-sweetened gravy.

 EATING & DRINKING IN LIÈGE: OUR PICKS

Brasserie {c}: Medieval buildings that are tasting rooms for Liège's Curtius beer range but also popular for Belgian food, burgers and *café liégeois. noon-11pm Thu-Sun* €€

Côté cour – Côté Jardin: Inviting Outremeuse brasserie with veg-friendly menu, garden seating, events and Thursday-night live music in summer. *11am-11pm Thu-Sun* €€

La Grand Poste: Combines a multicuisine food hall with good value student-deal meals, a beer-bar with over a dozen brews on tap and a lively rooftop cafe. *noon-11.30pm* €

Amon Nanesse: Rambling antique house serving satisfying local pub fare, and tasters of local gins. *9am-late, food noon-2pm & 6-10pm Thu-Mon* €

LIÈGE HIGHLIGHTS BY FOOT & BOAT

Explore central Liège starting from the Guillemins area, including a €2 Navette Fluviale river-boat ride. Return to Guillemins by tram from Grand Curtius.

START	END	LENGTH
Pôle Fluvial	Grand Curtius	3.5km, 90 mins

Arrive from Guillemins by Navette Fluviale boat at ① **Pôle Fluvial**. Peep inside the grand old ② **Institut Zoologique** and admire an important mural by Belgian surrealist Paul Delvaux, free if you don't also visit the building's science museum/aquarium. Cross the sweeping footbridge towards ③ **La Grand Poste**, a striking, 1901 former post office festooned with mock-Gothic heraldic figures. Heading southwest, pass notable buildings of the ④ **University**, ⑤ **Théâtre de Liège** and ⑥ **Emulation/Maison Renaissance**, an oddly hidden medieval building hosting pop-up contemporary art shows. Café-restaurants of the 'Latin Quarter' appear as you approach ⑦ **Cathédrale St-Paul** with its rich treasury,

then wander through ⑧ **Passage Lemonier**, an Art Deco shopping arcade. Visit the atmospheric if outwardly austere church ⑨ **Collégiale Saint-Denis**, then zigzag north via ⑩ **Wattitude**, a shop of made-in-Wallonia products. Get a first glimpse of the former ⑪ **Prince-Bishops' Palace**, then cross cafe-lined ⑫ **Place du Marché** to the ⑬ **Musée de la Vie Wallonne**. Pass gravity-defying ⑭ **Montagne de Bueren** on Rue Hors Chateau, nipping up intriguing tiny side alleys that hint at Liege's medieval heritage. Don't miss ⑮ **Impasse de l'Ange/Couronne** and ⑯ **Impasse de la Vignette**. End up on Place St Barthélemy with its celebrated ⑰ **church** and sprawling museum, ⑱ **Grand Curtius**.

Built between 1836 and 1838, Passage Lemonier was Belgium's first shopping arcade. Its current Art Deco look dates from a 1937 rebuild.

From several angles, you get tantalising views of the Prussian-hat spire atop 1772 **Église St-André**. However, the church is closed and entirely inaccessible.

The boats only leave six times daily, April to September, so time things carefully.

image surveys the lift shaft. If her statuette wasn't lit, miners would refuse to start work. These are just a few of the hard-hitting impressions you're left with after an unforgettable two-hour visit to this UNESCO-listed site, which produced coal up until the 1970s and retains much of the original equipment in working order.

The audio guide covers all major points in English but you'll get lots of extra insight if you can follow the French (or Dutch) commentary of the human guide who retells anecdotes from miners who worked here.

It's worth arriving well before your prebooked visiting slot to peruse the **Puits Marie** museum section (included) which illustrates important issues for miners such as lighting, air circulation and water removal: once pumping stopped in the 1980s, lower coal seams rapidly drowned.

There are copious play facilities for children and a nature path now climbs the nearest slag heap, illustrating how botany can conquer even the most awful pollution. Allow at least 20 minutes to drive here from Liège.

Valley of God
Recover with a blessed beer
Regain your equanimity after Blégny by driving on to contrastingly calming **Val-Dieu** *(abbaye-du-val-dieu.be/en)*, a rural neogothic basilica whose impressive buildings date from an 1885 rebuild, though the original was founded in 1216. Much of the complex is still an active Cistercian monastery producing an excellent abbey beer and set in tranquil parkland where iridescent dragonflies dart and hover over pretty ponds.

Historic castles
View fortresses around Liège
Château de Jehay rises from its moat like a gingerbread fantasy. At **Château de Modave** you'll pay to view the breathtaking interiors of the main castle, but it's free to walk through the extensive grounds and to access picnic areas in the front courtyard and former stables. Overshadowing the centre of Huy, the oppressively dour **Fort de Huy** was completed in 1823 and used by WWII German forces as an interrogation centre. Writer PG Wodehouse was held here and there's a fascinating if sombre museum. Access by a footpath zigzagging up from near Huy's impressive Gothic church, or from across the river on a 2023 cable car.

VISIT LIÈGE PASS PICKS

A total of 13 museums are included in the €18 Visit Liège pass, sold by the tourist office. Includes:

Musée des Transports en Commun de Wallonie: *(musee-transports.be; adult/student €6/5)* A treasure trove of nearly 50 public transport vehicles, mostly trams, spanning 150 years. You can climb aboard a dozen of them.

Maison de la Métallurgie: *(mmil.be; adult/student €5/4.50)* The key attraction here is a 1693 industrial iron forge, Belgium's oldest, salvaged and brilliantly reconstructed but not actually functioning.

Science Museum and Aquarium: *(masc.ulg.ac.be; adult/child €13/10)* See a living sturgeon and ray, and a collection of glass models of ephemeral creatures. Check times for the planetarium shows and the electrical experiences.

Musée de la Vie Wallonne: *(p248)* Arguably the best museum in Liège.

Grand Curtius: *(p248)* History of art in a distinctive building.

 DRINKING IN LIÈGE: OUR PICKS

Le Pot au Lait: Super-eccentric pub-cafe decorated with psychedelic murals and lamps resembling radioactive triffids. Lots of outdoor drinking space. *noon-4am*

Chez Moi: Morning coffee or evening cocktails in a mould-breaking cafe just beyond the boisterous Pot d'Or bar zone. Street BBQs, DJ weekends etc. *9am-late*

Blaes: Sleek yet unpretentious 20-somethings' favourite for organic wines, cocktails and an unusual selection of beers. Popular early evening. *5pm-1am*

Fragrances: Little changed since 1932, this beautifully perfumed mini-tearoom and shop is full of teapots, marmalades and 350 types of tea. *11am-6pm Mon-Sat, 11am-3pm Sun*

Places We Love to Stay

€ Budget   €€ Midrange   €€€ Top End

Waterloo   MAP p201

Van der Valk Hotel Waterloo €€ Business standard rooms in or beside a grand 1837 brick-vaulted building that was once a vast sugar factory.

Hotel 1815 €€ Compact rooms above the Maximus restaurant facing the battlefield, around 300m from the Lion's Mound.

Gîte Ferme d'Hougoumont €€€ Unique rental apartment above the south gateway of the historic Hougoumont farm-museum. Sleeps up to five.

Mons   MAP p207

Mons Dragon House € Guesthouse with stylish decor, very handy location, friendly hosts and communal sitting room/kitchen.

L'Olivier €€ New, slightly spartan but good-value hotel that's just paces from the Grand-Place. Great for nightlife but can prove noisy.

La Maison de la Duchesse de la Vallière €€ Genteel mansion B&B 600m south of the Grand-Place set back behind wrought-iron gates. Free private parking.

St Martins Dream Hotel €€ Converted from a historic chapel. The 'charming' rooms retain elements of these ecclesiastical origins.

Tournai

B&B Françoise Daniel € You won't find her place online, but pull the bell-handle on the unsigned 1673 townhouse at Rue des Soeurs Noires 35 for an intensely personal, slightly chaotic, art-filled experience. You'll need to like pets. Book by phone 0472-386972.

Villa Tournesol €€ Elegantly upper-market B&B in a leafy quarter a short walk from the Palais de Justice and museum area.

Hotel d'Alcantara €€ Compact music- and art-themed rooms, the inviting smell of fresh-baked pastries and a couple of free bikes for guest use.

Chimay

Hotel du Franc Bois € Typical old-style country hotel with simple rooms, perched above the pretty stream valley in lovely little Lompret hamlet, 6km northeast of Chimay.

Le Petit Chapitre €€ Charming central-Chimay B&B in a turreted, wisteria-draped house full of antiques and flamboyant furnishings.

Namur   MAP p223

Auberge de Jeunesse € It's hard to imagine a better HI hostel, facing the river with terrace, games room and generous breakfast.

Hôtel Les Tanneurs €€ Contemporary hotel in central Namur, artfully incorporating a series of 17th-century buildings.

Château de Namur €€ Sleep atop the citadel hill in castle-style architecture, even if the building is a 1931 caprice. Free parking.

Bouillon   MAP p228

Auberge de Jeunesse € Simple youth hostel with fabulous views from its breakfast room. It's a 15-minute climb by stairway (400m) from the town centre.

Gîtes Monmartre Breton € Three bargain value units in

antique stone cottages right on the Quartier Bretagne art alley. A per-stay cleaning fee applies.

La Ferronnière €€ Indulgent mansion hotel-restaurant overlooking town, with a wellness section (extra fee) in its extensive gardens.

Hotel de la Poste €€ Founded in 1730, Bouillon's most central riverside address is well modernised but retains some century-old wrought ironwork.

Redu & Around

Hotel Le Fournil €€ Modernised rooms above two of the restaurants (p231) in the centre of Redu. Various meal-deal options.

Château de Porcheresse €€ Inspiring B&B stays in an elegant family chateau. Great beds, shared bathrooms, bargain off-peak rates.

Rochefort

Hotel La Fayette € Reliable old-style auberge-hotel with decent-priced rooms a stone's throw from the castle.

La Malle Poste €€ Central Rochefort's 17th-century coaching inn with excellent restaurant and modern rooms, some complete with hot tubs.

Château de Mirwart €€€ Indulgent luxury in a gloriously upgraded grand chateau. All but three 'standard' rooms are in the former stables. Rural setting 16km south of Rochefort.

Durbuy

Aux 10 Clefs (p233) **€** Durbuy's best-value B&B with immaculate rooms, friendly welcome and a groaningly impressive breakfast.

Le Clos des Récollets €€
Boutique hotel linking three historic half-timbered houses in Durbuy's prettiest corner.

Le Sanglier des Ardennes €€€ Durbuy's landmark hotel is a super-suave oasis of contemporary urban chic with an incredible wine collection in the tunnel linking its two properties.

La Roche-en-Ardenne

Hôtel de Liège € Mural-fronted old-school hotel with friendly owners. Basic but perfectly functional budget option.

Hostellerie La Claire Fontaine €€ A 1930s roadside retreat totally reworked in 2023 with outdoor pool in an idyllic garden, hammam and view-sauna included in room price. Free parking.

Moulin de la Strument €€ Stone-built hotel incorporating a preserved former mill. Also has riverside camping spaces down a quiet lane from La Roche.

Spa
MAP p238

Villa des Fleurs €€ Intimate Napoleon III–style villa-hotel with original marble fireplaces and classically styled furniture.

Manoir de Lébioles €€€ Luxurious 1905 château-style mansion-hotel complex with spa and swimming pools, a 10-minute drive above Spa.

Les Bains de Spa (p239) €€€ Choose a 'heritage' room to sleep in the palatial UNESCO-listed 19th-century baths building, majestically revamped as a five-star hotel in 2025.

Villa Grand Maur €€€ Three guest rooms above a gourmet restaurant on the south edge of Spa, ideal for a gastronomic getaway.

Malmédy & Stavelot

Auberge de Jeunesse de Malmédy € Modern hostel in an outdoors activity park 2km northeast of Malmédy. Spacious bar area, generous breakfasts.

Bel Natura € Impressive B&B above an Italian deli in a 1869 Stavelot mansion with grand baronial-style breakfast room.

Hôtel Grand-Champ €€ Old-fashioned but well-kept basic hotel 3km from Malmédy with lovely rural setting, good walking and great views.

Hotel Dufays €€ Exquisitely restored 200-year-old stone

building in Stavelot where each lavish room has its own special character.

Daft Hotel €€€ Boutique rooms and glamping tents behind a prominent music-recording studio 2km south of Malmédy. Sauna and 'musical' swimming pool included.

Verviers

Au Clair Obscur €€ Gourmet getaway specialist in a splendid 19th-century mansion with contemporary makeover.

Le Petit Château Peltzer €€€ Grand yet personable B&B in a parkland setting in Verviers' leafy southern quarter. Free parking, handy for the motorway.

Liège
MAP p246

YUST Liège € Hostel accommodation taken to a swanky new level. The rooftop bar (p251) surveys Guillemins station. Free coffee in a comfy lounge area.

N° 5 Bed & Breakfast €€ Elegant B&B with sauna, entered through an 18th-century home in the city's most charming historic quarter.

Hotel Neuvice €€ Stylishly converted old houses combine to create this excellent boutique hotel right in Liège's commercial heart.

Hôtel Sélys Liège €€ Business hotel with glamorous, historic main building and indoor pool, but avoid the cheapest new-block rooms, which can be dark.

Manoir de Lébioles, Spa

Researched by
Mark Elliott

Luxembourg

THE WORLD'S RICHEST COUNTRY

Known for banking and cheap petrol, Luxembourg is also a wonderland of green hills, quaffable wines and loads of great castles.

Luxembourg's pretty woodland footpaths and quaint castle villages come as a surprise to many first-time visitors who most likely associated the Grand Duchy with banking or EU institutions. There's also a thriving wine industry creating beautiful vineyard landscapes on the hilly banks of the Moselle River. A superb dining scene ranges from hearty if mostly unsophisticated local cuisine to a glittering firmament of Michelin stars.

Luxembourg became an independent country almost by accident in the 19th century, having lost half of its territory to newly formed Belgium in 1830. It was pummelled during WWII, occupied by Nazi Germany, liberated, then briefly conquered again in Hitler's doomed last push in 1944 – a disastrous era remembered in many a memorial and museum. In the post-war period, a boom in the iron and steel industry shaped the southern Minett district, where mines and blast furnaces are now repurposed as visitor attractions. As steel-making waned, a lively banking sector arose. Well managed, resultant low taxes created a virtuous cycle leading to a society that's now wealthy enough to allow totally free public transport. Many museums are either free or great value, and there's a good network of youth hostels. Hotels in the capital can be fiercely expensive midweek, but most offer very substantial discounts at weekends. Most rural hotels are conversely cheaper midweek, so plan accordingly.

HANS-PETER MERTEN/GETTY IMAGES

THE MAIN AREAS

LUXEMBOURG CITY
Chasm of a fortress city and an EU hub. **p260**

SCHENGEN
An icon of Europe and gateway to Moselle wine country. **p271**

VIANDEN
A quaint base for discovering the northern castles. **p277**

For places to stay in Luxembourg, see p279

Left: vines, Moselle Valley (p272); Above: Vianden Castle (p274)

Find Your Way

Whether you're driving, cycling or using public transport, distances are modest. But remember that there are lots of hills to slow you down.

0 ——— 10 km
0 ——— 5 miles

La Roche-en-Ardenne

Houffalize

BELGIUM

Bastogne

Parc Naturel de la Haute Sûre

Sûre

Lac de la Haute Sûre

Troisvierges
N12 N7 E421
Heinerscheid
Clervaux
Dasburg
Derenbach
Hosingen
Untereisenbach
N12
Enscherange
N10
Wiltz
N15
Kautenbach
Hoscheid
Vianden
Esch-sur-Sûre
Bourscheid
N7
Vianden Castle
Insenborn
E421
Fouhren
N17
Eschdorf
Bourscheid-Moulin
Wallendorf
Bollendorf
N15
Diekirch
N12
Ettelbrück
N14
Beaufort
N10
Berdorf
Medernach
Echternach
Rosport
Christnach
Consdorf
N10
A7
Larochette
Born
Redange
Useldange
N11
Wasserbillig
N8
Mersch
E29
Bourglinster
Junglinster
N14
Hobscheid
N12
E421
Moselle
Steinfort
N7
Walferdange
Rammeldange
E44
Grevenmacher
Kopstal
N1
A1
E25 A6
N6
Bertrange
Sandweiler
N10
Clemency
Dippach
Oetrange
Wormeldange
E44
N5
Alzingen
E29
Ehnen
Pétange
A4
E25
N3
N2
Remich
Differdange
A13
Mondercange
A3
N13
Mondorf-les-Bains
Aspelt
Bettembourg
Rémerschen
Esch-sur-Alzette
Kayl
A13
Perl
Longuyon
Rumelange
Dudelange
Schengen
FRANCE

Vianden, p277

Home to the most authentically restored historic castle and a good alternative base from which to visit WWII battle memorials dotted all around the rural north of Luxembourg.

GERMANY

Sûre
Our

Alzette

Luxembourg City, p260

Fine dining and many free museums are dotted about an attractive, self-confident city whose deep-cut valley viewpoints rarely fail to impress.

LUXEMBOURG CITY

Schengen, p271

Symbolic as the place where European freedom of movement was agreed, and also a gateway to the very pretty vineyard terraces and tasting opportunities of the Moselle Valley.

TRAIN & BUS

All public transport is free, as long as you don't cross the border out of Luxembourg. Even most rural areas have a bus or train service, with connections accurately suggested through *mobiliteit.lu*.

BICYCLE

If you like hills, Luxembourg is a biking wonderland. Route possibilities are detailed through *provelo.lu/en/leisure*, and from April to November the brilliant *movewecarry.lu* system will transfer luggage between any two commercial accommodations in the Grand Duchy for €18 per piece.

Bock Casemates (p264), Luxembourg City

Plan Your Time

The Grand Duchy is small enough to visit in day trips from Luxembourg City. However, overnight stops in Echternach, Vianden, Clervaux, Esch-sur-Sûre and/or various other small towns add new perspectives.

Pressed for Time

● Get your bearings in **Luxembourg City** (p260), strolling 'Europe's most beautiful balcony' and visiting the casemates of the fortress remnants. Take in a selection of great museums and galleries, then jump on a free bus to **Schengen** (p271) or **Remich** (p273) and cycle the picturesque **Moselle Valley** (p272), tasting local sparklers from riverside wineries.

A Few Days to Explore

● Head south to experience Luxembourg's industrial underbelly. Prebook a subterranean adventure at the **National Mining Museum** (p271) and visit the **Belval** (p269) blast furnaces at Esch-sur-Alzette. Loop up the Moselle Valley and sleep in fascinating **Vianden** (p277). Explore castle villages and WWII museums in the northern part of the Grand Duchy.

Seasonal Highlights

SPRING

On Whit Tuesday, the **Springprozession** sees the culmination of a major pilgrimage with thousands dancing through the streets.

SUMMER

Luxembourg National Day (p266) explodes with fireworks and revelry in late June, and there's an arts or music festival most weekends.

AUTUMN

Autumn grape festivals take place. During late September's **Heritage Days** you can visit many usually-closed buildings.

WINTER

Drink *glühwäin* and eat *gromperekichelcher* and *mettwurscht* at several enchanting **Christmas markets**.

Luxembourg City

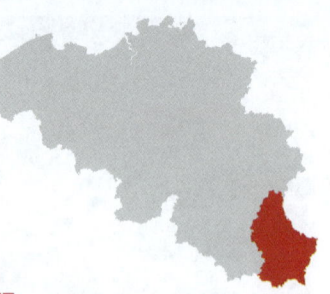

FORTIFICATIONS | MUSEUMS | FINE FOOD & FIZZ

If you were expecting a city dominated by high-rise banks and anonymous corporate HQ buildings, Luxembourg City will prove a refreshingly charming revelation. The old city is a UNESCO-listed layer-cake of bastion walls, footpaths and viewpoints terraced steeply down through parks and fortress remnants to the deep-cut Alzette and Pétrusse river valleys. These scenes are surveyed from many viewpoints and panoramic walkways, most notably the Chemin de la Corniche, which has been nicknamed the 'most beautiful balcony of Europe'. The atmospheric Grund quarter lies at the riverside below, and it's only when you cross the giant red road bridge (Pont-Grande-Duchesse Charlotte) that you reach the contrastingly brash glass towers of the EU quarter on the Kirchberg Plateau. Add in summer festivals, great art, fine museums and free public transport – you don't even pay for the funicular – and you have a gem of a discovery.

Fit for a Grand Duke

The Grand-Ducal palace, inside and out

Luxembourg's hereditary head of state has his office in the **Palais Grand-Ducal**, a palace building that's photogenically all aflutter with little pointy turrets. Built in 1572 as the town hall, an annex was added in 1860 that today houses the Luxembourg Chamber of Deputies (ie parliament). The main building has served as

  GETTING AROUND

Free transport around town includes a useful modern tram linking the main train station and airport via bus hubs and the Kirchberg EU district. Transport systems are completely integrated across the city and the whole Grand Duchy, with real-time best-choice connections given through the *mobiliteit.lu* app.

A funicular and two tall public elevators are handy for dealing with steep cliff ascents. These all run very frequently until 1am.

You do have to pay to use the **Velóh** *(myveloh.lu)* short-hop shared bicycle-hire scheme: €2/5 for one/three days, then free for rides of up to 30 minutes.

Palais Grand-Ducal

the royal palace since 1890. To get inside you'll need to prebook a 75-minute **guided tour** *(mid-July to late Aug only; adult/ under-13 €18/9)* online or via the **tourist office** *(luxembourg -city.com/en)*. Interior décor morphs from medieval-Gothic to sumptuous gilded romanticism as tour guides provide gently humorous insights into the Grand Duke's family.

Even if you can't get in, the palace façade beckons for selfie-taking and looks especially fine from the terrace of the **Chocolate House**.

Presiding over nearby **Place Guillaume II** is a bronze horseback **statue of William II**, the Grand Duke/Dutch King who in 1841 granted Luxembourg its then-liberal parliamentary constitution. Graves of the grand ducal family lie in the peaceful crypt of the **Cathédrale Notre-Dame**, guarded by bronze lions.

Formidable Fortifications

Going underground into the casemates

The defining feature of Luxembourg's extensive fortifications is the **casemates**, honeycombs of military tunnels and artificial caves. In 1867, when Dutch King/Grand Duke William III attempted to sell Luxembourg to France, international outrage forced Luxembourg to declare neutrality and its *continues on p264*

 EATING & DRINKING IN LUXEMBOURG CITY: OUR PICKS

Pizzeria Bacchus: Cheery, prompt service, decent portions and unusually good value for such a central spot. *noon-9.30pm Tue-Sat* €

Scott's Pub: Casual riverside watering hole with international pub food and grills. *kitchen 6-10pm Mon-Fri, noon-10pm Sat, noon-9pm Sun* €€

Beim Renert: Fox-themed local cafe-bar with popular terrace and unpretentious Belgo-Luxembourgish lunches. *10am-12.30am Tue-Sat, kitchen 11.30am-2.30pm* €€

Big Beer Company: Willy Wonka-esque microbrewery with Bavarian and Luxembourgish food in Rives de Clauseni nightlife zone. *5am-late Tue-Fri, from noon Sat & Sun* €€

LUXEMBOURG CITY

N 0 ———————————— 500 m
    0 ———————————— 0.25 miles

General Patton
Museum (35km);
National Museum of
Military History (40km)

57

Côte d'Eich

Blvd Paul Eyschen

Pont Grande-
Duchesse

7

20

14

58

PFAFFENTHAL

R Vauban

Alzette

15

Ave de la
Porte Neuve

Blvd de la Foire

Blvd Prince Henry

Blvd Royal

Côte d'Eich

R Mohrfels

27

R des Bains

Pl du
Théâtre

25

Av Emile Reuter

See Old Town Enlargement

Grand Rue

Blvd Joseph II

Blvd Royal

R Aldringen

R Philippe II

Pl d'Armes

R du Curé

Pl Guillaume II

OLD
TOWN

R du Fort Olizy

8

17

Ave Monterey

R Notre-Dame

Pl de la
Constitution

Blvd Roosevelt

R de Trèves

GRUN

46

37

51

R St Ulric

Blvd Grande-Duchesse Charlotte

Ave Marie-Thérèse

Pont
Adolphe **19**

*Citadel
Gardens*

23

Pétrusse

Blvd de la Pétrusse

R Goethe

R Michel Rodange

Blvd de la Pétrusse

Viaduc

R de Prague

Blvd d'Avranches

48

Pl de
Paris

Ave de la Gare

Ave de la Liberté

R de Bonnevoie

HOLLERICH

R Adolphe Fischer

R d'Anvers

R Glesener

GARE

36

31

Pl de
la Gare

Gare de Hollerich (600m);
Musée-Mémorial
de la Déportation (600m)

Pl de
Strasbourg

R du Fort Wedell

R Joseph
Junck

R de Strasbourg

**Gare
Centrale**

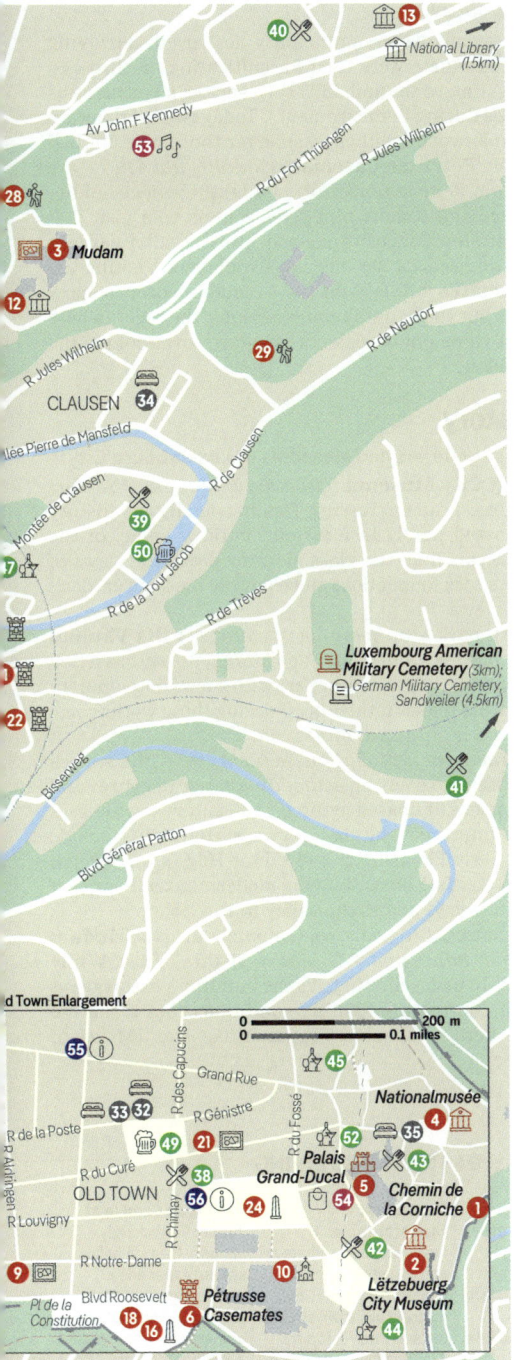

National Library (1.5km)

Av John F Kennedy

R du Fort Thüngen

R Jules Wilhelm

R de Neudorf

R Jules Wilhelm

CLAUSEN

Allée Pierre de Mansfeld

Montée de Clausen

R de Clausen

R de la Tour Jacob

R de Trèves

Luxembourg American
Military Cemetery (3km);
German Military Cemetery,
Sandweiler (4.5km)

Bisserweg

Blvd Général Patton

Old Town Enlargement

0 ————————— 200 m
0 ————————— 0.1 miles

Grand Rue

R des Capucins

R Génistre

R du Fossé

Nationalmusée

R de la Poste

R d'Allingen

R du Curé

OLD TOWN

R Chimay

Palais
Grand-Ducal

Chemin de
la Corniche

R Louvigny

R Notre-Dame

Pl de la
Constitution

Blvd Roosevelt

Pétrusse
Casemates

Lëtzebuerg
City Museum

continued from p261

THE UNLIKELY ROAD TO INDEPENDENCE

Luxembourg City's bastions and tunnels were once so indomitable that it was nicknamed the 'Gibraltar of the North'. Not quite impregnable, however, and the city fell to revolutionary France after a seven-month siege in 1792–93.

After Napoleon's demise in 1815, Luxembourg was declared a Grand Duchy to be ruled by the Dutch king through 'personal union', albeit diminished in size after the invention of Belgium. When Dutch King/Grand Duke William III died in 1890, his daughter Wilhelmina took the Dutch crown. However, Luxembourg's 'Salic' rules of succession (since changed) demanded a male heir. So Luxembourg's Grand Ducal line passed to Adolphe of Nassau. The 'personal union' with the Dutch crown ended, and Luxembourg's previously nominal independence became an unexpected reality.

vast fortifications were significantly destroyed. Surviving sections of casemate were used for cultivating mushrooms, ageing sparkling wines and, in WWII, sheltering as many as 35,000 locals during bombardments. Today two sections are open for exploration, neither feasible for those with limited mobility. The **Pétrusse Casemates** *(adult/child €18/12)* are accessed from Pl de la Constitution. Lighting effects add to the ambience and a short film gives context to a visit that descends 242 steps and exits one-way into the valley gardens below. Not advised for serious claustrophobes. Visiting the **Bock Casemates** *(adult/child €10/5)* could involve as many as 300 steps but you can skip some sections; the real fun here comes from views out of rock-cut 'windows' overlooking the valley far below.

Art & History

The greatest galleries and museums of Luxembourg City

Lëtzebuerg City Museum *(citymuseum.lu; adult/senior/child €5/3/free)* is an engrossing, family-friendly city history museum hosted partly in a former 'holiday home' of the Bishop of Orval. Take the glass elevator down for views of the building's rock foundations and enjoy the museum garden's panoramic views.

In a pretty park atop more fortifications, **Villa Vauban** *(villavauban.lu/en adult/under-26/child €5/3/free)* has a rich collection of 17th- to 19th-century art with a few contemporary extras. But what makes it thrilling is seeing those works come to life in a clever animated projection.

Nationalmusée *(nationalmusee.lu/en; free)*, the superb national museum, covers an astounding range of genres and crosses all epochs. It's based in three 17th-century townhouses confusingly interlinked by glass skyways. Highlights include some great early-Flemish art and Victor Hugo's 1871 sketch of Schengen Castle. Rooms showing modern Luxembourg art also have fine views across the valley to Kirchberg.

The city's most cutting-edge contemporary art is at **Mudam** *(mudam.com; adult/under-26/under-21 €10/7/free)*. While exhibitions can be fascinating, it's the building's extravagant spaces with contrasting lighting conditions that make the experience here so special. The architect was IM Pei of Louvre fame.

EATING IN LUXEMBOURG CITY: GASTRONOMIC DINING

Public House: Not a pub but a white-tablecloth dining experience within the historic Casino Luxembourg. *noon-2pm Tue-Sat & 6.30-8.30pm Wed-Sat* €€

Dans le Noir?: Dine in complete darkness at this mould-breaking experiential restaurant served by blind waitstaff in a Kirchberg Hotel. *6.45pm Thu, Fri & Sat* €€€

Restaurant Clairefontaine: Favourite of diplomats and ministers with a contemporary feel and discreet old-town street terrace. *noon-1.30pm & 7.15-9pm Mon-Fri* €€€

La Villa de Camille et Julien: Refreshingly unstuffy for a Michelin-starred experience, combining ecological awareness with culinary refinement. *noon-1.45pm & 7-8.45pm Tue-Sat* €€€

WALKING THE VIEWS

This walk shows you the city's contrasting main areas and many of the most photogenic viewpoints. To skip the more strenuous second half, return by tram from Mudam to the city centre.

START	END	LENGTH
Spuerkeess	Nationalmusée	6km, 2½ hours

Start beside the grand, round-towered **①** **Spuerkeess bank building** (1913). Cross the slightly older **②** **Pont Adolphe**, enjoying classic views of Vaubanesque star-point bastions and the leafy, deep-cut Pétrusse Valley. Views continue from triangular **③** **Place de la Constitution**. Look inside the **④** **cathedral**, consider a café-stop on **⑤** **Place d'Armes**, then cross Pl Guillaume and admire the **⑥** **Palais Grand-Ducal**. Follow off-beat bar-street Rue du Nord and pass the **⑦** **Badenstalt** spa-building, walking towards the **⑧** **Fondation Jean-Pierre Pescatore**, a monastery-like old-folks home where Patton installed his WWII command centre. A spectacular, toe-curling descent by **⑨** **Pfaffenthal Glass Elevator**

gets you near **⑩** **Porte d'Eich** stone tower. Cross the Alzette River on the Béinchen fortified walkway, then use the lift/funicular/walkway combination via **⑪** **Pfaffendal-Kirchberg station** to reach **⑫** **Mudam**. Descend through the hefty fortification-remnants of **⑬** **Fort Obergrünewald**, now a set of perched gardens. An easily missed, slightly overgrown **⑭** **stairway** descends to Allee de Mansfield. Climb past the **⑮** **Youth Hostel**, then steeply up to the Montee de Claussen for fabulous views all along the **⑯** **Bock** as you pass the **⑰** **casemates entrance** and stroll the glorious **⑱** **Chemin de la Corniche** pedestrian promenade. Loop back through old-town lanes to finish at the excellent, free **⑲** **Nationalmusée**.

Gëlle Fra, the wreath-bearing golden maiden here, commemorates Luxembourg's WWI casualties. Salvaged and hidden during WWII occupation, she was 'lost' until 1980, when discovered beneath the main stand of the national football stadium.

An architecturally original, sinuous 'passerelle' walkway-bridge is raised among the trees, adding appeal to this section of the walk to Mudam.

To enjoy a great view with a beer or cocktail, head for the hidden little terrace within the cosy music bar **Mirador**.

LUXEMBOURG CITY FOR FREE

There is a lot you don't have to pay for including all public transport, the brilliant **Nationalmusée** (p264), **Dräi Eechelen** (p261) and **Europa Experience** (p267).

There are free evenings at **Mudam** (p264; *6-8pm Wed*), **Lëtzebuerg City Museum** (p264; *6-8pm Thu*) and **Villa Vauban** (p264) *(6-9pm Fri)*.

Free contemporary art galleries include **Casino Luxembourg**, a former society mansion at which composer-virtuoso Franz Liszt gave his last concert in 1886, and **Ratskeller** in the cellar of the 1909 Cercle Cité building. **Free public toilets** next door.

Restaurants usually charge for water but there are free **drinking water** fountains notably opposite the Levi's store on Grand Rue.

SABINO PARENTE/SHUTTERSTOCK

Bars and restaurants in Luxembourg Old Town

Fireworks & Fizz

A city of celebrations

Luxembourg is often portrayed as a slightly staid place and it's true that on Sundays parts of the city can feel almost comatose. However, you'll quickly rethink this idea on Thursday to Saturday nights if you hit bars like **Urban** in the Old Town, or the seething **Rives de Clausen** pub-restaurant zone.

Throughout the summer there's the added boost of festivities that seem to come almost weekly. Particularly enjoyable is **Luxembourg National Day**, with revellers popping corks on bottles of fizz all around the city centre on 22 June in anticipation of the **Fakelzuch torchlight procession**. After a big firework display, parties continue into the night. And that's before the actual day, which is officially 23 June.

Earlier in June, the **Fête de la Musique** is a week-long series of free concerts, then in mid-July the joyous **Blues 'n' Jazz Rallye** sees two more days of partying around open-air stages and pub gigs.

Heart of Europe

Luxembourg and the EU

The EU's organisational structure, including commission, council and parliament, creates a complex bureaucracy that is mainly spread between Brussels, Strasbourg and Luxembourg.

Famed for its excellent carrot cake.

 DRINKING IN LUXEMBOURG CITY: OUR PICKS

Liquid Bar: Cosy house-pub in the Grund with great beers and live jazz/blues evenings on Tuesday and Thursday. *5pm-1am Tue-Fri, 1pm-1am Sat-Sun*

Paname: Multi-faceted, Art Deco-styled cafe with barista coffee, street terrace, cocktails and a great-value lunch-of-the-day. *10am-1am Mon-Fri, 9am-3am Sat, 9am-1am Sun*

De Gudde Wëllen: In summer, queue for their tree-shaded 'Gudde Weather' view terrace. In winter or on music nights, head inside one street above. *5pm-late Tue-Sat*

Konrad Café & Bar: Everyone seems to know each other in this Bohemian wonderland, equally inviting for wine or coffee. *10am-1am*

Curiously what's called the European Parliament buildings in Luxembourg don't actually host parliamentarians, just the offices for support staff such as document translators. This significant detail is barely mentioned in their **Europa Experience** (*europa-experience.eu; free),* a hi-tech if glitchy new museum designed to help European citizens understand the role of their MEPs and to see how EU decisions shape everyday life across the continent. There are some great ideas but the VR 'be-an-MEP' game feels contrived and the seven-minute 360° cinema experience raises more questions than it answers. Access requires passport/ID checks and an airport-style search.

The venue is one of many glass-walled EU and banking offices in the modernist Kirchberg quarter. Most are architecturally functional and closed to the public. The main exceptions are **Mudam** (p264), and the **Philharmonie** (*philharmonie.lu/en),* an eye-catching concert hall that looks like an architectural optical illusion. The **National Library** (*bnl.public.lu/en*) hosts occasional exhibitions.

Scars of War

Luxembourg City's WWII connections

The **Luxembourg American Military Cemetery** (*abmc.gov),* 4km from central Luxembourg City at Hamm, is a deeply moving sight. Over 5000 white graves and commemorative pillars remember the US soldiers who gave their lives for the double liberation of the Grand Duchy, first in September 1944 and again in the Battle of the Bulge that Christmas. Also here lies war hero General George Patton, who died not in battle but in a 1945 car accident. He was originally buried as just one of the many fallen. However, the large numbers of visitors who crowded the site led his grave to be moved to provide more access space.

For balance and further reflection, continue 1.5km further east to Sandweiler and contemplate the vast and equally sombre **German Military Cemetery** (*kriegsgraeberstaetten. volksbund.de/en/friedhof/sandweiler*) with nearly 11,000 graves.

In Luxembourg City centre, the former abbey of **Neimënster** (Abbaye de Neumünster; *neimenster.lu*) is now a multi-function arts and events space. However, during the period of Nazi occupation it had been used as a political prison. The sculptor **Lucien Wercollier** was incarcerated here in 1942 for refusing to produce pro-Nazi symbols, and later sent to a concentration camp. Though scarred, he survived and 25 of his works are now displayed here. Many others never returned. Luxembourg youths were forcibly conscripted to fight for Germany and some 800 Jews were sent to death camps. They generally departed from the **Gare de Hollerich** where there's a **Deportation Memorial** and permanent exhibition. Visits are Tuesday to Friday afternoons only or by appointment (*servicememoire@me.etat.lu*).

GENERAL PATTON

Famed for his swagger, ivory-handled pistol and almost comically foul-mouthed pronouncements, US General George Patton (1885–1945) is a WWII hero in Luxembourg. Daring and decisive, he pivoted the entire Third Army (250,000 men) to cut off the German counter-attack of December 1944. While based in Luxembourg City, he would stay at the **Hotel Alfa** and work from a command centre installed at the **Fondation Jean-Pierre Pescatore**, a grand monastery-like old people's home that dates from 1892. Some claim that Patton's prayers in the complex's chapel led to divine intervention, providing suitable weather for the battle's denouement.

He's buried at Hamm and there's the **General Patton Museum** (p270) at Ettelbruck.

OTHER WWII SITES

Other monuments and battle museums in northern Luxembourg and the Ardennes region of Belgium include a **Patton museum** (p270) at Ettelbruck, Luxembourg's **National Museum of Military History** at Diekirch and various experiences linked to the Battle of the Bulge at Bastogne (p235).

Beyond Luxembourg City

Wine to the west, castles north and post-industrial revivals to the south with plenty of music and attractive countryside in between.

An hour's ride from Luxembourg City you will find fascinating museums and regeneration projects in the post-industrial cities of the Minett. Discover castle villages in the west or north of the Grand Duchy. In the Mullerthal (aka Mëllerdall) region you can take brief strolls or longer woodland hikes that reveal intriguing micro-canyons. And in the east, it's fun to jump on a hired bicycle to trundle along the pretty Moselle Valley, stopping at wineries to taste the local fizz. Any sight is potentially a day trip from Luxembourg City, but your experience will generally prove more memorable if you stay overnight, perhaps in antique Vianden, magical little Esch-sur-Sûre or historic Clervaux.

Ansembourg

TIME FROM LUXEMBOURG CITY: **35MIN**

Driving through Castle Village

Ansembourg's **Grand Château** *(gcansembourg.eu; free)* is not Luxembourg's most dramatic castle-mansion, but its formal garden is an absolute delight. In a lush, mostly wooded valley of chestnut and copper beech, it twitters with birdsong with manicured terraces leading down to the (mostly hidden) river via an avenue of whitewashed statuary, espaliered fruit trees, a series of fountains and a tunnel of lilac.

As 20 minutes is enough to visit the gardens, it makes sense to combine Alsembourg with a low-key scenic drive via the very pretty Eisch Valley. Start in **Koerich**, whose hefty 14th-century castle ruin, **Gréiweschlass**, doubles as performance space for cultural events like mid-July's **Beautiful Decay festival**,

---

GETTING AROUND

Wherever you're going, the app/website *mobiliteit.lu/en* accurately identifies the best real-time public transport options. While trains and buses serve all main towns and villages, having your own wheels is helpful for linking outlying settlements or rural castles, especially if you don't want to return to Luxembourg City or other hub towns. Bicycle hire is well thought out in the Moselle Valley and around Echternach, with baggage transfers available for hikers and cyclists through *movewecarry.lu*.

Blast Furnace Belval, Esch-sur-Alzette

MINETT STORIES: STEEL & PEOPLE

Luxembourg's southwest Minett region is nicknamed the 'land of red rocks' and counterpoints a series of re-greened bio-reserves with the remnants of a once-powerful steel industry. The mining of iron ore deposits here took off in the 1840s in tandem with Europe's boom in railway building. It would come to totally reshape and dominate Luxembourg's economy until the mid-1970s.

As well as leaving physical remnants like old blast furnaces at Esch-sur-Alzette and mines at Rumelange, a major effect of the country's era of industrialisation was demographic: first farmers from the north moved south, then Germans, Italians and, from the 1960s, Portuguese came to fill labour shortages. Today almost 50% of Luxembourg's population are immigrants. Discover the region through personal tales at *minett-stories.lu/en*.

(beautifuldecay.lu). En route pass through **Septfontontaines** where you can glimpse but not visit the private **castle**.

Finish by ascending the steep lane from Alsembourg to **Hollenfels**, which has a good value cafe-pizzeria and a medieval **castle tower** with dry-moat ringed courtyard and great views (currently closed for long-term renovation).

Esch-sur-Alzette   TIME FROM LUXEMBOURG CITY: 25MIN 🚆

Discovering Belval's post-industrial regeneration

In 2022, Luxembourg's second city was European capital of culture. That might seem unlikely in a place best known for rusting steelworks, but in the post-industrial **Belval quarter**, two gigantic blast furnaces have now been very imaginatively preserved as the startling focus of an impressive new regeneration project. One has now been fused with a very contemporary facade to create **Blast Furnace Belval** *(fonds -belval.lu; adult/child €5/3)* where you can explore inside the looming giant. You can see sections of another furnace rising above and inside the stylishly retro-modernist **Café Saga** *(#sagabelval; noon-11pm Mon-Fri)*.

Also in Belval is **Rockhal** *(rockhal.lu),* Luxembourg's biggest live-music venue on a street sexily named Avenue du Rock'n'Roll. It's served directly by **Belval-Université** train station that looks like a 1960s vision of a UFO.

The 'wings' are made from cauliflower, not chicken.

 EATING IN MINETT REGION: OUR PICKS

Table du Chef:	La Maison Lefèvre:	Rucolino: All-vegan,	Brasserie Schmëdd:
Classy yet affordable Portuguese cuisine and bargain lunch deals in Dudelange town centre. *11am-2pm daily & 6-10pm Wed-Sat* €	Gourmet food at bistro prices in a splendidly restored 1897 Esch-sur-Alzette townhouse. *noon-1.30pm Tue-Sun & 6.30-9pm Tue-Sat* €€€	Italian-influenced snacks and meals with lots of imagination, also in Dudelange. Great value. *11.45am-2.30pm & 6.30pm-11pm Tue-Sat* €	Contemporary dining attached to the Ellergron nature centre. Lunch specials highlight local ingredients. *11am-11pm Wed-Sat,to 7pm Sun* €€

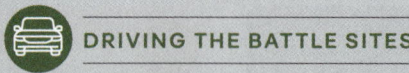

DRIVING THE BATTLE SITES

Visit key sites linked to 1944 WWII battles, interspersed with older castles and some lovely scenery.

START	END	LENGTH
Vianden	Vianden	125km, all day

Get to grips with events of the 1944 Battle of the Bulge and the wartime context at Luxembourg's two most important WWII museums, the **❶ National Museum of Military History** (MNMH) in Diekirch and the mural-fronted **❷ General Patton Museum** in Ettelbruck. Then drive Route 27 along the lovely Sûre Valley and climb to dramatic **❸ Bourscheid Castle**, Luxembourg's most memorable ruined fortress. Rollercoaster west through beautiful woodland hills, then unwind in the picturesque castle village of **❹ Esch-sur-Sûre**.

Route N12 brings you to WWII 'martyr town' Wiltz. Survey old Wiltz' ridge-top situation from beside **❺ 'Blood-and-Guts'**, a salvaged US Sherman Tank. Then descend Grande Rue to the **❻ Wiltz**

Castle Complex, which contains a small WWII museum plus microbrewery, historic tannery, and the amphitheatre that hosts the three-week Wiltz Festival in July. Nearby, the **❼ Streikdenkmal** climbable tower commemorates Luxembourg's 1942 general strike that started in Wiltz in protest at Nazi occupation/conscription. After a very pretty drive through soft woodland contours and riverside meadows, **❽ WWII artillery piece** announces your arrival in Clervaux, site of the first tank battle in the Battle of the Bulge. The gigantic whitewashed **❾ castle** is where Clervaux's valiant last US defenders finally surrendered on 18 December, 1944. Return to Vianden via charming riverside lanes following the German border.

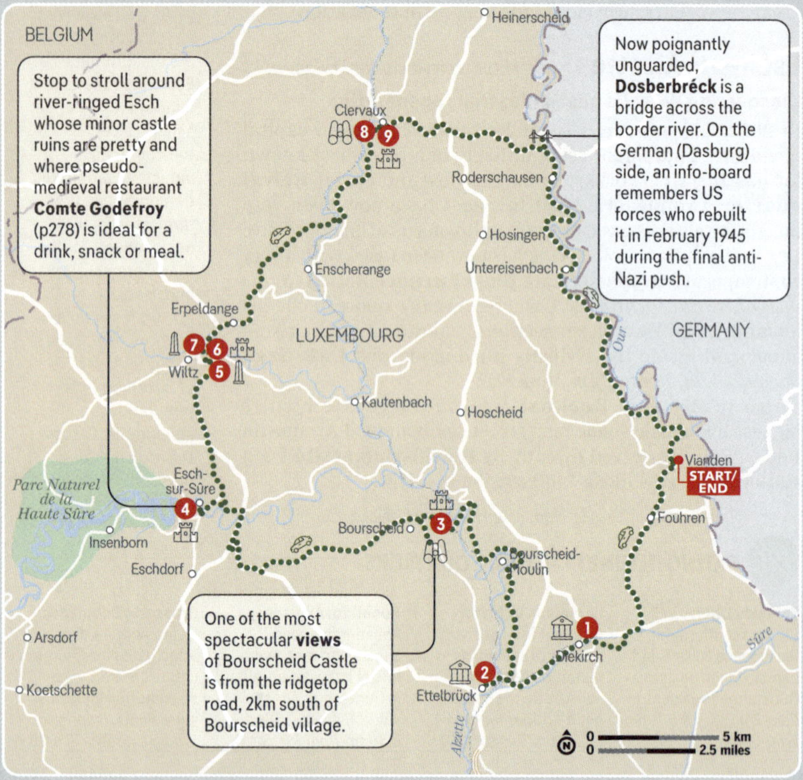

Stop to stroll around river-ringed Esch whose minor castle ruins are pretty and where pseudo-medieval restaurant **Comte Godefroy** (p278) is ideal for a drink, snack or meal.

Now poignantly unguarded, **Dosberbréck** is a bridge across the border river. On the German (Dasburg) side, an info-board remembers US forces who rebuilt it in February 1945 during the final anti-Nazi push.

One of the most spectacular **views** of Bourscheid Castle is from the ridgetop road, 2km south of Bourscheid village.

BELGIUM

Heinerscheid

Clervaux ❽ ❾

Roderschausen

Enscherange

Hosingen

Untereisenbach

Erpeldange

LUXEMBOURG

GERMANY

❼ ❻
Wiltz ❺

Kautenbach

Hoscheid

Esch-sur-Sûre

Parc Naturel de la Haute Sûre

❹

Insenborn

Eschdorf

Bourscheid

❸

Bourscheid-Moulin

Vianden
START/END

Fouhren

Arsdorf

Koetschette

❶

Diekirch

❷
Ettelbrück

Alzette

Sûre

Uur

0 ⎯⎯⎯⎯ 5 km
0 ⎯⎯⎯⎯ 2.5 miles

Mining memories

Central Esch, 3km southeast of Belval, can feel like a prosperous French provincial city if you stick to Rue de l'Alzette, but is significantly more ragged elsewhere. At the southernmost edge of town, where workers once laboured at the Katzenberg Mine (1881–1967), the small **Musée de la Mine Cockerill** *(cockerill. lu; free)* gives insights into the way they lived and worked, notably in the 1880s. Don't miss the clothes-chains. With delicious irony, this post-industrial site also hosts **Ellergronn** *(visitminett.lu/place/centre-d-accueil-ellergronn; free),* a cleverly conceived ecological centre where statistics highlight the ill effects of humanity on nature. A Greta Thunberg cut-out sits among flip charts addressing possible solutions, and the surrounding area is full of hikes and cycling trails.

Rumelange
TIME FROM LUXEMBOURG CITY: **45MIN**

Industrial underground

For Luxembourg's most immersive industrial experience, head to the **National Mining Museum** *(mnm.lu; adult/child €12/6)* in Rumelange. But do prebook; slots are limited and mostly in the afternoons. Dress for temperatures of around 12°C as you'll actually be going into the iron-ore mine, initially on a little narrow-gauge mineral-line train that starts above ground tootling past former open-cast pits now reclaimed by nature. There's a lot of equipment to observe and guides give comprehensive explanations of the mining process as you get off the train and walk through sections of workings.

Dudelange
TIME FROM LUXEMBOURG CITY: **20MIN**

Ironworks to festival town

The motto of Dudelange (aka Diddeling) is 'On dirait le sud', evoking to Francophone ears dreamy images of a laid-back Mediterranean landscape. That's quite a stretch for a post-industrial town formerly divided in half by mountainous piles of iron works slag waste. Today, however, Dudelange hosts several major music festivals, notably **Jazz Machine** (May), **Usina** (early June) and **Fête de la Musique** (mid-June). Its 'Italian Quarter', now more Portuguese than Italian, overlooks the Neischmelz regeneration zone where former factories house the **VEWA** *(vewa.lu)* craft workshops and **Kantin** *(kantin.lu),* a contemporary bar-café/microbrewery. Nearby, **CNA** *(cna.lu)* combines plush cinema and exhibition space.

Meanwhile don't miss looking inside central Dudelange's twin-towered **Église Saint-Martin**: behind a fairly standard church exterior lies a dazzling marvel of rich murals and stained glass above a gilded altar.

Schengen & Remerschen
TIME FROM LUXEMBOURG CITY: **1HR**

Home of hassle-free European travel

In the far southeast corner of Luxembourg lies the small town of Schengen in whose then ivy-draped 1779 **castle**

LUXEMBOURG FOR CHILDREN

Pirateschëff: Free playground in the Aire Jeux Avenue Monterey, one of Luxembourg City's central parks, with swings, slides and the big pirate ship.

Parc Merveilleux: *(parc-merveilleux. lu/en adult/ child €15/10)* This compact zoo/theme park lets children feed some of the animals, there's a miniature railway and an adventure playground.

Bambësch Forest Playground: *(luxembourg-city. com/en/place/ parc/playground-bambesch; free)* Recently renovated on Luxembourg City's northern outskirts with vintage merry-go-round, wooden fortress, climbing frames, ziplines and sandpits.

Park Sënnesräich: *(sennesraich.lu; adult/under-13 €9/7)* Small but well-designed 'sensory park' in the far north, aimed mostly at under-12s. Maize-maze in mid-summer.

BEST MOSELLE WINERY TASTINGS

Cep d'Or *(cepdor.lu; times vary)* Modernist concrete tasting platform facing the river at Hëttermillen. Don't miss sampling their richly oaked Pinot Blanc Barrique.

Poll-Fabaire *(vinsmoselle.lu; 11am-8pm)* Imposing winery building in Wormeldange offering 6-fizz tasters *(€14)* on the river-facing terrace. On Sunday afternoons, witness a sweetly time-warped wine dance in one of the cellar rooms. Walking the 3.2km viticulture circuit from here takes in the Koeppchen chapel-shrine viewpoint.

Caves Henri Ruppert *(domaine-ruppert.lu; 3pm-9pm Wed-Sun)* Tastings and light snack boards in a modernist salon with unbeatable pool-fronted river views above Schengen.

Kox Winery *(domainekox.lu/en; by appointment)* Experimental boutique winery in Remich. Range includes Georgian-style *qvevri* (amphora-based) 'straw' wines.

tower (p279) Victor Hugo once stayed. However, if the name Schengen sounds familiar, that's more likely due to the 1985 and 1990 treaties signed here. These led to the border-free travel agreement across large parts of Europe – known to this day as the Schengen Area. Actually the signing took place aboard a boat called the *Prinzessin Marie-Astrid*, moored very symbolically mid-river where France, Germany and the Benelux meet. For the treaty's 40th anniversary in June 2025, the boat was restored and returned to this location facing a free, interactive **European Museum** *(visitschengen.lu)*.

Nature, art & wine at Remerschen

Biodiversum *(biodiversum.lu; free)* is a wetlands area with 2.5km of partly boardwalked trails and bird-watching spots plus a pay-beach, view-cafe and 'Carpodrome' fishing pond. It's hard to believe that this attractive lakeland space used to be a series of gravel pits. It's near Remerschen, focussed on a free nature centre, introducing local ecology and birds in a very striking truncated pyramid-shaped building.

In central Remerschen is an even more dazzlingly contemporary structure, the **Valentiny Foundation Building** *(valentiny-foundation.com; free, 2-6pm Wed-Sat)*: a startling bleached-white building with lattice-like cut-out windows underlining architect François Valentiny's statement that 'architecture is a permanent revolt against boredom and mediocrity'.

Next door, facing the modern youth hostel, is the vast 1940s **Caves du Sud** winery building. Its extensive wine shop is centred upon a boat-shaped bar that's ideal for tasting local varieties at very reasonable prices.

River Moselle

TIME FROM LUXEMBOURG CITY: **DAY TRIP** 🚗

River of wine tasting

The banks of the River Moselle that form the Luxembourg–Germany border between Wasserbillig and Schengen are pillowed with emerald green vineyard-lined hillsides that by autumn are groaning with grapes. The vines produce excellent *crémants* (*méthode traditionelle* sparkling wines) as well as a wide range of whites. A special delight are the softly balanced *pinot blanc*s, almost unique to Luxembourg.

Though interrupted with a few less attractive sections, the scene is generally very appealing, especially south of Ehnen where the rebuilt **Wäinhaus** *(entente-moselle.lu/en/musee-du-vin)* is due to reopen by 2027 as a wine-discovery centre. An exhibition in the building shows the plans.

Winemakers, most with tempting tasting rooms, are dotted widely along the flat riverside road. There's also a parallel cycle path and handily you can do one-way bicycle hires with **Rentabike Miserland** *(rentabike-miselerland.lu; 24hr from €12, free with a LuxembourgPass)* collecting or dropping off at Schengen, Remerschen, Remich, Ehenen, Grevenmacher or Wasserbillig.

If you want a winery tour as well as a taster, there are two classic options Wednesday to Sunday. Book at least 48

Vineyards, Moselle river valley

hours ahead to visit the **Caves St-Martin** *(cavesstmartin. lu/en/visite-des-caves adult/child from €9.50/5)* with its atmospheric tunnel-cellars hewn directly into the riverside cliffs 1.5km north of Remich. A popular alternative is **Bernard-Massard** *(bernard-massard.lu; from €8)* by the bridge in Grevenmacher. Humorous tours start hourly on the hour from an art-filled reception area with drop-ins possible, though consider prebooking online as places are limited.

Many tourists are drawn to **Remich**, where there are river-boat trips and a selection of eateries. The town itself can become unpleasantly overcrowded, particularly on summer Sundays, but on quieter days the several viewpoints on the heights above are pleasant, notably **Point de Vue Remich picnic site** 3km southwest on Rte 16 where you might occasionally find a pop-up wine tasting terrace.

Echternach

TIME FROM LUXEMBOURG CITY: **50MIN**

History & spirituality

Set in a garden-softened bend of the River Sûre, Echternach is considered Luxembourg's oldest city and one of its loveliest. The heart of town is a square full of cafe-bars flanking the **Dënzelt**, a neo-medieval former law court rebuilt with Gothic

ST WILLIBRORD & SPRINGPROZESSION

Echternach has Roman roots but its abbey was founded in 698 CE by Northumbrian-born missionary Willibrord, then Bishop of Utrecht. Among Willibrord's saintly miracles was not getting beaten to death by angry guardians of the pagan temples that he vandalised in the name of his god.

The church became powerful in the 11th century, spawning a renowned scriptorium and huge abbey. Though sacked in the French invasion of 1794 and bombed by Nazis in WWII, both church and abbey were splendidly rebuilt. And there's still a St-Willibrord pilgrimage which culminates on Whit Tuesday (51 days after Easter Sunday) with Springprozession when thousands of people whip out their handkerchiefs and dance through the streets in formation.

 EATING & DRINKING AROUND MËLLERDALL

Fielser Stuff: Mountainous portions of honest, home-cooked classics plus Portuguese options in an unpretentious Larochette bar-restaurant. *9am-11pm Tue-Sun, to 3pm Mon* €

Beim Doktor: Traditional German-style beer-house serving schnitzels, sausage meals and more on a quiet but central Echternach square. *3-9pm Mon-Sat* €€

Auberge Rustique: Beaufort house-hotel (1790) serving excellent trout, sandwiches, quiches and more. Apple cake available between main meal times. *noon-7.30pm Apr-Oct* €€

Restaurant Mathes: Beautifully conceived, predominantly fish- and steak-based meals in a Moselle-facing dining room/terrace in Ahn. *noon-2pm Wed-Sun & 7-9pm Wed-Sat* €€€

273

Vianden's Reborn Castle

Luxembourg's best-restored castle utterly dominates the loveable old town of Vianden (p277). The gigantic structure had crumbled into a romantic ruin by the early 19th century and full reconstruction to its outwardly 13th-century form only started in 1977. But the result is a gem that looks fab from afar and feels genuine within, yet is relatively easy to explore: a lift allows some disabled access.

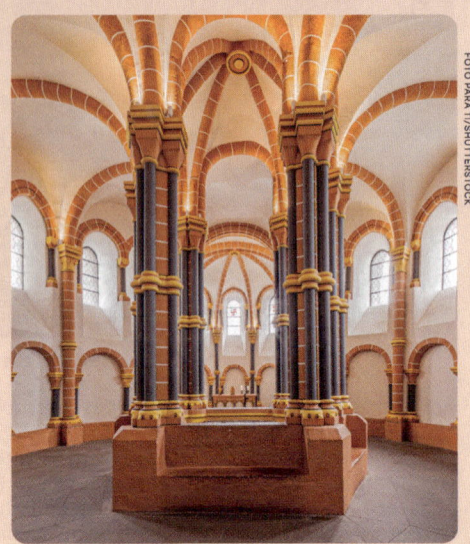

FOTO PARA TI/SHUTTERSTOCK

TOP TIPS

● Find the guest wi-fi code and optional luggage lockers (€2 coin deposit) behind the ticket booth on entry.

● The castle's visitor centre is bizarrely accessed through the cafe/shop from the Bailey, right near the start of the visit.

● Arrive early before the school groups and tour-coaches roll in.

PRACTICALITIES

● castle-vianden.lu/gb
● 10am-5.30pm Apr-Sep, to 4.30pm Mar & Oct, 10am-3.30pm Nov-Feb
● adult/student/under-13 €13/7/4

Inside the walls

Start in the easily overlooked visitor centre section where lots of trilingual, easy-to-grasp historical information adds to an exhibition area perched amid wall ruins. Discover that *caltrop* were something between land mines and barbed wire. But most importantly don't miss the utterly brilliant 10-minute wide-screen movie which uses CGI to recreate the castle in various epochs... and explains how archaeologists know what they know. Then use QR-coded explanations to explore the appealingly museumised heart of the castle on a 22-point self-guided tour, which gets more interesting as it progresses.

Views of the castle from outside

Even if you don't go inside, views of the crag-top castle are highly impressive. The building creates a looming presence when you stare up from the cluster of hotels and cafes around Vianden's central river-bridge. At night the fortifications are wistfully illuminated, taking on a lugubrious blue hue if you stand near Vianden's rather basic youth hostel. By day, a fun twist is to take Luxembourg's first **chairlift** *(adult/child €6.50/3.50)* up through the forests to a panoramic viewpoint, then walk 700m down to the castle entrance.

flourishes in 1895. Behind lies the imposing **Basilica of St Willibrord** *(willibrord.lu; free)*. Though it's a 20th-century rebuild after WWII bombing, its interior has a dark and convincingly understated neo-Romanesque magnificence augmented by 1950s stained glass. Descend to the crypt past two 7th-century sarcophagi to find the tomb of St Willibrord (p273) covered by an ornate white-stone canopy: his relics miraculously survived the WWII destruction. There's a free video to watch about Echternach's UNESCO-honoured Springprozession. And next door it's well worth the token entry fee to learn about the lives of medieval scribes in the abbey's former scriptorium.

The Basilica is at the heart of a vast former abbey site incorporating a **tourist office** but mostly used as a school. Peep through iron gates for glimpses of the fine 1736 **Orangery** or wander the riverside gardens to admire a 1761 **rococo pavilion**.

One kilometre south of the city centre, the **Villa Romane**, site of a 1st-century Roman villa, was discovered during the creation of the reservoir lake that now makes a popular boating and recreation area. The sparse, neatly maintained archaeological site is now set in a garden growing the kinds of medicinal species once used by Roman pharmacists.

On your bike, on your kayak

Bicycles can be hired through **Rentabike Mëllerdall** *(rentabike-mellerdall.lu)* which has a dozen pick-up and drop-off stations at campsites, hostels and tourist offices across the Mëllerdall (Mullerthal) region. While hills abound there's also an essentially flat riverside bicycle path following the River Sûre to Diekirch (27km). The PC2 route continues all the way to Luxembourg City, mostly following a former narrow-gauge railway line.

Alternatively kayakers can take bus 190 from Echternach to Dillingen and paddle back in a canoe rented from **Outdoor Freizeit** *(outdoorfreizeit.lu/en; one-/two-person canoe ride €25/40)*. You can usually paddle off between 10am and 2pm mid-June to mid-September, but call ahead to book and check appropriate water levels.

Müllerthal's woodlands & microcanyons

Across all the beautiful countryside in Luxembourg, no area is more magical than the woodlands of the **Mëllerdall** (**Mullerthal**) **region** with their pretty beech canopies and mossy rocks cut with streams and micro-canyons. The classic

BEST FOR CLASSIC MULLERTHAL GEOLOGY

Hohllay: (aka Huel Lee) Naturally formed cave-tunnels a 300m walk down from a small carpark outside Berdorf, yet visiting feels like you're bathing in birdsong.

Pérékop: Small parking area on the Echternach-Berdorf road lets you climb a scarily steep stairway through a narrow very tall micro-canyon. Return by the less perilous parallel stairway.

Schiessentümpel: Tiny stone bridge across a stream that's a famous if oversold beauty spot. The nearest carpark is a 600m (20-minute) walk south via a 'hanging stairway', which is the most interesting part of the experience.

Priedegtstull: One stairway leads to a rocky roadside overlook. Others climb the Werschrummschlëff micro-canyon.

 EATING & DRINKING NORTHEAST OF LUXEMBOURG CITY

| **Pizzeria Il Trio:** Inexpensive pizzas, pricier fish and meat dishes, and friendly service just north of Hollenfels castle. *noon-2pm & 6-9.30pm Wed-Sun* € | **Reilander Millen:** Brasserie fare from a roadside mill-restaurant right beside the main Mullerthal walking route. *noon-2pm & 6-9pm Wed-Sun* €€ | **Le Chalet:** Large informal multi-cuisine cafe-restaurant overlooking the beach-pools at Remerschen. *11am-10pm Tue-Sun* €€ | **Côté Cour:** Imaginative, mostly vegetarian gastronomy served in a tavern atmosphere within historic Bourglinster Castle. *noon-1.30pm & 7-9pm Wed-Sat* €€€ |

Kniddelen: Dumplings.

Lëtzebuerger Grillwurscht: White sausage. A BBQ favourite.

Blanne Jang: Bacon-wrapped cheese sausage.

Gromperekichelcher: Spiced pancakes made fritter-like from shredded potato.

Bouneschlupp: Green-bean soup with potatoes, onion and bacon.

Träipen: Luxembourg's take on black pudding, usually served with apple sauce.

Kachkéis: An intriguingly gloopy cheese spread.

Feiersténgszalot: Salad including beef and hard-boiled egg.

Rieslingspaschtéit: Slices of log-shaped meat-pie with wine-based jelly.

Bouchée à la reine: Vol-au-vent-based main course.

Judd mat Gaardebounen: Smoked pork with broad beans.

F'rell am Rèisleck: Trout in Riesling sauce.

Ham, Fritten an Zalot: Plate of cured meats with chips and salad.

Mëtschen: Various types of croissant-style pastry.

Hiecht mat Kraiderzooss: Pike-fish in a herb-based green sauce.

E1 walking route winds 6km from Echternach to Berdorf, passing through the **Wolfsschlucht** ('wolves' canyon') where a stone staircase leads to a fine viewpoint of such landscapes. Further on, the trail traverses the **Labyrinthe**, a succession of otherworldly cliffs and tight ravines, and there's a small open mini-cave system called **Hohllay** (aka Huel Lee; p275). Just beyond is Berdorf village with at least five cafes offering refreshment. You could then loop back to Echternach on the north side of the Aesbech Valley via the **Geierslee** viewpoint tower. Or simply take buses 191 or 211.

Beaufort
TIME FROM LUXEMBOURG CITY: **50MIN**

Castles & geology

Beaufort's former youth hostel is now home to the interactive **Geo Expo** (*naturpark-mellerdall.lu; free*), a modest info centre that highlights the special natural features of the region which, since 2022, has been designated the **Mëllerdall UNESCO Global Geopark**. The well-marked B1 round-trip hike here helps you discover the region's landscapes in about three hours. The starting point is near Beaufort's pair of valley-side **castles** (*beaufortcastles.com*): one a five-storey **medieval ruin** (*drop-in visits welcome, adult/student €7/4*), the other a 17th-century **Renaissance-style château** (*by guided tour only, up to three daily, adult/student €14/7 for both castles*).

Larochette
TIME FROM LUXEMBOURG CITY: **40MIN**

Commanding ruins

The ruins of **Château de Larochette** (*adult/student €7/4*) sit on a crag-top above the former mill-town of the same name. Up close, the castle is less complete than it had seemed from below and most of what you pay to see are stabilised wall stubs. However, the four-storey 1385 keep is intact with an interior that's sparse but offers a toe-curling view down the seemingly bottomless well within the hefty former kitchens. From central Larochette it's only 700m on climbing woodland footpaths, but by road it's 2km.

Luxembourg's blue jeans

Leave a deposit at the **tourist office** for a key to access the unstaffed, twin-site **Textil Museum** (*textilmuseelarochette.lu/ en*) that tells the intriguing tale of Larochette's former glories as a textile town. Who'd have guessed that it produced a leading brand of blue jeans until the 1980s?

Drachelay: a quieter taste of Mullerthal

One of Mëllerdall/Mullerthal's most delightful woodland walks is a 5km circular walk starting from a lonely **car park** 2km south of the church in **Nommern** or 4km west of Larochette. Steps help navigate the steepest micro-canyon sections, most memorably an outcrop called **Drachelay** where the path loops-the-loop with a tiny metal bridge. The whole area is far less frequented than equivalent walks nearer to Echternach.

TATIANA POPOVA/SHUTTERSTOCK

Ruins of medieval Beaufort Castle

Vianden

TIME FROM LUXEMBOURG CITY: **1-1½HR** 🚆 + 🚌

Victor Hugo gets everywhere

Vianden's big draw is its brooding **castle** (p274), which has been a tourist attraction for two centuries. It also hosts **Mittelalterfest**, Luxembourg's largest medieval festival In 1871, the castle's caretaker-architect was fired following complaints of substandard maintenance levelled by celebrity visitor Victor Hugo, who stayed several months in Vianden during his exile from France. The presence of the *Les Misérables* author is still celebrated. There's a bust, the **inn** where he would dine is now named after him, and across the road is a cute little **Victor Hugo Museum** *(visit-vianden.lu/ en/culture/victor-hugo-house; adult/under-26 €6/free)* in the house that hosted him. Walking the steep, cobbled **Grand-Rue** that rises from here to the castle entrance is an integral part of the Vianden experience.

Clervaux

TIME FROM LUXEMBOURG CITY: **1HR** 🚆

Rejoin the Family of Man

The **Family of Man** *(steichencollections-cna.lu/eng; adult/ under-22 €6/free)* is a black-and-white photo exhibition first unveiled in 1955 and so precious that, 70 years later,

FILLING STATION TOURISM

Luxembourg's fixed-price, low-tax policy on motor fuels makes it de rigueur for international motorists to fill up in the Grand Duchy. Coming from France on the A3 motorway, the **Aire de Berchem** is reputedly the world's biggest petrol station. Price differentials with Belgium are less significant, but a very bizarre sight awaits you at **Martelange**. Its banal main street is cut down the middle by the Luxembourg–Belgium border with unremarkable houses on one side and a surreally long strip of filling stations on the other.

Once you've refuelled, consider visiting the **Musée de l'Ardoise** *(ardoise.lu; adult/student/child €10/8/4)* at nearby Haute Martelange which details the town's pre-petrol-selling industry: slate mining. Wear warm clothes for the mine.

EATING IN VIANDEN: OUR PICKS

Fuku: Udon, sushi, and a range of Chinese and Thai dishes in a gently contemporary setting with reasonable prices. *11.30-2.20pm & 5.30-10pm Tue-Sun* €

Beim Hunn (Auberge Aal Veinen): Grill meals in a charming inn full of ancient beam work on the historic Grand Rue. *noon-3pm & 6-10pm Wed-Mon* €€

Pizzeria Petry: The Petry Hotel's restaurant has a range of great-value full meals but is especially renowned for its wood-fired, thin-crust pizza. *noon-2.30pm & 6-9pm* €

Hotel-Restaurant Victor Hugo: Castle-facing terrace or more staid interior for salads, trout and Luxembourgish food. Victor Hugo reputedly used to eat here. *noon-2.15pm & 6-9pm* €€

WHO WAS EDWARD STEICHEN?

Pioneering photographer Edward Steichen was world famous in the mid-20th century, having mixed with Rodin, Picasso and Richard Strauss. He saw photography as a window into the soul, and his portrait of Greta Garbo remains a classic. He also essentially 'invented' war photography.

However, his experience of the horrors of WWI and WWII led him to organise major exhibitions that sought instead to underline the overarching unity of the human experience. Though he had only spent the first 18 months of his life in his native Luxembourg before being taken to the US as a toddler (due to family poverty), he later returned as a hero to the Grand Duchy and bequeathed his collected works to the state.

it remains on display in almost its original format. And now with UNESCO honours. Painstakingly assembled by Edward Steichen, it was designed to be 'a show that you see with your heart', examining pictorially what it means to be human across all world cultures. Wi-fi and QR codes are provided to help you access a special app with child and adult versions of thought-provoking audio commentaries. Allow at least an hour here, and far more if you want to browse the library of photography books and Steichen volumes at the end of the tour.

The Family of Man is set within Clervaux's gigantic whitewashed **castle** authentically rebuilt after its destruction during the 1944 Battle of the Bulge. That history is covered by a second **museum** *(visit-clervaux.lu/en/patrimoine/ battle-and-castles-museum; adult/under-21 €5/free)* which also shows models of Luxembourg's many castles.

For more views of how the then-ruined castle looked in 1945, you could peruse photos behind the restored **Sherman tank** overlooking the central carpark just outside the castle's southwest wall. There's also a **GI statue** just east of Koener Hotel, showing a US serviceman whose relaxed-looking attitude recalls the calm-before-the-storm era of autumn 1944 when troops had thought that Clervaux would be an easy posting. Bronze townsfolk wave enthusiastically from a **'window' statue** opposite.

Let the spirit move you

A steep walk uphill from the castle takes you past the Church of Sts-Come and Damien, then through woodland to the **Abbaye de St Maurice** *(abbaye-clervaux.lu)*. Apart from the tree-framed views, the main attraction is that this is a working monastery that encourages visitors to attend their services. Timings are listed on the website's French-language page *(abbaye-clervaux.lu/fr/bienvenue)*. Each relatively short prayer session is chanted in Gregorian plainsong, and though there are generally only a dozen monks present, the ethereal sound resonates mellifluously around the large, 1909 neo-Romanesque church. In the crypt, a sweetly naive Expo celebrates (in French) the joys of monastic brotherhood and explains how, in WWII, Nazis commandeered the site as a Hitler Youth school.

EATING IN NORTHERN LUXEMBOURG: OUR PICKS

Beim Schlass: Gourmet-tinged dinners and fine-value set lunches with a summer street terrace near Wiltz's castle. *12.30-2.30pm Wed-Sun, 6.30-8pm Wed-Sat* €€

Brasserie de Vieux Moulin: Hearty local meals in a bierkeller beside the river a short drive from Bourscheid Castle. *11am-2pm & 6-10pm Tue-Sun* €€

Beim Luss: Excellent Clervaux bakery with unfussy interior and street terrace. Filled rolls, pancakes and a weekday €15.50 soup-and-meal lunch deal. *7am-6pm Tue-Sun* €

Restaurant Comte Godefroy: Heraldic details and the 1824 building add to the old-world charm of this quality brasserie-cafe in the heart of Esch-sur-Sûre. *noon-10pm* €€

Places We Love to Stay

€ Budget   €€ Midrange   €€€ Top End

Luxembourg City

MAP p262

Youth Hostel, Luxembourg City € State-of-the-art HI hostel whose terrace has great views up towards the Old Town (p265). Bring padlock for lockers.

Hôtel Perrin €€ One of several options on the Rue du Strasbourg near the central station. The easily missed reception retains elements of 1932 glasswork. Bargain prices some weekends.

Hôtel Français €€ Unpretentious but fair-value rooms above a classic brasserie in the city's cafe-life epicentre.

Hôtel Le Place d'Armes €€€ Appealingly renovated rooms retaining lots of hefty beams and gilt-work. It's right on the main cafe square.

Hôtel Parc Beaux Arts €€€ Exclusive historic property with original artworks and a 'secret' lounge in the eves. Brilliantly located in the heart of the old town.

La Pipistrelle €€€ Four gorgeous B&B suites in an 18th-century property that's essentially carved into the cliff between Grund and the old city.

Hotel Les Jardins d'Anaïs €€€ Oasis of cultured calm with a retro twist, sitting in gardens on a bend of the river, just beyond Claussen. Payable private parking.

Schengen

Youth Hostel Remerschen € One of Luxembourg's most impressive HI hostels fills a striking contemporary building in central Remerschen, 3km north of Schengen.

Hotel Château Schengen €€ Comfortable hotel in the rebuilt mansion-castle behind the tower sketched by Victor Hugo in 1871.

Bourscheid

Cocoon Hôtel Belair €€ Old-fashioned hotel in beautiful riverside lawns staring up towards the dramatic Bourscheid Castle ruins.

Echternach & Berdorf

Youth Hostel Echternach € Sports-oriented HI hostel at the lakeside on the edge of town with modern facilities, bike rental and 14m climbing wall.

Hotel Bel Air €€ Set in four hectares of parkland, 1.5km out of Echternach towards Berdorf, it's better value than most town-centre options and has a spa and pool.

Trail-Inn €€ Central Berdorf hotel has been given a youthful, clean-lines makeover to encourage nature fans and cyclists. Open year round.

Wollefstuerm €€ One of three medieval (if heavily rebuilt) city-wall towers in Echternach that have been converted into holiday rental apartments for families (you get three double rooms). Two-night minimum, €50 cleaning fee.

Wiltz & Esch-sur-Sûre

Hotel-Restaurant Beim Schlass €€ Ideally located family-style hotel right by the entrance to the castle-park in Wiltz. Excellent, fair-value restaurant.

Hôtel de la Sûre €€€ Rooms in antique houses dotted all around lovely Esch-sur-Sûre, with reception and atmospheric restaurant at the foot of the upper castle ruin.

Vianden

Auberge Aal Veinen € Shoehorns nine rooms into its medieval timbered building, all with quirks. It incorporates the upper town's liveliest cafe-restaurant.

Hotel Heinz €€ Renovated rooms in a former monastic brewery-inn with retained historic elements, wisteria-draped balconies and limited parking.

Hôtel-Restaurant Petry €€ Creates a country-rustic vibe while providing children's play-facilities, an umbrella-shaded terrace and free use of the swimming pool in nearby sister-hotel Belle-Vue.

Clervaux

Hotel Koener €€ Large, super-central hotel with indoor pool. For a modest supplement, upgrade from 1980s-style standard rooms to stylishly renovated 'superior' options.

Château d'Urspelt €€€ Romantic castle-hotel 3km northeast of Clervaux with spa and gastronomic restaurant. Part of profits fund a charity.

TOOLKIT

The chapters in this section cover the most important topics you'll need to know about in Belgium & Luxembourg. They're full of nuts-and-bolts information and valuable insights to help you understand and navigate Belgium & Luxembourg and get the most out of your trip.

Arriving
p282

Getting Around
p283

Money
p284

Accommodation
p285

Family Travel
p286

Health & Safe
Travel
p287

Food, Drink
& Nightlife
p288

Responsible
Travel
p290

Accessible
Travel
p292

LGBTIQ+
Travellers
p294

Nuts & Bolts
p295

Language
p296

Vismarkt (p130), Bruges

Arriving

The main ports of entry in Belgium and Luxembourg are Brussels Airport and Luxembourg Airport. Both are about 20 minutes away from their city centres, by train, tram or bus. Low-cost airlines mainly land at Brussels South Charleroi Airport, 45 minutes away from Brussels by bus. Careful when you book: many travellers confuse the two Brussels airports.

Visa

EU nationals don't need a visa for any length of stay. Those from the UK, Canada, New Zealand, the US and Australia can stay for up to 90 days in any six months without a visa.

SIM Card

EU residents benefit from the portability of their mobile plans. If you need a local SIM card, you can get one at Brussels Airport (there's no shop at Luxembourg airport).

Border Crossing

Belgium and Luxembourg are surrounded by fellow EU and Schengen countries. Once admitted into the Schengen area, you can freely move between one country and the next.

Wi-Fi

Free wi-fi is available at both airports and at main train stations. It's widely available everywhere else; you might just need to ask for a password.

Getting from the Airport

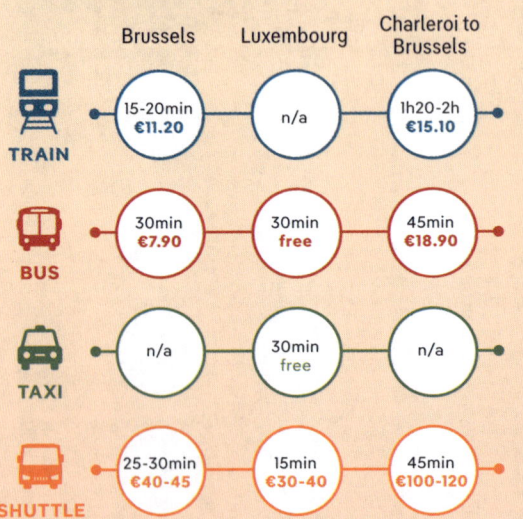

	Brussels	Luxembourg	Charleroi to Brussels
TRAIN	15-20min €11.20	n/a	1h20-2h €15.10
BUS	30min €7.90	30min free	45min €18.90
TAXI	n/a	30min free	n/a
SHUTTLE	25-30min €40-45	15min €30-40	45min €100-120

ETIAS

The European Travel Information and Authorisation System (ETIAS), also known as 'the European ESTA', has been delayed several times but should be implemented in 2026. Residents from visa-exempt countries will be required to have a travel authorisation to enter 30 European countries, including the EU, Iceland, Norway and Switzerland. The authorisation form will have to be filled out online prior to departure and submitted with a fee of €20. Make sure to check and get your ETIAS if it is in operation before your departure.

Scan to find out more

# Getting Around

You can easily move around by public transport in both countries, but the charming towns and villages of Wallonia and Luxembourg are more easily explored by car.

TRAVEL COSTS

Rental
Around €80 (B), €95 (L)

Petrol
Around €1.62L (B), €1.46 (L)

EV charging
48-53¢/kWh

Train from Brussels to Luxembourg
€26

Public Transport

Train and bus services are extensive and affordable, even free in Luxembourg *(mobiliteit.lu)*. Wallonia, being less populated, does not have the same coverage as Flanders and Brussels, but cities are well connected. Trains in Belgium are operated by SNCB/NMBS *(belgiantrains. be)* with no need to book in advance. Use the app for easy purchase. Other public transport is region-based: STIB/MIVB *(stib.be)* for Brussels, De Lijn for Flanders *(delijn. be),* and TEC for Wallonia *(letec.be).*

Train Deals in Belgium

Travelling by train on weekends (Friday 7pm to Sunday)? Enjoy a 50% discount on return tickets. For multiple destinations or group travel, the 10-trip Multipass (Standard, or Youth until 26 years of age) offers great value on longer journeys and can be shared between several persons. There are plans to change the pricing structure in the near future, so be sure to check *belgiantrains.be* for updates.

TIP

Bringing your bike on a Belgian train costs €4 per journey. Check the BikeOnTrain website for availability. It's free in Luxembourg.

RIGHT OF WAY

Belgium enforces strict right-of-way rules: priority is always given to vehicles coming from the right, even without signage – this is known as an 'absolute right'. A red-bordered triangle with a black X may mark such intersections. Drivers must yield at all times unless traffic lights, road signs or police override the rule.

DRIVING ESSENTIALS

Drive on the right.

Seatbelts must be worn by all occupants.

0.5/0.25

Blood alcohol limit is 0.5mg in Belgium, 0.25mg in Luxembourg.

Hiring a Car

Most rental companies require the driver to be 21 years old or over and to have a credit card. Airport hire is slightly more expensive than city hire, and the majority of cars are manual; an automatic will cost you extra.

Road Conditions

Belgium's motorway network is compact, toll-free and illuminated at night. The secondary roads are also good, but Wallonia's system is less maintained. Despite its small size, Luxembourg has six motorways (also toll-free) and excellent secondary roads.

Low Emission Zones

If you bring your own car, note that Brussels, Ghent and Antwerp have established Low Emission Zones to restrict older and more polluting vehicles from entering. Check if your car meets the criteria by registering it for free on the city's respective LEZ websites. It's mandatory.

Money

CURRENCY: EURO (€)

Taxes & Refunds

VAT is always included in both countries. Non-EU residents having bought goods with a minimum invoice of €125 (in Belgium) or €74 (in Luxembourg) are entitled to a refund. Don't forget to request your Tax Free Form. Have it stamped by customs and file it at the airport.

Digital Payment

Paying with your phone, smartwatch or contactless bank card is commonplace. For larger purchases, you will still be asked to enter your PIN. In Brussels and Flanders, public transport accepts contactless payment, but Wallonia's TEC still requires the purchase of tickets or passes (which can be done on their app).

Credit Card

Visa and Mastercard credit cards are accepted almost everywhere (it's not the case for American Express and Diners Club). Some smaller hotels or restaurants do not accept card payments.

Tipping

Service is included in prices at bars and restaurants, but if you are happy with it, tipping is appreciated.

Eating Out

Are you a foodie but intimidated by high menu prices? Many fine-dining restaurants offer affordable lunch menus, sometimes costing half of their dinner prices.

HOW MUCH FOR A...

Museum entry
€10–20 (B), €7–8 (L)

Discount card for attractions
from €39 (B), from €21 (L)

Train Brussels–Bruges **€17.50**

Train Luxembourg City–Esch-sur-Alzette
Free (second class), €3 (first)

HOW TO... Save Euros

Check museum policies for discounts (under-18, students, 65+). If you plan to visit a lot of museums, a city card (Brussels Card, LuxembourgPass, Musea Brugge Card) can save you money, and public transport is often included.

In Belgium, many museums are free on the first Sunday of the month. In Luxembourg, some open late on Tuesday or Wednesday for free night visits.

BUDGET

Belgium and Luxembourg are on the pricier side of Western Europe. Accommodation and eating out at a restaurant can cost you a pretty penny. If beer is cheap in Belgium, museums are expensive, and the opposite is true in Luxembourg! If you are travelling on a tight budget, many museums in Wallonia and Brussels are free on the first Wednesday or Sunday of the month. In Luxembourg, some open late on Tuesday or Wednesday for free night visits. If you are a student under 26, you're in luck: many museums in Luxembourg are free or at a discounted rate.

LOCAL TIP

Always keep loose change for the toilet attendants (known as 'Madame/Monsieur Pipi' at cinemas, clubs, public toilets or even some restaurants). They only take cash.

MONEY TOOLKIT

Accommodation

Old Stones Stays

Belgium and Luxembourg are full of historic buildings (castles, monasteries, almshouses) and some of them have found a second life as tourist accommodation. There are options for every budget, from luxury resorts to boutique hotels, B&Bs and even hostels. The Flemish art cities are particularly blessed with choices.

Unusual Places to Stay

Experiential tourism is all the rage – be it a yurt, a tiny house in the countryside, a cabin in the trees, a caravan in a park, a safari tent – and both countries understood the message. The green surroundings of the Belgian Ardennes and Namur province make them prime locations for a unique stay. Luxembourg has a few options too.

B&Bs

Fancy trying some Belgian or Luxembourg hospitality with a slice of insider tips about your destination? Then we cannot recommend staying at a B&B enough. You can find them everywhere: by the sea, in cities and towns, in the countryside, from the most luxurious to the most casual. They are a great solution in rural areas where hotels are scarce.

Bike Hotels

Biking is an essential part of Belgian (and especially Flemish) culture, and with growing interest in slow tourism, it's no surprise that the network of bike-friendly hotels is expanding. Different labels have been developed across the country: Fietsvriendelijke logies (Flanders), Bienvenue Vélo (Wallonia), Bike Friendly (Brussels) and Bed&Bike (Ostbelgien). Luxembourg has also introduced its own Bed+Bike label.

HOW MUCH FOR A NIGHT IN BELGIUM AND LUXEMBOURG

Hostel dorm
€35 (B & L)

Midrange hotel
€130 (B & L)

Luxury hotel
**€300 (B),
€380 (L)**

Camping

Wild camping isn't allowed, but Luxembourg tolerates one-night stays off-trail (away from homes and paths, except around the Haute-Sûre lakes). In Wallonia, the Nature & Forests Department has arranged several public overnight bivouac spots, especially along multiday itineraries such as those in the Pays des Lacs. The Flemish equivalent, Natuur en Bos, has done the same.

ACCOMMODATION TIPS

Brussels and Luxembourg City have a unique characteristic: both are congress towns filled with business travellers during the working week and so, often, spending the night in hotels is cheaper during the weekend than during the week, especially on Sunday night.

Airbnb is widespread across both countries but think before you book, especially for accommodation in tourist-focussed cities where a large swathe of housing capacities has been co-opted for the benefit of tourists while there is a raging housing shortage for locals, with skyrocketing rent prices as consequences. In Belgium, check out *fairbnb.coop*.

Family Travel

Travelling as a family is rarely an issue in Belgium and Luxembourg. Many hotels and hostels offer family rooms, and there are also numerous attractions to keep children entertained, ranging from comic museums to amusement parks and outdoor activities. With discounts available for different age groups and categories, you can enjoy a family getaway without exceeding your budget.

Eating

You won't have to stick to fast food, as many restaurants (especially casual ones) offer children's menus and are well-prepared to accommodate their youngest customers with highchairs and diaper-changing facilities in the restrooms. In Belgian cities such as Mechelen, Ghent, Leuven, Liège and Brussels, food courts have become increasingly popular and are a great option for families.

Guesthouses

Guesthouses are ideal for families and extended stays. Just make sure you book months in advance as they are popular. Oftentimes, guesthouses have children's beds, cots and baby chairs, but it's better to double-check if they are available.

COMIC STRIP CAPITAL OF THE WORLD

Since the interwar period, Belgium (especially the French-speaking part) has developed a love for comic strips, earning the country a reputation as the Comic Strip Capital of the World. Known locally as 'bande dessinée' or 'stripverhaal' or even 'the 9th art', it has flourished here for decades, producing iconic characters like Tintin, The Smurfs and Lucky Luke. Belgian comic artists have achieved global recognition for their creativity and storytelling prowess. Kids will love to visit the **Comics Art Museum** (p61) in Brussels, the **Hergé Museum** (p205) in Louvain-la-Neuve, or discover Brussels along the comics' murals trail.

Transport

If you are using public transport, travelling through Luxembourg will be a breeze, as buses and trains are free. In Belgian trains, up to four kids under 12 can travel for free when accompanied by an adult. For youth aged between 12 and 26, the Youth Ticket offers a flat price of €7.70 per journey to any destination.

Attractions

Almost everywhere, concession rates are applied to young visitors. Institutional museums (such as fine-art museums in Brussels or Antwerp) are free for visitors under 18. In Luxembourg, entry is free under 21 for similar museums.

BEST KID-FRIENDLY PICKS

Institut des Sciences Naturelles
Dinosaurs! Need we say more? (p67)

Mini-Europe
A grand tour of the EU (and the UK) on a small scale. (p95)

Garnaalsvissers te paard
Kids will love seeing the shrimp fisherfolk in yellow raincoats bringing in shrimp in horse-drawn nets. (p144)

Euro Space Center
The chance to be an astronaut for a day. (p230)

Parc Merveilleux Luxembourg
Compact little theme park and zoo with animal-feeding opportunities. (p271)

Health & Safe Travel

INSURANCE

We hope you won't need it, but purchasing travel insurance is strongly recommended, especially for non-EU residents. EU citizens (including Iceland, Liechtenstein, Norway, Switzerland) should carry the free European Health Insurance Card (EHIC) for local-rate medical care. UK residents should use the UK Global Health Insurance Card (GHIC), which replaces the EHIC and provides similar coverage across most European countries.

Petty Crimes

Belgium and especially Luxembourg are pretty safe destinations, but pickpocketing and bag-snatching can and do happen, mostly in cities. Keep your wits about you, especially at train stations and while on public transportation. Conditions in Brussels' Gare du Nord and Gare du Midi's neighbourhoods are a little rough, especially at night. We recommend using public transportation to get to your destination.

Cannabis Policy

Contrary to the general perception, possession of cannabis is still illegal in Belgium– it's merely decriminalised. However, carrying a small amount for personal use (3g) is tolerated if you're over 18 years. Luxembourg just passed a similar law. Smoking cannabis in public, even if some people indulge, is still prohibited.

TAP WATER

Locals buy bottled water and few restaurants offer free water, but tap water is perfectly safe in Belgium and Luxembourg.

FEMALE SOLO TRAVELLERS

With a safe environment, efficient transportation systems and plenty of accommodations with female-only dorms, Belgium and Luxembourg are both great destinations for female solo travellers. While exploring cities, take the usual precautions as you would in any other urban area. Women might get some unwanted attention (especially in Brussels); the best thing to do is to ignore it and carry on confidently. Going out on your own? Many restaurants, bars and nightclub participate in the 'Ask for Angela' campaign. If you feel unsafe, head for the bar and ask for 'Angela'. The staff will be there to assist you.

Terrorism

Ever since the March 2013 Brussels terrorist attacks, Belgium has been on high alert to protect its citizens and visitors. It is currently at Level 3 (serious threat). As for Luxembourg, despite its status as an EU centre of power, it has only faced low levels of threats.

CARS & BIKES CRIME

Unfortunately, both Belgium and Luxembourg have seen an increase in car theft, including theft of vehicles and items left inside cars. Be cautious not to leave anything too valuable inside your vehicle. Bicycles, especially e-bikes, are particularly easy targets for thieves. Cities like Brussels, Luxembourg and Antwerp provide bike parking spots or boxes to safely park your bike.

Food, Drink & Nightlife

When to Eat

Petit-déjeuner/Ontbijt (7am to 10am)
Breakfast is usually bread-based with sweet
or savoury spreads, cold cuts and/or cheese.

Dîner/Lunch (noon to 2pm) From a light
snack to a three-course lunch menu.

Apéritif/Aperitief (6pm to 8pm) Time
to have a beer, Moselle wine and some
finger food.

Souper/Dinner, avondeten (6pm to 10pm)
Dinner tends to be a more consistent meal,
with several courses when dining out.

Where to Eat

**Restaurant
gastronomique /
Gastronomische
restaurant** Celebrating
cuisine with quality
dishes, fine wine
selection, attentive
service and a charming
ambiance.

Bistrot / Eetcafé A
small place for eating
and drinking, offering a
concise menu, some at a
gastronomic level.

Brasserie Can be either
a brewery or a non-stop
restaurant, serving classic
dishes.

Bar-café Serves drinks
(from coffees to cocktails)
with optional casual
dining and finger food.

Boulangerie / Bakerij
Bakery

Pâtisserie A bakery
focused on cakes, pies
and other sweet treats.

MENU DECODER

**Plat du jour /
Dagschotel** Dish of
the day

**Menu de dégustation
/ Degustatiemenu**
Sampling menu

**Entrées /
Voorgerechten**
Starters

**Entrées froides /
Koude voorgerechten**
Cold starters

**Entrées chaudes /
Warme voorgerechten**
Hot starters

**Plats /
Hoofdgerechten**
Main dishes

**Accompagnements /
Bijgerechten**
Side dishes

Pain / Brood Bread

Poissons / Vis Fish

Viandes / Vlees Meat

Volailles / Gevogelte
Poultry

**Fruits de mer /
Zeevruchten** Seafood

Dessert Dessert

**Fait-maison /
Huisgemaakte**
Homemade

**Eau minérale (plate
ou pétillante) /
Mineraalwater (plat
of bruisend)** Mineral
water (flat or sparkling)

Bière au fût / Tapbier
Beer from tap

**Bière en bouteille /
Bier op fles**
Bottled beer

Vin blanc / Witte wijn
White wine

Vin rouge / Rode wijn
Red wine

HOW TO… Settle the Bill

Paying the bill at restaurants, bars
or cafes in Belgium and Luxembourg
is pretty straightforward: everything is
included (taxes and service charges). What
you get is what you've paid for, and tipping
is not necessary unless you want to reward
exceptional service. If you're at a restaurant and
want the bill, you'll need to request it, as it's
common for customers to linger after the meal
(having dinner is not to be rushed here). When
a waitstaff member enquires if you'd like coffee
or after-dinner liquor, take the opportunity to
ask for the bill. Splitting the bill should not be
a problem either for your dining partners or for
the restaurant, but some establishments may
not accept it, especially if you mix cash and card
payments. It's always best to ask beforehand, so
you and your party can decide how to settle it.

HOW MUCH FOR A...

Croissant
(in a bakery)
€1.75

Deli sandwich
**€6-8 (B),
€6.5-9 (L)**

Dish of the day
at lunch
€18 (B), €20 (L)

Three-course
dinner
€50 (B), €57 (L)

Three-course
gastronomical
dinner
**€70-€175 (B),
€85-200 (L)**

Beer (Pils)
**€3 (B, 25cl),
€4 (L, 33cl)**

Beer
(special, 33cl)
**€4.50-6 (B),
€7.5 (L)**

Glass of wine
**€5-8 (B),
€7.5-12 (L)**

HOW TO...

Eat Mussels Properly

The Belgian national dish is a sacred thing and should be eaten with the utmost reverence – which means with a mussel's shell. Eat your first mussel (choose a large and sturdy one) using your hands or a fish fork. The now empty shell will serve as a pair of claws to grab your *frites* and shell the other mussels. Mussels are usually served in large saucepans, and its upturned lid collects the empty shells. If you spot a closed shell, do not eat it as it means the mollusk is not cooked. Discard it right away with the empty shells. Once finished, the mussels' broth can be eaten with a spoon (don't overlook it, it's where all the best flavours are located). A welcome finger rinse is always provided.

Mussels can be enjoyed in a variety of sauces:

Moules marinières/Mosselen à la marinière (natuur) The classic of classics, with onions, celery, parsley and butter

Moules au vin blanc/Mosselen met witte wijn in a white wine sauce

Moules à la bière/Mosselen met bier in a beer sauce

Moules à la provencale/Mosselen Provençaals with tomatoes, bell pepper and garlic

Moules à la crème/ Mosselen met room in a cream sauce

Moules à l'ardennaise/Mosselen ardennaise with bits of bacon, veggies, cream and mushrooms

Mussels Season

Did you know that almost all the mussels eaten in Belgium are from Zeeland in the Netherlands? The mussels season lasts from July to February. Outside of those months, they are not fresh.

GOING OUT

Belgians have the reputation to know how to party (Luxembourgers are a little more on the quiet side but that does not mean they frown upon a good night out). Typically, the evening starts around 6pm with a beer in a cosy bar or aperitif in a bar-café or cocktail bar, just to set the mood for the night. If you feel a bit hungry, you can usually order finger food but don't overdo it if you have plans to go to a restaurant. In the evening, restaurants usually offer at least three courses, so make sure you're hungry and have plenty of time to enjoy your meal. If you're planning to go to a movie, theatre or concert (these often start at 8pm), arrive at the restaurant early (many open at 6pm), so you can enjoy your meal without feeling rushed. Don't hesitate to mention you have something planned when you order so the staff can ask the kitchen to speed things up. When the weather is nice, locals will flock the terraces – you should do the same. After dinner or a show, it's time to carry on the evening with a little partying. From music bars, disco bars to clubs (such as the **Fuse** in Brussels or the **Lenox Club** in Luxembourg City), there's something for everyone. The nightlife lasts until the wee hours, so, if you're heading to a club, don't think about going before midnight.

Responsible Travel

Climate Change & Travel

It's impossible to ignore the impact we have when travelling; Lonely Planet urges all travellers to engage with their travel carbon footprint, which will mainly come from air travel. While there often isn't an alternative, travellers can look to minimise the number of flights they take, opt for newer aircrafts and use cleaner ground transport, such as trains. One proposed solution — purchasing carbon offsets — unfortunately does not cancel out the impact of individual flights. While most destinations will depend on air travel for the foreseeable future, for now, pursuing ground-based travel where possible is the best course of action.

The **UN carbon footprint calculator** shows how flying impacts a household's emissions.

The **ICAO Carbon Emissions Calculator (ICEC)** allows visitors to analyse the CO_2 generated by point-to-point journeys.

Train Travel

Belgium and Luxembourg are blessed with extensive railway networks connecting their respective cities, towns and neighbouring countries, making travelling by train a breeze. While affordable in Belgium, trains (and buses) are free in Luxembourg.

Brussels Greeters

Discover Brussels from a local's perspective with a **Greeter**. These volunteers dedicate their free time to share their slice of Brussels. It's a wonderful way to get to know the city and its inhabitants.

The **Brussels Makers Fair** takes place several times a year at the Gare Maritime of Tour & Taxis (p80). Find local and sustainable designers, creators and their wares.

Browse through regional products at the biweekly **Stater Maart**, right on Luxembourg City's Place Guillaume II. Delicious hams and cheeses, Moselle wines and a food village for those who cannot wait to eat.

FOOD WITH A MEANING

Have a wonderful and affordable meal at Brussels' **Belmundo** (p83) in Molenbeek. Most of the veggies are grown in their garden and most of the rest is locally sourced. The restaurant trains jobseekers as cooks and waitstaff.

SUSTAINABLE STAYS

Luxembourg's EcoLabel Lux *(ecolabel.lu/lecolabel-lu)* certifies tourist accommodation that makes significant efforts to reduce its impact on the environment and the climate. From camping to châteaux, you'll find an extensive list of establishments.

Look for Good Food

In Brussels, look for restaurants with the **Good Food label** *(goodfood.brussels),* awarded to establishments promoting local and seasonal produce, alternatives to animal proteins and food produced in an environmentally friendly way, while minimising food waste.

Cycling in Belgium

With many kilometres of cycling routes and relatively flat terrain, Flanders is easy to get around by bike. For information and itineraries: *visitflanders.com/en/discover -flanders/cycling.* In Wallonia, RAVel *(ravel. wallonie.be)* is a network of former light rail tracks turned into protected cycling paths.

Make for the Villages

Leave the crowded Flemish art cities and head for **Wallonia's Most Beautiful Villages**. This award is bestowed to villages with an outstanding architectural and natural heritage, such as Limbourg or Aubechies. More info at *beauxvillages.be.*

Green Music

Catch a concert at **4AD Muziekclub** *(4ad. be)* in Diksmuide. In addition to on-point lineups, they are sustainability pioneers with practices going from carbon offset to proposing local and fair-trade food or recuperating rain water.

Cups of Goodness

Exploring Luxembourg City, you might need to refuel with a hot drink on the go. **Cup2Go** are reusable cups you can fill up at participating establishments with rewards in store. Find them at *cup2go.vdl.lu.*

Twenty Belgian beaches hold the **Blue Flag** environment label. Check the list at *blueflag.global.*

GR412, dubbed the 'Black Loop', is an unusual hiking trail through Charleroi's industrial landscape.

5th

Luxembourg is ranked fifth in the **Global Sustainable Index**. Its success stems from sustainable finance – for instance, by selling green bonds for eco-friendly projects. Free public transport also helps in reducing car usage and CO_2 emissions.

RESOURCES

fietssnelwegen.be/en/
Everything you need to know about Flanders' cycle highways.

visitwallonia.com/en-gb/3/i -love/sustainable-holidays
Sustainable activities and accommodation in Wallonia.

visit.brussels/en/visitors/what -to-do/sustainable-brussels
Visiting Brussels, the sustainable way.

Accessible Travel

Belgium and Luxembourg, especially the cities, are increasing their efforts to improve accessibility. Belgium is a little less exemplary than its neighbour, but things are gradually improving.

Cobblestones Everywhere

One thing both countries have in common is cities with plenty of cobblestone streets. These streets can be challenging for wheelchairs and the vision-impaired due to their uneven surfaces.

AIRPORT

Contact your airline or travel agent at least 48 hours in advance (72 hours for Luxembourg) to request PMR assistance. At Brussels Airport, find the Special Assistance Welcome Desk behind check-in row 2. Brussels South Charleroi has PMR Corners at both terminals. At Luxembourg Airport, report to your check-in desk.

METRO AND TRAMS

Brussels metro stations have Braille signs and tactile tiles leading up to the platforms. Personal assistance is available at stations with lifts, but advance request is needed (+32 2515 2365). Station staff can also provide help upon request. Most trams are accessible, especially as the older ones tend to disappear.

Accessible Museum Experiences

Brussels' Fine Arts Museum (p57) offers 'made-to-measure' tours for vision- or hearing-impaired visitors. **Huis van Alijn** (p115) in Ghent caters to various needs, with a dedicated accessibility officer. Luxembourg's **Mudam** (p264) provides adapted activities for visitors on the autistic spectrum.

Accommodation

Large hotels and well-established brands have accessible rooms. For smaller hotels, historical buildings, B&Bs or short-term rentals, it might not be the case. Check in advance.

Bars & Restaurant

When hotels and museums are largely accessible to mobility-impaired visitors, it's not the case for bars and restaurants, as toilets are often located in basements or on a floor above.

Public Transportation

Luxembourg City offers accessible public transportation with low-floor buses, trams and an easy-to-use funicular. Trains provide free assistance for mobility-impaired passengers; requests should be made 24 hours in advance in Belgium (+32 2607 3000) and one hour in Luxembourg (+352 2489 2489; pmr@cfl.lu).

MUSEUM ACCESS

Museums are widely accessible to wheelchairs (although bear in mind some rooms might not be). If you are visiting the **Atomium** in Brussels, only the top sphere is accessible to wheelchairs via elevators.

RESOURCES

Visit Brussels *(visit.brussels/en/ visitors/plan-your-trip/practical-info/ accessibility)* Plenty of tips to discover the capital.

Visit Flanders *(visitflanders.com/en/ travel-information/ accessibility)* Prepare your visit to Flanders according to your needs.

Access-i *(access-i.be)* Lists accessible accommodation, buildings, events and trails in Wallonia, based on disability types.

Info-Handicap *(info-handicap.lu)* Luxembourg's representative organisation for people with disabilities. In French or German.

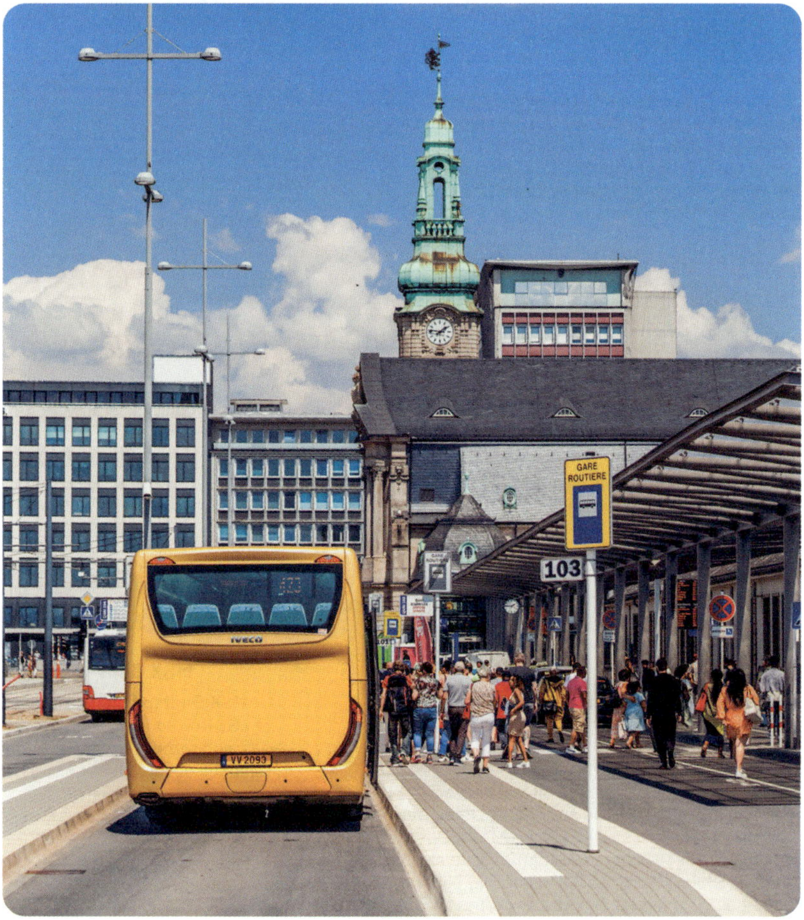

Public transportation, Luxembourg City (p260)

LGBTIQ+ Travellers

Belgium and Luxembourg are among the most welcoming destinations in the world for LGBTIQ+ travellers. With progressive attitudes and legal protections in place (Belgium was the second country, after the Netherlands, to legalise same-sex marriage), both countries offer an inclusive atmosphere and larger cities have thriving queer communities. However, be aware that prejudice still does exist.

Pride

Pride is the highlight of a busy calendar for the queer community. **Brussels Pride** is the largest Pride in the country, with over 150,000 participants during the weekend around 20 May. Pride festivities are loaded with events, conference and exhibition during the week leading up to the march. **Antwerp and Ghent** also host their own Pride events. **Luxembourg Pride** follows the same model but takes place during the first week of July, culminating with the Equality March on Saturday. Brussels also holds **Bear Pride** in October.

COMMUNITY HOUSES

Brussels has its **Rainbow House** (*rainbowhouse.be*), and Luxembourg City its **Rainbow Center** (*rainbowcenter. lu*). Both provide information, assistance and a safe place for LGBTIQ+ community members. They also serve as a meeting point. **Cavaria** (*cavaria.be*) and **Prisme** (*federation-prisme.be*) are the umbrella organisations federating Rainbow Houses and smaller, or more specific, associations, in Flanders and in Wallonia, respectively.

La Démence

One of Europe's biggest gay parties has been going on for years, taking place every last Friday of the month at the famed **Fuse** club in Brussels. With three floors, several bars, a dark room and a tight DJ lineup, guests are here to party hard.

BRUSSELS' RAINBOW VILLAGE

Brussels has a 'gay neighbourhood' centred around Rue du Marché au Charbon, Plattesteen and Rue du Lombard. Bars, disco-bars, shops (kinky or not), a sauna – whatever you're after, it's always a good place to have fun and make new friends in the local community along the way.

MSK Gent

MSK Gent (p117) offers an LGBTIQ+ tour highlighting 7 works from its collection and the queer stories behind them. Curated by members of the LGBTIQ+ community, the tour is available in English, providing an inclusive and enriching experience for visitors.

IN LUXEMBOURG

The LGBTIQ+ scene may be small and discreet but there's plenty of fun to be had. **We Are Family Luxembourg** has taken up the torch of several initiatives that closed recently. This LGBT collective organises parties several times a year at **Lenox Club**. Another spot (the only gay bar remaining in Luxembourg City): **Letz Boys** holds parties and drag shows.

Nuts & Bolts

OPENING HOURS

This is for indications only, as schedules may vary.

Banks 9am–4/5pm

Bars 6pm–midnight/1am

Cafes 8am–8pm

Clubs 10pm–3am (L)/6am (B)

Restaurants noon–2pm and 6pm–10pm

Shopping malls 9/10am–7pm

Shops 10am–6pm (with a possible midday break)

Supermarkets 8am–8pm

Internet
Wi-fi is usually available in airports, large train stations, restaurants, cafes and in some public areas.

PUBLIC HOLIDAYS

Luxembourg and Belgium share a significant number of public holidays. On these days, most stores and services are likely to be closed.

New Year's Day 1 January

Easter Monday March/April

Labour Day 1 May

Europe Day (Luxembourg) 9 May

Ascension Day May

Whit Monday May/June

Luxembourg National Day 23 June

Belgian National Day 21 July

Assumption Day 15 August

All Saints' Day 1 November

Armistice Day (Belgium) 11 November

Christmas Day 25 December

Second Day of Christmas (Luxembourg) 26 December

Weight & Measures
Both countries use the metric system. Also, pay attention: the decimal place is indicated by a comma and the thousand by a dot.

Smoking
Smoking is prohibited indoors, everywhere, and on outdoor station platforms in Belgium.

Electricity 230V/50Hz

Type E (Belgium)

Type F (Luxembourg)

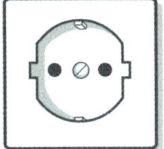

Language

Belgium is split into Dutch-speaking Flanders (*Vlaanderen* in Dutch) and French-speaking Wallonia (*la Wallonie* in French), as well as a small German-speaking region. French, German and Lëtzebuergesch are spoken in Luxembourg.

DUTCH

The Dutch spoken in Belgium is also called 'Flemish'. The grammar and spelling rules of Dutch in Belgium and in the Netherlands are the same, and 'Flemish' (Vlaams) is not a separate language in itself.

Basics
Hello. Dag./Hallo. dakh/ha·loh
Goodbye. Dag. dakh
Yes./No. Ja./Nee. yaa/ney
Please. Alstublieft. al·stew·bleeft
Thank you. Dank u. dangk ew
Excuse me. Excuseer mij. eks·kew·zeyr mey
Do you speak English? Spreekt u Engels? spreykt ew eng·uhls
I don't understand. Ik begrijp het niet. ik buh·khreyp huht neet

Time
What time is it? Hoe laat is het? hoo laat is huht
It's (10) o'clock. Het is (tien) uur. huht is (teen) ewr
morning ochtends sokh·tuhns
afternoon middags smi·dakhs
evening avonds saa·vonts
yesterday gistere khis·tuh·ruhn
today vandaag van·daakh
tomorrow morgen mor·khuhn

Directions
Where is ...? Waar is ...? waar is ...
What is the address? Wat is het adres? wat is huht a·dres
Can you show me (on the map)? Kunt u het mij tonen (op de kaart)? kunt ew huht mey toh·nuhn (op duh kaart)

Signs
Entrance Ingang / **Exit** Uitgang
Open Open / **Closed** Gesloten
Prohibited Verboden / **Toilets** Toiletten

Emergencies
Help! Help! help
Leave me alone! Laat me met rust! laat muh met rust
Call the police! Bel de politie! bel duh poh·lee·see
Call a doctor! Bel een dokter! bel uhn dok·tuhr
I'm sick. Ik ben ziek. ik ben zeek

FRENCH

In Wallonia, a grasp of French will prove important. Brussels is officially bilingual, though French has long been the city's dominant language.

Basics
Hello. Bonjour. bon·zhoor
Goodbye. Au revoir. o·rer·vwa
Yes/No. Oui/Non. wee/non
Please. S'il vous plaît. seel voo play
Thank you. Merci. mair·see
Excuse me. Excusez-moi. ek·skew·zay·mwa
Do you speak English? Parlez-vous anglais? par·lay·voo ong·glay

I don't understand. Je ne comprends pas. zher ner kom·pron pa

Directions
Where is ...? Où est ...? oo ay ...
What is the address? Quelle est l'adresse? kel ay la·dres
Can you show me (on the map)? Pouvez-vous m'indiquer (sur la carte)? poo·vay·voo mun·dee·kay (sewr la kart)

Signs

Entrance Entrée / **Exit** Sortie
Open Ouvert / **Closed** Fermé
Prohibited Interdit / **Toilets** Toilettes

Time

What time is it? Quelle heure est-il? kel er ay til
It's (eight) o'clock. Il est (huit) heures. er il ay (weet)
morning matin ma·tun
afternoon après-midi a·pray·mee·dee

evening soir swar
yesterday hier yair
today aujourd'hui o·zhoor·dwee
tomorrow demain der·mun

Emergencies

Help! Au secours! o skoor
Call the police! Appelez la police! a·play la po·lees
Call a doctor! Appelez un médecin! a·play un mayd·sun
I'm sick. Je suis malade. zher swee ma·lad
I'm lost. Je suis perdu/perdue. (m/f) zhe swee·pair·dew

GERMAN

Around 70,000 German speakers live in Wallonia's Eastern Cantons (Ost Kantonen).

Basics

Hello. Guten Tag. goo·ten tahk
Goodbye. Auf wiedersehen. owf vee·der·zay·en
Yes/No. Ja/Nein. yah/nain
Please. Bitte. bi·te
Thank you. Danke. dang·ke
Excuse me. Entschuldigung. ent·shul·di·gung
Do you speak English? Sprechen Sie Englisch? shpre·khen zee eng·lish
I don't understand. Ich verstehe nicht. ikh fer·shtay·e nikht

Time

What time is it? Wie spät ist es? vee shpayt ist es
It's (10) o'clock. Es ist (zehn) Uhr. es ist (tsayn) oor
morning Morgen mor·gen
afternoon Nachmittag nahkh·mi·tahk
evening Abend ah·bent
yesterday Gestern ges·tern
today Heute hoy·te
tomorrow Morgen mor·gen

Directions

Where is (the station)? Wo ist (der Bahnhof)? vor ist (der bahn·hawf)
What is the address? Wie ist die Adresse? vee ist dee a·dre·se
Can you show me (on the map)? Können Sie es mir (auf der Karte) zeige? ker·nen zee es meer (owf dair kar·te) tsai·gen

Signs

Exit Ausgang / **Entrance** Eingang
Open Offen / **Closed** Geschlossen
Prohibited Verboten / **Toilets** Toiletten

Emergencies

Help! Hilfe! hil·fe
Go away! Gehen Sie weg! gay·en zee vek
Call the police! Rufen Sie die Polizei! roo·fen zee dee po·li·tsai
Call a doctor! Rufen Sie einen Arzt! roo·fen zee ai·nen artst
I'm ill. Ich bin krank. ikh bin krangk

NUMBERS	1	2	3	4	5	6	7	8	9	10
Dutch	één	twee	drie	vier	vijf	zes	zeven	acht	negen	tien
	eyn	twey	dree	veer	veyf	zes	zey·vuhn	akht	ney·khuhn	teen
French	un	deux	trois	quatre	cinq	six	sept	huit	neuf	dix
	un	der	trwa	ka·tre	sungk	sees	set	weet	nerf	dees
German	eins	zwei	drei	vier	fünf	sechs	sieben	acht	neun	zehn
	ains	tsvai	drai	feer	fünf	zeks	zee·ben	akht	noyn	tsayn

STORYBOOK

Our writers delve deep into different aspects of
Belgian & Luxembourgish life

Maison de la Radio (p313), Brussels
FINECKI/SHUTTERSTOCK

A HISTORY OF BELGIUM & LUXEMBOURG IN

15 PLACES

From the mists of time, what's now Belgium and Luxembourg has been an area both fertile and strategic. The castle-filled region has been an almost eternal battleground through which armies have passed, often surprised by the plucky resistance of a people who finally got their own nations almost by accident in two twists of 19th-century geopolitics. By Mark Elliott

AS A COUNTRY, Belgium didn't exist before 1830. Then, an almost accidental rebellion ignited by a vocal group of opera-goers led to a new Belgian state being thrust into unexpected independence. A German king was provided to counteract a rather liberal constitution. Belgium grabbed part of Luxembourg but the rest of Luxembourg stayed Dutch until a quirk in the then rules of accession gave the Grand Duchy an equally unlikely chance to go it alone. Both countries rapidly industrialised thanks to rich deposits of coal and iron ore, Belgium also enriching itself from King Leopold II's heartless exploitation of his African colonies.

Much later, cooperation between Belgium, Luxembourg and the Netherlands would form the Benelux, a model that helped inspire the future EU.

But don't imagine that there was no history here pre-1830. The name Belgium comes from a throwback to the semi-mythical Belgae, a confederation of Gallic tribes who briefly resisted the Romans. Far later, the area's duchies became part of Burgundy, then Hapsburg Spain. After the 16th-century Dutch Revolt, the Protestant Netherlands broke away but future Belgium/Luxembourg remained Spanish-ruled, with Catholicism becoming entrenched and eventually reinforcing a stark cultural division with the Netherlands. The Hapsburg empire later split over Spanish royal succession, then a period of Austrian rule ended as revolutionary France invaded and destroyed the monasteries. After Napoleon lost Waterloo, the Dutch took over but only lasted 15 years.

1. Silex's

SIGNS OF NEOLITHIC BUSINESS CULTURE

If you thought that stone-age people were simply isolated groups of mutually antagonistic cavemen, a surprise awaits at Silex's near Mons, Belgium. In 1867, railway engineers digging a cutting close to Spiennes village found a series of hand-dug shafts which proved to be as much as 6000 years old. Clever archaeologists saw here apparent proof that Neolithic humans had a culture sufficiently developed that they could organise complex mining operations as well as developing long-distance trade in flint – the raw material of the day for knives and weaponry.

For more on Silex's see p210

2. Ambiorix Statue, Tongeren

A REAL-LIFE ASTERIX

As every Belgian schoolchild learns, no people were as brave – or perhaps foolhardy – as the Belgae, a Germano-Celtic tribal confederation who briefly resisted the Roman legions. The group's semi-mythical leader was Ambiorix, whose vague memory was dusted off when Belgium emerged as a country in 1830. A slightly cartoonish statue of the hero stands proudly in central Tongeren which, ironically, is now the town with the most significant remnants of time under Roman rule. It's also home to an excellent Gallo-Roman Museum. Though it's a wild over-simplification, today's linguistic divide between Francophones and Flemish speakers can be approximately linked to the northeast Roman frontier established near here around 50 BCE.

For more about Roman Tongeren see p188

3. Beffroi de Tournai

CIVIC RIGHTS WRITTEN IN STONE

In Tournai, another Belgian city with Roman roots, an ornate *beffroi* (belfry) first built in 1188 rises 72m high. But it isn't part of a church. Indeed, it provides a remarkable secular counterpoint to the Tournai's vast, multi-spired Romanesque cathedral across the way. The non-religious belfry was the Low Countries' first, but in rapid succession many more towers, along with fine guildhalls, became widespread symbols of a town's civic rights, pushed by guilds of skilled workers who had the impudent idea that wealth should allow a degree of privilege. Within a feudal system that generally assumed the birthrights of counts, dukes and the distant French crown, that was novel.

For more on Tournai see p213

4. Kortrijk 1302 Museum

FRENCH CHIVALRY, TAKE THAT!

As the 13th century ended, wealthy Flanders was in a conundrum. Its weaving economy depended on wool imports from

Inner courtyard of Mechelen Courthouse

WALENCIENNE/SHUTTERSTOCK

England; however, the Count of Flanders officially owed allegiance to France, whose king was at war with England. This supposedly meant imposing what today we'd call 'sanctions'. The unwilling Flemish revolted. In a messy fight, the high point (from the Flemish point of view) was the Battle of the Golden Spurs on 11 July 1302, a day still celebrated as a holiday in Flanders. Sweet if temporary victory saw a rag-tag force of peasants and weavers outwit the heavily armed French by getting the aristocratic cavalry bogged down in cunningly disguised marshland.

For more about Kortrijk see p149

5. Mechelen Courthouse

WHERE CHARLES V PLAYED AS A BOY

The *Gerechtsgebouw* (courthouse) in Mechelen was once the palace of Margaret of Austria. Who? Well, in the 14th and 15th centuries, local counties and duchies had steadily amalgamated, mostly through intermarriage. By the 15th century most of the Low Countries had become part of the then extensive Burgundian empire. Born at Ghent, a 'Burgundian' prince called Charles (Karel) was destined to be heir to the Hapsburg/Spanish empire and would go on to become Holy Roman Emperor Charles V, history's most powerful teenager since Alexander the Great. However, he was brought up in Mechelen by his young aunt Margaret who for a while acted as regent administering the Low Countries in his name.

For more about Mechelen see p178

6. Museum Plantin-Moretus

ANTWERP LEADS THE WORLD'S 16TH-CENTURY TECH REVOLUTION

Antwerp's Museum Plantin-Moretus was one of Europe's earliest major printing houses and retains the world's oldest surviving presses. Printing in its day was like AI today, threatening to upend social order. Mass-printed Bibles in the 16th century unleashed a revolt against perceived corruption of the Catholic Church and the growth of Protestantism. Charles V, with humanist advisors like Erasmus, had proved tolerant as the educated Low Countries rapidly embraced the new-fangled ideas. But Charles's Spain-based son Phillip II was ultra-Catholic and tried to crush them. The result was decades of war and the loss of the Netherlands, but the heavy-handed re-Catholicisation of proto-Belgium.

For more on the Museum Plantin-Moretus see p171

7. Archéoforum, Liège

A HOLE WHERE A CATHEDRAL SHOULD BE
Through many centuries, Liège (and its patchwork of dependencies) remained aloof from the politics of dukes, emperors and reformations, being an ecclesiastical territory ruled by a Catholic prince-bishop. Low taxes encouraged loyalty as well as experimental metallurgy and beer production, notably in distant exclaves like Hoegaarden. However, in the anti-religious fervour following the 1789 French Revolution, the prince-bishops were ousted and the symbol of their power – the vast Cathedral St-Lambert – was destroyed after a vote of the city folk. Where it once stood is now the Archéoforum, a subterranean archaeological visitor experience.

For more on the Archéoforum and former prince-bishops see p248

8. Theatre de la Monnae

MONTY PYTHON-STYLE REVOLUTION
French forces took over, destroyed monasteries and generally ripped up any remnants of the Hapsburg system, but Napoleon's defeat at Waterloo in 1815 saw the region come under the Dutch crown. Then, just 15 years later, history took a whacky turn at La Monnae, still Brussels' foremost opera house. Following a performance of a Daniel Auber composition, tipsy theatre-goers, fired up with patriotic sentiments, poured out of the grand building joining demonstrating workers on the street outside. Together the crowd chased Dutch troops out of key locations and raised the flag of Brabant. Belgium was born – or so the very simplified story goes.

For more about Brussels' theatres see p61

9. National Mining Museum, Rumelange, Luxembourg

INDUSTRIALISATION IN FULL SWING
Going into the former iron-ore mine at Rumelange in southernmost Luxembourg is now a fun museum experience, but for miners in the 19th and 20th centuries, conditions were incredibly tough. It was in great part through the sweat of such folks, of coal

miners in the Borinage (Mons, Charleroi) and steel workers at Seraing, Charleroi and Belval, that massive infrastructure development was funded, including continental Europe's first train service and a network of canals that now include a series of remarkable UNESCO-listed boat lifts.

For more about Luxembourg's industrial regeneration zone see p271

10. AfricaMuseum, Tervuren

LEOPOLD'S COLONIAL LOOT FUNDS ART NOUVEAU BRUSSELS
An Africa Museum on the outskirts of Brussels? While now on the road to improving its relationship with the continent, the grand establishment at Tervuren has a history that makes one wince (it once exhibited Congolese people in the gardens like zoo animals). But that's nothing compared to the history of how King Leopold II personally amassed vast swathes of colonial territory under the guise of Christian charity. The disingenuous name, Congo Free State (from 1885), hid appalling human rights abuses. Locals became essentially enslaved to produce rubber and other products. The profits helped fund the incredible flowering of Art Nouveau architecture in Brussels and Antwerp. International outrage shamed Brussels into annexing Leopold's African holdings in 1908, but while forced labour was abolished, Congolese copper, diamonds and other resources were plundered by the colonial regime until 1960.

For more on the AfricaMuseum see p98

11. Lakenhalle, Ypres (Ieper)

WWI GETS BOGGED DOWN
One of the most glorious medieval buildings in Belgium is the huge, fanciful cloth hall in Ypres (Ieper). Except, what you see was totally rebuilt after WWI when it had been left as rubble after endless bombardment. Whole villages disappeared into the mud where for several years soldiers rotted in sodden trenches in Flanders fields. The whole course of WWI could have been very different if plucky Liège had not previously delayed German advances by 12 valuable days. And if the coastal route towards France had not been flooded when the sluice gates at Nieuwpoort were opened to block further advance.

For more about Ypres see p146

AfricaMuseum (p98), Tervuren

12. McAuliffe's Bust & Sherman Tank in Bastogne

NUTS TO HITLER

During WWII, German forces once again surged across Belgium and Luxembourg, this time fully occupying both countries from May 1940. Jewish and Roma communities were decimated, many victims 'processed' (sent to death camps) through an infamous deportation camp at Mechelen. 1944 saw liberation by an apparently unstoppable Allied force pushing full tilt towards Berlin. Then at Christmas, Hitler launched a last-gasp counteroffensive across the snowy Ardennes. Dozens of towns in Luxembourg and southeast Belgium were caught up in renewed fighting but in surrounded Bastogne, when invited to surrender, the US commander Anthony McAuliffe rebuffed the German emissary with one word: 'Nuts!'

For more about Bastogne see p98

13. The Atomium, Brussels

POSTWAR OPTIMISM

The Atomium is one of the oddest buildings anywhere, a futuristic series of nine great metal balls linked in an architectural lattice to form the centrepiece for the 1958 Brussels World Fair. At the time it was a celebration of technology, underlining how Belgium had raced ahead in developing a prosperous modern economy in the wake of WWII. Again this was fuelled by coal and steel, reserves that Luxembourg also enjoyed. The prosperity was felt less by the migrant mine workers who flooded in from Italy (and later Portugal, Turkey and North Africa) and laboured under conditions that were often arduous and dangerous.

For more about the Atomium see p95

14. Schengen Pier

FREEDOM OF MOVEMENT STARTS HERE

When growth faltered in the 1970s, little Luxembourg cleverly diversified into banking and grew ever more affluent. Slow to adapt, the once-wealthy heavy industrial areas of French-speaking Wallonia slumped, while Flanders was contrastingly responsive. As the economic balance shifted, so historical Flemish grievances against Francophone dominance developed into a growing tension across Belgium's linguistic divide. However, Brussels and Luxembourg had meanwhile become important bureaucratic hubs for the EEC (later EU) and it was in a barge in the river at Schengen, Luxembourg, where a 1995 agreement unlocked the free movement of people within most of the block.

For more about Schengen see p271

15. Havenhuis, Antwerp

MULTICULTURAL ARCHITECTURE

Few places better symbolise the positives of multicultural, globally linked 21st-century Belgium than the dramatic Havenhuis building in Antwerp. Combining futuristic and historic elements and designed by British-Iraqi architect Dame Zaha Hadid (1950–2016), it serves as the new management hub for a port which cleverly reinvented itself through massive expansion to regain its historic status as a global trade hub. However, while Luxembourg continues to prosper, parts of Belgium remain economically sluggish and Belgium's arcane political system remains prone to paralysis. In 2020, at the peak of the COVID pandemic, a national government was finally assembled, a world record 652 days after the previous administration threw in the towel.

For more about Antwerp Port see p167

MEET THE BELGIANS

How do you describe a multicultural country's inhabitants? Let us try. MELISSA MONACO introduces her people.

ASK FOREIGNERS WHAT they think of Belgians and you'll often hear: 'Friendly, but a little hard to get to know.' It's true that Belgians value personal space and that breaking into their close-knit social circles can take time. But once you do – perhaps over a couple of beers – you'll discover warmth, generosity and a sharp, dry humour that is often ironic and self-deprecating.

Belgium sits at the crossroads of Europe, blending Northern pragmatism with Southern expressiveness, layered with traditions shaped by centuries of foreign rule and waves of migration. In the north, Dutch-speaking Flemings are known for their directness, entrepreneurship and a rich artistic heritage. In the south, French-speaking Walloons have a reputation for being more expressive and laid-back, with an industrial past that shaped their identity. In the east, a small but vibrant German-speaking community adds yet another cultural thread.

Then there is Brussels – the multilingual, cosmopolitan capital that both Flemings and Walloons like to grumble about – where a laissez-faire spirit floats in the air, endearing to some, maddening to others. Despite these differences, a shared 'Belgianness' unites them: collective humility, a taste for life's simple pleasures (good food, good company, a well-kept home) and a fondness for folklore, music and festivals.

Belgium's political complexity has also fostered a national talent for pragmatism, negotiation, and compromise – the famed *compromis à la belge* – visible in everything from village councils to the EU presidency, held by Belgians Herman Van Rompuy and Charles Michel.

For all its international connections, Belgium is deeply local at heart. It's a country of villages and mid-sized towns, where many people maintain friendships from primary school and settle close to where they grew up. This rootedness helps explain why social circles can feel impenetrable to newcomers – they've simply been in place for decades.

Centuries of foreign rule, coupled with today's intricate federal system and sense of egalitarianism, have also bred a healthy scepticism toward authority. Belgians respect laws and institutions, but they are quick to challenge pretension or overreach, often with satire. Boast too loudly or flaunt your position, and you'll likely be cut down with a well-placed joke. While it's not anarchism, there's an instinctive resistance to putting anyone on a pedestal just because of a title or uniform.

Finally, there is a lack of Belgian nationalism (even though Flemish nationalism is quite strong) that makes this a country open to influences from abroad and a certain freedom to create, free from constraints. No wonder the artistic scene is so vibrant.

To understand Belgians is to appreciate subtlety: like their beers, they come in different flavours, each with its own singularities, and equally delicious to know.

Who & How Many

On 1 January 2025, Belgium's population amounted to 11,825,551 inhabitants: 58% live in Flanders, 31% in Wallonia (the 0.67% of German-speaking community members included) and 11% in the Brussels-Capital Region. More than a third is of foreign heritage.

I'M A BELGIAN ZINNEKE

A *Zinneke,* in Brussels' dialect, is a mongrel dog whose destiny often ended in drowning in the Senne (Zenne in Dutch) river. Nowadays, it's a badge worn with pride by *Bruxellois,* most of whom have diverse origins.

I am part of it: my paternal grandparents and father came here during a large 1950s migration, when Belgium turned to Italy to provide coal miners in exchange for coal. My maternal grandfather was Flemish, my grandmother French; my mother was born in Brussels, and my brother and I grew up in a tranquil village in western Wallonia, living in a former coal-mining district where one in two inhabitants was of foreign origin. A perfect example of a contemporary Belgian!

No wonder that ever since I have arrived in Brussels for my studies, I felt at home in this city with its kaleidoscope of nationalities – yet with a small-town feel. Though I've lived abroad for years, I've finally returned, with no plans to leave.

MEET THE LUXEMBOURGERS

In this Q&A, ALISHA JEGEN and STEVEN MASON explain some of the hidden complexities behind what it means to be Luxembourgers, Europe's richest people per capita… on paper at least.

Do you both speak Luxembourgish? Is it really a 'living language'?

Yes, we're both fluent, and so are all of our friends. Luxembourgish is Alisha's mother tongue. Although Steven grew up speaking English at home, he's now just as fluent in Luxembourgish. We both use Luxembourgish when talking to each other… and every day at work too, as our jobs have Luxembourgish as one of the vehicular languages.

Are most Luxembourgers really multi-lingual? What language(s) do you use when?

At state-run schools and colleges, children learn Luxembourgish, German, French and English, so yes, pretty much everyone can speak all four of those languages. Most lessons are conducted in German or French, but the spoken language between lessons is Luxembourgish. We both studied abroad and didn't really need any extra language tuition before going.

In shops, it depends where in the country you are and what language the shop staff speak. For example in the Moselle Valley, a lot of cross-border workers speak German. However, most of the time it's French. Luxembourgish is also possible, and English is becoming more frequently used.

Leisure activities (for example sports, music, Scouts) are nearly always conducted in Luxembourgish. Going to hospital can be quite challenging, as the nurse might speak German while the doctor speaks French, so

being able to switch between languages is a necessary skill in Luxembourg.

These days, speaking four languages is really a minimum. Many people speak more: Portuguese and Italian are also quite common. And, you can hear an increasing number of Slavic languages, especially Serbian and Bosnian.

What are the pluses and minuses of living in Luxembourg?

Not everyone in the country is rich. In fact there's quite a lot of hidden poverty, especially for people with children who are often reliant on social financial measures. Very high rents and astronomical property prices are a big headache. Many of our friends in their early 30s are still forced to live with their parents because they can't afford to move out. How to bring property prices under control is a huge political issue. Luxembourg can also be a stressful place to live: people can be snobby and there are very high expectations to perform at work and at school. Sometimes the weather gets us down.

But there are many positives. Life is very multicultural. There's good health care and a social safety net. Work is mostly well-paid, there's child support and six months' leave after the birth of a child for *both* parents. Everything in the country is close, there is free transport, beautiful hiking and great cycling trails. Plus a cool Luxembourgish music scene… and *keelen* (a skittle game) in pubs.

Who & How Many

Official statistics from January 2024 gave Luxembourg's fast-growing population as 670,050. Only 354,372 [ME1] are Luxembourgers. The other 47.3% includes 170 nationalities, most significantly a community of over 90,000 Portuguese. In addition, nearly 230,000 [ME2] non-resident foreigners commute into Luxembourg for work on a daily basis.

HAPPY TO BE LUXEMBOURGERS

Alisha works at the Ministry of Family Affairs, Steven is a teacher. Both were born in Luxembourg, though their different ancestries reflect the many strands of immigration that have forged so many of today's Luxembourgers.

Alisha: One side of my family has always lived here, but my grandparents all had at least some roots in different countries (Germany, Italy, France), arriving over the generations in different areas of Luxembourg. The person who moved here most recently was my grandfather, who grew up in Germany.

Steven: I am the first in my family to be born in Luxembourg. My parents, who originally came here for work with the EU, are from the UK, which means that I have dual citizenship (British and Luxembourgish). My dad did find out that we are related to Count Siegfried, the founder of Luxembourg, dating back to 963. That probably doesn't count but I think it's a cool fact. I officially became a Luxembourger at the age of 21.

THE ART OF
ZWANZE

In Brussels, *zwanze* is not just a word; it embodies the spirit of the city itself. By Mélissa Monaco

ROOTED IN POPULAR culture, *zwanze* refers to the art of playful banter, witty humour, good-natured teasing and practical jokes. Mixing French, Dutch and Brussels' dialect, spoken with that irresistible Brussels accent, it also demands a good sense of self-mockery, for 'blessed are those able to laugh at themselves, because they are not done laughing'.

To be a *zwanzeur* or *zwanzeuse* is to possess quick wit and a knack for comedic timing. It's about cleverly responding to any situation with a lighthearted jest, even in the face of challenges. It means creating an atmosphere of warmth and camaraderie, where laughter is central to daily interactions.

The first *zwanzeur* is, of course, Manneken Pis, the little peeing boy who unapologetically relieves himself in front of strangers. A few days after the bombing of Brussels by the troops of the King of France, Louis XIV, in 1695, a humorous pamphlet called *Manneken Pis' lament* circulated among the ruins of the city, showing that in the face of tragedy, Brussels' population had enough resilience to make light of it.

Manneken Pis (p53), Brussels

Zwanze has much to do with the earthiness of the French Bruxellois (inhabitants of Brussels; often called 'Beulemans' after a famous theatre play). In the 19th and early 20th century, French became the language of power in Brussels, which had predominantly Flemish or Flemish-dialect-speaking inhabitants. More than willing to adapt to the new order of things, the bourgeoisie started to learn French, giving rise to a creole language mixing Dutch grammatical structure, French vocabulary (sometimes translated literally from Dutch) and dialect words. It spread to the rest of the population, making it a language of the people. This mix of odd phrasing and clever retort forms the basis of *zwanze*.

Examples of *zwanze* can be found throughout Brussels but it's often associated with the Marolles, the most popular and rebellious neighbourhood, where the spirit of old Brussels is still alive. Imagine entering an old brown cafe like Le Petit Lion on Rue Haute and ordering a strong coffee. You might get a response like this: 'Do you want a double shot or a coffee strong enough to lift weights?'

As *zwanze* is essentially spoken (or played as a joke), it found its place in theatre, famously in the 1910 *Le Mariage de Mademoiselle Beulemans*. The play, by Frantz Fonson and Fernand Wicheler, tells the story of a young Frenchman sent to Brussels to learn the brewing trade. He falls in love with the daughter of his boss, the truculent, hot-tempered Monsieur Beulemans.

In one scene, Mr Beulemans struggles to put on his suit and gets angry with his wife's clumsy attempts to help.

> *Mr Beulemans: You're going to give me a heart attack. Maybe that's what you want.*
> *Mrs. Beulemans: Yes! I want you dead, don't I?*
> *Mr. Beulemans: Well, I do have life insurance.*

Another way to understand *zwanze* is by attending a puppet show at the Théâtre Royal de Toone, performed in Bruxellois or Brusselvloms (the original Brussels dialect). However, it requires mastery of French or Dutch.

Zwanze can also be found on the streets. One of its best ambassadors is Brussels-born sculptor Tom Frantzen. His work is spread around town, and one of his most famous sculptures is the *Zinneke Pis,* depicting a mongrel dog (*zinneke* in Brussels dialect) lifting its hind leg against a bollard to pee. But the sculpture that best embodies *zwanze* is the *Vaartkapoen* (Canal's Rascal). This sculpture depicts a man coming out of a sewer and tripping a policeman, who seems to fly in the air before falling, symbolising youth challenging authority.

More than just having fun, *zwanze* is a state of mind and truly captures the essence of Brussels – a city that celebrates the simple things, cherishes its unique identity, and finds humour in every aspect of everyday life.

THE ART OF PLAYFUL BANTER, WITTY HUMOUR, GOOD-NATURED TEASING AND PRACTICAL JOKES

Théâtre Royal de Toone (p61), Brussels

MARVIN GAYE
IN OSTEND

A Belgian seaside town isn't the first location you'd think of for a legendary soul singer to write one of the most erotic songs of the 20th century. But for 18 months, this out-of-the-way place hosted Marvin Gaye and – temporarily – saved his life. By Helena Smith

'THERE ARE PLACES I'd probably rather be, but I probably need to be here.'

In early 1981 Marvin Gaye was stuck in London and on the ropes: creatively stifled by Motown, four million dollars in debt to the IRS, going through a painful second marriage breakup and addicted to cocaine. Frail and unstable, he took a call from Belgian promoter and long-time fan Freddy Cousaert. Cousaert wanted the star to perform at the Kuursal Casino in Ostend, on the condition that he clean up and quit drugs.

Recovery

Gaye arrived in Ostend by ferry on Valentine's Day and was put up in the Cousaert's hotel. Concerned about Gaye's thinness, Cousaert's wife cooked for him, his apt favourite being sole. Gaye gradually returned to health, doing boxing training with Freddy's brother and playing basketball. Richard Olivier's documentary *Transit Ostende* (1989) shows the singer running over sand dunes and chinwagging with intrigued but un-star-struck locals in a pub. Escaping fame, he found acceptance

Marvin Gaye performing at the Kuursal Casino Concert, 1981

and peace here. 'I'm an orphan at the moment, and Ostend is my orphanage,' he said.

The Kuursal Casino Concert

Cousaert linked Gaye up with local musicians, and they began to work towards the Kursaal concert to be held on 4 July 1981. Gaye, elegant and slim in a black tuxedo with a white ruffled shirt and maroon bow tie, put on a fantastic show. His voice was restored, and it soared in a slowed down sensual version of 'Come Get to This', and in a beautiful medley of songs in memory of Tammi Terrell. However, the show didn't sell out – something for which the population of Ostend will surely eternally kick itself.

Sexual Healing and Midnight Love

While the Kursaal concert wasn't the money spinner both men must have been hoping for, it marked a transformation in Gaye's creative life in Ostend. In the spring of 1982, in an apartment overlooking the North Sea, he and David Ritz wrote 'Sexual Healing' after an intimate conversation about the childhood beatings Gaye endured from his violent father. The song went on to become his best-selling single. It was the first release

Kursaal Casino, Ostend (p138)

FROM LEFT: GIE KNAEPS/GETTY IMAGES, ARTERRA/UNIVERSAL IMAGES GROUP VIA GETTY IMAGES

from the album *Midnight Love*. Gaye had jammed this material into existence with Belgian musicians, but when it came to the recording, established artists were flown in to Belgium from the US. Released in November 1982 by Columbia Records (Gaye had been liberated from his contract with Motown), *Midnight Love* was a triple-platinum success.

Leaving Ostend

While this must have eased Gaye's financial woes, his renaissance was sadly short lived. Visa issues meant he had to leave Ostend and return to the US, where his addictions resurfaced. Within 18 months Marvin Gaye was dead, shot by his father in a cocaine-fuelled argument.

In Ostend, the singer is memorialised by a life-sized and inappropriately ugly statue of him at the piano – and by the excellent Midnight Love walking tour app, which shows intimate footage of the singer at locations around the city. In one of the most tender scenes, he sings soulfully for the tiny and staid-looking congregation of a local church, and the shots of him rehearsing the *Midnight Love* songs still crackle with the energy of his meticulous musicality.

In the end Ostend couldn't quite save Marvin Gaye. But the city – and the Cousaert family in particular – gave him respite, and a few more years of life. And Marvin gave the world 'Sexual Healing'.

A new song?

In a curious postscript, in 2024 a collection of cassettes, apparently containing 66 demos by Gaye made just before 'Sexual Healing' was written, was uncovered in Ostend. They were given to Belgian musician Charles Dumolin by Gaye in gratitude for housing him for part of his Ostend stay. The prospect of a future Marvin Gaye hit is tantalising. But legal wrangles over copyright mean it may be a long time coming.

Follow the *Midnight Love* tour in Ostend

See Marvin Gaye's 1981 concert at the Kursaal

100 YEARS OF
ART DECO IN BRUSSELS

In 2025, Brussels celebrated Art Deco's centenary, a style that shaped its architectural landscape. By Mélissa Monaco

IT'S TRUE THAT Brussels is known for its Gothic churches, Flemish Renaissance guild houses, Haussmannian-style boulevards, Art Nouveau mansions, and brutalist buildings. But if you look closely, you'll quickly notice that one style is scattered evenly across the city's 19 municipalities: Art Deco.

The Style of Optimism

Born in the aftermath of World War I, the name Art Deco was coined after the 1925 Exposition Internationale des Arts Décoratifs et Industriels Modernes held in Paris. The exhibition marked the triumph of this young architectural style. A symbol of optimism, its clean lines, geometric forms, and stylised ornamentation reflected the interwar years of fascination with speed, progress and modern living.

Before that, Art Nouveau – with its curves, natural shapes, and lush decorations – was the *en vogue* style. But as years went by, Art Nouveau became increasingly tame and abstract. Even its master, Victor Horta, in the later stages of his career, designed buildings such as the Palais des Beaux-Arts and Gare Centrale in a style foreshadowing Art Deco.

In Brussels, the style took root in a city eager to reinvent itself after the upheavals of the war. The population was growing, and housing was in high demand. The result was a real explosion of Art Deco buildings across an expanding city.

Grand Eldorado Cinema Hall, UGC De Brouckère

A Democratic Style

Unlike Art Nouveau, often reserved for the wealthy, Art Deco was more democratic in spirit. You'll find it on grand public buildings (Koekelberg Basilica, Flagey's Maison de la Radio) and small private homes alike: in bourgeois suburbs (Villa Empain, Van Buuren House) as well as working class districts. Even industrial and apartment buildings followed suit. Local architects embraced the style's versatility – sometimes dressing facades with elegant stone reliefs, sometimes opting for streamlined brickwork punctuated with porthole windows or metal railings. The Congo also inspired architects and decorators, such as in the Grand Eldorado Hall – UGC De Brouckère's largest cinema room.

A Timeless Style

Unlike Art Nouveau, Art Deco weathered Brussels' 1950s and 1960s wave of demolitions relatively well. The city still recalls with shame the loss of Victor Horta's Maison du Peuple, razed in 1965 to make way for an unremarkable apartment block. In the post-war decades, Art Nouveau was dismissed as 'too extravagant', 'outdated' and 'overly decorative'. Art Deco, with its clean lines and geometric elegance, was considered more modern and versatile. Its streamlined forms blended more easily with the emerging modernist and brutalist architecture, sparing many of its buildings from the wrecking ball.

Celebrating a Centenary and Beyond

While the official 2025 'Year of Art Deco' has come to a close, its celebration is far from over. Each March, the BANAD Festival (Brussels Art Nouveau & Art Deco) organises a month of activities: guided visits (some in places usually closed to the public), walks, conferences, and more – dedicated to both architectural styles.

The Musée Art & Histoire has also opened a new gallery showcasing decorative items, furniture – and a recreated Jean Cousin winter garden by Victor Horta – spanning from the late 19th century to 1940.

See Art Deco in Brussels

Because Art Deco was so popular, there is no single walking route to follow. Here are some architectural highlights to look out for.

The Pentagon: The Pathé-Palace cinema theatre; warehouses and apartment buildings on Boulevard d'Ypres and Boulevard de Dixmude.

EU Quarter: Résidence Palace (Brussels' first luxury apartment building, now a press centre); Quartier des Fleurs and Sainte-Suzanne Church in Schaerbeek.

Ixelles, Saint-Gilles & Forest: Flagey's Maison de la Radio; buildings along Ave Franklin Rooselt; Villa Empain (Michel Polak's masterpiece), Palais de la Folle Chanson; Forest Municipal Hall, Wiels Brewery and Saint-Augustin Church.

Along the Canal: Saint-Jean-Baptiste Church in Molenbeek; Meir neighbourhood in Anderlecht.

South & East Brussels: Kapelleveld Garden City in Woluwe-Saint-Lambert; Henri Lacoste villa and surrounding residential area near Beaulieu metro; Square Coghen and its mix of Art Deco and Modernist villas in Uccle.

Northwest Brussels: Koekelberg Basilica, Brussels' largest Art Deco building and one of the largest churches in the world; the Fondation Médicale Reine Elisabeth building and Palais des Expositions du Heysel in Laeken.

Koekelberg Basilica (p96)

LEFT & RIGHT: WERNER LEROOY/SHUTTERSTOCK

INDEX

Map Pages **000**

"Taking the train out of Bruges (p121) I had an hour to spare, so I took a refreshing dip in the Coupure canal."

HELENA SMITH

"Until I asked Google Maps a few years ago, I did not realise that it's sometimes faster to get around Brussels (p44) by train. The region boasts 35 stations."

MÉLISSA MONACO

Mapping data sources:
© Lonely Planet
© OpenStreetMap http://openstreetmap.org/copyright

THIS BOOK

Destination Editor
Annemarie McCarthy

Production Editor
Aileen Cudmore

Image Researcher
Ania Lenihan

Cartographer
Dave Connolly

Coordinating Editor
Tasmin Waby

Assisting Editors
Paul Harding, Karyn Noble

Cover Researcher
Stefanie Delgado

Thanks Sofie Andersen, Alice Barnes-Brown, Gwen Cotter, Fergal Condon, Sandie Kestell,

Alison Killilea, Darren O'Connell, Charlotte Orr, Saralinda Turner, Maja Vatrić

Paper in this book is certified against the Forest Stewardship Council™ standards. FSC™ promotes environmentally responsible, socially beneficial and economically viable management of the world's forests.

Published by Lonely Planet Global Limited
CRN 554153
10th edition – June 2026
ISBN 978 1 83869 678 8
© Lonely Planet 2026
10 9 8 7 6 5 4 3 2 1
Printed in Malaysia